A History of the Archaic Gr

Blackwell History of the Ancient World

This series provides a new narrative history of the ancient world, from the beginnings of civilization in the ancient Near East and Egypt to the fall of Constantinople. Written by experts in their fields, the books in the series offer authoritative accessible surveys for students and general readers alike.

Published

A History of the Archaic Greek World
Jonathan M. Hall

A History of the Later Roman Empire, AD 284–621
Stephen Mitchell

A History of the Classical Greek World
P. J. Rhodes

A History of the Ancient Near East, second edition
Marc Van De Mieroop

A History of Byzantium
Timothy E. Gregory

In Preparation

A History of the Persian Empire
Christopher Tuplin

A History of the Hellenistic World
Malcolm Errington

A History of the Roman Republic
John Rich

A History of the Roman Empire
Michael Peachin

A History of the Archaic Greek World

ca. 1200–479 BCE

Jonathan M. Hall

Blackwell
Publishing

BLACKWELL PUBLISHING
350 Main Street, Malden, MA 02148-5020, USA
9600 Garsington Road, Oxford OX4 2DQ, UK
550 Swanston Street, Carlton, Victoria 3053, Australia

The right of Jonathan M. Hall to be identified as the Author of this Work has been asserted in accordance with the UK Copyright, Designs, and Patents Act 1988.

First published 2007 by Blackwell Publishing Ltd

4   2009

Library of Congress Cataloging-in-Publication Data

Hall, Jonathan M.
   A history of the archaic Greek world / Jonathan M. Hall.
      p.   cm. — (Blackwell history of the ancient world)
   Includes bibliographical references and index.
   ISBN 978-0-631-22667-3 (hardback : alk. paper)
   ISBN 978-0-631-22668-0 (paperback : alk. paper)
   1. Greece—History—To 146 B.C.   I. Title.   II. Series.

   DF221.2.H35 2006
   938—dc22

                                        2006004753

A catalogue record for this title is available from the British Library.

Set in 10^1/$_2$/12^1/$_2$pt Plantin
by Graphicraft Limited, Hong Kong
Printed and bound in Singapore
by Ho Printing Singapore Pte Ltd

For further information on
Blackwell Publishing, visit our website:
www.blackwellpublishing.com

To Gregorio

Contents

Maps

Figures

Documents

Preface

I had not intended to write a revisionist history of the Archaic Greek world and I hope that I have not, since that would imply that what I offer here is intended as a definitive reconstruction of early Greek history. Rather, my intention was always to introduce the reader to some of the excitement (and frustration) that accompanies the practice of history. If readers are interested simply in "what actually happened" in this formative period of Greek history, there is no shortage of good, narrative accounts to which they can turn. If, on the other hand, they are interested in venturing into the historian's laboratory, in familiarizing themselves with the evidential materials and tools of the trade and in learning to interpret those materials in ways that are meaningful in the present, then I hope that they will find this book of some value. In engaging directly with the source materials rather than obediently following the authority of a secondary work of reference, it is inevitable that some hallowed orthodoxies are going to be challenged. On the other hand, if this book equips the reader with the critical skills to challenge even the reconstructions offered here, it will have served its purpose.

For my interest in Archaic Greece and in issues of historical method, I owe a particular debt to three people: to Nicholas Purcell, who was my tutor in Ancient History at Oxford and who eloquently dispelled my delusion that history was just "one damn thing after another"; to George Forrest, whose paper on early leagues and amphictionies (posthumously published in Brock and Hodkinson 2000, 280–92) inspired my doctoral research and who was first responsible for my initiation into American academia; and to Anthony Snodgrass, who was my PhD supervisor at Cambridge and whose success in pioneering a new synthesis between ancient history and archaeology will continue to influence generations of classicists to come. I am especially grateful for the comments that have been offered by, among others, Greg Anderson, Paul Cartledge, Sara Forsdyke, John Hyland, Irad Malkin, Glenn Most, and the two anonymous readers for Blackwell, as well as by audiences at the University of Michigan at Ann Arbor, Stanford University, Harvard University, the University of California at Berkeley and, of course, the University of Chicago. For Blackwell, Al Bertrand's persistent faith in the project has provided welcome reassurance, as has the efficient and friendly professionalism of Angela Cohen and Louise Spencely. As always, my wife, Ilaria, has offered invaluable encouragement and support. This book is dedicated to my son, Gregorio – not in the expectation or hope that he too, like his father or maternal grandfather, will become a historian but rather as an insufficient recompense for all the days that were spent in the study rather than the park.

Note on spelling: Proper names that appear in the third edition of the *Oxford Classical Dictionary* (Oxford and New York, 1996) are given in the Latinized forms to be found there. All other proper names are transliterated in their Greek, rather than Latin, forms.

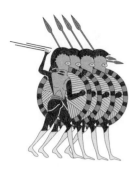

Timeline

525	Cleisthenes holds archonship in Athens
514	Assassination of Hipparchus
510	Spartan expulsion of Hippias from Athens
508	Reforms of Cleisthenes
506	Athenians defeat Boeotians and Chalcidians
499	Outbreak of Ionian revolt
494	Ionians defeated at Lade. Sack of Miletus
490	Battle of Marathon
487	First ostracism held at Athens
483	Discovery of new silver vein at Laurium allows the Athenians to equip themselves with a new navy
480	Persian invasion of Greece, Battles of Thermopylae, Artemisium, and Salamis
479	Battles of Plataea and Mykale. Expulsion of the Persians from Greece

Map 0.1 The Aegean

1

The Practice of History

The Lelantine War

To the modern visitor the Lelantine plain might seem an unlikely setting for a conflict of epic dimensions. Flanking the southern coast of the island of Euboea, just across from the mainland regions of Attica and Boeotia, the plain is today dotted with holiday villas and summer homes as well as the odd physical remnant of the area's earlier importance for the brick-making industry, but its economy – now, as in antiquity – is dominated by the cultivation of cereals, olives, figs, and vines. The ancient cities of Chalcis and Eretria, like their modern namesakes, lay at either end of the plain, twenty-four kilometers apart. Relations between the two were initially cordial enough: according to Strabo (5.4.9), Pithecusae, on the Italian island of Ischia, was a joint foundation of Eretrians and Chalcidians, probably in the second quarter of the eighth century. But both cities had expanding populations that they needed to feed and in the final decades of the eighth century the two came to blows over possession of the plain that lay between them.

The aristocrats of Euboea were renowned for their horsemanship and for their skill with the spear. Both Aristotle (*Pol.* 4.3.2) and Plutarch (*Mor.* 760e–761b) refer to cavalry engagements, but the Archaic poet Archilochus (fr. 3) implies that the warriors also fought on foot and at close quarters with swords, rather than relying upon slings and bows. Indeed, Strabo (10.1.12) claims to have seen an inscription, set up in the sanctuary of Artemis at Amarynthos (eight kilometers east of Eretria), which recorded the original decision to ban the use of long-range weapons such as slings, bows, or javelins. It was a war, then, conducted according to a chivalric code we normally attribute to medieval knights.

Those who sacrificed their lives for their cities were treated like heroes. Around 720, an anonymous Eretrian warrior was accorded funerary honors that parallel closely the Homeric description of Patroclus' funeral in the *Iliad*. The warrior's ashes had been wrapped in a cloth along with jewellery and a gold and serpentine scarab, then placed in a bronze cauldron, covered by a larger bronze vessel, and buried on the western perimeter of the settlement, next to the road that led to Chalcis. With the cinerary urn were buried swords and spearheads, which denoted the deceased's martial prowess, and a bronze staff or "scepter," dating to the Late Bronze Age, whose antique status probably served to express the authority he had formerly held in his home community. Charred bones indicate that animals – including a horse, to judge from an equine tooth – were sacrificed at the site of the grave, probably on the occasion of the funeral. Over the next generation, six further cremations of adults (presumably members of the same family) were placed in an arc around the first, while slightly to the west were situated the inhumation burials of youths, arranged in two parallel rows. In both cases, the funerary rites differ from those that were then in vogue in the city's main necropolis by the sea. In the Harbor Cemetery, the corpses of infants had been stuffed into pots whereas at the West Gate they had been afforded the more dignified facility of a pit grave, accompanied by toys and miniature vases, and whereas adults in the Harbor Cemetery were also cremated, their ashes were not placed in cinerary urns nor were their burials accompanied by costly grave goods. After the last burial, ca. 680, a triangular limestone monument was constructed above the cremation burials and from the deposits of ash, carbonized wood, animal bones, drinking cups, and figurines found in the immediate vicinity, we can assume that ritual meals continued to take place in honor of the dead here until the fifth century.

Chalcis had its war heroes too. The poet Hesiod (*WD* 654–5) recounts how he had once crossed over from Boeotia to Chalcis to attend the funeral contests held in honor of "wise" Amphidamas and won a tripod for a song he had composed. Plutarch (*Mor.* 153f) adds that many famous poets attended these funerary games and that Amphidamas "inflicted many ills upon the Eretrians and fell in the battles for the Lelantine plain." Elsewhere (760e–761b), he tells of horsemen from Thessaly, the great upland plain of northern-central Greece, who had been summoned by the Chalcidians, fearful of the Eretrian cavalry's superiority. Their general, Kleomakhos, was killed in the fighting and was granted the signal honor of being buried in the agora of Chalcis, his tomb marked by a tall pillar.

The war was no purely local affair. According to Thucydides (1.15), the entire Greek world was divided in alliance with one or other of the two protagonists in a collective effort that would not be seen again until the great wars of the fifth century (Figure 1.1). Herodotus (5.99) mentions a war between Eretria and Chalcis in which Miletus, the most important Ionian foundation on the coast of Asia Minor, had taken the side of Eretria and Miletos' island neighbor, Samos, that of Chalcis. Other allies can only be assigned to sides on evidence that is more circumstantial. Given that Corinthian settlers are supposed to have expelled Eretrians from Corcyra (the modern island of Corfu) in 733 (Plutarch, *Mor.* 293b), that Megarian colonists are said to have

Eretria	Chalcis
Miletus	Samos
Megara	Corinth and colonies (Corcyra, Syracuse)
Boeotia	Thessaly
Aegina	Athens
Argos	Sparta and colonies (Melos, Thera, Taras, Cyrene)
Chios	Erythrae
Mytilene	Chalcidian colonies (Naxos, Catana, Leontini, Zancle, Rhegium, Cumae)

Figure 1.1 The alliances that have been proposed for Eretria and Chalcis in the Lelantine War

been driven out of Sicilian Leontini by Chalcidians five years later (Thucydides 6.4), and that the hostility between Corinth and its neighbor, Megara, was proverbial, one can assume that Megara was allied with Eretria and Corinth with Chalcis. Thessaly, as we have seen, came to the aid of Chalcis, which might suggest that Thessaly's neighbor and enemy, Boeotia, was on the side of Eretria, along with the island of Aegina, which claimed a special relationship with Boeotia (Herodotus 5.80) and had itself engaged in hostilities with Samos (3.59). The Peloponnesian city of Argos, an ally of Aegina (5.86) and an enemy of Corinth, probably sided with Eretria while Argos' enemy Sparta, which had been assisted by Samos during the Messenian War (3.47), would have favored Chalcis, as would Aegina's enemy Athens. Since Mytilene on the island of Lesbos contested control of the Hellespontine city of Sigeum with Athens (5.95), it is unlikely to have fought alongside Athens on the side of Chalcis, and Miletus' ancient alliance with the island of Chios against the Ionian city of Erythrae (1.18) may allow us to assign Chios to the Eretrian contingent and Erythrae to the Chalcidian. Finally, it is to be expected that "colonial" foundations would have taken the side of their mother-cities: thus Chalcis is likely to have been supported by her own colonies in the west (Naxos, Catana, Leontini, and Zancle on Sicily, Rhegium and Cumae on the Italian mainland), as well as by the Corinthian colonies of Corcyra and Syracuse and the Spartan colonies of Melos, Thera, Taras, and Cyrene.

History does not record the outcome of the conflict. It is possible that hostilities continued intermittently for some considerable time because Archilochus (fr. 3), conventionally assigned to the middle of the seventh century, appears to imply a resumption of combat in his own day while verses attributed to the Megarian poet Theognis (891–4) protest that "the fine vineyards of Lelanton are being shorn" and assign the blame to the descendants of Cypselus, who seized power at Corinth around the middle of the seventh century. There are, however, hints that Eretria fared worse than Chalcis. Firstly, the site of Lefkandi, which is situated on the coast between Chalcis and Eretria and had been a flourishing and wealthy community in the eleventh and tenth centuries, appears to have been destroyed around 700. Strabo (9.2.6) makes a distinction between an Old Eretria and a Modern Eretria, and given that Lefkandi begins to go into decline ca. 825 – that is, at about the same time that Eretria develops as a center of settlement – it has been argued that Lefkandi had been Old Eretria and that it was a casualty of Chalcidian action towards the end of the eighth century. Secondly, the cooperation between Eretria and Chalcis in overseas ventures came to an abrupt end in the last third of the eighth century. The Chalcidians who had settled Pithecusae are said to have transferred to the Italian mainland where they founded Cumae (Livy 8.22.6), but for the remainder of the century it is Chalcis rather than Eretria that continues to play a pivotal role in such western ventures. A Delphic oracle (*Palatine Anthology* 14.73), perhaps dating to the seventh century, lavishes praise on "the men who drink the water of holy Arethousa" (a spring near Chalcis) and the land that Athens confiscated from Chalcis in 506 BCE lay in the Lelantine plain (Aelian, *HM* 6.1).

The foregoing sketch would appear to offer an impressive demonstration of how historians can assemble fragments of evidence from various literary authors and combine them with the findings of archaeologists to draw a vivid picture of past events – no mean achievement for a period in which literacy was still in its infancy and for which contemporary documentation is practically nonexistent. Unfortunately, this whole reconstruction is probably little more than a modern historian's fantasy, cobbled together from isolated pieces of information that, both singly and in combination, command little confidence.

The Lelantine War Deconstructed

To begin with, the authors whose notices are culled to generate this composite picture span a period of some nine centuries – roughly the same amount of time as from the Battle of Hastings to the present day. The poems of Hesiod, Archilochus, and Theognis probably date to the seventh century (though see below); Herodotus and Thucydides were writing in the later fifth century, Aristotle in the middle of the fourth, Livy towards the end of the first century, Strabo around the turn of the Common Era, Plutarch at the turn of the second century CE, and Aelian at the beginning of the third. The testimony of late authors is less weighty if they are merely deriving their information from that of the earlier authors we possess rather than from an independent tradition. While it is unlikely that Thucydides was reckless enough to base his belief in the Panhellenic nature of the war on Herodotus' notice that Miletus had once fought with Eretria against Chalcis and Samos, Plutarch's description of the poetic contests at the funeral of Amphidamas stands a good chance of representing an elaboration on the testimony of Hesiod, who never actually mentions the Lelantine War.

Nor is it likely that Thucydides invented out of thin air a tradition about widespread participation in a Lelantine War. He mentions this early war in order to justify his contention that the Peloponnesian War of 431–404 was the greatest upheaval to have ever affected the Greek world, notwithstanding the great military campaigns of the past. The Lelantine War stands in the same relationship to the Peloponnesian War as the Trojan War does to the Persian War: the former are wars among Greeks while the latter are wars between Greeks and their eastern neighbors, but in each set the more recent war is greater in scope than the former. Clearly, the rhetoric here could not have been effective unless Thucydides' readership was already familiar with a story in which Eretria and Chalcis had been joined by many allies in their war against each other. Yet the existence of a tradition that predates Thucydides does not guarantee its authenticity. It is surely not insignificant that none of our earlier literary sources implies a broader conflict. Furthermore, Thucydides compares the Lelantine War with the Trojan War and while some historians and archaeologists might be prepared to accept that a genuine Mycenaean raid on the Anatolian coast underlies the elaborated traditions about the Trojan War, few believe that the conflict was as epic or as global as myth and epic remembered. Why should the Lelantine War have been any different? In fact, the impressive roster of alliances hypothesized above is built on scattered notices about alliances and hostilities that were anything but contemporary: the Corinthian expulsion of Eretrians from Corcyra is supposed to have taken place in 733 but the alliance between Argos and Aegina dates to around 500, some seven generations later. Are we to believe that Greeks in the Archaic period were so consistent in their loyalties? And how seriously, in any case, should we take such notices? The Eretrian settlement on Corcyra is mentioned only by Plutarch and has, up to now, received absolutely no corroboration from archaeological investigations on the island.

Plutarch is also our only source for the intervention of Thessaly on the side of Chalcis. This testimony is not incompatible with Thucydides' picture of a broader conflict, but neither is it exactly an exhaustive endorsement of the grand alliances that he suggests. In fact, there is a good chance that Plutarch's information derives not from a tradition that was also known to Thucydides but from a story attached to a monument at Chalcis – namely, the column that supposedly marked the tomb of the Thessalian hero Kleomakhos in the agora. Whether or not the tomb really contained the remains of a warrior who fell in the Lelantine War is as unverifiable for us as it was for Plutarch. For example, when Jacob Spon and George Wheler visited Athens in 1676 CE, the so-called "Tower of the Winds" outside the Roman Agora was commonly believed to be the tomb of the fifth-century philosopher Socrates (it is now identified as a water-clock, designed by the Macedonian astronomer Andronikos Kyrrhestes in either the second or first century). Monuments may create, as much as perpetuate, social memory.

Similarly, it is far from apparent that Herodotus, in his description of the alliance between Eretria and Miletus against Chalcis and Samos, has in mind the more global conflict recorded by Thucydides. The earlier alliance is mentioned in order to explain why the Eretrians joined the Athenians in providing support to the Ionians of East Greece on the occasion of the latter's revolt in 499: "they did not campaign with them out of any goodwill towards the

Athenians but rather to pay back a debt owed to the Milesians, for the Milesians had earlier joined the Eretrians in waging the war against the Chalcidians, on exactly the same occasion as the Samians helped the Chalcidians against the Eretrians and Milesians" (5.99). The wording appears to leave little scope for the participation of additional combatants, but neither can we exclude the possibility that the earlier, undated alliance was invented to justify Eretrian intervention at the beginning of the fifth century. As for Aristotle, it is difficult to maintain that his reference to a cavalry war between Eretria and Chalcis is derived from Archilochus, whose mention of the use of swords clearly implies an infantry engagement. He could be following an independent source but it is more likely that he has made the inference on the basis of the names given to the elite classes at Eretria and Chalcis – the *Hippeis* (horsemen) and *Hippobotai* (horse-rearers) respectively. From there, the idea that the war had involved both cavalry and infantry could have passed to Plutarch, for whom Aristotle was often an important authority.

It might be thought that we are on firmer ground with those poets who are supposedly contemporary with the events they describe: Hesiod, Archilochus, and Theognis. Yet, here too we encounter difficulties. In most standard works of reference, Hesiod is dated to around 700, but how is this date derived? It relies in part on certain stylistic and thematic correspondences between the Hesiodic poems and the epics of Homer – though the dating of Homer and the relative chronological relationship between Homer and Hesiod are hotly contested by scholars (see pp. 24–5) – but it is also based on the assumption that Hesiod was a contemporary of the Lelantine War! Such circular reasoning cannot command much faith, especially since it is not Hesiod but Plutarch who associates Amphidamas with the Lelantine War. Archilochus is conventionally dated to the middle of the seventh century. One of his poems describes a total solar eclipse which is probably to be associated with that calculated as having occurred on April 6, 648, while one of his addressees, a certain Glaukos, son of Leptinos, is mentioned in a late seventh-century inscription found in the agora of Thasos, Archilochus' adopted home. Some literary scholars are, however, dubious that Archaic poetry can be read so autobiographically and consider such works to be the products of a cumulative synthesis of a city's poetic traditions which is continuously recreated over several generations and attached to the name of an original poet of almost heroic status. The fragmentary poems attributed to Archilochus were probably performed at the hero shrine established to the poet on his native island of Paros towards the end of the sixth century. Some elements of the *oeuvre* may well date back to the mid-seventh century but others could be a good deal later. This is even clearer in the case of the poetry ascribed to Theognis: the repetition of entire verses, the inclusion of couplets ascribed by other sources to poets such as Solon or Mimnermus, and the fact that some verses seem to refer to events of the seventh century while others allude to events that cannot predate the fifth century all give us reason to suspect that the *Theognidea* is more of a compendium of Archaic Greek poetry than the work of a single author.

There is a concrete quality to archaeological evidence that sometimes encourages us to believe that it can provide "scientific" confirmation or refutation of inferences made on the basis of literary texts. This is, unfortunately, a little optimistic. While it is essential that historians examine both the material and the literary records, the understandable urge to associate material items with textual correlates runs the risk of committing what Anthony Snodgrass has called the "positivist fallacy" – that is, of automatically equating what is archaeologically visible with what is historically significant. We need to remember that, just as only a tiny fraction of the texts that were known in antiquity has survived to the present day, so too the evidence that is studied by archaeologists represents only a minute proportion of the totality of human behavior in the past. The recovery of such material depends upon whether it was consciously or unconsciously disposed of at a particular moment in the past, whether it has been subject to degradation over several centuries or is instead imperishable, whether it has been located and retrieved by the archaeologist and whether it has been correctly classified and identified, let alone interpreted. The burials that were subsequently honored by the West Gate at Eretria may be those of warriors who died defending their city in the Lelantine War, but they could just as easily be associated with the thousands of episodes of Eretrian history of which we know absolutely nothing.

A more particular consideration holds in the case of Lefkandi. The assumption that settlement at the site ceased ca. 700 is based on the excavators' observation that a house, situated on the eastern slopes of the headland, was destroyed and abandoned towards the end of the Late Geometric pottery phase; further to the west, another structure seems to have been abandoned at the same time, though there are no indications there of a destruction. But since perhaps no more than 2 percent of the settlement at Lefkandi has been excavated and since sixth-century pottery has also been reported, even if its exact context is unclear, it is entirely possible that the so-called "destruction" of the site was merely a local conflagration and that other, unexcavated parts of the settlement continued to be occupied into the seventh century. Indeed, this is precisely what preliminary results of renewed investigation at the site of Lefkandi-Xeropolis, begun in 2003, now appear to suggest. Nor is it at all certain that Lefkandi should be identified with Strabo's Old Eretria. Elsewhere (10.1.10), the geographer seems to imply that Old Eretria was simply a quarter of Modern Eretria.

Finally, even if we were to take all this evidence at face value, there is a conspicuous lack of chronological synchronisms. The first warrior burial at the West Gate of Eretria dates to ca. 720, probably around two decades before the house at Lefkandi was destroyed. Archaeological dating is never, of course, precise and it is possible that the burial (and consequently the destruction) could be ten or fifteen years earlier – around the time, say, of the alleged expulsions of Eretrians from Corcyra and of Megarians from Chalcidian Leontini. The testimony of Hesiod could fit this early date – if we accept that Amphidamas was connected with the war and suppose that Hesiod attended his funeral games very early on in his career – but there are no compelling literary grounds for precluding a lower date in the early seventh century. The testimony of Archilochus, however, drags us down to the middle of the seventh century, while the reference to the descendants of Cypselus by the author of the *Theognidea* takes us into the second half of the seventh century, if not the beginning of the sixth. If this was a war waged continuously over a century and a half, it is remarkable that its lengthy duration was not commented upon by ancient authors. Perhaps ancient authors confused a series of separate encounters between Eretria and Chalcis, aided occasionally by an outside ally. Or perhaps a relatively unspectacular confrontation of unknown date between the two cities was invested with more heroic dimensions and a more global outreach for the purposes of glorifying the victor. In short, we do not know when – or even whether – the Lelantine War occurred.

That sort of agnostic confession can often strike either the student who is new to history or the interested general reader as deeply unsatisfying, if not frustrating. Many come to the study of history in order to "know" the past and to deal in facts and certainties, not hypotheses and revisionist critiques. The reaction is entirely understandable but it rests, I would suggest, on a rather narrow understanding of what history is.

What is History?

The English word "history" has two principal meanings. In the first place it is commonly used as a synonym for "the past." When we talk about "great men and women in history," we are referring to individuals whose deeds and achievements took place in the past; the "historic streetcars" of San Francisco are antique vehicles from around the world that have been preserved and pressed back into service; and when we say that someone or something "is history," we mean that they no longer possess any relevance in the present. A subsidiary definition of this first meaning of history involves the notion of progress or development in the past – histories of art, for instance, are concerned with studying the art of the past but generally seek to trace the evolution of artistic themes and styles over time. The second meaning of "history" indicates the *study* of the past – a definition that is closest to the etymological derivation of the word (from the Greek *historia*, meaning "inquiry"). In this case, the term denotes the act, or practice, of study rather than its object. In English, the distinction between these two meanings is not always clear-cut. When, for example, we say that "history teaches us that the denial of national or ethnic self-determination is likely to provoke separatist movements," we are stating that the *study* of the past suggests to us that this is a likely consequence but we are also implying that *the past itself* presents documented examples whose lessons we should heed. This definitional ambiguity arises from a widespread assumption that the practice of history is simply to "unearth" the past – in other words, that the past is capable of speaking for itself, provided that the historian rescues it from oblivion and assists in giving it a voice. In this sense, "history as practice" is dependent upon, and derivative of, "history as the past."

That interpretation of history was challenged in 1961 by Edward Hallett Carr in a book entitled *What is History?* – a revised version of the George Macaulay Trevelyan Lectures that he had delivered earlier that year at the University of Cambridge. A former civil servant with the British Foreign Office, editorial writer for the London *Times*, professor of politics, and author of the fourteen-volume *History of Soviet Russia*, Carr defined history as "a continuous interaction between the historian and his facts, an unending dialogue between the present and the past" (1987: 30). His definition of a historical fact, however, was anything but conventional for his day. Attacking what he characterized as a "nineteenth-century fetishism of facts" – represented above all by the German historian Leopold von Ranke's insistence that the historian's task was to show "how it actually was" (*wie es eigentlich gewesen*) – as well as the positivist tendency to draw conclusions from facts (i.e. the "inductive method") and the British empiricist tradition which posited a sharp distinction between subject and object, Carr argued that not all facts in the past are historical facts and that it is the historian who decides which facts should be considered significant and in what order of significance they should be ranked. In short, it was ridiculous to imagine that there existed any objective historical facts "out there," independent of the interpretation of the historian.

At first sight, Carr would seem to have been giving priority to the practice of history over the establishment of what actually happened in the past and, indeed, he is sometimes regarded as a relativist – as someone, that is, who believes that every truth claim or historical interpretation possesses equal validity. As such, his work is often contrasted to that of his conservative contemporary Geoffrey Elton (the son of the classicist Victor Ehrenberg), who argued that the subject matter of history was events themselves rather than the evidence for them that the historian needs to interpret. In reality, however, Carr did believe in an objective truth and his efforts to challenge the self-evident nature of historical facts were actually attempts to discredit earlier "liberal" histories against which, as a Marxist, he was ideologically predisposed. For Carr, an "objective" history could not be divined from events of the past alone but only from understanding them in a broader perspective that comprehended the evolutionary progress of history and could make sense of past actions and events through reference to the future directions that history would take. In other words, a superior history depended upon the historical skill of the practitioner but this was itself a function of the historian's ability to mediate between the events of the past and the emerging goals of the future.

Like the English "history," the German word *Geschichte* describes both the past and the study of the past, but it can also mean a "story," "tale," or "fable," and this triple meaning of "history as the past," "history as practice," and "history as narrative" is also inherent in the French word *histoire*, the Italian *storia*, and the Modern Greek *istoría*. To Anglophones this inability to distinguish between "factual" and "fictional" accounts can appear decidedly odd, even if the English word "history" was also once used in the same sense. This third meaning of history "as narrative" is one that has, in recent decades, been championed by the American theorist Hayden White.

For White the past is vanished and can never be represented mimetically or in its totality in any historical account. All that remains of it are fragmentary "traces" which are normally themselves already textualized (i.e. represented in narrative form in documents or other records). These isolated traces, or what White calls the "unprocessed historical record," have no meaning in them-selves – they tell no story. What the historian does is, firstly, to arrange them into a chronological sequence or "chronicle"; secondly, to shape the chronicle into a story with a beginning, middle, and end; and, thirdly, to transform the story into a narrative by means of a series of standard devices. These devices include the ideological stance that the historian adopts (conservative; liberal; radical; anarchist), the mode of argument employed (organicist; contextua-list; mechanistic; formist), and the specific type of emplotment chosen (com-edy; satire; tragedy; romance). White believes, however, that the choice between these various options is not entirely contingent; rather, it is linguistically pre-determined by the "trope," or rhetorical mode of representation, in which the historian writes (metaphor; metonymy; synecdoche; irony). The historical text is, therefore, primarily a literary artifact – the techniques by which it is produced vary little, if at all, from those employed by novelists – and this is because the historian needs to code what is essentially unfamiliar (the traces of the past) in a literary form that is both familiar to, and recognizable by, an audience. The traces or "facts" may be "discovered" by the historian, but the narrative created from them is largely imagined and invented, and this means that moral or aesthetic considerations, rather than issues of evidence, are the only criteria available for judging the relative merits of different interpretations or visions of history.

White's interpretation of history has been enthusiastically endorsed by post-modernist scholars, dissatisfied with what they consider the uncritical certainties and epistemological *naiveté* of more traditional historians. Keith Jenkins, for example, argues that no history – or historian – is ideologically disinterested or neutral, that all histories are compiled from the standpoint of the present, that all histories are imagined rather than discovered, that no history can truly correspond to the actuality of a now absent past, and that all history is really his-toriography – the product of the historian rather than of the past. Unsurprisingly, such interpretations have also provoked an equally trenchant reaction from more traditional historians who resent what they see as the encroachment upon their discipline by literary critics and social theorists. Books with titles such as *Telling the Truth About History*, *In Defense of History*, and *The Killing of History* seek – with varying degrees of sobriety – to defend cherished notions such as truth, objective knowledge, and disinterested science against what is dubbed the agnosticism, relativism, and nihilism of postmodernist scholars.

Ironically, the radically different interpretations of both the postmodernists and the traditionalists are the product of the same "emplotment" of how history has been studied. That is to say, for both parties the three definitions of history outlined above are often regarded as three different chronological stages in the philosophy of history. First there was the straightforward view of history "as the past," as espoused by Ranke; then, greater emphasis was placed on the subjective interpretation of the historian – a move associated in British scholarship with the name of Carr, though the American historians Charles Beard and Carl Becker had made similar pronouncements before the First World War; and finally, the practice of history was divorced from the past by stressing the imaginative and fictive nature of historical writing. For postmodernists, the basic story is one of an emancipation from the tyranny of the past, whereas for traditionalists it is a flight of fantasy away from common-sense realities. Yet, as we have already seen, in many languages the word for history denotes all three meanings simultaneously, and if we take this tripartite definition more seriously then the central tenets of the postmodernist critique are considerably less radical than their proponents pretend but also potentially more illuminating than many traditionalists are prepared to concede.

History as Literature

Let us consider the late fifth-century Athenian historian Thucydides. Long regarded as the father of "scientific" history, Thucydides is perhaps studied less by ancient historians today than he was a generation or two ago, though he is currently enjoying considerable popularity among more philologically-minded scholars, who have justly drawn attention to the highly accomplished literary qualities of his work. The account of the disastrous Athenian expedition to Sicily in 415 is a case in point. Apart from the fact that this particular episode is very deliberately emplotted as a tragedy, whose squalid outcome is poignantly counterposed to the pomp and optimism surrounding its inception, Thucydides' account consciously employs echoes taken from his predecessor Herodotus' description of the Persian invasion of Greece in 480. For example, Herodotus (7.44) tells how, upon reaching the Hellespont, the Persian king Xerxes presided over a race between the ships in his fleet; in Thucydides (6.32.2), the Athenian ships race each other as far as the island of Aegina. According to Herodotus (8.75), the Athenian general Themistocles forced the naval battle in the straits of Salamis by sending a secret message to the Persian command, advising them to attack before the Greeks abandoned their station. Thucydides (7.73) recounts how the Syracusan statesman Hermocrates prevented the defeated Athenians from escaping by having his men pretend to befriend them and warn them not to retreat immediately because the roads were being guarded. Even Thucydides' description (7.70–71) of the naval battle in the Great Harbor of Syracuse echoes the chaotic and crowded conditions that characterize Herodotus' portrayal of the Battle of Salamis (8.84–96). This is no act of plagiarism: by deliberately evoking the account of Herodotus – an account that would certainly have been familiar to his readership

– Thucydides was in a sense comparing the imperialist designs of Athens with those of the Persian Empire earlier; and everybody knew how that campaign had ended.

Such literary devices are certainly not limited to the description of the Sicilian Expedition. Thucydides crafts the speeches which he presents in such a way as to reveal the character of those who are made to utter them. Thus, the sober and cautious speech of the Spartan king Archidamus (1.80–85) is designed to reflect the dilatory – not to say sluggish – tendencies that the Athenians attributed to the Spartans, while the confession of the Spartan ephor Sthenelaidas that he could not understand "those long speeches of the Athenians" (1.86) illustrates the Spartans' proverbial economy with words (the word "laconic" derives from the Greek word *Lakôn*, meaning "Spartan"). Furthermore, certain events are anticipated, deferred, or juxtaposed outside their strict chronological occurrence for the purposes of providing a more contoured account of the war. Pericles, for example, is made to utter his final speech one year before his death from the plague in order to have him safely off the stage prior to the entrance of Cleon, the demagogic politician whom Thucydides compares unfavorably to Pericles. Yet does this recognition of Thucydides' literary artistry provide sufficient grounds for denying that the events which Thucydides describes ever happened? When we are faced with divergences between Thucydides' account and other testimony – be it the contemporary evidence of comic satirists such as Aristophanes, the public inscriptions that the Athenian democracy set up, or the later history of Diodorus of Sicily – are the criteria on which we make our ultimate judgment really only moral or aesthetic?

As I write this sentence (on Monday March 24, 2003), bombs and missiles are raining down on Baghdad. As you read these words, the conflict will (one hopes) be part of the past though what the final outcome will be is, at this stage, far from certain. The statement I have just made is undoubtedly one of those traces by which we access the past, but to insist that the past has no reality independent of those traces is to dishonor not only the Iraqi citizens killed or maimed by coalition firepower but also the American, British, Australian, Iraqi, and other servicemen and servicewomen compelled to risk their lives for their country. How one chooses to represent Operation "Iraqi Freedom" is, of course, open to a variety of choices. One might begin the story with the attempted assassination of Saddam Hussein on the morning of March 20, 2003, with the adoption of Resolution 1441 by the United Nations Security Council on November 8, 2002, with the Gulf War of 1991 or perhaps even with an examination of British colonial policy in the early twentieth century. Obviously one's ideological commitments cannot but play a role in how one interprets the war and a historical treatment could certainly be emplotted in a variety of ways – whether as a "romantic" struggle to cast off oppression (be it that of an Iraqi dictator or of a western superpower) or, more "satirically," as a venture in which there were only losers and victims. History can be a messy business and an interpretation which focuses on just one of these interpretations to the exclusion of others is unlikely to be as satisfactory as one that seeks to take account of variant, often contradictory factors. But it will certainly be more satisfactory than an analysis that displays little interest in attempting to determine what did and did not happen in the course of the war.

Of course we cannot hope to recapitulate the past "in its totality": the context against which we frame individual events is to a certain degree imagined. But in this respect the past is no different from the present. After all, I have no firsthand knowledge that bombs and missiles are currently raining down on Baghdad. I am sitting at a computer in my study in Rome and such information as I have derives from what (I think) I understand from Italian news reports on the television and from internet sites. My personal experience of the present is every bit as subjective and partial (in both senses of the word) as the historian's perception of the past, but these are not sufficient grounds for resigning myself to ignorance and refusing to attempt to comprehend what is happening. In spite of – and no doubt because of – the plethora of information available from a variety of media, strategies of disinformation are rampant on both sides of the conflict, yet the reason why facts are disputed so vehemently is because it *is* important to establish their authenticity in order to evaluate the claims that are based upon them.

White himself is not as averse to the idea of historical facts as are some of his acolytes. At a conference, held at the University of California, Los Angeles in 1990, he acknowledged that outright acceptance of his view that the grounds for distinguishing between alternative historical accounts were moral and aesthetic rather than epistemological could feasibly lend credibility to revisionist histories that denied the reality of the Holocaust. He therefore conceded that in some – though not all – cases, the type of emplotment available to the historian might actually be limited by the "real" facts, though this concession obviously undermined the view that history is entirely reducible to its narrative representation. To be fair, despite his emphasis on the literary strategies through which historical accounts are crafted, White had never denied the reality of the historical traces that the historian discovers and has even suggested that "responsibility to the rules of evidence" can help the reader "distinguish between good and bad historiography" (Canary and Kozicki 1978: 59). That is clearly not the view of other postmodernist scholars such as Jenkins, who argues that "there is a range of methods without any agreed criteria for choosing" (2003: 15).

Method and Theory

In his enumeration of feminist, *Annaliste*, neo-Marxist, structuralist, and post-structuralist "methods," Jenkins reveals a basic inability to distinguish between method and theory. Theory is essentially an explanatory tool that is applied to sets of data in order to make them comprehensible. Often, theories are generated from circumstances, situations, and contexts that are independent of the

data-sets to which they are applied. The explanatory function of theory inevitably endows it with a "presentist" quality – meaning that the theories historians
select tend to echo contemporary concerns (e.g. feminism; postcolonialism;
queer theory) while theories employed by earlier generations can fairly swiftly
appear to become outmoded (e.g. classical Marxism). The type of theory
selected will inevitably influence the form of interpretation and mode of argu-
mentation employed but it will also determine which facts are considered
relevant for the current purpose of the study. Thus a Marxist history will
obviously focus more on issues of class and class conflict while a structuralist
history will concern itself more with myths, rituals, and mentalities. To the
extent that different theories pursue different interests by means of different interpretive strategies, there are no epistemological grounds for choosing
between them. However, any theory that felt itself entirely unconstrained by
such historical facts as have survived would rightly be condemned as either
insufficient or misrepresentative. For example, a feminist history that ignored
facts unrelated to women, not because they were irrelevant to the case but
precisely because they contradicted it, would be far inferior to one that sought
to take account of the awkward counterexamples. In these cases, it is not the
theory that has been violated, but the "rules of evidence," the "critical standard" – in short, the historical method.

Perhaps I can illustrate what I mean with a musical example. A mute manuscript is given audible musical form by a pianist in the course of a recital. The
pianist decides what to play – be it Mozart, Rachmaninov, or Gershwin – and
the talented pianist will give his or her own interpretive expression to the
musical notation on the page in order to communicate with his or her audience. At the end of the day, though, there is a correct way to play the piano
(striking the keys sequentially) and an incorrect way (e.g. taking a chainsaw to
it). No doubt the latter makes for an interesting artistic expression, but only
the senselessly wealthy or acutely tone-deaf would pay money night after night
and still pretend they were listening to a pianist. By the same token, any
literary critic who espouses a particular postmodernist theory but refuses to
believe in, let alone practice, historical method cannot seriously expect to be
regarded as a historian.

Jenkins is right to say that there is no single definitive method but this is not
– or should not be – a function of which theory a historian decides to employ
but rather of the nature of the surviving historical evidence. Tchaikovsky's
music can be played on any number of instruments, but a violin is not played
in the same way as a piano, a flute, or a glockenspiel. Carr noted that he was
sometimes tempted to envy the competence of his colleagues who wrote
ancient or medieval history, but then consoled himself with the thought "that
they are so competent mainly because they are so ignorant of their subject"
(1987: 14). The remark was obviously not intended as a compliment but it
nevertheless underscores the important point that the study of modern or
contemporary history, which enjoins its practitioners to scour new or insuf-
ficiently known archival materials, requires an entirely different method from

that needed to study ancient history, where the written documentation is scant (and consequently familiar to a larger number of scholars) and where there is generally greater recourse to non-written, material evidence. And this is especially true of the Archaic period of Greek history, where such written testimony as exists is largely the product of later periods.

This book is concerned primarily with the practice of history, and especially with method. It assumes that there is a past which we can access, however incompletely, from historical traces and it accepts that the writing of history is a literary pursuit that requires a certain amount of imagination, though all interpretation – however imaginative – is to some degree constrained, or at least framed, by the available historical evidence. The fundamental question that I wish to ask is not so much "what happened?" in the Archaic period of Greek history but rather "how do we know what (we think) happened?" In fact, one of the conclusions to emerge will be that the evidence we have at our disposal is insufficient to support the sort of political–military narratives that can be written about later periods where the documentation is fuller.

On the other hand, the evidence is more amenable to the treatment of longer-term social, economic, and cultural processes. One conclusion to emerge from the chapters that follow is that an attachment to place was a more significant basis of cohesion in the earliest protohistorical communities than has previously been recognized and that this was probably a longer-term legacy of Late Bronze Age administrative organization that survived in spite of – or perhaps precisely because of – the unsettled conditions of the intervening Dark Age. Conversely, the communities that emerged from the Dark Age were relatively underdeveloped in terms of social complexity and seem not to have possessed the level of organization that is attributed to them by those later literary accounts that tell of colonial ventures in the eighth century. Instead, it is not until well into the seventh century that contemporary poetry and the earliest inscribed laws attest to the transition from a "ranked" society, in which local communities coalesced around charismatic chieftains, to a stratified society in which a true aristocratic ruling class emerged. A direct consequence of this was a more politicized consciousness among non-elite members of the community, though it is only towards the end of the Archaic period that this political consciousness was translated into action – and then only in certain cities such as Athens.

Throughout much of the Archaic period, a relatively small elite class, whose membership was recruited according to landholding and descent (the primary mechanism for the transmission of property), enacted the most important decisions within a political community which was predominantly composed of peasant landholders; beneath these were dependent laborers, serfs, and chattel slaves. Economic opportunities overseas offered new sources of wealth and, although these were initially exploited largely by aristocrats, by the sixth century there had emerged a new class of non-agricultural producers who demanded a social and political status concomitant with their wealth. Long-distance trade becomes more visible, while an examination of settlement patterns and land use suggests an intensification of agricultural practices aimed at producing a surplus for market exchange. These developments fostered, and were facilitated by, the invention of coinage, which also allowed city-states to make public expenditures on a greater scale than ever before and to invest more in monumentalizing urban centers. It is these more processual developments, rather than individual events, that the combined testimony of contemporary but fragmentary literature, inscriptions, and archaeology is best able to illuminate.

Needless to say, the historian hopes to understand the past better. It would obviously be satisfying if we could establish once and for all whether, when, and how the Lelantine War was fought, but what I hope to demonstrate in the pages that follow is that actually "doing" history, regardless of the results obtained, is also a worthwhile pursuit in itself. The practice of history is often compared with the act of translation. The fact that one is able to translate at all would suggest that the past is not entirely incommensurable or incomprehensible to the present; the fact that one needs to translate, however, underpins the fundamental differences between past and present. The historian's task is not simply to uncover the past in its own terms (even if this were possible), just as a translator cannot render an English version of Tolstoy by finding Russian synonyms. Instead, the historian must make sense of the past in terms that carry meaning in the present. In the act of translation there are often words, phrases, and concepts which are not directly translatable into another language and which reveal both the expressive nuances and the limitations of the respective languages. So, too, the practice of history, aside from yielding valuable information about the past, can impel us to become more self-aware about the assumptions, priorities, and values that our own society holds to be self-evident.

FURTHER READING

Lelantine War: Parker 1997. Eretria: Bérard 1970. Lefkandi: Popham, Sackett, and Themelis 1980.

Discussion of Archaic poetry: V. Cobb-Stevens, T. J. Figueira, and G. Nagy, "Introduction," in Figueira and Nagy 1985, 1–8. "Positivist fallacy": Snodgrass 1987: 37–8.

Theories of history: Carr 1987; Elton 1967; Jenkins 1995, 2003; White 1973; "The historical text as literary artifact," in Canary and Kozicki 1978, 41–72; "Historical emplotment and the problem of truth," in Friedländer 1992, 37–53. Reactions: Appleby, Hunt, and Jacob 1994; Windschuttle 1996; Evans 1999.

Thucydides: Connor 1984; Hornblower 1987; "Narratology and narrative techniques in Thucydides," in Hornblower 1994, 131–66.

Good recent treatments of Archaic Greece: Snodgrass 1980; Murray 1993; Osborne 1996; Mitchell and Rhodes 1997; Fisher and van Wees 1998.

2

Sources, Evidence, Dates

Evaluating Sources

Historians are often fond of distinguishing themselves from those they rather disparagingly call "antiquarians." Antiquarians, it is argued, are interested in facts for their own sake while real historians are more concerned with interpreting those facts from a broader perspective that seeks to identify interconnections, causes, and consequences. As we have seen in the previous chapter, however, facts are not "out there," waiting to be discovered by the historian; rather, they too are established through a process of interpretation. Those interpretations that command near universal acceptance – for instance, that the Greeks defeated the Persians near the Boeotian city of Plataea in the spring of 479 – are easily accorded the status of a fact. By contrast, other so-called facts – for example, that tyrants came to power in Greek cities with the support of citizen militias – are not nearly as incontrovertible. The standard, or benchmark, by which factual status is judged is the degree to which an interpretative reconstruction of a past event can claim authority from the available evidence. Such evidence exists in a wide variety of forms but pride of place has traditionally been given to written accounts or sources.

Conventionally a distinction is drawn between primary sources and secondary sources. Primary sources typically designate written materials that are contemporary to the events that they describe – normally with little in the way of interpretation or commentary. Secondary sources, instead, indicate "second hand" works of synthesis based on primary sources and normally compiled at a later date. The cardinal sin in historical practice is to confuse the two and to cite a secondary source as an authority for an argument. So, for example, an essay on the Persian War of 480–479 that cited as its only reference A. R. Burn's *Persia and the Greeks* – magisterial though it may be – would not be graded very highly. Burn's book provides an excellent introduction to the topic and presents some original hypotheses that should certainly be taken into account, but ultimately the student of history must construct a narrative on the basis of his or her interpretation of ancient accounts such as Diodorus, Plutarch, and especially Herodotus. The same is obviously true of this book. The historical conclusions that are found in the pages that follow should not be accepted uncritically but should instead be examined to see whether they provide a satisfactory interpretation of the available evidence. To repeat, the primary aim of this book is not so much to explain "what actually happened" in the Archaic Greek world but rather to illustrate how we go about writing a history of this period. This inevitably involves us in engaging with the primary sources in order to gauge the relative plausibility of the various interpretations they have generated.

This distinction between primary and secondary sources is useful – but only up to a certain point. The common tendency to regard ancient authors as primary sources is not entirely accurate. Herodotus was not an eyewitness to the great war between Greece and Persia that constitutes the central theme of his work. The *Histories* were written around the start of the Peloponnesian War in 431, almost fifty years after the Persian War, so it is clear that Herodotus' account – which actually includes plenty of commentary and interpretation – is reliant on the reports of others, and these technically count as Herodotus' primary sources. Strictly speaking, then, the *Histories* are a secondary source and, by extension, a book such as Burn's, which seeks to provide a narrative of the war on the basis of the testimony of Herodotus and other authors, is more properly to be regarded as a tertiary source. But perhaps the employment of the term "source" to describe Burns' book is not entirely appropriate either. The word "source" implies a starting-point or origin whereas it is quite clear that Burns' work of synthesis constitutes more of an end product. It is, then, probably preferable to reserve the use of the word "source" for those written materials that represent our most proximate entry-point into the ancient world.

Another problem with the primary–secondary source distinction is that it can sometimes endow ancient sources with an aura of infallibility that they do not always deserve. Historians generally regard Herodotus' account of the Persian War as more reliable than the narratives of Diodorus or Plutarch but that is not to say that Herodotus' credibility has never been called into question. Few believe that the invading Persian forces totalled 1,700,000 as Herodotus (7.60) claims, and it is generally supposed that this figure is based on a mixture of unreliable witnesses, faulty calculation, and a desire to exaggerate further the Greek achievement. It is important, then, to remember that the quality and reliability of sources may vary widely, thus necessitating what German scholars call *Quellenkritik*, or "source criticism." Sometimes it is a matter of gauging the relative merits of two or more sources that provide different or even contradictory information. More often than not, however (and especially for the Archaic period), all we have is a single, solitary source. In such cases, the best tactic is to steer a middle course between an excessive credulity, which holds that every piece of information furnished by an ancient author should be accepted on trust so long as no contradictory evidence is available, and a paralyzing hypercriticism that would admit no evidence at all.

There is no foolproof method for establishing the reliability of a source. If there were, historians would have little to occupy their time. There is, however, a set of tools or tests that at least make explicit the presuppositions one entertains when employing a particular source. The first test is that of *temporal proximity*. Was our informant an eyewitness to the events he (very rarely she) describes or was he at least contemporary to them so that he may have been able to glean information from others who were present? If not, how long after the events that are described did he write? It is an often noted – though seldom resolved – fact that most narrative histories of the Archaic Greek world are heavily dependent upon isolated notices provided by authors writing many centuries later. To take an example, in the eighth chapter of her *Archaic Greece: The City-States c. 700–500 BC*, published in 1976, Lilian Jeffery discusses the history of Sparta in the seventh and sixth centuries. Of 112 literary sources cited, only two date to the Archaic period – namely, Tyrtaeus' claim (fr. 5) that the conquest of Messenia lasted twenty years and a reference by the Corinthian poet Eumelus (fr. 11) to the fact that Apollo was originally worshipped in the form of a column. Almost 43 percent of the cited sources date to the fifth century – the vast majority deriving from Herodotus – but well over one third date to the late first century CE or later. This is less a criticism of Jeffery – who, it should be said, supplemented literary evidence with epigraphic testimony and material evidence – as it is a characterization of the difficulties that face the historian of Archaic Greece with respect to sources.

It should be stressed that there need not be any direct correlation between a source's reliability and its temporal proximity to the events it relates. A writer might, for any number of reasons, decide wilfully to misrepresent a situation. But, even in the absence of deliberate duplicity, no two eyewitnesses will normally perceive – let alone remember – the same event in identical ways. Thucydides (1.22.3) famously observed that it was no simple matter to verify the truth of eyewitness reports of the Peloponnesian War "because those who were present at the various events did not say the same things about them, whether out of goodwill to one side or the other or else as a result of faulty memory." On the other hand, later authors were not always as creative or inventive as modern scholars would have us believe. Writers such as Strabo, Plutarch, and Pausanias often consulted earlier works and in some cases it is possible to hunt down those earlier authorities – a practice that is known in German scholarship as *Quellenforschung*, or "the search for sources." For example, our principal source for the constitution of Sparta in the Archaic period is Plutarch (*Lyc.* 6), writing in the late first and early second centuries CE, who cites a document that has come to be known as the "Great Rhetra." Since, however, Plutarch cites the fourth-century philosopher Aristotle in explaining some of the more arcane provisions of the Rhetra and since we know that Aristotle – or rather one of his pupils – wrote a now lost *Constitution of the Spartans*, it is not an unreasonable inference that Plutarch's information derives from an earlier work of at least the fourth century. Whether or not the Aristotelian work was itself based on earlier information is a more difficult question to answer (see further pp. 184–7). In fact, it is generally difficult to trace back beyond the fourth or fifth centuries the sources employed by writers living under the Roman Empire without resorting to conjectural lines of trans- mission between shadowy authors who are little more than names to us. And more often than not, the search for the sources on which Roman imperial writers drew carries us back only as far as the Hellenistic period of the third and second centuries. The test of temporal proximity comes with no guaran- tees as to reliability but it remains the case that the employment of a late source demands a greater burden of proof in establishing its authoritative credentials.

The second test is that of *contextual fit*. How well does the source fit against the general context or background of what we think we know about either the period in which the described events occurred or else the period in which the author was writing? Alternatively, how does a specific piece of information relate to other writings by the same author? If, for example, we are confronted by an author whom we know to have been a committed anti-Athenian or a staunch supporter of aristocratic rule, then we will probably not be misled into assuming that such information is necessarily representative of wider opinion. "Contextualist" approaches have recently come under fire from postmodernist scholars, who argue that since a historical context is itself constructed out of numerous individual sources, it is fallacious to regard it as a more "objective" or "real" set of circumstances against which the authenticity of any individual source can be measured. Yet the issue of objectivity is a red herring: since historical practice is by nature interpretative, it is necessarily subjective (which is not to say that it bears no relation to underlying historical realities). It is perfectly legitimate to interpret an individual source in light of the broader understanding we have gained from the study of other sources just as our cognitive faculties process new information on the basis of earlier (subjective) sensory perceptions. When we come across a source that cannot be accommod- ated within what we imagine to be the broader historical context, we should certainly be prepared to entertain the possibility that the context we have constructed is unsatisfactory. But more often than not, the most common reason why a source cannot be accommodated within a broader context is because it never belonged to that context in the first place.

Let us consider a couple of concrete examples. As we saw in chapter 1, Plutarch (*Mor.* 760e–761b) relates how the Thessalian cavalry commander Kleomakhos was killed while aiding the Chalcidians in the Lelantine War and adds that he was granted the honour of burial in the agora at Chalcis, where his tomb was marked by a tall column. This piece of information clearly scores poorly in the test of temporal proximity, but what about that of contextual fit? Let us assume for the sake of argument that the Lelantine War was a real event that occurred around or shortly after 700. Would Thessalians have aided

Chalcidians in the early seventh century? Would warriors be granted elaborate burial rites in the agora at this date? And did tall columns typically serve as grave markers in this period? Given their geographical proximity, the idea of Thessalian military support for a Euboean city is not, in principle, unthinkable, though we know next to nothing about interstate relations in this period. That warriors might be granted elaborate, even "heroizing" burials finds confirmation in the West Gate cemetery at Eretria (p. 2), but there is no evidence at this date that distinguished luminaries were buried in the heart of the city or even that the agora was a common feature of early cities (pp. 80–2). As for grave monuments, certitude is impossible but tall columns are unlikely to have served as tomb markers until the sixth century at the earliest.

The principle of contextual fit does not always need to operate negatively. A first-century geographical account in iambic meter, once attributed to Scymnus of Chios (589), relates how a hero named Physkos was the son of Aetolos. The notice might, at first sight, appear trivial but genealogical expressions such as this were the standard mode through which the ancient Greeks conceived of relationships between peoples and settlements.

Physkeis was, in the Classical period, the principal federal sanctuary for the Western Locrians so the genealogy implies some sort of derivative or sub-ordinate relationship of the Western Locrians vis-à-vis the Aetolians. Around two centuries later, Plutarch (*Mor.* 294e) claimed that Physkos was the son not of Aetolos but of Amphiktyon. The test of temporal proximity might lend more credence to the account attributed to Scymnus but the test of contextual fit suggests that it was Plutarch who was following the more ancient tradition. A number of ancient authors, from at least the fifth century onwards, regarded Amphiktyon as the original founder of the Pylaian Amphictiony, a league of predominantly central Greek states – including West Locris – that adminis-tered Apollo's sanctuary at Delphi. A genealogical tradition that makes Physkos the son of Amphiktyon almost certainly symbolizes the role that the Locrians played within the early development of this league, prior to Thessalian domin-ance in the later seventh and sixth centuries, and this provides the best pos-itive contextual fit for the genealogical tradition furnished by Plutarch. The notice attributed to Scymnus, on the other hand, fits most plausibly within a third-century context, after the Aetolians had seized control of Delphi and annexed Locris.

The third test is that of *intentionality*. What is it that our source deliberately wants to communicate and what prior knowledge or presuppositions are casually assumed? Both Herodotus (5.62–65; 6.123) and Thucydides (1.20; 6.53–59) go to great lengths to argue that the tyranny at Athens was ended not by Harmodius' and Aristogiton's assassination of Pisistratus' younger son Hipparchus in 514 but by the Spartan expulsion of Hipparchus' older brother Hippias in 510. The Spartan intervention, we are told, was prompted by the Delphic oracle which had been bribed by the Athenian aristocratic family of the Alcmaeonidae (see pp. 210–12). The fact that both authors are so insistent could suggest one – or perhaps even both – of two things. Either the two historians had invested considerable time and energies in ascertaining the truth of the matter and were frustrated by what they regarded as widespread popular ignorance in this regard or else they had a personal or political agenda to promote, be it their own or that of their informants. There are good grounds for believing that Thucydides – and perhaps also Herodotus – had close relations with members of the Alcmaeonid family which might lead one to suspect the latter option, though the former is not necessarily thereby excluded. In either case, the intentionality behind this information – which is not entirely germane to the general narrative of either author – reveals that a large part of the Athenian public thought otherwise and that also is a fact that deserves further historical interpretation.

On the other hand, there is much information in these passages that is not so marked by intentionality. When Thucydides (6.54.6) talks about the Pisistratus, son of Hippias, "who dedicated the altar of the Twelve Gods in the *agora* and that of Apollo in the Pythion," we can presume that the location of these altars was common knowledge to his readership (unless Thucydides was prone to careless or imprecise lapses, which the test of contextual fit would seem to rule out). The attribution of the altars to Pisistratus is more intentionally marked than their location, though far less so than the identity of those who put an end to the tyranny and, in fact, the inscription from the Python that Thucydides cites verbatim ("Pisistratus, son of Hippias, dedicated this memorial of his magistracy in the precinct of Pythian Apollo") was discovered near the Ilissos river in 1877 and is now in the Epigraphic Museum of Athens (ML 11 = Fornara 37). As we shall see, much of the contemporary literary evidence available for the Archaic period tends to fall within the unintentional category.

Dating Archaic Poets

The first work to be written in prose rather than poetry is generally believed to be an astronomical treatise, now known only from fragments, composed by Anaximander of Miletus around the middle of the sixth century. The first complete prose work to have survived to the present, however, is Herodotus' *Histories*, written more than a century later. In acclaiming Herodotus the "father of history," Cicero (*Laws* 1.1.5) also admitted that his account contained many tales (*fabulae*) and this tendency was further impugned by writers such as Plutarch and Lucian. By the time of the Renaissance, the evidently fabulous quality of many of the descriptions and accounts included in the *Histories* failed to persuade the Tuscan scholar Francesco Petrarca of Herodotus' credentials as a historian; indeed, the sixteenth-century Spanish humanist Juan Luis Vives argued that he should more properly be regarded as the father of lies than as the father of history. Herodotus' fortunes revived in the age of exploration when the opening up of the New World spawned travel accounts that seemed no less fabulous than those to be found in the *Histories*, but with the rise of "positivist" history in the nineteenth century, Herodotus' qualities could hardly fail to suffer in comparison with Thucydides, considered to be the first truly "scientific" historian.

In recent decades Herodotus' reputation has been rehabilitated as scholars have come to recognize that he was concerned with such fundamental historical considerations as source criticism (to the extent that this was possible) and causation. Nonetheless, although Herodotus' work has frequently been mined for information concerning the Archaic period, it is important to remember that his principal aim was not to document the earlier history of Greece for its own sake but to record the great conflict between Greece and Persia in 480–479 and to explore the reasons why they fought one another. Chronologically distanced from the war he describes, let alone the events that had occurred previously, his intention in discussing earlier events and personalities is almost invariably dictated by the consequences that he believed these had for the origins and course of the great war and this makes the tests of contextual fit and intentionality especially urgent.

Our only contemporary literary evidence for the Archaic period is almost exclusively poetic in character. Although largely anonymous epic narratives such as the *Homeric Hymns* or the *Shield of Heracles* have survived, the predominant literary expression in this period is what is generally dubbed "lyric poetry." These poems share the characteristic that they were intended to be chanted or else accompanied by the lyre or double-pipe, but in other respects the category of lyric poetry embraces a wide diversity of types. Some poets (e.g. Alcman, Simonides, and Pindar) composed choral verses for religious and civic festivals and we can probably assume that the values expressed are broadly representative of wider social opinion. Others (e.g. Sappho, Alcaeus, Anacreon, Phocylides, and Xenophanes) composed solo songs, especially for the *symposium* or male drinking-party, and these inevitably exhibit more factional interests or personal viewpoints; the verses ascribed to Theognis of Megara purport to represent the last-ditch attempt of an embattled aristocrat to defend traditional values against the growing influence of the nouveaux riches. Poets such as Tyrtaeus of Sparta or Callinus of Ephesus composed exhortatory martial poetry while those such as Mimnermus of Colophon or Solon of Athens turned their hand to didactic poetry. The poems of Archilochus of Paros treat the popular lyric themes of love, sex, and inebriation but employ an ironic and satirical stance that was exploited further in the abusive and often obscene verses of Hipponax of Ephesus.

With the partial exception of Pindar, no complete works have survived from any of these lyric poets. All we have are fragments. These may be fragments in the literal sense – scraps of papyrus, normally preserved in the arid conditions of Egypt, on which Hellenistic or Roman scholars copied verses from earlier texts. More frequently, however, we employ the term "fragments" to denote citations in the works of later authors. Nearly all of the verses ascribed to Solon, for example, are quotations from the fourth-century Aristotelian *Athenian Constitution*, Plutarch's *Life of Solon*, and the *Anthology* compiled by the fifth-century CE scholar Stobaeus. With fragments of now lost prose works it is sometimes difficult to determine whether a later author is citing his source verbatim or merely paraphrasing it, but the fact that poetry was written in meter and often in a rather distinctive literary dialect means that it is generally easy to identify where the quotation begins and ends.

Archaic poets score well on the test of temporal proximity and, given that their intention was seldom to provide for posterity the sort of information that the historian seeks, this testimony is potentially extremely valuable for documenting ideas, attitudes, and values among various sectors of society in the Archaic period. Unfortunately, the recent philological challenge to the "auto-biographical" nature of lyric poetry and the suggestion that the verses ascribed to Archilochus or Theognis are more a cumulative synthesis of a city's poetic traditions than the *oeuvre* of a single, historical individual (see p. 6) mean that it is hazardous to use them to date events. Take Tyrtaeus: one of his poems (fr. 4), preserved in the sixth chapter of Plutarch's *Life of Lycurgus*, has often been taken to paraphrase some of the wording of the Great Rhetra. Since a Byzantine encyclopaedia known as the *Suda* dates Tyrtaeus to the thirty-fifth Olympiad (640–637), scholars have generally assumed that the Great Rhetra must therefore predate the mid-seventh century. But we cannot be entirely sure how the *Suda* derived its date for Tyrtaeus and if the poems traditionally attributed to Tyrtaeus were not, in fact, the work of a single individual but part of a continuous poetic tradition at Sparta, then we lose an important chronological indication for the adoption of the Spartan constitution. The anti-autobiographical viewpoint is, of course, only a hypothesis (though one that carries conviction in the case of Theognis), but until such time as the matter can be resolved to near satisfaction, the historian would be well advised to exercise caution in using the evidence of Archaic poets to date events with any precision.

It is in some senses surprising that our most complete poetic works from the Archaic period are also the earliest – the *Iliad* and the *Odyssey*, traditionally ascribed to Homer, and the *Theogony* and *Works and Days*, assigned to Hesiod. Although there is some debate as to whether each pair of works was really composed by the same author, there is general agreement that the *Iliad* precedes the *Odyssey* and that the *Theogony* precedes *Works and Days*. Most scholars also now believe that, save for the closing verses of the *Theogony* and perhaps the final section of the *Works and Days*, the internal artistic and literary unity of the four poems points to a single composer for each rather than a continuous poetic tradition (though the Homeric epics certainly employed motifs and narratives that had been circulating orally for centuries). What meets with less consensus is the relative dating of the Hesiodic poems vis-à-vis the Homeric epics and the absolute dates that should be assigned to each. Modern scholarship has generally favoured the anteriority of the Homeric poems and stylistic analysis of the diction in the four works would appear to argue for the traditional sequence: *Iliad, Odyssey, Theogony, Works and Days*. But several ancient authors list Hesiod before Homer when citing the earliest Greek poets and it has recently been argued that several passages of the *Iliad* actually echo Hesiodic poetry rather than vice versa.

In terms of absolute dates, ancient authors provide varying estimates for when Homer and Hesiod lived: Herodotus (2.53.2) dates them to the later ninth century, Strabo (1.2.9) to the mid-seventh. For this reason scholars have turned to independent, external indications, though here too consensus has proved elusive. It was once thought that the appearance of mythical scenes known from Homer on pottery dating to the second half of the eighth century and the contemporary appearance of votive offerings at Late Bronze Age tombs betrayed an awakened interest in the mythical age, inspired by the dissemination of the Homeric epics. However, the pictorial scenes could represent mythical episodes that were independently followed by both artist and poet while the tomb offerings are probably to be connected with cults to anonymous ancestors rather than named, Homeric heroes. A late eighth-century East Greek *kotylê*, found in a grave at Pithecusae, carries a metrical inscription which seems at first sight to echo the Homeric description of Nestor's drinking cup in the *Iliad* (11.632–37), though several scholars believe that the Pithecusae cup follows in an entirely different tradition. For some, Odysseus' wanderings reflect the great age of colonization in the last third of the eighth century, but others regard them as more indicative of a "protocolonial" phase dating to the late ninth century. Hesiod's reference (*Th.* 490–500) to the sanctuary at Delphi could belong to any time after ca. 800 – the date from which cultic activity is first attested at the shrine. Descriptions in the Homeric epics of weaponry and battle tactics seem to presuppose the advent of hoplite warfare, which is normally dated to the first half of the seventh century (see pp. 157–63). Finally, it has been suggested that the Homeric description of Achilles' shield (*Il.* 18.468–608) parallels early seventh-century Cypro-Phoenician metal vessels and that the premonition of the sack of Troy in the *Iliad* (12.17–32) consciously echoes accounts of the sack of Babylon at the hands of the Assyrian king Sennacherib in 689. For these reasons, there is a growing view among scholars that the Homeric and Hesiod poems date to the first half of the seventh century but no universal agreement has been reached and detailed chronological arguments based exclusively on the supposed dates of the poems are untenable.

In the case of the Homeric epics, problems are compounded by the fact that both the *Iliad* and the *Odyssey* purport to portray the distant world of a Heroic Age. Earlier assumptions that this world matched the Mycenaean palatial civilization of the sixteenth to thirteenth centuries were finally dispelled after the decipherment, in 1952, of Late Bronze Age documents (the so-called Linear B tablets) revealed a society that was structured and organized very differently from that depicted by Homer (see pp. 42–3). Moses Finley, the ancient historian who had already anticipated the implications of the decipherment of Linear B, believed that the society portrayed in the epics was, from the standpoint of sociological and anthropological analysis, coherent and consistent and to be dated to the Dark Age of the tenth and ninth centuries. He urged this date partly because the *polis* or city-state barely figures in the epics and partly because he believed that other features represented in the poems – for example, the emphasis on bronze tripods and cauldrons, the practice of cremation burial and the apparent monopoly that Phoenicians exercise over trade – could hardly date as late as the eighth century. Yet tripods continued to be manufactured and dedicated in the eighth century, cremation remained in many areas an elite mode of funerary disposal even after the reintroduction of inhumation in the eighth century and it is now no longer certain that the Phoenicians were traversing the seas so much earlier than the Greeks. As for the *polis*, there is some danger of a circular argument since many scholars have attempted to date its emergence on the basis of the Homeric epics. Neither poem has any intrinsic reason for being concerned with the *polis*: the *Iliad* focuses on the tenth year of an overseas military campaign waged in Asia Minor while the *Odyssey* is about the wanderings of an individual and the survival of his *oikos* or "household." Yet, for all this, the *polis* does feature in the *Odyssey* and many have observed how, in the *Iliad*, both the city of Troy and the makeshift camp of the besieging Achaeans betray features normally associated with the *polis*.

Archaeologists have typically paid attention to objects or institutions mentioned by the epics that can be dated by independent means; observing that they belong to widely divergent periods, they assume that "Homeric society" is composite in nature – a sort of fantastic or utopian community that existed in no single place or point in time. More recently, however, historians have argued that the social structures and behavioral values portrayed in the Homeric epics are broadly consistent and that the apparent anachronisms or artificial elements identified by archaeologists are deliberately employed by the poet(s) as an archaizing "patina," intended to provide epic distance from the here and now. Ultimately, they argue, the society depicted by Homer, for all its apparent remoteness in time, had to make sense to a contemporary audience much in the same way that science fiction seldom represents a world that is incomprehensible to a modern audience or readership (we are expected to identify with the values and ideals held by the crew of the Starship Enterprise). If so, the society that Homer portrays should match to some degree the historical conditions of the late eighth century. Again, however, caution is required.

Of the two poems ascribed to Hesiod, the *Theogony* is valuable for the conception it projects of the relationship between gods and mortals – particularly with regard to divine justice – and for what it reveals about Greek religious thought and practice in the early period (though it is a moot point whether Hesiod describes or prescribes conventional thinking in this regard). Of more interest to the social historian, however, is *Works and Days* – a poem that takes a supposed inheritance dispute between the author and his brother Perses as a starting-point for a discussion of moral behavior. Whether the poem should really be read autobiographically is the subject of dispute. One wonders how an individual who, in some senses, conforms to all the characteristics of a peasant society and continuously urges the necessity of labor to avoid falling below the breadline managed to find the time to compete in poetic contests (*WD* 650–9). One may also wonder whether Boeotian smallholders were typically imbued in the sort of oriental myths and aphorisms from Near Eastern wisdom literature that are so prevalent in the poem and it is for this reason that some scholars regard "Hesiod" as a poetic *persona*, adopted by the author of *Works and Days* for narrative purposes. Nevertheless, it is quite clear that the world depicted by the poet is the contemporary world – the moral and didactic purpose of the poem would make no sense otherwise – and for this reason, *Works and Days* can rightfully be regarded as one of the most significant literary documents for the historian of the Archaic Greek world.

Non-Literary Evidence

By epigraphic evidence, we mean texts that were inscribed or painted on surfaces of stone, metal, or terracotta (inscriptions were presumably also written on wood and wax though this seldom survives in the archaeological record). Technically, the distinction between epigraphic and literary testimony is not entirely accurate: as we have seen, the inscription on the so-called "Nestor's Cup" at Pithecusae was metrical and epitaphs were often composed in verse. A more precise distinction between the two categories of evidence is that inscriptions provide us with direct and unmediated access to the moment of their production whereas literary texts have come down to us through a long and complicated process of textual transmission, in which copying errors and editorial choices have intervened. Inscriptions may be either public (decrees; law codes; civic dedications or commemorations) or private (personal dedications; epitaphs; graffiti). The test of intentionality must always be applied but the fact that most inscriptions are contemporary with the information they communicate serves to endow them with a particular reliability. The principal factor that compromises this reliability is their state of preservation. Metal corrodes or is recycled, while stone wears, splinters, and fractures and this means that many inscriptions are not entirely legible, requiring "restorations" (indicated within square brackets) on the part of the editor. Such restorations are more than mere guesswork – they rely on an extensive knowledge of typical formulae and expressions employed in similar inscriptions – but they must always be approached with caution.

Inscriptions are next to useless for historical purposes unless they can be dated. From the Classical period, public decrees often specified the name of the magistrate who presided in the year they were proposed (see below), but this seldom happens in the Archaic period and, when it does, we invariably lack external evidence that would allow us to assign any named magistrate to a specific year. Occasionally a monument which can be dated by archaeological means allows us to date inscriptions that were displayed on it, though very many inscriptions are found detached from their original archaeological context because they were reused as building materials – either in antiquity or in more modern periods – or else excavated illegally and sold on the antiquities market. For these reasons, a large number of Archaic inscriptions are dated on the basis of letter-forms. Much like pottery styles (see below), the shapes of alphabetic letters varied between regions and over time. Some indications for the rate at which such letter forms evolved are provided by external chronological checks: the Nestor inscription can be dated by the style of the vase on which it appears while the use of inscriptions as building materials in the Athenian fortifications of the 470s provides a *terminus ante quem* (a latest possible date) for the shapes of the letters attested on the stones. The method is not precise and is generally insensitive to calligraphic differences between individuals, so the dating ascribed to the vast majority of Archaic inscriptions should usually be regarded as very approximate.

Inscriptions generally furnish information that is qualitatively different from that to be found in literary sources but they can also make up for gaps in our historical knowledge, especially in the Classical and Hellenistic periods and especially outside of Athens. Even in Classical Athens, however, much of our knowledge for how the Athenian Empire functioned is owed not to literary sources but to inscriptions – in particular, the annual lists of tribute paid to the Treasury of Athena by Athens' allies. By contrast, epigraphic evidence has played a less prominent role in Archaic Greece. Although more than 5,000 inscriptions are known from the period, the vast majority are simply names, indicating possession, or short dedications – e.g. "Hariknidas dedicated (this) to the white-armed goddess, Hera" (*SEG* 36.341). Nevertheless, as we shall see, epigraphic testimony has provided some valuable evidence for the nature of early laws and constitutions, relations between states and religious and commemorative practices.

Numismatic evidence (i.e. coins) has also played a relatively minor role in studying the history of the Archaic Greek world. There are two reasons for this. Firstly, coinage appears fairly late in the period – around the middle of the sixth century in a few states in mainland Greece. Secondly, unlike coins of the Hellenistic and Roman periods, which often commemorated specific events, reigns, or dynasties, the earliest issues of coins appear to be longer-lived and more concerned with establishing a widely recognizable standard than with communicating propaganda. In later periods, coins can provide important dating standards for archaeological contexts (though care needs to be exercised since coins might be hoarded and their small size may easily result in them appearing in archaeological contexts dating to an entirely different period from that in which they were minted). In the Archaic period, by contrast, coins often have to be dated by other archaeological artifacts found with them – though, once again, this technique is unavailable for those many coins that have been acquired illegally and sold on the antiques market with no note of their original provenance. For all that, Archaic coins do provide important information about the self-image that city-states wished to project and both distribution charts of known issues and comparison of varying weight-standards allow us to draw important conclusions about the nature of Archaic trade (see chapter 10).

Given the ubiquitous and contemporary nature of the material record, it may seem surprising that ancient historians should have resisted employing archaeological evidence until comparatively recently. This has much to do with the historical development of the two disciplines. For so long as classical archaeologists concerned themselves chiefly with great objects of art, their subject matter served as convenient illustrations for the scholarly preoccupations of historians who tended to focus primarily on political and military matters and the rise and fall of civilizations. The Parthenon exhibited the grandiose but serene splendor of Athenian hegemony while the exuberance of Hellenistic sculpture reflected the decadence of a Greek world in the twilight of its years, subjected to Macedonian despots. But as archaeologists began to interest themselves in the totality of material culture and in issues such as the function and meaning of objects, many preferred to affiliate themselves with anthropologists rather than historians (who failed to find much excitement in the questions archaeologists were asking). It is only really in the past two decades – and largely due to the so-called "Cambridge School" associated with Anthony Snodgrass – that a new synthesis has arisen between classical archaeologists and ancient historians as the former have once again recognized the importance of the historical dimension and the latter have turned to more social and cultural issues.

It is obvious that archaeology has a particularly crucial role to play in periods or in regions for which there is little in the way of literary, epigraphic, or numismatic evidence, but Finley's proclamation that "[i]t is self-evident that the potential contribution of archaeology to history is, in a rough way, inversely proportional to the quantity and quality of the available written sources" (1986: 93) is anything but self-evident. The misconception arises from a commonly held belief that the role of archaeological evidence is merely to illustrate written materials. Archaeology has been summoned in from the cold but all too often only to serve as a handmaid to – rather than a bedfellow of – ancient history. There are two reasons why this understanding of the relationship between the two disciplines is flawed. Firstly, archaeology highlights a whole range of issues that are often quite different from those emphasized in literary sources. New, more meticulous techniques of excavation, trace element analysis, petrology, and floral and faunal analysis have yielded vital information about settlement use, public and domestic space, diet, environmental conditions, and cultural and commercial exchange that are barely hinted at in literary sources. Field survey, a non-intrusive investigation in which teams of walkers traverse fields in search of surface material – normally pottery sherds and roof tiles – which is then dated by ceramic experts, provides answers to questions concerning regional settlement patterns and land use that are seldom raised by ancient authors. There is a good deal more to archaeology than providing dates for historians – though that too is important (see below).

Secondly, the old distinction between "subjective" literary sources and the "objective" archaeological evidence that can confirm or refute them has receded somewhat. Most critically aware archaeologists have now come to recognize that interpretation of the material record is every bit as subjective as the historical interpretation of sources. Furthermore, material culture is not merely the passive "footprint" of past human behavior. People use material objects for particular purposes. In modern parlance, archaeology is a "discourse" but one that is entirely different from the discourse to which literary sources belong – what people say they do and what they actually do in practice are often two different things. This – together with the extremely fragmentary character of both written and material evidence – is why historians need to be careful to avoid the "positivist fallacy" of mechanically equating what we find in the archaeological record with what we know from the literary sources (see p. 7). Any given artifact or cultural feature should first be examined in its own context – both the archaeological context in which it was originally deposited and the broader context of contemporary materials among which it previously circulated – before any attempt is made to match it with information deriving from written sources. Occasionally there is a happy congruence, though cases where words and things do not appear to converge are no less interesting from the historian's point of view.

Ancient Chronography

The historian's apparent obsession with dates arises not from a passion for trivia but from the fact that "the study of history is a study of causes" (Carr 1987: 87). Establishing which events came first and which occurred later is an essential first step in determining whether or not a causal relationship exists between them. This is not to say that because a certain event succeeds another, it is necessarily a consequence of it: an old historical adage warns against the assumption *post hoc ergo propter hoc* (literally, "after this and therefore on account of this"). On the other hand, it is no good positing that an event is the cause of another if it is patently clear that it came after, not before, it. For most practical purposes it would be sufficient merely to establish a relative sequence of events, though this is normally only possible if we know absolute dates by years and – where possible – months and days.

In most regions of ancient Greece, the year was divided into twelve lunar months (Figure 2.1), though the names of these months varied from city to city, as did the conventions governing how years were reckoned. Generally speaking, the political systems of most Greek states, democratic or oligarchic, were characterized to some degree by the principle of rotation of political office and each year was named after the most important magistrate who presided in that period. At Sparta the senior of the five annually-elected ephors ("overseers") gave his name to the year while of the nine archons ("rulers") at Athens, the highest ranking was known as the "eponymous archon" because

	Athens	Miletus	Rhodes	Epidaurus
1	Hekatombaion	Panemos	Panamos	Azosios
2	Metageitnion	Metageitnion	Karneios	Karneios
3	Boedromion	Boedromion	Dalios	Proratios
4	Pyanepsion	Pyanopsion	Thesmophorios	Hermaios
5	Maimakterion	Apatourion	Diosthyos	Gamos
6	Poseideon	Poseideon	Theudaisios	Teleos
7	Gamelion	Lenaion	Pedageitnios	Posidauos
8	Anthesterion	Anthesterion	Badromios	Artamitios
9	Elaphebolion	Artemision	Sminthios	Agrianios
10	Mounykhion	Taureon	Artamitios	Panamos
11	Thargelion	Thargelion	Agrianios	Kuklios
12	Skirophorion	Kalamaion	Hyakinthios	Apellaios

Figure 2.1 List of months at Athens, Miletus, Rhodes, and Epidaurus (n.b. the year began in mid-summer)

it was his name that was recorded in connection with events that occurred during his tenure of office. So, for example, the Parian Marble, an inscribed table of events set up on the Cycladic island of Paros in the mid-third century, says that the Pisistratid tyrants of Athens had been expelled from the city 248 years earlier "when the archon at Athens was Harpaktides" (Fornara 1A). Since the archons assumed their duties in the summer, Greek years are often given a double notation – in this case, 511/10.

A list of archons was set up in the Athenian agora ca. 425. Today, all that survives of it are four fragments of marble on which the names of known archons of the sixth and early fifth centuries are recorded (ML 6 = Fornara 23), though it is normally assumed that the inscription originally carried the names of all the archons stretching back to 683/2 – the year in which, according to the Parian Marble, archons were appointed on an annual basis rather than for ten-year terms. It is possible that the inscription "updated" earlier lists of archons but other indications suggest that the Greeks only really acquired an interest in chronography towards the end of the fifth century (see below). Presumably, the custom of recording the eponymous archon for each year became regular thereafter, meaning that we can be fairly confident about events dated to archon years subsequent to ca. 425. It is also reasonable to suppose that the names of archons and the order in which they held office over the previous two, and perhaps even three, generations was a matter of public memory. Beyond that, however, it is difficult to know how credible our information is. The compiler of the list might have come across informants who had reason to believe that their great-grandfather had been eponymous archon 140 years earlier but, in the absence of official lists, such testimony would surely have been unverifiable. The fact that the name Kreon – traditionally recorded as the first of the annually appointed archons – is a synonym for "archon" hardly dispels such suspicions.

Another way of reckoning years was by major Panhellenic festivals. Aristotle and his nephew Callisthenes were said to have compiled a register of victors at the Pythian Games of Delphi in the third quarter of the fourth century. Still earlier, towards the end of the fifth century, the sophist Hippias of Elis published a list of those who had won the *stadion* (the 200 meter race) at each Olympic festival, stretching back to the supposed first Olympic Games of 776. Hippias' list has not survived but it is widely believed that it was used for the early part of a list of Olympic victors from 776 to 211 CE, recorded by the third-century CE Christian philosopher Sextus Julius Africanus and preserved in the *Chronicle* of Eusebius, the fourth-century bishop of Caesarea. As in the case of the Athenian archons, Africanus' list implies that victories were regularly recorded from the time of Hippias onwards but it is less clear how much credibility should be given to Hippias' original list. We can assume fundamental accuracy for the fifth-century and perhaps even late sixth-century victors and it is entirely possible that it was easier to remember that a family member had won the *stadion* thirty-five Olympiads ago than that he had been archon 140 years earlier. It is, however, difficult to believe that all of the names in Hippias' list rest on unimpeachable testimony and many doubt whether the Olympic Games were really as ancient as Hippias pretended – especially since the other great Panhellenic games at Delphi, Isthmia, and Nemea were only organized formally in the early sixth century. Even Plutarch (*Num.* 1), whose anecdotes are too often and too uncritically employed to write the history of the Archaic period, was skeptical about the veracity of Hippias' work.

A third way of dating events to years was by the tenure of religious office. This is the method that was adopted by a contemporary of Hippias, Hellanicus of Mytilene, for his *Hiereiai* – a chronicle of historical events organized according to the successive years of office served by the priestess at the sanctuary of Hera outside Argos. Only around eleven fragments, all references by later authors, have survived of this originally three-volume work but there is reason to believe that Hellanicus provided a series of synchronisms that anchored his chronological scheme both to the Athenian archon list and to the Spartan list of ephors. Indeed, it is sometimes claimed that it was Hellanicus who was responsible for the publication of the Athenian archon list ca. 425. Either way, it was almost certainly on Hellanicus' *Hiereiai* that Thucydides (2.2.1) drew when he wrote that the Peloponnesian War broke out "when Khrysis had held the priestess-hood at Argos for forty-eight years and Ainesios was ephor at Sparta and when there were still two months remaining of the archonship of Pythodoros at Athens" (431 in our terms). Surprisingly, perhaps, these lists of officials were not synchronized with the Olympic victors lists until the beginning of the third century. According to Polybius (12.11.1), it was the Sicilian historian Timaeus of Tauromenium who first matched the Olympic victors lists to the lists of Argive priestesses, Spartan ephors, and Athenian archons though dating by Olympiads was not truly exploited until the chronographic works of Eratosthenes of Cyrene later in the century.

The synchronisms established by Hellanicus, Timaeus, and Eratosthenes only produced correspondences between relative chronological systems. Three further developments were required before ancient reckonings of years could be translated into our modern western chronological scheme (based on Pope Gregory XIII's modification of the Julian calendar in 1582 CE, though the "Gregorian Calendar" was not introduced in Britain or America until 1752). The first, achieved by Eusebius in his *Chronika*, was the synchronism of Olympiads with both the Hebrew system of dating by years "after Abraham" and the Roman annalistic traditions of years that had elapsed since the city of Rome had been founded (*ab urbe condita*). This work only exists today in a fragmentary Byzantine Greek edition, an Armenian edition, and a Latin translation undertaken by Jerome in the early fifth century CE, and unfortunately these different versions do not always furnish the same date. The second was the calculation by the sixth-century Scythian monk Dionysius Exiguus that 248 years had elapsed since the Roman emperor Diocletian had come to power and that 532 years had passed *ab incarnatione Domini* ("from the incarnation of the lord" – i.e. since the birth of Christ). Working backwards from a base line of 532 CE, Diocletian's reign would therefore have begun in 284 CE. The third was the extension, in the early seventeenth century, of Dionysius Exiguus' calculations back into the pre-common era by the French Jesuit theologian Dionysius Petavius. Since Diocletian was acclaimed emperor 1,037 years after the date Varro assigns for the foundation of Rome, then Rome was founded in 753. And since Rome was said to have been founded in the third year of the sixth Olympiad, then the first Olympic Games took place in 776.

It is worth pointing out that, since all chronographic systems are to a certain degree arbitrary and conventional, the accuracy or even historicity of Christ's birth is irrelevant. Had Dionysius Exiguus decided to rename the 248th year of the Diocletianic era, say, year nine of the papacy of John I, the basic chronological scheme would not be affected. The first Olympic Games would still have been dated 1,308 years earlier and the foundation of Rome would still have been dated twenty-three years after that. The uncertainties that arise derive not from the chronographic system in itself but from the credibility of the dates that are assigned to events. For example, we are on firm ground when Pausanias (10.2.1) dates the Phocian capture of Delphi to "the fourth year of the 105th Olympiad, when Proros of Cyrene won the *stadion*" (357/6 in our calendar). But when, elsewhere (4.15.1), he dates the outbreak of the Second Messenian War to the fourth year of the twenty-third Olympiad (685), we are entitled to wonder how reliable this date is, given that it predates the compilation of the Olympic victors lists by more than two and a half centuries. Furthermore, the synchronisms that were established in the later fifth century only really work if the Olympic Games were held without fail every four years or if magistrates always succeeded one another on an annual basis. There are some indications that this was not always the case and, unless such aberrations were explicitly noted in the registers, the correlations between different chronological schemes in their earlier phases would be less secure. As a general rule of thumb, it is probably prudent to regard with some suspicion all precise calendar dates prior to the middle of the sixth century.

Archaeological Dating

The scarcity and possible unreliability of dates offered by literary sources for the earlier Archaic period mean that dates derived from archaeological evidence are of the utmost importance. In theory, material objects can be dated by a battery of scientific techniques, of which the best known is radiocarbon dating, pioneered by Willard Libby in 1949. Applied to organic materials, this technique measures the rate of decay of the radioactive Carbon[14] isotope compared with the more stable Carbon[12] and Carbon[13] isotopes. By comparing the amount of Carbon[14] that still remains in the object to the known half-life of the isotope, it is possible to calculate how many years have elapsed since the object ceased to exist and absorb carbon – in the case of timber, for example, this would be when the tree was felled. In practice, the results can be vitiated by a number of factors such as cross-contamination between samples or fluctuations across time in the level of cosmic radiation. The standard deviation, or margin of error, that accompanies radiocarbon dates is often so wide that the technique is more useful in prehistory, where chronological precision is seldom as crucial, than for more historical periods where standard deviations of sixty or so years are not terribly helpful. Similar criticisms hold with regard to thermoluminescence dating, which measures the build-up of electrons to determine when a ceramic vessel was fired. Considerable advances have been made recently in dendrochronology (tree-ring dating), though gaps in the dendrochronological sequence still remain and timber seldom survives at archaeological sites in the Greek world.

The basic foundation of Greek archaeological dating is therefore style and, in particular, the principle that the style of any given object changes over time (think of cars, cellular phones, or Coca Cola bottles). Although stylistic evolution occurs in all artifacts, painted ceramics have traditionally been privileged for three reasons. Firstly, unlike organic materials which decay or metal objects which may corrode, kiln-fired clay is practically indestructible. Secondly, the intrinsic low value of painted pottery meant that it was used widely in antiquity and discarded freely. Metal objects, on the other hand, would often be melted down and recycled. This, together with its indestructibility, means that ceramic material appears in vast quantities at every archaeological site in the Greek world. Thirdly, painted ceramic vessels generally offer far more variables for stylistic comparison – be it the shape of the vessel or the choice and placement of decorative design – than is the case with other classes of material.

Figure 2.2 shows the various stylistic phases of the two best-known pottery sequences – those of Attica and Corinth. The names given to the successive stylistic phases generally derive from the painted decoration applied to vases. "Geometric" designates a class of pottery on which bands and panels are

Fixed points	Attica	Corinthia	BCE
			1200
	Late Helladic IIIC	Late Helladic IIIC	1150
			1100
End of XX Dynasty in Egypt (1070)			
			1050
	Submycenaean	Submycenaean	
			1000
	Early Protogeometric	Early Protogeometric	
	Middle Protogeometric	Middle Protogeometric	950
	Late Protogeometric	Late Protogeometric	
			900
	Early Geometric I		
	Early Geometric II	Early Geometric	850
	Middle Geometric I		
		Middle Geometric I	800
	Middle Geometric II	Middle Geometric II	
	Late Geometric Ia		750
Foundation of Syracuse (733)	Late Geometric Ib	Late Geometric	
Destruction of Hama (720)	Late Geometric IIa		
Bokkhoris Scarab (718–712)	Late Geometric IIb	Early Protocorinthian	700
Destruction of Tarsus? (696)			
	Early Protoattic	Middle Protocorinthian I	
	Middle Protoattic	Middle Protocorinthian II	650
Foundation of Selinus (628)	Late Protoattic	Late Protocorinthian Transitional	
Destruction of Ashkelon (604)		Early Ripe Corinthian	600
	Black Figure	Middle Ripe Corinthian	
			550
		Late Ripe Corinthian	
	Red Figure		500
Persian Sack of Athens (480)		Red Figure	480

Figure 2.2   Ceramic chronology for Attica and Corinthia

Figure 2.3   Argive Late Geometric *pyxis*. Ecole Française d'Athènes, photo: E. Sécafis/C.209

decorated with wavy-lines, meanders, battlements, lozenges, squares, and triangles and – in its later phases – stylized representations of human and animal figures (Figure 2.3). "Protogeometric" owes its name to the fact that this class of pottery was identified only after the classification of the Geometric styles. In the Black Figure style, pioneered by Attic painters but influenced by earlier Corinthian fashions, silhouettes of figures were painted in black against the background of the red clay and details were rendered by incision, allowing the natural colour of the clay to show through (Figure 2.4). The Red Figure style, instead, reverses the technique: here, it is the background that is painted black while the figures are depicted by reserving the red clay and then applying details in black paint with a fine brush.

Stylistic evolution does not proceed at the same pace in all areas of Greece. The sequences of Attica and Corinth follow a similar development, though Attica seems to move from Protogeometric to Geometric styles earlier than Corinth while it was some time before Protoattic pottery took its cue from the widely popular Protocorinthian style. In other regions, the pace of development could be quite different. Euboea and Laconia, for example, do not really produce pottery that can be classified as Early or Middle Geometric. Instead, a lingering Protogeometric tradition persists until the adoption of Late

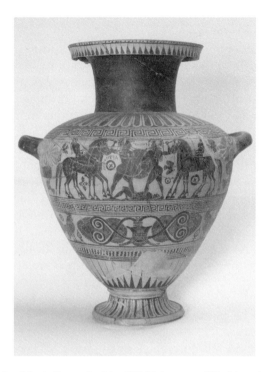

Figure 2.4 Laconian black-figure *hydria*. KB Ephorate of Prehistoric and Classical Antiquities, Rhodes

Geometric styles. The different tempos can be registered by cases in which pots from different regions are found in the same archaeological context – for instance, as grave goods in a tomb. So, the presence of Early Protocorinthian cups alongside local Late Geometric II pots in Argive tombs indicates that Corinthian potters had abandoned a properly Geometric style of decoration before their Argive counterparts.

The progression of these ceramic styles is not difficult to discern on a museum shelf but it can also be confirmed by excavation. Most settlements in the Greek world were situated with a view to defense, water sources, and access to agricultural land and harbors. For this reason, sites tended to be occupied over long periods of time and if a settlement was destroyed or abandoned it was normally rebuilt or reoccupied fairly swiftly afterwards. With each successive phase of occupation a habitation layer, or "stratum," was deposited above the ruins of the previous settlement. At Troy, when excavations began in 1870, the ground level was as much as sixteen meters above the natural bedrock. Stratigraphy denotes the practice of identifying these various habitation levels in an excavation, and although there are exceptions, the general principle is that the deeper a layer is, the earlier it is. In such cases, the relative stylistic sequence of ceramic classes can be cross-checked against stratigraphy, the expectation being that Submycenaean pottery will be found in lower levels than Protogeometric pottery and Red Figure pottery in higher levels than Geometric wares.

Although painted ceramics offer the fullest and most continuous evidence, stylistic sequences can be identified for all classes of material. Bronze pins, for example, become ever more ornamental as time passes and the evolution of architectural styles can be charted by such techniques as measuring the ratio between the height and diameter of columns or examining the profile of column capitals. If such monumental buildings also supported sculpture, then the evolution of artistic styles can be correlated against the evolution of architectural forms. Again, these sequences can be "pegged" onto the ceramic series through cross-dating. A certain type of pin or fibula (brooch), for example, may be commonly found in graves containing Middle Geometric II pottery, in which case pins that appear, on stylistic grounds, to be just slightly later are probably contemporary with Late Geometric wares. Architectural structures can be dated by the pottery found beneath them: so, if Middle Protocorinthian sherds are found in the foundation trenches of a temple, the temple cannot predate the period in which Middle Protocorinthian styles were in vogue. All this, however, leaves us with a loosely connected series of floating relative sequences. We can be pretty certain as to which styles of pottery are earlier and which are later as well as to which ceramic phases other classes of material belong but we have no absolute dates nor – aside from educated intuition – can we establish how long each stylistic phase lasted. These floating relative sequences need to be pinned down to a precise chronological scheme and this is achieved by means of what are called "fixed points" (Figure 2.2).

The first set of fixed points comes from destruction levels at Near Eastern sites. Because the destructions of these cities are often recorded in Assyrian and Babylonian annals or in the Old Testament, burnt layers of debris should theoretically provide fairly precise dates for pottery found immediately above and below them. So, for example, Euboean Subprotogeometric *skyphoi* (cups with two horizontal handles) and an Attic Middle Geometric II *krater* (mixing-bowl) were found in the destruction horizon of Hama in Syria. According to Assyrian records, Sargon II sacked Hama ca. 720 and if it is this act that is signaled by the destruction level then we have a *terminus ante quem* for Euboean Subprotogeometric and Attic Middle Geometric II pottery. A destruction level at Tarsus in Turkey may reflect an attack on the city by another Assyrian king, Sennacherib, in 696; if so, this would provide a *terminus ante quem* for an Early Protocorinthian *aryballos* found among the destruction debris. Similarly, Babylonian records inform us that King Nebuchadnezzar sacked the southern Palestinian city of Ashkelon in 604; the latest pottery here included Transitional Corinthian pottery, implying that the transition from Protocorinthian to Ripe Corinthian styles occurred before the end of the seventh century.

The second set of fixed points comes from colonial foundations in the west. At the beginning of his account of the Sicilian Expedition of 415, Thucydides (6.1–5) describes the populations of Sicily, including the first permanent Greek settlers on the island (Figure 2.5). These colonial foundations are dated in

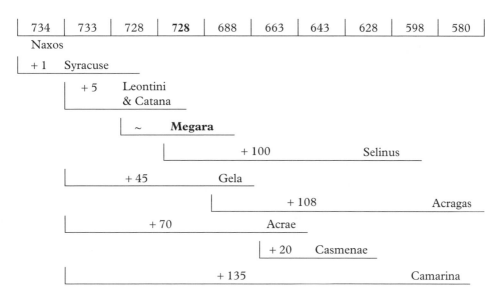

734	733	728	**728**	688	663	643	628	598	580

Naxos

+ 1   Syracuse

+ 5   Leontini & Catana

~   **Megara**

+ 100   Selinus

+ 45   Gela

+ 108   Acragas

+ 70   Acrae

+ 20   Casmenae

+ 135   Camarina

Figure 2.5   Thucydides' dates for the foundations in Sicily

relation to one another. So, Thucydides tells us that Syracuse was founded one year after Naxos; Leontini and Catana five years after Syracuse, with Megara Hyblaea following shortly afterwards; Gela forty-five years after Syracuse; Acragas 108 years after Gela; Acrae seventy years after Syracuse; Casmenae almost twenty years after Acrae; and Camarina 135 years after Syracuse. Since he also tells us that Megara Hyblaea was settled for 245 years before its destruction by Gelon, the tyrant of Syracuse, and since we know that this latter event occurred in 483, then we have an absolute date for Megara Hyblaea (728), allowing us to calculate dates for the other Greek cities on Sicily. This should mean that the Corinthian Late Geometric and Early Protocorinthian pottery found at Syracuse and Megara Hyblaea was in vogue in the last third of the eighth century. The apparent absence of Protocorinthian pottery from Selinus, on the other hand, should indicate that the transition from Proto-corinthian to Ripe Corinthian styles took place around, or just before, 628.

Another fixed point derives from an imported Egyptian scarab, marked with the cartouche of the Pharaoh Bokkhoris, which was found in an infant burial at Pithecusae. On the assumption that the scarab was deposited in the burial soon after Bokkhoris' short reign (718–712), the Early Protocorinthian *aryballoi* also found in the grave should date to the last quarter of the eighth century. Finally, a number of refuse pits found on the Athenian acropolis are probably to be connected with cleaning operations following the Persian sacks of Athens in 480 and 479, meaning that most of the debris found in the pits should predate 480. Shortly after the withdrawal of the Persians, the Athenians hastily constructed a fortification circuit (the so-called "Themistoclean walls"), incorporating fragments of funerary sculpture and inscriptions that had been damaged during the Persian invasion, thus providing an important *terminus ante quem* for Late Archaic sculpture and epigraphic letter-forms (see above).

It should be noted that not all of these fixed points are unassailable. Doubt has often been expressed concerning the accuracy of Thucydides' dates for western foundations (see pp. 104–6); the match between destruction horizons at Near Eastern sites and events described in Assyrian or Babylonian records is seldom self-apparent and the evidence from Tarsus and Samaria has recently been challenged; the Bokkhoris scarab could have been in circulation some time before its final deposition; and since the refuse pits on the Athenian acropolis were not eventually sealed until the Periclean building operations of the 440s, it is entirely possible that material dating to after 480 found its way into the deposits. On the other hand, the traditional ceramic chronology does seem to possess an internal coherence that has withstood various attempts to downdate the whole sequence and its strength appears to derive from the sum of its parts rather than from individual fixed points. It is not as fine-grained as some historians might like – generally ceramic phases are assigned to quarter-centuries – though this at least offers a degree of latitude that would probably not be radically affected by future chronological adjustments.

To conclude: while it is essential that the historian be aware of the potential pitfalls that each type of evidence presents, the judicious employment of as many categories of evidence as possible can flesh out an otherwise bleak perspective on the past and offer a more multidimensional – if broadly sketched – picture of the Archaic Greek world and especially its more important processual developments.

FURTHER READING

Use of sources: Crawford 1983; Morley 1999, 53–95.

Divergent views on dating Homer and Hesiod: Janko 1982; M. L. West, "The date of the *Iliad*," *Museum Helveticum* 52 (1995), 203–19; J.-P. Crielaard, "Homer, history and archaeology: Some remarks on the date of the Homeric world," in Crielaard 1995, 201–88; Powell 1991. Composite nature of Homeric society: A. M. Snodgrass, "An historical Homeric society?" *Journal of Hellenic Studies* 94 (1974), 114–25. For the unitary view: I. Morris, "The use and abuse of Homer," *Classical Antiquity* 5 (1986), 81–138; K. A. Raaflaub, "A historian's headache? How to read 'Homeric society'," in Fisher and van Wees 1998, 169–93. Hesiod as a persona: R. Martin, "Hesiod's metanastic poetics," *Ramus* 21 (1992), 11–33.

Epigraphy: Woodhead 1981; Bodel 2001. Issues of dating and development: Jeffery 1990. Numismatics: Howgego 1995. Relationship between history and archaeology: Finley 1986, 87–101; Morris 2000, 37–76; Whitley 2001, 3–59.

Chronology: Bickerman 1980; Biers 1992. Olympic victors lists: Hall 2002, 241–6.

Archaeological dating: Whitley 2001, 60–74. Protogeometric chronology: Lemos 2002, 24–6. Regional Geometric pottery chronologies: Coldstream 1968. Doubts on Near Eastern "fixed points": Forsberg 1995.

3

The End of the Mycenaean World and its Aftermath

Mycenaean Greece

There is currently a great deal of interest among historians in issues of "periodization" – that is, why we carve up historical time into periods the way we do. Until recently, accounts of Archaic Greece tended to begin in the eighth century because it was widely believed that this is when the *polis* or city-state first emerged in the Greek world. In the next four chapters, I will suggest that the development of the *polis* was a far more gradual phenomenon that played out over the course of several centuries, and that to understand its origins we need to examine not only the unsettled centuries that preceded it (the "Dark Age") but also the Late Bronze Age "Mycenaean" civilization that flourished in mainland Greece in the second half of the second millennium.

On November 28, 1876, the German businessman Heinrich Schliemann wrote to George I, King of the Hellenes, grandiosely announcing his discovery of the graves of Agamemnon, the Homeric king of Mycenae, and his companions. The five shaft graves (supplemented by a sixth the following year) were grouped inside a funerary circle, known as Grave Circle A, immediately inside the famous "Lion Gate" at Mycenae, and contained between them nineteen bodies, accompanied by costly weapons and gold jewellery, vessels and death masks (Figure 3.1). Dating to the sixteenth and early fifteenth centuries – and thus too early to be associated with any historical Agamemnon – the exotic nature and extraneous origin of many of the grave offerings initially prompted speculation that the burials were those of newcomers to Greece, and some have even suggested that these warriors were the first Greek-speakers in the peninsula. In 1952, however, a second funerary enclosure of twenty-five graves (Grave Circle B) was discovered some fifty meters to the northwest of the first. The later burials overlap with those in Grave Circle A, but the earliest date back to the later seventeenth century and establish beyond much reasonable

Figure 3.1   Grave Circle A, Mycenae (photo by author)

doubt a continuous cultural tradition, stretching back into the Middle Bronze Age, to which the warriors inhumed in Grave Circle A were the heirs. It is preferable, then, to regard the burials as indications not for the arrival of an outside population but for the emergence of a new elite class from within the ranks of the existing population.

From the fourteenth century, the Mycenaean elites began to invest their wealth in the construction of palaces and impressive fortifications at mainland Greek sites such as Mycenae, Tiryns, and Midea in the Argolid, Pylos in Messenia, Thebes and Gla in Boeotia, and Volos in Thessaly. Although the "type-site" of Mycenae has given its name to the generally common culture that these palatial centers share, there is no compelling evidence that Greece was politically unified in the Late Bronze Age. The idea of the palace itself is one that almost certainly derived from Minoan Crete – a civilization with which the Mycenaeans were in close contact – and, beyond there, from the Near East. The Mycenaean palaces are far less impressive and generally much smaller than their Cretan counterparts, but like the Minoan palaces, the Mycenaean citadels functioned as economic centers. Production and manufacture were under the direct control of the palace administration and the palaces themselves served as centers for the storage and redistribution of mainly agricultural products, extracted in taxes from rural communities. Our evidence for the redistributive nature of the Mycenaean economy comes from both the storage magazines excavated in various palaces and from detailed inventories of what was stored, recorded on clay tablets in a syllabic script known as Linear B.

Since the decipherment of Linear B in 1952, the clay tablets – especially those from Pylos, Cnossus, and Thebes – have revealed much about the administration of the Mycenaean kingdoms. A number of different occupations are mentioned, including weaving, carpentry, leather-working, metal-working, and arms manufacture, thus attesting to a relatively complex and specialized division of labor. An extensive hierarchy of named administrative offices, headed by the *wa-na-ka* ("lord"), exercised military, judicial, fiscal, and religious functions. At Pylos, we learn that the territory controlled by the palace was divided into two provinces, governed by a *da-mo-ko-ro* and a *du-ma*, with each province being further subdivided into districts under the authority of a *ko-re-te*, assisted by a *po-ro-ko-re-te*. We also know that most – though perhaps not all – of the names of the deities that Greeks of the Archaic and Classical periods worshipped were already known in the Mycenaean period.

Around 1200, however, towards the end of a ceramic phase known as Late Helladic IIIB (LHIIIB), the Mycenaean world was overwhelmed by a mysterious catastrophe. The palaces at Mycenae, Tiryns, Midea, Pylos, and Volos, together with a building dubbed the "Mycenaean mansion" at Therapne in Laconia, appear to have been destroyed in violent conflagrations (Thebes may have been a rather earlier casualty). There are indications that some sort of impending disaster was anticipated. In the second half of the thirteenth century, the fortifications at both Mycenae and Tiryns were strengthened and extended, and provisions were taken to safeguard the water supply through the construction of concealed passageways leading to underground cisterns. What appears to be a wall running across the Corinthian isthmus has been interpreted as a preventive measure against attack from the north and Linear B tablets from Pylos refer to the stationing of watchers and rowers. Periodic destructions, partial or complete, were certainly not unusual at Late Bronze Age sites in Greece: Mycenae may have suffered damage, perhaps as a result of earthquakes, on three occasions in the thirteenth century prior to the final disaster, while Tiryns experienced no fewer than eight destructions between the middle of the thirteenth century and the first quarter of the eleventh century, six of which date to the LHIIIC phase (ca. 1190–1070). What distinguishes the series of destructions ca. 1200 is their violence and their approximately simultaneous occurrence. The causes of the catastrophe continue to be debated, though when evidence for the palatial destructions first came to light in the late nineteenth century suspicion immediately fell upon the Dorians.

Gauging the Historicity of the Dorian Migration

By the fifth century, various cities in the eastern and southern Peloponnese, the southern Aegean islands of Crete, Melos, and Thera, the Dodecanese, southwest Asia Minor, North Africa, South Italy, and Sicily proclaimed their allegiance to a shared Dorian heritage. Indeed, rallying-calls to this heritage served to cement alliances between the Spartans and their allies – especially the Syracusans – at the time of the Peloponnesian War. This sense of Dorian kinship was chartered by a migration tradition which told how the ancestors of the Dorians had originally inhabited a region of northern-central Greece but had been led into the Peloponnese by the Heraclidae, descendants of Heracles who were seeking to regain their ancestral possessions in southern Greece. Thucydides (1.12.3) dates the migration to eighty years after the Trojan War. According to the tradition, the arrival of the Dorians in the Argolid and Laconia forced the former Achaean population to leave and settle the northern Peloponnesian region of Achaea, where they displaced Ionians who fled first to Athens and then further eastwards, settling the Cyclades and the central coastal belt of Asia Minor (Map 3.1). From the Peloponnese, later expeditions settled

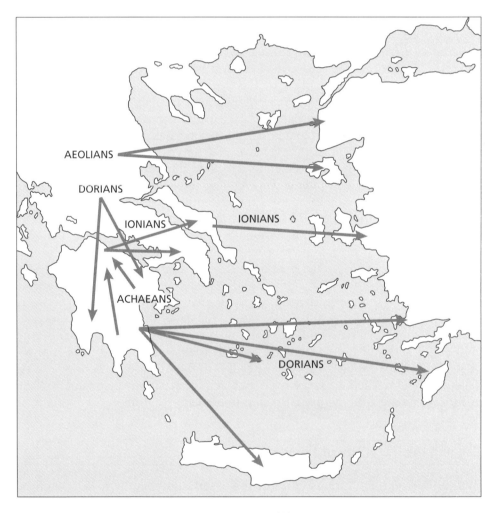

Map 3.1   Migrations according to the literary tradition

the other Dorian cities of the Aegean and central Mediterranean. There are two issues here. The first is whether the Dorians were responsible for the disasters that befell the Mycenaean palaces. The second is whether the tradition for the migration itself is credible. Since any doubt concerning the latter must necessarily weaken the case for the former, it is on the credibility of the migration tradition that we shall focus.

It is widely believed that the historical distribution of the Greek dialects supports the literary traditions for the migrations. Every Greek city possessed its own local or "epichoric" dialect but, on the basis of certain shared characteristics, linguists have identified four principal dialect groups (Map 3.2): the West Greek dialects, spoken in northwestern and central Greece, most of the Peloponnese, the Southern Aegean islands of Melos, Thera, and Crete, the Dodecanese, and southwest Asia Minor; the Aeolic dialects, spoken in Thessaly, Boeotia, Lesbos, and northwest Asia Minor; the Attic–Ionic dialects, spoken in Attica, Euboea, the Cyclades, and the central seaboard of Asia Minor; and the Arcado-Cypriot dialects, spoken in Arcadia and on Cyprus.

In one case, the linguistic evidence fails completely to match up with the literary tradition. On the basis of the ancient belief that Achaeans had inhabited Laconia and the Argolid before the arrival of the Dorians, we would have expected the Achaean dialect to resemble closely the Mycenaean dialect represented on the Linear B tablets. In fact, the historical dialect that was closest to Mycenaean was Arcadian, while the Achaean dialect belonged to the West Greek group, loosely related to the Doric dialects of Laconia and the Argolid. In other respects, however, the distribution of the dialects tallies closely with the distribution of groups that professed the same ethnic heritage. The most economical hypothesis would be to assume that these dialects were spread by new migrant populations and that the differences that arose between dialects belonging to the same group were due to the various admixtures that resulted in each zone from the imposition of the "adstrate" dialect of the immigrants on the "substrate" dialect of the previous inhabitants. Unfortunately, economical hypotheses are not always correct hypotheses. Firstly, it does not take a massive wave of immigration to introduce a new dialect into a region – especially when the newcomers occupy the dominant positions in the community: in Britain, the Normans would be a case in point. The history of a language or dialect is not necessarily the same as the history of those who speak it. Secondly, a closer look at the dialect map reveals that the zones where the West Greek, Aeolic, and Attic–Ionic groups of dialects were spoken form, by and large, three broad strips of contiguous territories, stretching from west to east. This raises the possibility that linguistic features shared by the dialects in these groups need not all be the inheritance of a proto-dialect, originally spoken in a primordial homeland, but rather the product of diffusional convergence between speakers who came into continuous and repeated contact with one another. A detailed study of the dialects spoken in the Argolid, for example, has concluded that the "Doric" dialects of the region evolved through contact with other West Greek and non-West Greek dialects.

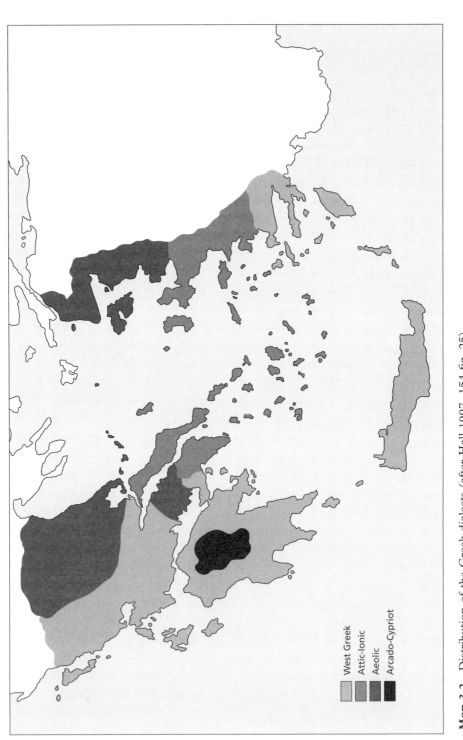

West Greek

Attic-Ionic

Aeolic

Arcado-Cypriot

Map 3.2 Distribution of the Greek dialects (after Hall 1997, 154 fig. 25)

Institutional features have also been invoked in support of the ultimately historical quality of the migration traditions. In the Classical period, the citizens of most cities were distributed among "tribes" (*phylai*) which served as administrative units for political and military organization. At Sparta, the "Dorian" tribes of the Hylleis, Pamphyloi, and almost certainly the Dymanes (though there is a lacuna in the papyrus) are named already by Tyrtaeus (fr. 19). The same names occur at Megara, Cos, and Calymnos and, alongside other tribal names, at Sicyon, Argos, probably Issa, and perhaps Troezen, Thera, and the Cretan cities of Hierapytna and Olous (Figure 3.2). It is often assumed that the recurrence of the same names represents the fossilized relic of an earlier, premigratory tribal organization in use among the Dorians, but there are difficulties with this view. Firstly, these tribal names are not attested everywhere. By the Classical period the citizen body of Dorian Corinth was distributed among eight tribes and the assumption that this was due

City	Hylleis	Dymanes	Pamphyloi	Date (century)	Other tribes
Sparta	x	x	x	7	
Sicyon	x	x	x	6	Arkhelaoi
Megara	x	x	x	5	
Argos	x	x	x	5	Hyrnathioi
Corcyra				5	Aoreis; Makkhidai; ?Antheia; ?Philoxenoi
Corinth				4/3	Aoreis
Epidaurus	x	x		4/3	Azantioi; Hysminatai
Troezen	x	x		4/3	Skheliadai
Thera	x	?		4/3	
Cos	x	x	x	4/3	
West Locris		x		3	
Issa	?	x	x	3	
Acragas	x			3	
Gortyn		x		3	Aithaleis; Ap[-]yma[-]; Arkheia; Dek[-]
Lyttos		x		3/2	Diphyloi
Calymnos	x	x	x	3/2	
Hierapytna		x	x	2	Kamiris
Olous		x	x	2	[-]on
Cnossus			x	2	Aithaleis; Arkheia; E[-]
Lato	x			2	Aiskheis; Ekhanoreis; Synameis
Oleros			x	2/1	

Figure 3.2   The tribal organization of selected Dorian cities

to a reform that replaced an earlier tripartite structure is pure speculation, conditioned by *a priori* suppositions about the primordially "tribal" nature of Dorian communities. Secondly, evidence for the existence of the tribal names is generally late, rarely predating the fifth century. This may simply be a consequence of the fact that inscriptions – our primary source of information for civic organization – are relatively uncommon before the Classical period but neither can we exclude the possibility that the names were borrowed rather than inherited. Thirdly, and most importantly, the fact that tribes served as the basis for military and political units presumes that they were approximately equal in size and this "rational" division of the citizen-body into roughly equivalent groups implies that the tribal system can only have developed within the context of already organized socio-political communities.

Archaeology offers fewer solutions to the problem than was once thought. Before further excavations refined our knowledge of the chronological phases of the Late Bronze Age, the appearance of new artifacts and cultural forms at the transition to the Iron Age was thought to reflect the arrival of newcomers from the north. A type of domestic pottery called Handmade Burnished Ware, a bronze fibula in the form of a violin bow, a slashing sword known as the Naue II or *Griffzungenschwert*, the employment of cremation, the practice of single inhumation in cist graves and even the knowledge of ironworking were all thought to mark a decisive break with the Mycenaean way of life and were therefore attributed to a new intrusive population. Yet some of these items – e.g. Handmade Burnished Ware, the violin-bow fibula, and the Naue II sword – are now attested within the Mycenaean world in archaeological contexts dated to before the destructions ca. 1200. Cremation tends to be avoided in the predominantly Dorian Peloponnese but is favored in "Ionian" areas such as Attica and Euboea while single inhumation in cist graves is popular in both Dorian and non-Dorian areas but was, in any case, already practiced by the Mycenaeans prior to the collapse of the palaces. Iron implements were not entirely unknown in the Mycenaean world though iron was not generally used for weapons until the eleventh century, becoming more common in the tenth. But in any case, the technology of ironworking seems to have arrived, via Cyprus, from the Near East rather than from the northern Balkans and central Europe as was once believed.

In LHIIIC, after the destruction of the palaces, new sites appear at Perati in eastern Attica, Lefkandi, Emborio on Chios, Ialysus on Rhodes, and Enkomi and Kition on Cyprus as well as in Achaea. Sometimes interpreted as refugee settlements, they might lend some support to the traditions concerning the expulsions of the Achaeans and the Ionians from their former homelands. On the other hand, the material culture of twelfth-century Achaea does not appear to display any particular debt to the Argolid while there is little evidence that the Argolid itself was depopulated – in fact, the area of settlement around Tiryns in LHIIIC has been estimated at around twenty-five hectares, as opposed to eight hectares in the preceding LHIIIB phase. One might have interpreted this as indicating the arrival of a new population ca. 1200 were it not for the evident continuity in material cultural styles – not only at Tiryns but also at other sites – and this suggests that the residents of twelfth-century Tiryns had abandoned the surrounding rural villages and sought protection in the shadow of the mighty fortress.

One archaeological fact is indisputable: most of the Mycenaean palaces were violently destroyed at the end of LHIIIB. Yet even this fact is at variance with the literary tradition, which credits the Dorians and Heraclidae with ousting Agamemnon's grandson, Tisamenus, but makes no reference to the physical destruction of any city. Indeed, destructions are attested at some sites – for example, Koukounaries on the island of Paros – which were never to be inhabited by Dorian populations. One solution might be to dissociate the Dorians from the palatial destructions but still preserve the credibility of the migration tradition by assuming that they arrived around a century after the catastrophe, easily overwhelming a civilization that had already been severely weakened by other parties or causes. Hostile action would undoubtedly have been involved – numerous arrowheads were found in the last LHIIIC destruction level in the Lower Citadel at Tiryns – but of far less magnitude than a century earlier. At Mycenae, for example, the fire that destroyed the Granary at the end of LHIIIC does not seem to have been particularly widespread and at both Tiryns and Argos occupation continues into the eleventh century, albeit at greatly reduced levels and perhaps after a very short break. It is true that there is not really any more evidence for "intrusive northern elements" in southern Greece during the eleventh century than there is during the twelfth, but then again, there are historically documented examples of migrations that have left little if any material trace – for example, the Celtic invasion of Asia Minor in the third century or the Slavic invasions of Greece from the late sixth century CE.

However, the situation in Laconia and, to a lesser extent, Messenia – both regions that were considered Dorian in the Classical period – hardly squares with such a hypothesis. Far from finding evidence for the arrival of a new population, either in the twelfth or in the eleventh century, these regions actually witness a steep decline in the number of archaeologically identifiable sites, suggesting widespread abandonment. Although a few fragments of Mycenaean pottery have been recovered from the Spartan acropolis, there is no convincing evidence for settlement there until around the second half of the tenth century. The decision to found a new city on the west bank of the Eurotas River, across from where the earlier Mycenaean center of Therapne had stood, might possibly indicate the arrival of a new population and finds a parallel at Corinth, where intensive habitation around Temple Hill from the tenth century onwards marked a shift in settlement from the earlier Mycenaean site of Korakou. But the tenth- and ninth-century pottery of Laconia and Messenia displays stylistic affinities not with northern-central Greece but with West Greek areas such as Ithaca, Achaea, Elis, and Aetolia, and it is entirely unrelated to the Protogeometric and Geometric wares of other Dorian cities such as Argos or Corinth.

In the face of such equivocal evidence, some historians have maintained that the strongest argument for the historicity of the Dorian migration is the fundamentally consistent nature of the literary tradition, which persists over a time period that spans some nine centuries. Predictably, perhaps, our most detailed sources are late: the fullest accounts are provided by the first-century historian Diodorus of Sicily (4.57–58) and in a slightly later compendium known as *The Library*, erroneously attributed by Byzantine commentators to Apollodorus of Athens (2.8.2–4). Yet the information provided by fifth-century authors such as Pindar (*Pyth.* 1.62–65; 5.69–72; *Isthm.* 9.1–3), Herodotus (6.52.1; 9.26–27), and Thucydides (1.9.2; 1.12.3), while far more fragmentary, is not significantly at odds with the fuller narratives we meet later. Still earlier, Tyrtaeus (fr. 2) refers to the foundation of Sparta by "the descendants of Heracles, with whom we [Dorians] left windy Erineos and arrived in the broad Peloponnese," and even Homer (*Od.* 19.177), whose subject-matter is supposed to predate the migration of the Dorians, lets his guard slip once and attests the presence of Dorians on Crete. The fundamental elements of the tradition, then, if not all of its details, were clearly well established early in the Archaic period. This marks a strong contrast from the traditions concerning the Ionians of Asia Minor, whose origins are variously assigned to Athens (Solon fr. 4a; Pherecydes fr. 155), Achaea (Herodotus 1.145), Messenian Pylos (Mimnermus fr. 9) and Boeotian Thebes (Hellanicus fr. 101; cf. Homer, *Il.* 13.685).

It nevertheless remains the case that we are still faced with a gap of at least four centuries between the date at which the migration is supposed to have taken place and our earliest literary testimony for it and, in fact, a close analysis of the internal logic of the tradition reveals that it cannot have been so unitary in its initial, pre-literary phases. Firstly, there is the distinction between the Dorians and the descendants of Heracles. In the accounts that have come down to us, this is conceived in terms of an expedition manned by Dorian warriors but commanded by unrelated Heraclid leaders. That the traditions concerning the two groups were originally independent of one another is betrayed by the awkward manner in which they were conjoined. According to the fourth-century historian Ephorus (fr. 15), Aegimius, the king of the Dorians, adopted Heracles' son Hyllus alongside his own sons, Pamphylos and Dymas. The names serve as eponyms to explain the existence in many cities of the three Dorian tribes (see above). Yet the three half-brothers do not originally seem to have been contemporaries: according to Herodotus (9.26.2), Hyllus was killed during an earlier abortive attempt to regain his ancestral homeland, three generations before the successful return to the Peloponnese during which Pamphylos and Dymas lost their lives.

Secondly, our sources reveal a certain indeterminacy with regard to the original homeland of the Dorians. Tyrtaeus tells how the Dorians arrived from "windy Erineos," a town located in the region of Doris, north of Phocis. The region around Doris is also named as the Dorian homeland by Ephorus (fr. 15), Strabo (9.4.10), and Pausanias (5.1.2), and in 457, the Spartans sent 1,500 soldiers to their "metropolis" of Doris to defend it from a Phocian attack

(Thucydides 1.107.2). But Diodorus (4.37.3–4) says that the Dorians originally lived under the rule of Aegimius in the region of Hestiaeotis, which constitutes the western zone of Thessaly and lies about one hundred kilometers to the north of Doris. Ancient authors were not oblivious to the discrepancy: Herodotus (1.56.3) hypothesized that the Dorians had wandered ceaselessly before their arrival in the Peloponnese while Strabo (9.5.17) suggested that Hestiaeotis had formerly been called Doris. The clue to the conundrum, however, is provided by the figure of Aegimius, who is regularly associated with Hestiaeotis rather than Doris. In the developed tradition, Aegimius is the son of Doros, who gave his name to the Dorians, and the father of the tribal eponyms Hyllus, Pamphylos, and Dymas, but he does not give his own name to any group. Yet this actually defies the logic of eponymous genealogy. Take, for example, the case of the Ionians, where the sons of the eponymous Ion are the tribal eponyms, Geleon, Hopletes, Argades, and Aigikores, thus expressing the straightforward view that Ionians are divided into four constituent groups. By analogy, Hyllus, Pamphylos, and Dymas should be the adopted and natural sons of Doros, not Aegimius. The intrusion, then, of the non-eponymous Aegimius almost certainly indicates a conflation between a tradition that told of the Dorians of Doris, presumably originally ruled by Doros himself, and another tradition concerning a group located in Hestiaeotis, under the rule of Aegimius.

There can be little doubt that the collapse of the political and economic system centered on the Mycenaean palaces provoked a climate of instability and insecurity and that some people – whether for reasons of safety or economic necessity – decided to abandon their former homes and seek a living elsewhere. But it is also clear that the developed literary narrative for the Dorian migration is the end product of a cumulative synthesis of originally independent traditions. As such, it need not reflect a dim and hazy memory of a genuine single movement of a population from north to south, even if it captures the general instability and mobility of this period. Rather, it seeks to establish a common identity for a plethora of communities whose pedigrees were undoubtedly far from uniform in origin.

Alternative Explanations

With the Dorians absolved of responsibility for the destruction of the Mycenaean palaces, suspicion has turned upon raiders from further afield and especially the so-called "Sea Peoples." The important thing about the palatial collapse in Greece is that it seems, by and large, to coincide with a series of destructions at numerous other cities on Cyprus, in Anatolia, and in the Levant. An inscription from the great temple at Karnak commemorates a victory by the Egyptian pharaoh Merneptah, in the fifth year of his reign (1208), over Libyan invaders of the western delta. We are told that the Libyans were led by their chief, Meryre, and were accompanied by northerners named as the Ekwesh (Achaean Greeks?), Teresh (Etruscans?), Luka (Lycians?), Sherden

(Sardinians?), and Shekelesh (Sicilians?). The Shekelesh are also listed, along-side the Peleset, Tjeker, Denyen, and Weshesh, in another inscription, set up at Medinet Habu to commemorate further victories by land and sea – this time by Rameses III over Levantine invaders in 1179. There are, however, prob-lems in assuming that these two inscriptions reveal the identity of the agents responsible for the widespread catastrophes at the end of the thirteenth cen-tury. Although the ubiquity of the turmoil could be accounted for by the apparently far-flung origins of the invaders, the temptation to "identify," simply on the basis of apparent lexical similarity, correspondences between Hittite and Egyptian names, on the one hand, and Greek names, on the other, has a long but not necessarily creditable history. The equation, for example, of the people that Homer calls Achaeans with a kingdom of Ahhiyawa mentioned in Hittite texts, or of both with the Ekwesh of the Karnak inscription, is not accepted by everyone. And if we were to accept that the Ekwesh who invaded the western Delta were not only Achaeans from Greece but the inhabitants of the Hittite Ahhiyawa and that they were responsible for the more widespread catastrophes, then we would also have to assume that the Mycenaean palaces were destroyed by the very people who are supposed to have built them. Furthermore, Egyptologists are suspicious about the Medinet Habu inscrip-tion. Rameses III's claim that Carchemish was a casualty of the invaders appears to be belied by archaeology, while we know from earlier inscriptions that groups such as the Peleset and Shekelesh, far from sweeping into Syria in 1179, were already resident in the region, serving as mercenaries in Egyptian and Hittite armies. It has been suggested that Rameses invented his heroic defense of Egypt out of a series of minor local clashes and even that he claimed the earlier victories of Merneptah for himself.

Another variation of the Sea Peoples hypothesis has, however, recently been put forward. The twelfth century sees the appearance of new weapons such as the Naue II slashing sword and the javelin as well as defensive armor like the waist-length corselet, greaves, and the round shield. On this basis, it has been suggested that the introduction of mass infantry tactics allowed the raiders and pirates – "barbarian hill people" – to overwhelm the chariot forces employed by the Late Bronze Age kingdoms. The insistence that the appearance of these new types of weapons signals new modes of combat is probably apposite, though can only really be linked to external raiders if one assumes that chariot warfare and mass infantry tactics were each the exclusive preserve of different populations. The paucity of evidence for infantry warfare in Mycenaean Greece is not entirely surprising: if foot soldiers were employed in Mycenaean armies they were probably lightly armed and presumably of too low a status to be represented in pictorial scenes, which tend instead to focus on more unusual – and perhaps mythical – scenes of individual combat. It is true that infantrymen become more prominent on LHIIIC vases – notably the famous Warrior Vase from Mycenae – but the new attention given to humble foot warriors could be a consequence of the disappearance of an elite class rather than an indication for an entirely novel mode of combat.

As for chariots, while it is clear from the Linear B tablets at Cnossus and Pylos that they were a familiar vehicle in Mycenaean Greece, it is not absolutely certain that they were employed primarily, if at all, in a military function. It has been argued that the Homeric depiction of the chariot – as a "taxi" for infantrymen – was probably true of the twelfth century but that earlier chariots performed the same combat functions in Mycenaean Greece as they did in Egypt and the Near East. Yet such pictorial representations as survive from this earlier period in Greece invariably portray chariots in a more ceremonial role. Nor is the terrain of Greece particularly suited to wheeling chariot formations. The Argive plain, for example, is crossed by seasonal torrent beds and in antiquity a good part of it was marshy. In fact, a recent study of the Mycenaean roads in the region concludes that they were designed for heavy-wheeled traffic – presumably the carts that conveyed agricultural produce to and from the palatial center – rather than for military purposes. The whole hypothesis is also heavily dependent upon a characterization of the Sea Peoples as freebooting raiders rather than immigrants – a judgment based largely on the earlier attestations of Peleset and Shekelesh mercenaries – but the Karnak inscription explicitly mentions that the invaders were accompanied by their families and cattle.

Some scholars have supposed that the destruction of the Mycenaean palaces was caused not by external invaders or raiders but rather by internal factors. This shift of perspective can only really be understood within the context of theoretical and ideological developments that took place in the middle decades of the twentieth century. Marxism, for example, tended to eschew explanations that attributed change to external conquerors and invaders in favor of those that privileged technological factors and internal class-based revolutions. Thus, Gordon Childe hypothesized in the 1940s that the Hittite Empire collapsed when the masses acquired the knowledge of ironworking, previously restricted to the elite, and then employed it in forging weapons against their former masters; buoyed by success, they subsequently took to the seas and overran other Late Bronze Age kingdoms. The problem with the hypothesis as far as Greece is concerned is that iron, as we have seen, did not enter into mass use until considerably later than the palatial destructions.

From the 1950s, environmental factors came to be invoked more frequently in explaining culture change. According to one theory, a contraction of the polar ice caps towards the end of the Bronze Age led to the northward displacement of the jet stream during the autumn and winter months; the consequence would have been arid conditions, followed by drought and famine. The palatial centers were destroyed by hungry populations desperate for the grain that was stored in the magazines, but the higher mortality rates that accompanied the famine led to depopulation and to the abandonment of many Bronze Age centers of habitation. Some environmental evidence in support of the drought hypothesis has been marshalled – for instance, tree ring patterns in Californian bristle-cone pines, the diminution of lake levels in Switzerland and the advance and recession of glaciers in the Himalayas – but some climatologists are equally convinced that the end of the Bronze Age witnessed a mini ice age. A food shortage appears to be indicated in Merneptah's inscription at Karnak though the Pylos tablets contain no hint of provisions being taken to avert famine.

Another theory appeals to economic factors and systems collapse, normally in conjunction with other variables. According to one view, the Mycenaean palaces encouraged excessive specialization in a limited number of crops with the result that a series of bad harvests left them unable to feed their dependent populations. According to another, the palatial centers engaged in a spiralling increase of expenditure that compelled them to exact ever higher rates of taxes from the surrounding countryside until the system could no longer cope and the palace elites, left resourceless, also lost their status and authority. In such circumstances, the weakened palatial centers presented attractive and easy pickings for raiders and looters.

Finally, it has been suggested that the collapse of the Mycenaean palaces was due to unusually violent seismic action. The suggestion was first made by Spyridon Iakovides, the excavator of Mycenae, and then extended to Tiryns by Klaus Kilian. There have been a number of objections to the earthquake hypothesis. Cities, it is argued, are seldom completely destroyed by earthquakes and are normally swiftly repaired by the survivors. Ash and blackened destruction levels indicate that the Mycenaean palaces were destroyed in a fierce conflagration but, prior to the advent of electricity and gas, it is unlikely that earthquakes in antiquity would have been accompanied by such devastating fires. Had the palaces been destroyed by an earthquake, we would expect to find the remains of those who were trapped by falling masonry while trying to make their escape; the absence of skeletons, instead, should suggest that the populations of the palaces were able to flee before marauders set fire to the cities. At Mycenae and Tiryns, the chief casualties seem to have been houses; the massive fortification walls, by contrast, appear to have remained completely unscathed by the hypothesized earthquake. Finally, given that earthquakes not infrequently trigger tidal waves, it is strange that LHIIIC survivors of the disaster should have chosen to build their settlements so close to coastlines.

Not all of these objections are, however, equally valid. Earthquakes strike with varying intensities and with various results. In 1953, much of the island of Kephallenia – including entire villages – was destroyed by an earthquake and new settlements built in different areas. But this is clearly not what happened at sites such as Tiryns and Mycenae, where rebuilding and repair are attested for LHIIIC. It is not impossible that the massive fortification walls withstood a seismic shock that proved too much for ordinary dwellings. Of fifteen houses excavated in the Lower Citadel of Tiryns, only one showed clear effects of fire damage and, in fact, one skeleton was found crushed beneath the masonry of one of the buildings. One casualty hardly amounts to a catastrophe, but it should be remembered that only a fraction of the Lower Citadel has been excavated and that earthquakes can often inflict heavy physical damage with comparatively light loss of human life, depending upon the season and time of day at which they strike. Some indications for more localized fires, perhaps resulting from toppled lamps and braziers, rather than a massive conflagration also come from Mycenae, where the Citadel House was the casualty of an incendiary destruction while the mud brick and plaster walls of the cult center next door showed no evidence of burning. As for the wisdom of situating new settlements in coastal areas, we cannot discount the possibility that Bronze Age Greeks displayed the same blend of fatalism and optimism that can be found today among residents of California's Bay Area. In fact, evidence for two inundations, probably caused by tidal waves, is attested for the Lower Citadel of Tiryns during the first phase of LHIIIC. The fact that the zone continued to be inhabited for approximately another century offers some clue to the Tirynthians' mentality in this regard.

If Tiryns really did suffer an earthquake ca. 1200, it is almost certain that Mycenae, which is less than twenty kilometers away, and Midea, which is even nearer, shared the same fate. It is less likely, however, that the mansion at Therapne or the palaces at Pylos or Volos were casualties of the same tremor, and this serves to illustrate the limitations of unicausal and universal explanations. We tend to talk about simultaneous destructions ca. 1200 but what we actually have is a series of episodes that date towards the end of the LHIIIB ceramic phase. In real terms, the destructions could have taken place over a period as long as thirty years or so and this allows for more complex causes, effects, and consequences. It is still significant that so many Late Bronze Age centers could have been delivered an ultimately fatal blow within the course of a single generation, but the apparent ubiquity of the catastrophe may be due not so much to there being a single cause as to the fact that the palatial economies of centers in the Aegean and the Near East were interlocked. In other words, a systems approach that focuses on the economic relations not only between the palatial center and its rural periphery but also between different palatial centers probably offers a more powerful explanation as to why the catastrophe was so widespread, but there can be little doubt that a systems collapse, if it occurred, was both the cause and the result of a wide range of factors that varied from region to region. Raiders and pirates could well have been responsible for harrying or even severing important economic networks between kingdoms and it is hard to believe that they would have refrained from preying on those already debilitated, but it would surely be a mistake to assume, on the basis of two Egyptian texts, that the identity of these raiders was the same in southern Greece as it was in the southern Levant. Earthquakes that destroyed palace storage rooms would have had a deleterious effect on the economic functioning of the palaces, just as they would have further demoralized and left even more vulnerable to external attack a population on the brink of starvation. And drought and famine could have served as either a preliminary trigger or the final death knell for a redistributive system that could no longer sustain itself. Whatever the causes behind the collapse of the Mycenaean palaces, the answer must lie in the complexity of the world that the Bronze Age Greeks and their Near Eastern neighbors had created.

The Loss and Recovery of Writing

The skilled laborers who built the fortified palaces and the craft specialists who produced the luxury goods through which the elite both affirmed its status and boosted its wealth were supported by the agricultural surpluses that the palatial centers exacted from the countryside. With the collapse of the palaces as effective political, administrative, and economic centers, those skills were no longer required. Monumental architecture, figured representations on pottery, engraving of precious metals, and ivoryworking all disappear from the material record, not to resurface for at least another three centuries. From the point of view of the historian, one of the most significant skills to fall into abeyance is that of writing.

Linear B was a cumbersome script with some sixty ideograms and at least a further eighty-nine signs, most of which stand for syllables rather than individual phonemes. It must have been a comparatively difficult system to learn and, given that it seems to have been employed solely for commercial and accounting purposes, demand for people literate in it can never have been high. These considerations, together with the fact that only a limited number of different handwritings can be identified in the tablets, make it virtually certain that literate competence was restricted to a small number of scribes, probably no more than a handful at any one time in each palatial center. There is no reason to suppose that future excavations will reveal the persistence of literacy into the Early Iron Age. Faced with the realization that their skills were redundant after the disappearance of the palaces, the scribes would have needed to make provisions for their own livelihood. Some may well have passed their expertise onto their children but, in the absence of any functional application, it is unlikely that competence in Linear B would have survived more than a generation or so.

Quite when, how, and where writing returned to Greece is a matter of some dispute. Let us start with what we know. The earliest known graffiti are written on pottery that generally appears to belong to around the middle of the eighth century, though slightly earlier dates have been claimed for graffiti from Eretria, Naxos, and Lefkandi, while a small, globular flask, incised with what seem to be four or five Greek letters and found in a grave at Osteria dell'Osa, east of Rome, is unlikely to be later than ca. 800–775 BCE. Technically, a graffito could be scratched on a pot some time after its manufacture, meaning that the decorative style of the pot would offer little assistance in dating the inscription. In practice, however, many of the earliest graffiti appear on vessels that served as grave offerings and the latest vases in the assemblage will normally date the closure of the tomb and thus serve as a *terminus ante quem* for the inscription. Furthermore, the fact that dipinti – inscriptions painted on pots prior to firing – appear on ceramics dating to the third quarter of the eighth century at Pithecusae provides some reassurance that most graffiti were probably roughly contemporary with the pots on which they were scratched.

Nor is there much dispute concerning the origin of the Greek alphabet. Despite a claim that it was borrowed from a Canaanite alphabet ca. 1150, most scholars are agreed that it is an adaptation of the later Phoenician, or Northwest Semitic, script. Greek scripts display notable local characteristics – principally with regard to the shape of letters but also in the matter of the phonetic values attributed to signs such as *san*, *sigma*, *khi*, and *psi*. All local Greek scripts, however, share important divergences from the Phoenician proto-type, notably in the reutilization of certain Semitic consonantal symbols to represent vowels and perhaps – though the evidence for the Southern Aegean scripts is ambiguous – in the creation of three new symbols to represent aspirated plosives (*phi*, *khi*, and *psi*). These shared divergences would suggest that the Greek alphabet was born in one place only, in a single moment and perhaps as a result of the initiative of a single creator. Local differences would have arisen only subsequently. What is less clear is where such a transmission took place and whether our earliest extant graffiti are really the first examples of writing or whether writing was actually practised earlier but on more perish-able items such as skins or wood that have not survived in the archaeological record.

In terms of the place of transmission, the Eastern Mediterranean has gener-ally been favored as a place where Greeks and Phoenicians came into regular contact with one another. Crete is situated in an advantageous position to dis-seminate the alphabet to other Greek regions, and at Kommos, on the southern coast, there is evidence for the construction of a Phoenician tripillar shrine, dated to the last quarter of the tenth century. Cyprus, where permanent Phoenician settlements appear from the ninth century, is another candidate, but the early attestation of graffiti at Eretria, Lefkandi, and Pithecusae gives some reason to suppose that it was a Euboean who was responsible for adapt-ing the Phoenician alphabet to fit the Greek language. Attention has often focused on Al Mina, a trading-post on the mouth of the River Orontes in modern Turkey, where large quantities of imported Euboean pottery have been excavated (see pp. 96–8). Alternatively, the Osteria dell'Osa inscription must at least raise the possibility of a transmission in Italy, where Euboeans undoubtedly lived alongside Phoenicians and others in the trading-post of Pithecusae. Some have objected that the letters on the Osteria dell'Osa flask make no sense and may not, therefore, represent the Greek language. On the other hand, one could argue that this sort of unintelligibility is exactly what one ought to expect to find when a population attempts to come to grips with an entirely new skill. For all that, it is worth pointing out that the theory of an individual adapter does not require the documented existence of intense interaction between Greeks and Phoenicians. Unfortunately, the archaeological record is not always capable of identifying the activity of single individuals, as opposed to groups, meaning that the transmission of the alphabet could theoretically have occurred anywhere.

The issue of an earlier, epigraphically invisible transmission is more difficult. It has been suggested that the shapes of the letters on the earliest Greek graffiti resemble most closely the shapes that Phoenician letters assumed ca. 800, implying that the alphabet was transmitted only very shortly before its earliest attestations on painted pottery. Since, however, there exists only a handful of extant Phoenician inscriptions that predate 500, it is difficult to establish a reliable stylistic sequence of letter forms. Furthermore, the stylistic comparison would only be valid if we could be absolutely certain that our earliest surviving Greek inscriptions truly belong to the first generation of Greek scripts. Ultimately, it is a matter of plausibility. While it is entirely possible that the Greeks wrote on perishable materials, it is perhaps less likely that they studiously avoided scratching graffiti on ceramic vessels until the eighth century.

From a broader historical perspective, however, it is far from clear how consequential the discovery of earlier graffiti would really be. The fact is that our earliest inscriptions are remarkably uninformative. Aside from "Nestor's Cup" (see p. 25) and an Attic Late Geometric *oinokhoe* (wine-jug), found in the Kerameikos district of Athens (Figure 3.3), which carries the metrical graffito "Whoever of all the dancers now dances most daintily, of him this . . . ," the vast majority of eighth-century inscriptions simply involve names. There is nothing to match the detailed record-keeping of the Linear B tablets.

Figure 3.3   Attic Late Geometric *oinokhoe*. National Archaeological Museum, Athens, Archaeological Receipts and Fund (TAP Service)

Furthermore, the effect that the advent of literacy had on Greek society now appears less revolutionary than was once thought. Traditionally, anthropologists used to draw a sharp distinction between the cognitive faculties employed by oral and literate societies respectively, but this dichotomy appears to have been rather overstated in general and is certainly unsatisfactory for the Greek world. The existence of literacy may have created favorable preconditions for the development of rational thought, detailed administrative and financial accounting, and a more historical consciousness but none of these applications was truly realized until several centuries later. Notwithstanding what appears to be a fairly early and relatively pervasive literate competence in regions such as Attica, Greece remained an essentially oral society until well into the Classical period.

Whose Dark Age?

With the possible, but dubious, exception of Homer (see pp. 25–6), ancient authors preserved no memory of the four or so centuries that followed the collapse of the Mycenaean palaces. Save for the locations of the impressive citadels whose remains continued to be visible, they display little recollection of the Mycenaean period either, but at least here we have the testimony of the Linear B tablets to supplement the material record. For the succeeding centuries we have only archaeological evidence, though recent decades of archaeological exploration have seen impressive advances in our knowledge of this period. This has persuaded some that the term "Dark Age," conventionally employed to designate the period ca. 1200–750, is now a misnomer. The Dark Age, it is argued, is defined less by the material conditions of the immediate post-Mycenaean period as it is by our ignorance of those conditions on account of the absence of contemporary written documents. Since, however, archaeology has stepped in to compensate for the lack of literary evidence, the Dark Age has now been illuminated. That we know more about this period now than we did several decades ago is indisputable. Nevertheless, while it would be futile to deny that some continuities are traceable across the centuries of darkness, such information as has come to light serves only to confirm a general picture of isolation, introversion, and instability.

This is most apparent from settlement patterns. The data in Figure 3.4 are taken from a survey of sites in southern-central Greece (including the Cyclades but excluding the Ionian islands, Epirus, Macedonia, Thrace, and Thessaly). Earlier estimates of site numbers for the entire Aegean area are broadly compatible. What we find is a steep decline in the number of archaeologically identifiable sites, beginning in LHIIIC and continuing to a low point in the succeeding Submycenaean phase (ca. 1070–1000). There is then a recovery in the Protogeometric period (ca. 1000–900) and a further increase in the Geometric period (ca. 900–700), though the total number of sites is still well below the level attested for LHIIIB, prior to the palatial destructions.

Period	Percentage increase/decrease from previous period
Late Helladic IIIC	−62.5%
Submycenaean	−61.9%
Protogeometric	+104.4%
Geometric	+111.9%

Figure 3.4   Increases/decreases in site numbers from the twelfth to the seventh centuries

It would be unwise to assume a direct correlation between site numbers and population levels. As we have seen, the settlement area around the citadel of Tiryns was far more extensive in LHIIIC than it had been in LHIIIB and this suggests that the decline in the overall number of sites in the twelfth century was due in part to processes of settlement nucleation whereby small rural sites were abandoned in favor of larger, more defensible locations. But were settlement nucleation the only explanation, we would expect the few sites that are attested in the eleventh century to be even larger, and this is not generally what we find. Even those sites that continued to be occupied throughout the Dark Age were only sparsely settled. Numbers of graves are a notoriously unreliable indicator for population levels but the fact that the number of eleventh-century graves at Argos is less than half the number attested for the tenth century is at least consistent with the settlement evidence. An estimate of between 600 and 1,200 for the Dark Age population of Argos is probably in the right range if we regard the lower figure as an absolute maximum for the eleventh century.

Argos was among the larger Dark Age settlements. More typical, perhaps, is Nikhoria in Messenia. A site of some importance in the Late Bronze Age – it may even have been the administrative center of the "Further Province" mentioned in the Pylos tablets – Nikhoria suffered a destruction ca. 1200 though was not entirely abandoned. In its first Dark Age phase (ca. 1075–975), simple one-room dwellings were erected in haphazard fashion directly above the ruined foundations of the Mycenaean settlement. The excavators estimated that Nikhoria was at this time home to some thirteen or fourteen families, or eighty-five to ninety people in all. In the next phase (ca. 975–800), clusters of apsidal houses sprang up, providing home for up to forty families, or 200 people, though the community appears to have dwindled again in the final phase (ca. 800–750) with an estimated population of 100 people, or twenty families. There is no particular reason to suppose that there were more populous settlements in Messenia at this time: survey results suggest that the Dark Age population of the region was little more than 10 percent of what it had been during LHIIIB. What, then, had happened to the Bronze Age population of Messenia?

It is possible that some died in the disturbances ca. 1200, but this cannot be the whole story. People evidently left and since there are few indications in eleventh-century Greece for the emergence of new settlements, it is not unlikely that some of them were among the settlers who established new communities in Asia Minor in the eleventh and tenth centuries (see p. 96). Another possibility is that part of the population adopted a more transient way of life within Greece, occupying on a temporary or seasonal basis sites in marginal areas. The peripheral location of such sites and the non-permanent nature of their occupation would certainly make them correspondingly more difficult to identify in the archaeological record. Telling in this respect, per- haps, is the scarcity of identifiable cult locations in this period, notwithstand- ing the clear evidence that the religious ideas and practices we find attested in the later Archaic and Classical periods preserve important continuities with those of Bronze Age Greece. Evidence for continuous cultic activity across the Dark Age is indicated for only a handful of sites: Kalapodhi in Phocis, Kato Symi, and perhaps the Diktaian Cave on Crete. More sanctuaries appear in the course of the eleventh and tenth centuries (e.g. Amyclae in Laconia, Isthmia, Kombothekra, and Olympia in Elis, Mount Hymettus and Munychia in Attica, the Polis Cave on Ithaca), but it is not until the eighth century that there is a veritable explosion in the numbers of permanent cult places. At several sanctuaries where we believe there to have been Bronze Age cultic activity – Agia Irini on Ceos, the Maleatas sanctuary at Epidaurus in the Argolid, and perhaps Delphi – there is a complete lack of evidence for Dark Age worship.

The hypothesis of a more mobile population is closely connected to the view that subsistence strategies in the Dark Age were dominated by pastoralism. The evidence for pastoralism is, admittedly, far from overwhelming and is predominantly based on faunal analysis from Nikhoria which indicates a sharp rise in bovine consumption between the latter part of the thirteenth century and the Dark Age. Pastoralism, it is argued, would have been an obvious subsistence option when agricultural regimes were threatened by the instability that accompanied the palatial destructions but it would also have required greater mobility and the seasonal or periodic occupation of sites as grazing areas became exhausted. Furthermore, a meat-rich diet was less nutritionally beneficial than one based on grain, pulses, and vegetables and this dietary change would have had deleterious effects on reproduction rates, thus contrib- uting further to demographic decline.

Whatever the merits of the pastoralist hypothesis, it is clear that not every- body adopted a more transient lifestyle. The pottery styles of LHIIIC continue many Mycenaean traditions but they also display for the first time regional differentiations that are maintained into subsequent centuries and that are normally interpreted as indications for isolation and introversion. The vast majority of the material at Nikhoria – as at many other sites – is locally produced, and there are very few imports from other Greek regions. Similarly, while the diffusion of iron technology from Cyprus and the appearance of Near Eastern imports in tenth- and ninth-century graves from Attica, Euboea, Crete, and the Dodecanese testify to a certain maintenance of overseas con- tacts, there can be little doubt that such contacts were far less intensive and frequent than they had been in the Mycenaean period or than they would prove to be from the eighth century onwards.

It was not all doom and gloom. The site most frequently invoked by those who deny that there was a true Dark Age in Greece is Lefkandi, excavated since 1964 by Greek and British archaeologists. To the east of the modern village, the Xeropolis headland was first settled on a permanent basis towards the end of the Early Bronze Age (ca. 2000). Rebuilt ca. 1200, perhaps by refugees fleeing the disturbances on the mainland, the excavated settlement appears to have been abandoned around a century later, although continued activity in the area is attested by the presence of Submycenaean cist graves in the Skoubris plot, situated on the hills to the northwest of Xeropolis.

Shortly after 1000, an impressive apsidal building, forty-five meters long and ten meters wide, was constructed on a leveled rock platform in the Toumba plot, southeast of the Skoubris cemetery. With plastered mud brick walls standing on stone foundations, its gabled thatched roof was supported by a row of internal central columns and by an exterior wooden colonnade, making it not only the earliest known peripteral (colonnaded) building in Greece but also the only structure in the whole period that can justifiably warrant being described as monumental. Divided into five rooms, two shafts, 2.75 meters deep, were discovered in the middle of the largest, central room. In the more southerly shaft were the skeletons of four horses, two with iron bits still in their mouths. In the other were two burials. One was the cremation burial of a male, aged thirty to forty-five: his ashes had been gathered in a linen cloth and placed within a twelfth-century bronze amphora of probably Cypriot manufacture; closed by a bronze bowl, the urn was accompanied by a whetstone and an iron razor, spearhead, and sword, the latter originally sheathed in a wooden scabbard. The other burial was the supine inhumation of a female, aged twenty-five to thirty, who wore bronze and iron pins, a gold and faience necklace, an electrum ring and a gold ring, gold hair-spirals, and a gold brassiere. By her head was an ivory-handled iron knife, which suggested to the excavators that she might have been sacrificed during the funeral of the warrior whose remains were found beside her.

The interpretation of the building is fraught with difficulties – not least because it appears to have been partially dismantled shortly after its construction and deliberately buried beneath a huge earth tumulus. Many believe that it was the house of a "big man" – that is, a leader of a small, fairly egalitarian community who achieved his status on account of his military prowess and competitive generosity (see further pp. 122–7). The status of the big man is always fragile, rarely outliving him, and the suggestion is that the obliteration of the Toumba building, immediately after its occupant's death, visibly signaled the end of his authority. The excavators, however, have noted that there are scorch marks on the bedrock below the clay floor of the building, suggesting that the funeral took place *before* the construction of the building – a conclusion that may be strengthened by the observation that there is a slightly wider gap between the two internal supports either side of the shafts than between any of the other supporting posts. They suggest that the building was designed as a type of mausoleum but that it was buried out of fear after some unforeseen circumstance – perhaps subsidence in the zone.

Immediately after the construction of the tumulus, a new cemetery was laid out at its eastern end and, by about 950, there is evidence that Xeropolis was once again occupied. The second half of the tenth century is, in fact, the great heyday of Lefkandi: the influence of Attic – alongside Thessalian and Cypriot – styles on the local pottery is particularly noticeable and the practice of inurned cremation may also derive from Attica, but the most distinctive feature of this period is the voluminous presence of precious metals, especially gold, and of imported luxury items from Egypt, Cyprus, and the Near East. Those imports continue into the ninth century, even if local ceramic styles become more resistant to the influence of other Greek regions, but around 825 the excavated cemeteries are abandoned and Xeropolis appears to go into decline. The settlement becomes open once more to influences from Attica, Thessaly, and now Corinth in the second half of the eighth century, before being for the most part abandoned ca. 700 (though see p. 7).

How typical is Lefkandi? The human resources that the warrior evidently commanded, the wealth that the community – or at least part of it – possessed and the long-distance contacts that are attested with Egypt and the Near East are unmatched on this scale anywhere else in Greece during this period. It is always possible that there are further sites like Lefkandi waiting to be discovered, although it would be hard to claim that the archaeology of Early Iron Age Greece has been neglected in recent decades and the few parallels that have been suggested for the Toumba building – for instance, Megaron B at Thermon in Aetolia – hardly measure up. There is some debate about the size and the nature of the community that lived at Lefkandi. Assuming that the excavated graves are a representative sample, the population should have been smaller than Argos and perhaps closer in size to the community at Nikhoria. One estimate would even put the population below fifty. On the other hand, it has been calculated that the tumulus that covered the Toumba building would have required between 500 and 2,000 days of human labor. Unless the inhabitants of Lefkandi could rely on outside labor, it is difficult to imagine that they could have accomplished the task with so small a population. While it is possible that there are many more cemeteries awaiting discovery in the area around Lefkandi, it is also not unthinkable that a substantial part of the local population has not been recognized in the archaeological record because it was not afforded formal burial – a possibility that has been proposed for nearby Attica in this period (see pp. 78–9).

Those who argue for a small community tend to envisage it as broadly egalitarian, save for the pre-eminent authority of the warrior buried beneath the Toumba building. Yet there are some indications to the contrary. Figure 3.5 shows the percentage of graves that contained metal objects in the three principal cemeteries at Lefkandi, while Figure 3.6 tabulates the average number of metal artifacts in those graves together with the standard deviation

	1100–950 BCE	950–828 BCE
Skoubris Plot	54.1%	61.5%
Palia Perivolia Plot	60%	38.6%
Toumba Plot	–	60.6%

Figure 3.5 Percentages of graves with metal items at Lefkandi by cemetery and period

	1100–950 BCE		950–825 BCE	
	Mean	SD	Mean	SD
Skoubris Plot	4.25	4.1	6.75	8.76
Palia Perivolia Plot	–	–	2.29	1.26
Toumba Plot	–	–	7.9	6.58

Figure 3.6 Average number of metal items in graves at Lefkandi by cemetery and period together with the standard deviation around the mean

(a measurement which serves as an index of variance). The figure of 60 per-cent for the earliest graves in the Palia Perivolia cemetery is not terribly signific-ant because the sample includes only five graves. What is more interesting is that far fewer of the Late Protogeometric (ca. 950–900) and Subprotogeometric I–II (ca. 900–825) graves in this plot contained metal objects than is the case with either the Skoubris or the Toumba cemeteries. Furthermore, the average number of artifacts in graves in the Palia Perivolia cemetery is well below that in the other two burial grounds and there is far less variance between the grave assemblages there. Mere numbers cannot capture the wealth of some of the burials in the Toumba cemetery, especially in its later phases: Tomb 36, for example, contained a gold diadem and ten gold attachments, alongside two gold rings, three bronze fibulae, a bronze bracelet, and pieces of faience, amber, and crystal. Nevertheless, the differential in wealth between – and, in the case of the Skoubris and Toumba plots, within – cemeteries might lead one to suspect that the community at Lefkandi qualifies at least as a ranked society (see p. 123). Set within a broader context, however, the apparent exceptionality of Lefkandi only indicates that in the Dark Age an aggregately lower amount of wealth was distributed less evenly between communities than was the case in either the Mycenaean period or the period from the eighth century onwards. Lefkandi hardly serves to refute the concept of a Dark Age.

Unless, that is, the Dark Age is simply a historiographical mirage, generated by faulty chronological reckoning. This is precisely the suggestion made in 1991 by a consortium of historians and archaeologists. Struck by the seemingly seamless resumption, after three or four centuries, of certain craft skills such as ivoryworking, figured pictorial representations on pottery, monumental stone architecture, and even literacy itself, they wondered whether the palatial destructions may not have taken place considerably later, thereby compressing the period of time normally allotted to the Dark Age. In their view, the source of the problem lies with Egyptian chronology, upon which all the dating-systems of the Mediterranean and Near East are, to a greater or lesser degree, dependent. The relative chronology of Egypt is derived from late epitomes of a text, originally written ca. 280 by an Egyptian high priest named Manetho, which records the names of all the kings of the thirty dynasties together with the number of years that they reigned. This chronology is then pegged to absolute dates by what is known as the Sothic theory. The Egyptian year began with the flooding of the Nile. Ideally this should coincide with the rising of the Sirius star on the eastern horizon immediately before dawn – something that did, in fact, occur in 1321 and 139 CE – but since the solar and lunar years are not the same length, the two events would have diverged from one another at a rate of one day every four years unless the Egyptians practiced intercalation (e.g. the insertion of an extra day every fourth year). Thus, when Egyptian documents name the calendar date on which Sirius rose, we are able to count the number of days that separated this event from the New Year, multiply the result by four and arrive at the number of years that had elapsed since the start of the Sothic cycle. If the same document also records in which regnal year of which pharaoh an event took place, then we are able to synchronize Manetho's list with absolute dates.

The objections to this system are that we cannot be sure the Egyptians did not practice intercalation, that the rising of Sirius would have been visible on different days depending on where one was in Egypt, and that Manetho's king list may not be reliable in the first place. By some ingenious number-crunching – and a few wild guesses – it is proposed that the dates of the eighteenth, nineteenth, and twentieth dynasties should be lowered by about 250 years. The consequence for the Aegean is that the Mycenaean period would then have ended ca. 900, slashing in half at one stroke the Dark Age. The thesis offers a salutary reminder about the contingent nature of our chronology (see p. 40), but Egyptologists have disputed the claim that New Kingdom/Late Period chronology is entirely dependent upon Sothic dating and Greek archaeologists note not only that it is difficult to squeeze the eight chronological sub-phases of the Geometric style into a mere one hundred years but that radiocarbon dates broadly seem to support the traditional chronology. Perhaps the ultimate failing, however, is the belief that a Dark Age is in some sense problematic and needs to be explained away. Dark Ages are attested for various historical periods around the world and only those who are unremittingly committed to a unidirectional evolutionist view of progress would seek to attribute every one of them to present-day ignorance. There were, as we shall see, many important underlying continuities that spanned the Dark Age, but it remains the case that Greece in the eighth, seventh, and sixth centuries was a very different place from what it had been in the Late Bronze Age. The explanation for this undoubtedly lies in the unstable conditions of the Dark Age, when centralized authority vanished, when obligations and loyalties lay nearer to home, and when self-reliance became essential rather than desirable.

FURTHER READING

Mycenaeans as first Greek-speakers: Drews 1988. For the discovery of Mycenaean civilization: McDonald and Thomas 1990.

Archaeological evidence and literary traditions concerning migrations: Vanschoonwinkel 1991. Critique: Hall 1997, 114–28, 143–81; 2002, 56–89. Greek dialects: J. Chadwick, "The prehistory of the Greek language," *Cambridge Ancient History*, vol. 2.2, third edn. (Cambridge, 1975), 805–19. Information in Figure 3.2: Roussel 1976; Jones 1987.

Various reasons for palatial collapse: Drews 1993.

Introduction of Greek alphabet: A. W. Johnston, "The extent and use of literacy: The archaeological evidence," in Hägg 1983, 63–8; Powell 1991, 5–67.

The Dark Age as a historiographical mirage: J. K. Papadopoulos, "To kill a cemetery: The Athenian Kerameikos and the Early Iron Age in the Aegean," *Journal of Mediterranean Archaeology* 6 (1993), 175–206. Data in Figure 3.4 based on Syriopoulos 1983, 307–17. Estimate of Argive population: I. Morris, "The early polis as city and state," in Rich and Wallace-Hadrill 1991, 25–57. Nikhoria: McDonald, Coulson, and Rosser 1983; Thomas and Conant 1999, 32–59. Pastoralist hypothesis: Snodgrass 1987, 190–209; Tandy 1997, 19 43. Lefkandi: Popham, Sackett, and Themelis 1980; 1993; Thomas and Conant 1999, 85–114; J. Whitley, "Social diversity in Dark Age Greece," *Annual of the British School at Athens* 86 (1991), 341–65. Megaron B at Thermon: Morris 2000, 225–8. Population of Lefkandi: A. M. Snodgrass, "Two demographic notes," in Hägg 1983, 167–71. Chronological revisionism: James et al. 1991.

4

Communities of Place

Defining the *Polis*

Greece's status as a single sovereign nation is a realization of the modern age. Even under Roman occupation, what now constitutes the Hellenic Republic was administratively divided between the provinces of Achaea, Macedonia, and Crete-Cyrene. Before that, Greece comprised a plurality of small citizen communities with varying degrees of autonomy known as *poleis* (singular: *polis*) of which, for the period down to the death of Alexander the Great in 323, no fewer than 1,035 are known by name throughout the Mediterranean and Black Sea areas (though not all of these existed concurrently). Often considered to be the dominant and most characteristic political formation in the ancient Greek world, it is hardly surprising that considerable effort should have been expended in attempting to determine how, why, and especially when the *polis* emerged.

Scholarly interest in this question can be traced back to 1937 and an article entitled "When did the *polis* rise?" written by Victor Ehrenberg. Disputing the claim, advanced by the German historian Helmut Berve, that the *polis* first emerged out of conflicts between major political leaders ca. 500 and that its evolution was still not complete by 450, Ehrenberg argued that the internal dissolution of the *polis* was already discernible in the time of Pericles and the sophists in the fifth century, meaning that its acme should be situated much earlier. Presupposed in sixth-century laws and decrees as well as in the poems of Solon, dated to the beginning of that century, Ehrenberg thought that the concept of the *polis* was a little hazier in the Boeotia that is depicted in Hesiod's *Works and Days*; nevertheless, he reasoned that it may have been more developed in those regions that were less "backward." Ultimately, he resorted to Homeric evidence: claiming that the *polis* is absent from the *Iliad* but plays a central role in the *Odyssey* – and adopting a somewhat high dating for the Homeric epics – he proposed a date of ca. 800 for its emergence.

As we have seen (pp. 24–5), it is notoriously difficult to make chronological arguments on the basis of the Homeric poems. Few today would date the epics so early and many are unconvinced that the *polis* is entirely absent from the *Iliad*. In the late 1970s and 1980s, however, the question of when the *polis* arose was given a new lease of life by classical archaeologists, who noted that the middle decades of the eighth century witnessed a number of material changes that could possibly be attributed to socio-political development – notably, the construction of monumental temples, shifts in the location of cemeteries, the reappearance of crafts skills that had fallen into disuse since the Late Bronze Age, and the re-establishment of intensive overseas communications. It is this resumption of cultural practices that had remained dormant throughout the Dark Age that has inspired some to talk in terms of an eighth-century Greek "renaissance."

It is not entirely surprising that such an intensive focus on the origins of the *polis* would have provoked a backlash. On the one hand, those who believe that the Dark Age is little more than a mirage (see pp. 59–66) criticize excessive attention to the origins of the *polis* on the grounds that it establishes an artificial disjunction in what they regard as a more gradual and continuous process of state formation. On the other hand, those whose research is focused principally on the so-called *ethnos* regions of northern and western Greece, where the *polis* is generally believed to have emerged much later, complain that a disproportionate emphasis on the *polis* has diverted attention away from other forms of state organization that were no less complex or functionally efficient. It is, then, worth asking how important a watershed the eighth century was for the development of the *polis* as well as assessing the validity of the distinction that is traditionally drawn between *polis* and *ethnos* forms of organization.

Most modern treatments of the early *polis* are based, directly or indirectly, on the definitions offered by Aristotle in the *Politics*. Thus, while the *polis* is regarded as resulting from the physical fusion of villages (*kômai*), it is its characterization as a community of citizens that is typically given the most emphasis. The community should ideally be small enough that office-holders are familiar to voters but large enough to encourage labor specialization in order to achieve self-sufficiency (*autarkeia*). Perhaps most importantly from the modern perspective, the *polis* should be self-governing and independent (*autonomos*). Aristotle recognized the importance of employing historical evidence: the *Athenian Constitution*, written by a member of his school, is the sole surviving example of the originally 158 accounts that described the constitutional histories of different Greek *poleis* and served as the empirical database for the *Politics*. But the *Politics* itself is a work of political theory, not history, and we cannot automatically assume that the "ideal type" of *polis* that it depicts is strictly representative of any single actual *polis* in Aristotle's day – let alone in earlier centuries.

In a massive undertaking which, in some senses, offers a modern parallel to the research project of Aristotle and his school, the Copenhagen Polis Center, under the direction of the Danish historian Mogens Herman Hansen, has collected all known attestations of the term *polis* and its derivatives in the period ca. 650 to ca. 323. The aim is both to determine what the ancient Greeks thought a *polis* was and to identify those communities that they expressly defined as *poleis*. The results have challenged certain orthodoxies: self-sufficiency, for example, was rarely achievable in practice while external autonomy was not a defining characteristic of the *polis* since there are many communities that were politically or militarily dependent on more powerful neighbors but are still named as *poleis* in ancient sources. Above all else, the term *polis* – at least by the Classical period – seems to have signified three things simultaneously: it could be used synonymously with *astu* to indicate an urban center and with *gê* or *khôra* to denote a territory which included both the urban center and its hinterland, but it also signified a political community in the Aristotelian sense. The equation of *polis* with a territory is not terribly common but the urban connotations of the term would appear to be just as important as the social associations. In fact, one of the conclusions to have emerged is that the term *polis* was not indiscriminately applied to any urban center but only to an urban center that served as a center for the political community. Conversely, and with very few exceptions, only those political communities that possessed an urban center could be described as *poleis*. As both an urban center and a political community, then, the translation of *polis* as "city-state" – an equation that was immortalized with the publication, in 1898, of Jacob Burckhardt's *Griechische Kulturgeschichte* – is not as inappropriate as is sometimes claimed. It is true that the Greek *poleis* differed in several important respects from medieval Italian *comuni* or German *Reichsstädte*. Yet the similarities between these various city-state cultures far outweigh the differences and serve to distinguish this type of political formation from nation-states, nomadic states, or feudal systems.

It should, nevertheless, be pointed out that the vast majority of the Copenhagen Polis Center's evidence derives from texts of the fifth and fourth centuries. We cannot be completely certain that the three meanings of *polis* that can be identified in Classical sources were all inherent in the term from the outset. In fact, it has been argued that since urbanization in early Greece was limited and proceeded at such a slow pace, it makes little sense to talk about "cities" before the late sixth century. Conversely, the argument continues, certain features in the material record of Dark Age settlements such as Lefkandi or Khora on Naxos could be taken to indicate complex political and social hierarchies that might have survived the collapse of the Mycenaean palaces ca. 1200. According to this view, the "state" aspects of the *polis* preceded its urban characteristics.

There is, however, some evidence to suggest a different reconstruction. On the basis of cognates in other Indo-European languages – e.g. Old Indian *púr*; Lithuanian *pilìs*; Latvian *pils* – it seems likely that the original meaning of *polis* was "stronghold." Indeed, in some literary and epigraphic texts the term *p(t)olis* is used interchangeably with "acropolis" in contexts that suggest that this was its signification in the Late Bronze Age. This should indicate, then,

Document 4.1

It is a fine thing for a man to die after falling in the front ranks fighting for his fatherland (*patris*), while the most grievous thing of all is for him to leave his *polis* and rich fields and beg, wandering with his dear mother and aged father and with his small children and wedded wife. (Tyrtaeus fr. 10)

that the meaning of the term was extended to denote the urban settlement that sprang up around the foot of the acropolis and then the surrounding territory more generally before coming to be applied to the political community of that territory.

It is probably no accident that in the *Iliad*, *polis* is only very occasionally used to indicate a community: upon recognizing Hector's lifeless body, for example, Cassandra laments the hero's death, describing him as a "delight to the *polis* and to all the people" (24.706). In the vast majority of cases, however, *polis* is employed synonymously with *astu* to denote a physical place. When, in the *Odyssey* (8.555), the Phaeaecian king Alcinous asks Odysseus to name his *gaia* ("land" or perhaps "region"), *dêmos* (probably "territory" to judge from the term's Mycenaean ancestor), and *polis*, it is clear that he is "zooming in" on an ever more precise identification of his guest's origins, in which *polis* can only really refer to a specific settlement. Nor is this more restrictive sense of *polis* limited to Homer. Tyrtaeus (Document 4.1) employs the term *patris* rather than *polis* when glorifying the warrior who sacrifices his life for his homeland and his juxtaposition of the term *polis* with "rich fields" (*pionas agrous*) clearly indicates that he had a physical, rather than social, connotation in mind. One cannot discount the possibility that Tyrtaeus is here consciously employing "Homeric" language, but that is not sufficient to discredit the inference that the term *polis* designated an urban center before coming to denote a political community. Even before embarking on an examination of when the *polis* may have emerged, it is already clear that we are dealing with a phenomenon that was far from instantaneous. We shall discuss the emergence of political communities in subsequent chapters; here, the main focus will be on the importance of place to concepts of the *polis*.

The Urban Aspect of the *Polis*: Houses, Graves, and Walls

Homer's portrayal of Scheria (Document 4.2), with its high city-walls, paved agora, sanctuary of Poseidon, and twin harbors, is often cited as providing an accurate snapshot of what a *polis* of the late eighth or early seventh century might have looked like. So vivid is the depiction that some have assumed that

Document 4.2

Then we will reach the *polis*, which is surrounded by a high bastion. There is a good harbor on each side of the city and a narrow causeway; the curved ships are dragged up along the road and there is a berth for each person. Here, next to the fair sanctuary of Poseidon, is their *agora*, constructed from transported blocks of stone set firmly into the ground. And there they attend to the tackle of their black ships, the cables and sails, and they smooth their oars, for the Phaeacians care little for the bow or quiver, but rather for the masts and oars and the well-balanced ships in which they rejoice as they sail across the grey sea. (Homer, *Od.* 6.262–72)

it was based on a real life model: Old Smyrna in Asia Minor, Palaiokastritsa on the island of Corcyra, and even Corcyra town itself have all been proposed as possible candidates. Yet, while it is almost certainly true that Homer's world had to be recognizable enough to contemporary audiences to be in any sense meaningful, it is emphatically not the case that Homer's heroes rubbed shoulders with his listeners. This is especially true of Scheria, which represents an almost utopian society: the Phaeacian inhabitants of the island are "close to the gods" (*Od.* 5.35) and their omniscient ships require no helmsmen or rudders to guide them overseas to distant lands (8.555–63). In this and many other respects they are the precise opposite of the Cyclopes, their former neighbors (6.4–6), who have no ships, no agriculture, no assemblies, and no laws (9.105–29). In other words, the "superhuman" Phaeacians and the savage Cyclopes define the absolute cultural limits within which human societies conduct their daily life and relations. This is not to say that individual features such as harbors, sacred precincts, fortification walls, and perhaps even paved *agorai* were unfamiliar to Homer's audience – merely that it would be rash to regard their specific conjunction in this passage as an accurate description of any particular contemporary *polis*.

Attempts to define a city and to distinguish it from lower order settlements such as towns or villages are beset by difficulties. Absolute thresholds in terms of physical size or population density are not always very helpful: while there can be little doubt that sprawling *metropoleis* such as New York, Los Angeles, or Chicago qualify as cities, in Vermont the title "city" is often bestowed upon urban settlements that would barely rank as medium-sized towns in Britain (where civic status can only be granted by a royal charter). One of the most influential definitions of the pre-industrial city is that provided by the German sociologist Max Weber in his posthumously published *Die Stadt: Eine soziologische Untersuchung*. According to Weber, the ancient city was a fortified, densely occupied settlement in which the population was too large for "reciprocal personal acquaintance." It was, to a greater or lesser extent, a self-governing community that housed political and administrative institutions. And it served as a market center in which craft products and traded items could be acquired and in which farmers, who constituted the greater part of the urban population, could sell surplus agricultural products.

Sites such as Athens, Argos, and Corinth continued to be inhabited throughout the Dark Age but they lacked fortification circuits. There are several references to fortification walls in the Homeric epics, notably in connection with Troy – which in most respects is treated exactly like a Greek city – but also with regard to Tiryns, Gortyn, Calydon, Phaia, and Thebes. The Achaean heroes are often described as "sackers of well-walled cities" and a walled city under siege features on the ornate shield that the god Hephaestus makes for Achilles (Homer, *Il.* 18.509–40). The evidence is ambiguous, however, since the more significant cities that appear in the epics were also important Mycenaean settlements whose impressive fortifications remained largely visible to Greeks of the eighth and seventh centuries. We cannot, in other words, be sure that Homer describes contemporary urban settlements. On the other hand, there are also numerous references to walled settlements in other Archaic Greek poets. Hesiod (*WD* 241–7) explains how Zeus often destroys a city's army, ships, or walls for the sake of a single transgressor and Alcaeus' maxim (fr. 426; cf. fr. 112) that men and not walls make the *polis* presumes a familiarity with walled settlements. Echoes of Achilles' shield resurface in the pseudo-Hesiodic *Shield of Heracles* (270–2) with its "well-turreted *polis* of men, guarded by seven golden gates, fitted to the lintels" while Theognis (233–4) rants that a noble man is an acropolis and rampart for an empty-headed populace and elsewhere (951) describes scaling the high walls of a city.

According to a recent survey, around 43 percent of Archaic settlements had walls, although it is often difficult to date them with any accuracy and sometimes it is not even possible to determine their disposition. Old Smyrna was for a long time credited with the earliest circuit though it is not continuous and some suspect that the scant remains to the north and northeast of the settlement actually belong to a terrace wall rather than a fortification circuit. But Old Smyrna certainly had walls by the middle of the eighth century, followed closely by the Ionian city of Melie, Minoa on Amorgos, Agios Andreas on Siphnos, Emborio on Chios, Zagora on Andros, Asine in the Argolid and, at the beginning of the seventh century, Eretria. It has been suggested that the geographical distribution of these early fortifications – principally in Asia Minor and the Cycladic islands – is a consequence of the fact that such settlements were constantly threatened by non-Greek or piratical neighbors who could not be expected to respect the highly formalized conventions of hoplite warfare, which privileged infantry encounters on broad plains rather than siege operations. It is, however, disputable whether hoplite warfare was already common in the eighth century and its highly ritualized nature has recently been contested, at least for the early period (p. 157). By the end of the sixth century, walls had become a more common feature on the Greek mainland, with fortifications attested at Halai in Boeotia, Amphanai in Thessaly, Pistyros in Macedonia,

and Eleusis in Attica. We are remarkably ill-informed about the earliest fortifications in some of the larger urban settlements such as Athens or Argos,
though Argos probably had walls before the end of the sixth century as did
Athens – at least to judge from Thucydides' comment (1.89) that only portions of the circuit remained standing after the Persian sacks of 480 and 479.
Combining the literary and archaeological evidence we can probably infer that
the *idea* of city walls was widely disseminated even if more than a half of
Archaic *poleis* remained unfortified.

In theory, walls should provide a reliable guide to the size of a settlement.
In practice, matters are less straightforward because early fortification walls
did not necessarily enclose the entire settlement. At Zagora, the sheer cliffs that
surround the settlement on three sides provided sufficient protection and a
wall was constructed only across the flatter neck of land to the northeast. At
Emborio, Larissa on Hermos, and perhaps Halai and Megara, only the acropolis
was walled, while in the Potters' Quarter at Corinth, a stretch of wall, dated
ca. 650–625, may belong to a city circuit though the extensive and dispersed
pattern of early settlement at Corinth makes it at least possible that the wall
enclosed only this zone. Some idea of a settlement's extent can be derived
from the location of cemeteries which, from the eighth century onwards, tended
to be situated outside habitation areas. Here too, however, matters are complicated by the fact that many ancient settlements lie either wholly or partially
under modern conurbations (e.g. Argos, Athens, Eretria, Sparta). Our knowledge of such sites is normally a result of "rescue excavations," occasioned by
new construction or repair work to utilities, but while this has the unintentional benefit of providing a random sample of archaeological material, it is
seldom possible to obtain a complete overview of the extent or spatial mor-
phology of an ancient urban center.

Even in those cases where we do have a rough idea as to the extent of an
urban center, it is not always easy to estimate the number of inhabitants that
might have been accommodated within the settlement. Firstly, notions of
space are culturally relative and may vary greatly from place to place or from
period to period. Modern "guesstimates" of population density are no less
variable: so, for example, figures as low as twelve and as high as fifty inhabitants per hectare have been proposed for Early Iron Age settlements, which
would yield anything from 540 to 2,250 inhabitants for Eretria or from ninety
to 375 inhabitants at Zagora (Figure 4.1).

Secondly, density of occupation is dependent upon house-type. Conglomerations of abutting units, for example, house more people in less space than
detached residences and among the latter, residences with apsidal or oval
plans (e.g. Assiros in Macedonia; Antissa on Lesbos; Eretria; Old Smyrna;
Miletus; Lefkandi) tend to occupy more space than those with rectilinear plans
(e.g. Emborio; Corinth; Aegina; Kastanas in Macedonia). In general, archaeological evidence suggests that detached houses with apsidal plans tend to be
typical of Dark Age settlements: at Eretria, Old Smyrna, and Miletus, such
residences were replaced by rectilinear houses in the course of the seventh

Settlement	Size (ha)	Population (low: 12–25 people/ha)	Population (high: 30–50 people/ha)
Sparta	300	3,600–7,500	9,000–15,000
Athens	200	2,400–5,000	6,000–10,000
Cnossus	100	1,200–2,500	3,000–5,000
Argos	50	600–1,250	1,500–2,500
Eretria	45	540–1,125	1,350–2,250
Ascra	20	240–500	600–1,000
Zagora	7.5	90–188	225–375

Figure 4.1 Estimated sizes and population levels for eighth-century settlements

century. Conglomerations of units, on the other hand, appear to be an innovation of the eighth century, appearing at Agios Andreas, Kastanas, Prinias on Crete, and Thoricus in Attica, and perhaps testify to increasing pressure on available space. Typically, such dwellings consisted of one room only which had to serve multiple functions. In the seventh century, however, Vroulia on the island of Rhodes offers an early example of multiple-room houses, arranged in single rows lining streets or allies, while by the sixth century, *pastas* or courtyard houses – already attested for the eighth century at Zagora and for the seventh at Corinth – become common in most areas of Greece. It has been estimated that 80 percent of eighth-century settlements covered an area less than ten hectares in extent, while the figure drops to 20 percent for the sixth century. Given, however, that courtyard houses typically occupy more space than single-roomed detached residences, we cannot necessarily assume that the increase in the inhabited area is directly proportional to an increase in population.

Thirdly, it is clear that not all urban centers were continuously inhabited across the entire area of the settlement. Some settlements – for example, Cnossus on Crete or Haliartus and Ascra in Boeotia – do seem to have simply expanded from a single Early Iron Age nucleus. It is this type of compact settlement that is portrayed on Achilles' shield in the *Iliad* (18.484–607) and that the sixth-century poet Phocylides (fr. 4) has in mind when he maintains that "a small and orderly *polis* on a rock is better than foolish Nineveh." But many other sites exhibited a more dispersed pattern of settlement with several clusters of habitation separated by open spaces. Since eighth-century houses were constructed from modest materials such as timber, mud-brick, and thatch, they rarely survive intact in the archaeological record. Instead, our reconstruction of early Greek settlement plans is generally based on more archaeologically recognizable features such as wells and especially graves, which offer in a certain sense a "negative image" of settlement patterns. At Corinth, for example, clusters of activity appear in the vicinity of water sources such as the Peirene and Sacred springs and beside long-established routes like the road

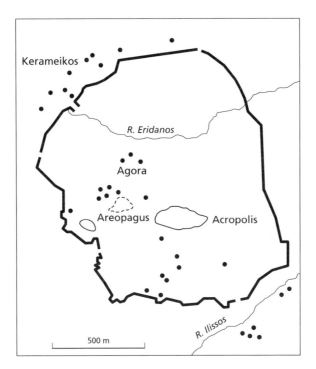

Map 4.1   Distribution of Late Geometric burials at Athens (after Morris 1987, 64 fig. 17, 66 fig. 18)

that led to Lechaeum. Similarly, at Athens graves have been found in clusters focusing on principal lines of communication (Map 4.1). In ninth- and eighth-century Argos (Map 4.2), the distribution of cemeteries seems to indicate detached foci of settlement in the area of the ancient agora, at the foot of the Aspis hill to the north and on the eastern side of the town where the cathedral of Agios Petros now stands.

Perhaps the most famous case of a dispersed settlement pattern is that of Sparta. Even as late as the fifth century, Thucydides (Document 4.3) described it as being "settled in villages (*kômai*) according to the old custom in Greece." One of these villages, Amyclae, was situated about five kilometers south of the Spartan acropolis but the other four – Limnai, Pitana, Mesoa, and Kynosoura – were all located on the west bank of the River Eurotas where the modern town stands today, occupying an area of around 300 hectares in total. Throughout the Archaic period, the populations of Sparta and Athens were probably roughly comparable; the fact, however, that settlement at Sparta extended over a greater area than at Athens only goes to show that distinct, bounded villages remained visible at Sparta long after separate clusters of settlement at Athens had been absorbed by urban expansion. An even more striking case is presented by Thespiae in Boeotia. Here, habitation during the

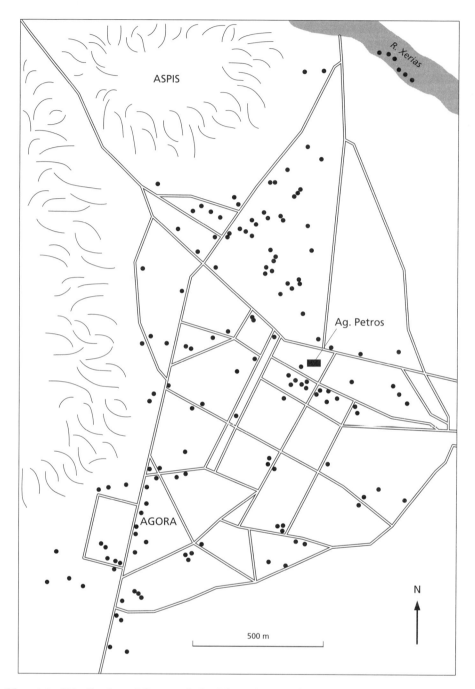

Map 4.2 Distribution of Geometric burials at Argos (after Piérart and Touchais 1996, 23)

Document 4.3

For if the *polis* of the Lacedaemonians were abandoned, and only the sanctuaries and the foundations of the buildings were left, I think that, as time passed, there would be great disbelief among the generations to come that their power measured up to their reputation. And yet they occupy two-fifths of the Peloponnese and exercise hegemony over all of it as well as over many allies outside. Nevertheless, because their *polis* is not synoecized and lacks monumental sanctuaries and buildings, being settled instead by villages according to the old way of life in Greece, it would appear to be less impressive. (Thucydides 1.10.2)

Archaic period seems to have been divided between four settlement clusters which extend across an area some three times the size of Sparta, though it would obviously be unreasonable to hypothesize that the inhabitants of Thespiae outnumbered the Spartans three times over.

In contrasting the settlement plans and monumentality of Athens and Sparta, Thucydides describes the latter as a *polis* that had not been synoecized. The anglicized term "synoecism" is applied to a variety of processes. In reference to the early unification of Attica, which myth attributed to the hero Theseus, Thucydides (2.15.2) uses the term in a political sense. He tells how the inhabitants of Attic towns were persuaded by Theseus to give up local deliberative councils in favor of a single *bouleuterion* ("council chamber") and *prytaneion* ("town hall") in Athens itself (see pp. 218–25). This political type of synoecism is, however, exceedingly rare in our written sources. Far more common is a situation in which a new *polis* is created from either the merging or the absorption of neighboring *poleis*. In 408/7, for example, the citizens of the Rhodian *poleis* of Camirus, Ialysus, and Lindus united to found the new city of Rhodes on the northernmost cape of the island. Although the earlier urban centers were not entirely abandoned, their function was largely limited to the religious sphere. It is possible that a similar phenomenon is attested earlier, albeit on a much smaller scale. Zagora, inhabited since ca. 925, was abandoned ca. 700 and it is often suspected that its inhabitants – like those of nearby Hypsele, which was abandoned at the same time – decided that their needs would be better met by relocating to the principal settlement of Andros at Palaiopolis. Only the sanctuary of Athena, located in the center of the settlement, continued to function down until the fifth century. A similar picture emerges from Koukounaries, situated on the southwest side of Naoussa Bay on the island of Paros. Here, the tenth-century settlement was abandoned towards the end of the eighth century, perhaps as a result of an earthquake; its seventh-century successor was short-lived but the fact that the contents of the houses appear to have been emptied suggests strongly a coordinated abandonment whereby the inhabitants of Koukounaries probably moved to Paros town. Again, however, the temple of Athena, constructed ca. 700 on the southeast slope of the settlement, continued in use until the end of the third century.

With regard to Sparta, however, Thucydides seems to entertain a rather different model of synoecism whereby settlement clusters or villages, often in close proximity to one another, expanded until they merged to form a single, continuous habitation. Some classical archaeologists, comparing this model with Aristotle's claim (*Pol.* 1.1.4–11) that the *polis* was formed from a coalescence of villages, have sought to identify such a process in the material record. Between the eleventh and the eighth centuries, burial plots are found scattered throughout the area later enclosed by the city walls at Athens – notably to the south of the acropolis and in what would eventually become the Classical agora. From around 700, however, save for some infant graves, burial in these locations ceases while there seems to be a preference for cemeteries completely outside the settlement area, especially to the northeast of the city and to the northwest in the Kerameikos quarter. The assumption is that formerly discrete settlement clusters had merged to create a single conurbation. A similar interpretation has been offered for Argos, where the shift to using outlying cemeteries to the north and south of the city begins ca. 800 but is not completed until about a century later. The eighth century also sees an increase in the level of activity among the scattered foci of Corinth, together with the extension of settlement to new areas such as the Potters' Quarter and the Panagia field. Here, however, it is clear that settlement continued to be rather dispersed well into the seventh century. Evidently, not all urban centers developed in the same way or at the same pace.

For all the above reasons, estimates of eighth-century populations can be little more than guesses, yet even guesses can be informative. Figure 4.1 tabulates the estimated size of seven eighth-century settlements together with possible population levels based on a low estimate (twelve to twenty-five inhabitants per hectare) and a high estimate (thirty to fifty inhabitants per hectare). What the figures suggest is that Weber's criterion of a lack of "reciprocal mutual acquaintance" may just have been the case in urban centers such as Sparta, Athens, Cnossus, and possibly Argos and Eretria (though the body of male citizens, which should constitute between a sixth and a quarter of the total population, is more likely to have been a "face-to-face" community). Conversely, Ascra – which is not, in fact, classified by ancient sources as a *polis* – would not qualify and neither would Zagora, even if its densely packed settlement fulfils another of Weber's criteria.

It is now generally agreed that, following centuries of depopulation (pp. 59–61), the eighth century witnessed a rise in population levels. Initially, this thesis was argued on the basis that the number of known burials in Athens and Attica increases sevenfold in the period 780–720. The interpretation of this phenomenon, however, has subsequently been questioned. According to one view, the increase in burials should actually indicate higher death rates rather than higher birth rates – especially since the number of known burials tails off significantly in the seventh century. Given that a number of wells in the area of the later Athenian agora were filled in towards the end of the eighth century and that the same period sees a substantial increase in dedications at the sanctuary of Zeus Ombrios ("Bearer of Rain") on Mount Hymettus, outside Athens, it has been suggested that Attica was hit by a devastating drought. Another view is that the increase in burials need not represent a corresponding rise in the number of mortuary disposals actually made but could signal the extension of a more formal mode of burial to a wider cross-section of the population. Prior to the eighth century, it is argued, the corpses of the less advantaged members of Attic communities were disposed of in more casual ways that have left little or no trace in the archaeological record. As the political community began to take collective cognizance of itself in the eighth century, however, it began to demand for itself the sorts of funerary practices that had previously been monopolized by the elites; in the seventh century, conversely, the elites reacted and formal burial was again denied to large sections of the population.

That there was some increase in population levels in the eighth century is strongly indicated by the settlement evidence. Those settlements that had been occupied throughout the Dark Age clearly experience some expansion in this period. One might be tempted to interpret this pattern as one of settlement nucleation – akin to what happened immediately after the collapse of the Mycenaean palaces (see pp. 48–9) – by which small rural settlements were abandoned in favor of larger urban settlements. As we have seen, this may have been the case on Andros and Paros. But the general picture that emerges from archaeological field survey is that isolated houses, hamlets, and outlying cemeteries are extremely rare in the Dark Age. Furthermore, in many regions there is evidence for renewed rural settlement at exactly the same time that urban centers expanded. The archaeological record suggests that in most areas this took place in the course of the eighth century and it is perhaps interesting that the first evidence for a settlement hierarchy and for the distinction between a *polis* and a *kômê* appears not in the archaizing world of Homer but in Hesiod's depiction of the contemporary world (*WD* 639). A rise in population would have had obvious consequences: "[a] loose organization under a dominant family, with ad hoc decisions taken by a local ruler and only occasional assemblies of any larger group, becomes unworkable when the community more than doubles in size within a single generation" (Snodgrass 1980: 24). Ideally, one might hope to find traces of the new institutional and administrative functions that were demanded by a growing population.

Political and Economic Functions

Evidence for public buildings that served administrative functions rarely predates the sixth century. A theatral-like wooden structure at Metapontum in South Italy, dating to ca. 600, has been interpreted as an *ekklêsiastêrion* – i.e. a building housing the popular assembly – while an inscription, dated to 575–550, from Proconnesus in the Propontis refers to a *prytaneion* – a building that served as the headquarters for the highest magistrates of a city (Fornara 20). For what it is worth, tradition held that Larikhos, the brother of the poetess Sappho, had once served wine in the *prytaneion* of Mytilene on the island of Lesbos (Athenaeus 10.425a). Sixth-century *bouleutêria* (council chambers) have been identified at Agia Pelagia on Crete, Delos, Delphi, and Olympia. Possibly earlier examples of public buildings are a four-room structure, erected in the seventh century to the north of the temple of Athena at Koukounaries, which has been variously described as a banqueting-hall or *bouleutêrion* and a complex of small rectangular rooms in the southern part of what would later become the agora at Argos, in which were found votive materials, inscribed lead plaques, and weights. The complex may date back to the seventh century but no earlier since the location had been used for habitation in the later eighth century.

It is difficult to know how to interpret the apparent lack of eighth-century buildings with an overtly administrative function. It could simply be due to the fact that the earliest public buildings were of flimsy construction and have not survived – or been accurately identified – in the archaeological record. But it is equally likely that the political communities of eighth-century Greece were not yet complex enough to warrant housing specific administrative functions in designated buildings. Such functions were probably originally discharged from the house of the community's leader. At Nikhoria, for example, the tenth-century houses clustered around a larger structure (Unit IV.1), originally 10.5 meters long but extended to 15.9 meters in the ninth century by the addition of an apse. In the eighth century this building was replaced by an adjacent apsidal structure with a courtyard, measuring 20.2 meters in length, which was destroyed along with the rest of the settlement ca. 750. Similar "chiefly" dwellings have been recognized at Zagora, Emborio, and Eretria (Figure 4.2). In some cases, it is argued, ritual functions were eventually assumed by temples that were usually constructed over, or close to, the now defunct ruler's house. At Eretria, however, the mid-eighth-century apsidal house (Building 1) that has plausibly been identified as a ruler's dwelling seems to have continued in use even after the construction ca. 725 of a monumental temple adjacent to it.

The political and administrative hub of the *polis* in the Classical period was the agora. The word originally meant an "assembly" or "gathering" (from the Greek verb *ageirein*: "to gather together") and it is in this sense that it is generally employed in the *Iliad*. In the Homeric assembly, the people (*laoi*) throng together in an open space while the elders sit on polished stones in a circle; orderliness is maintained by heralds who place a staff in the hands of each speaker (*Od.* 2.1–260). To judge from the harsh treatment that Odysseus metes out to Thersites in the *Iliad* (2.265–69), discussion was largely restricted to leaders and elders (see p. 182). It seems, however, that the assembled onlookers were expected to ratify by verbal assent the proposals put before it

Figure 4.2 "Chiefly" dwelling at Eretria (photo by author)

and it would not be stretching the imagination too far to infer that the practice of a chieftain seeking broader support for his decisions was one that had existed in most communities during the Dark Age.

We may assume that any open space might serve as a location for meetings of the community assembly but at a certain point, the term agora came to designate a determinate place that was specifically reserved for this purpose. Unfortunately, this transition is hard to date precisely because it is not always clear in which sense the term is used in our written sources. The Thessalian general Kleomakhos is said to have been buried in the agora of Chalcis in recognition of his valor in the war against the Eretrians (Plutarch, *Mor.* 760e–761b), but we have already had reason to question the credibility of this evidence (p. 5). Similarly, Ephorus' notice (fr. 216) that the Laconian dissidents who founded Taras in the last decade of the eighth century launched their coup d'état in the Spartan agora could be anachronistic, given the lateness of the testimony. In the Homeric epics, Scheria is clearly equipped with a purpose-built agora near the harbor (Document 4.2), and Troy also seems to have had a permanent agora next to Priam's palace (*Il.* 18.274), while Theognis' observation (826) that the boundary of Megara's territory is visible from the agora surely indicates a fixed location. When, on the other hand, Hesiod advises Perses to avoid the "quarrels of the agora" (WD. 29), it is far from clear that the poet has in mind a specific, reserved space – especially since the term recurs in the plural in the following verse. Likewise, when the *Homeric Hymn to Demeter* (296) describes how Celeus "summoned the vast throng to an agora and ordered them to construct a rich temple for fair-tressed Demeter" or when Xenophanes (fr. 3) chides his fellow Colophonians for going to the agora in Lydian robes of purple, we cannot necessarily assume that a permanent location for assembly meetings is intended.

Archaeology offers surprisingly little help in this regard. By the Classical period, the agora of a *polis* tended to be demarcated by monumental buildings, stoas (porticos), and temples, but originally it was simply an open space and is therefore difficult to identify in the archaeological record. It is sometimes argued that Megara Hyblaea in Sicily had a formal agora from the moment of its foundation in or around 728, though – as we shall see (pp. 107–10) – the argument is not entirely compelling. There do appear to have been open spaces within the eighth-century settlements of Zagora, Emborio, Koukounaries, and Dreros on Crete, though their proximity to cult buildings probably indicates that their primary function was to host ritual observances; the same goes for the Cretan site of Lato where, in any case, the structures do not predate the fourth century. At Argos, a formal agora seems not to have been laid out prior to the sixth century, when the marshy area at the foot of the Larissa acropolis was drained, and the earliest monument building here – a square edifice with internal columns, probably designed to house the council – was not constructed until 475–450. Similarly, at Athens, the younger Pisistratus' dedication in 522/1 of the altar of the Twelve Gods (see p. 22) and the installation, a couple of decades later, of boundary stones (*horoi*) probably marks the formal beginnings of the Classical agora (Map 4.1). Later authors, however, refer to a quarter on the eastern side of the acropolis, under the modern Plaka district, as the "old (*arkhaia*) agora" and, if the late fifth-century republication of Dracon's homicide law is genuine (ML 86 = Fornara 15), Athens should have possessed an agora by the last decades of the seventh century.

That the economy of Archaic *poleis* was based predominantly on agriculture can hardly be refuted. Phocylides (fr. 7) advises his listeners that if they desire wealth, they should give their attention to a rich farm. Yet, this observation has sometimes prompted modern scholars to downplay the significance of markets. In describing how "potter strives with potter, carpenter with carpenter, beggar with beggar and bard with bard," Hesiod (*WD* 25–6) testifies to a basic division of labor; elsewhere (493), he mentions a blacksmith's forge. Solon (fr. 13) refers to traders, craftsmen, bards, seers, and doctors alongside farmers but, much earlier, Homer (*Il.* 23.834–35) implies that metalworkers procured their raw supplies in the urban center. Indeed, while potters normally set up their kilns on the outskirts of urban settlements, eighth-century metal workshops have been identified within urban centers at Zagora, Argos, and Athens. At Eretria, a goldsmith's workshop has been recognized in a late eighth-century house, under the apse of which was discovered a cracked *skyphos* (two-handled cup) filled with gold ingots, pieces of electrum, and distorted pieces of jewellery, weighing 510 grams in total. The specialization of function that is implied by a division of labor necessitates an exchange of products in markets, and it is surely no accident that even the makeshift camp of the Achaeans who are besieging Troy is described as possessing a market where wine is exchanged for bronze, iron, hides, cattle, and slaves (*Il.* 7.467–75). At the same time, it is clear from *Works and Days* that – save for crop crises or irresponsible indolence – farmers were expected to produce a surplus that they could exchange for tools and other specialized products in markets (see further chapter 10).

That said, it is not entirely clear that such markets were always located in urban centers as the Weberian definition of the pre-industrial city would pre-scribe. In the Classical period, commercial activity was focused above all on the agora, but at present our earliest evidence for an agora fulfilling an eco-nomic function comes from the early fifth-century Law Code found at Gortyn in Crete. Conversely, there are indications that sanctuaries may earlier have played a prominent role in market transactions. There is evidence for bronze casting at Olympia from at least the seventh century, while a small bronze workshop in the sanctuary of Athena Alea at Tegea in Arcadia probably dates back to the eighth century. In a pre-monetary economy, these goods clearly had to be purchased with other products, suggesting at the very least the existence of temporary or seasonal non-urban markets.

In comparing the evidence for the early *polis* with Weber's definition of the pre-industrial city, it is clear that the eighth century witnesses some significant developments. But it is also evident that these developments can only be understood within a longer-term perspective that stretches back into the Dark Age and was still barely completed by as late as the sixth century. Sites such as Old Smyrna and Zagora or certain zones within the later cities of Athens and Argos were densely occupied prior to the eighth century even if there are clear indications of settlement expansion at this time. Even then, however, conurbations such as Sparta or Corinth continued to display dispersed settle-ment patterns. Fortifications rarely predate the eighth century but walls are not a common feature on the Greek mainland until the sixth century at the earliest. There are some reasons for believing that population levels reached a threshold by the eighth century that put an end to strictly face-to-face communities, though – with a few exceptions such as Athens – the corps of male citizens never became so large that mutual acquaintance was impossible. It is sometimes assumed that a larger eighth-century population would have necessitated a change in decision-making procedures but the fact that there is little evidence for the permanent location of complex political, admin-istrative, and economic functions in the urban center until the seventh or even sixth century should cause us to question that assumption. Contrary to common belief, the evidence of cultic activity does not tell a fundamentally different story.

Cultic Communities

It has become something of an orthodoxy that the fundamental framework in which Greek religion functioned was the *polis*. Every *polis*, it is argued, had its own system of cults and rituals and possessed its own sacred calendar. Several *poleis* – notably Athens but also Cos – were placed under the tutelage of Zeus Polieus and Athena Polias; at Sparta, the pre-eminent deity was Athena

Thessalians
Boeotians
Dorians (Dorion; Kytenion; Sparta)
Ionians (Athens; Eretria; Priene)
Perrhaebi
Magnesians
Dolopes
Locrians
Aenianes/Oitaioi
Phthiotid Achaeans
Malians
Phocians

Figure 4.3   The members of the Delphic Amphictyony (after Hall 2002, 135–9)

Polioukhos ("Athena who protects the *polis*"). Priests might often be prominent civic officials as in the case of the Molpoi, a board of officials who administered the cult of Apollo Delphinios at Miletus and whose leader, according to some scholars, served as *aisymnêtês* – the eponymous magistrate of the city (*Milet* I.3 122). *Xenoi*, or "outsiders," were often denied permission to enter civic sanctuaries: in the 490s, the priest of the Argive Heraion apparently attempted to prevent the Spartan king Cleomenes from sacrificing on the grounds that he was a *xenos* (Herodotus 6.81), and fourth-century inscriptions from the islands of Delos (*ID* 68) and Amorgos (*IG* XII.7 2) specify that access to the sanctuary is prohibited to *xenoi*. At the great "Panhellenic" sanctuaries such as Olympia and Delphi or at those interregional shrines that served as foci for "amphictionies" or religious leagues, it was supposedly the *polis* that mediated the participation of its citizens in ritual activity.

It is not that this picture of the *polis* as anchoring, legitimating, and mediating all religious activity is entirely inaccurate. But it is somewhat misleading – even for the better-documented Classical period. The Amphictiony which administered Apollo's sanctuary at Delphi (Figure 4.3) was organized according to *ethnê*, not *poleis* (Aeschines, *On the Embassy* 116), and *ethnê* such as the Thessalians, Boeotians, Dorians, and Ionians comprised several *poleis* which cannot all have had an equal deliberative voice even if they were all guaranteed protection. As for *xenoi*, it is not always certain that it was affiliation with a specific *polis* that guaranteed exclusion. A mid-fifth century inscription from Paros (*IG* XII.5 225) stipulated that it is Dorian *xenoi* who are to be excluded from the sanctuary of Kore, and when Cleomenes is also denied access to the sanctuary of Athena Polias on the acropolis at Athens it is not because he is a Spartan but because he is a Dorian (Herodotus 5.72.3). In other cases – notably the Thesmophoria festival celebrated by married women in honor of Demeter – it is clear that the grounds for exclusion were based on gender rather than civic affiliation. If we move further back in time, however, it is not at all patent that the *polis* constituted the primary or basic level of ritual activity.

A great deal of attention has been given in recent scholarship to the emergence of sanctuaries and the construction of monumental temples. Every Greek
polis, it is reasoned, was a community of cult, presided over by a patron deity
(often, though not always, female). A crucial element in such an official cult
was a hallowed space where the cultic community could come together and
sacrifice, and the initial establishment of cult can be identified by the date of
the earliest dedications made to the patron deity. At many sanctuaries, it is the
eighth century that witnesses a sharp increase in – if not the actual commencement of – offerings and, from this period, metal dedications in particular
gradually begin to be deposited in the more public domain of the sanctuary
rather than in individual graves, as had been the practice in the preceding
centuries. An altar and a demarcated space were the *sine qua non* for religious
activity in the ancient Greek world. A temple, whose function was normally to
house an image of the deity, was not indispensable but the construction of
monumental cult buildings has often been taken to indicate a confident self-
assertion, not to say mutual rivalry, on the part of nascent political communities. The temple, it is argued, testifies not only that the state has assumed
responsibility for the cult of its presiding deity but also that it can command
the loyalty of its citizen community. The two examples normally cited are the
temple of Hera on Samos and the temple of Apollo Daphnephoros at Eretria.
On Samos, the first Heraion, situated eight kilometers southwest of the modern town of Pithagório, probably dates to the early part of the eighth century.
One hundred feet in length (*hekatompedon*) and rectangular in plan, it had
mud-brick walls standing on a stone socle and a central row of columns
supporting a roof that was almost certainly thatched; shortly after its construction, it was encircled by a wooden peristyle (colonnade). The temple at Eretria,
dated to ca. 725, is also a *hekatompedon* of similar construction though it has
an apsidal plan and lacks a peristyle. Both buildings are taken as an indication,
along with the evidence of dedications, for the emergence of the *polis* in the
eighth century.

The problem with this hypothesis is that, while the eighth century undoubtedly witnesses an intensification of ritual activity, it is by no means certain that
this is the formative period for the cultic practices with which we are more
familiar in later periods. We have already seen (p. 61) that many sanctuaries
were already hosting ritual activity in the Dark Age – i.e. prior to the date
conventionally assigned to the rise of the *polis*. In some instances – for example,
Kombothekra and Olympia – cultic activity is attested in areas where the
polis was especially slow to develop. Kalapodhi in Phocis is another good
example. Ritual activity here began shortly before 1200 and, to judge from
floral and faunal analysis, involved the consumption of meat – especially deer
and tortoise – and cereals. In the middle of the tenth century the sacred
precinct was extended by means of terracing while a hearth altar was erected
in the eighth century, followed by two mud-brick temples in the course of the
seventh century. In the Classical period, the shrine at Kalapodhi was controlled
by the *polis* of Hyampolis but there is at present little evidence to suggest

that Phocis was organized by *poleis* prior to this and the archaeological material from Kalapodhi hints at close associations in the earlier period with Ithaca, Thessaly, Euboea, and especially East Locris.

Furthermore, undue emphasis on the Samian and Eretrian temples conceals the fact that many of the oldest cult buildings are not in fact found in areas where early *poleis* are attested. At Mende-Poseidi in the Chalcidice, for example, a long apsidal mud-brick temple (Building Στ) has been dated to the tenth century. The double-apsidal *hekatompedon* with wooden peristyle at Ano Mazaraki-Rakita, located some twenty kilometers south of Aegium in Achaea and perhaps dedicated to Apollo and Artemis, probably dates to the later eighth century, making it one of the first peripteral (colonnaded) temples in the Greek mainland. Yet there is no evidence for the emergence of *poleis* in Achaea until the very end of the sixth or beginning of the fifth century. A similar case may be presented at Thermon in Aetolia – a region where *poleis* are not attested in literary sources until the fifth or even fourth centuries. Here, there are some indications that a peripteral apsidal temple was, in the course of the eighth century, constructed above the ruins of Megaron B, an Early Iron Age building whose function – if not monumentality – may be compared to the Toumba building at Lefkandi (pp. 62–3).

Nor is it entirely clear that the construction of a monumental temple testifies to a collective effort on the part of a neonate citizen community rather than signaling, for example, the ability of a powerful individual to mobilize labor and resources. In the literary tradition, the construction of monumental temples is often attributed to tyrants (pp. 140–1). The observation that the earliest cult buildings are difficult to distinguish from contemporary rulers' dwellings has suggested that cultic activity during the Dark Age was in the hands of local chieftains. The common belief, however, that the construction of the first temples signaled the termination of the ruler's authority by the emergent political community is less patent. Although Tiryns, Thermon, and Eleusis are sometimes cited as cases where a ruler's dwelling was converted into a temple, the archaeological evidence is ambiguous. Conversely, as we have seen, the ruler's dwelling at Eretria appears to have continued in use after the construction of the adjacent *hekatompedon* and the same may be true at Koukounaries, Prinias, and Lathoureza in Attica. We cannot, in other words, rule out the possibility that the construction of at least some urban temples was an expression of singular authority rather than communal consciousness.

Sanctuary evidence has also been invoked in tracing the emergence of the *polis* in its territorial aspect. This thesis starts with the observation that the earliest and most important sanctuaries were very often not situated in urban centers but in rural locations some distance from the principal settlement. It is argued that the placement of these "extra-urban" sanctuaries serves, firstly, a symbolic function as a point of mediation between the "civilized" agricultural domain of the *polis* and the "wilder," more marginal land beyond the *polis'* frontiers (e.g. mountains, marshes, or the sea) and, secondly, a political function in physically marking out the territorial boundaries of the *polis*. Among the examples that have been suggested are the sanctuaries of Hera at Perachora and Poseidon at Isthmia (Corinth), Apollo Hyacinthius at Amyclae (Sparta), Artemis at Amarynthos (Eretria), Apollo at Didyma (Miletus), and Hera on the island of Samos (Samos town). The archetypal example, however, is the sanctuary of Hera, located thirteen kilometers northeast of Argos. For some, the establishment of this sanctuary in the eighth century signals Argos' claims to possession of the entire Argive plain and the annual procession of armed youths, maidens, and cattle that later authors (e.g. Aeneas Tacticus 17.1; Dionysius of Halicarnassus, *RA* 1.21) describe as making its way from the urban center to the sanctuary of Hera is deemed to constitute a very physical celebration of that possession.

The thesis is immensely attractive – not least, because there is precious little other evidence that might indicate the territorial extent of the *polis* in this period. Unfortunately, however, it has not stood up to further testing. The sanctuary at Isthmia, for example, was already functioning in the middle of the eleventh century, some two to three centuries before any urban activity can be recognized at Corinth. The sanctuary of Perachora is more or less contemporary with developments at Corinth but here around 75 percent of the early metal offerings are of predominantly Levantine origin and the dedication of Egyptian mirrors with hieroglyphic inscriptions to Mut – a goddess whose identification with Hera was certainly known to later authors – suggests a more international rather than exclusively Corinthian constituency. A similar case is presented by the Samian Heraion, where 85 percent of the eighth- and early seventh-century metal artifacts is of non-Greek manufacture. It is, in any case, difficult to comprehend why the Heraion served a boundary-marking function when the island of Samos supported only one *polis*. Detailed analysis of the literary, archaeological, epigraphic, and mythical evidence suggests that the "Argive" Heraion originally functioned as a shared sanctuary for the various *poleis* that occupied the Argive plain (Mycenae; Tiryns; Midea) and that it was not until Argos destroyed these neighboring communities in the 460s that it took exclusive possession of both the plain and the sanctuary.

In fact, it now seems that extra-urban sanctuaries acted as arenas in which leaders from various surrounding settlements could compete in the display of pre-eminence. When we combine this conclusion with the fact that, during the eighth century, dedications at Corinthian sanctuaries appear to communicate more visibly gender, wealth, and status roles – that, for example, the martial and athletic character of the weapons, armor, and tripods dedicated at Isthmia contrasts with the more feminine offerings of jewelry and clay *koulouria* (breadrings) at Perachora – then some rethinking is evidently required. While there can be little doubt that ritual activity served to demarcate "cultic communities" and that such groups could theoretically be coterminous with the citizen-body, it is also readily apparent that the boundaries of cultic communities often cross-cut and intersected with one or several citizen communities. Put another way, the mere emergence of sanctuaries, temples, and ritual practices need not be the unambiguous reflection of the rise of the *polis*.

Polis and Ethnos

When one reads the Archaic poets, it is easy to gain the impression that the *polis* was ubiquitous and that it constituted one of the most important points of reference for the Greeks. In reality, however, there were many regions of Greece where the evidence suggests that the *polis* did not emerge until late in the Archaic period or even well into the succeeding Classical period. Conventionally, scholars have termed such regions *ethnos* states. Viewed as survivals from an earlier, "tribal" past, *ethnê* are typically defined as populations "scattered thinly over a territory without urban centres, united politically and in customs and religion, normally governed by means of some periodical assembly at a single centre, and worshipping a tribal deity at a common religious centre" (Snodgrass 1980: 42). As such, they are often regarded as an alternative form of state organization to the *polis*. This conventional distinction between the *polis* and the *ethnos* seems to have arisen from a rather difficult passage in Aristotle's *Politics* (Document 4.4). Yet, Aristotle is here comparing an alliance (*symmakhia*) with an *ethnos*: both are constituted by elements that are the same in kind. And since we know from another passage in the *Politics* (3.5.11) that the basic element that constituted the alliance was the *polis*, then Aristotle must have in mind a situation where an *ethnos* is constituted by a plurality of *poleis*. In other words, far from establishing a mutual opposition between *poleis* and *ethnê* as alternative forms of political organization, Aristotle is here distinguishing between *ethnê* settled in villages and *ethnê*, like the Arcadians, settled in *poleis*.

That *ethnê* might be organized by *poleis* seems to find further textual support. According to Thucydides (3.92.2), the Malians of central Greece, defined as an *ethnos* by Aeschines (*On the Embassy* 115–16), were divided into three parts – the Paralioi, the Iries, and the Trachinians – and Herodotus (7.199.1) explicitly describes Trachis as a *polis*. Elsewhere, Herodotus explains that the Peloponnese was inhabited by seven *ethnê*: the Arcadians, the Cynurians, the

---

Document 4.4

For a *polis* does not arise from a collection of men who are all alike: there is a difference between an alliance and a *polis*. What is useful for an alliance is quantity, even if all the elements are the same in kind (for the alliance has come into being for the sake of assistance), just as a heavier weight tips the scales. It is also in this way that a *polis* is different from an *ethnos*, when the population is not scattered among villages (*kômai*) but like the Arcadians. The components that make up a unity, on the other hand, should differ among themselves. (Aristotle, *Pol.* 2.1.4–5)

Achaeans, the Dorians, the Aetolians, the Dryopes, and the Lemnians. The *poleis* of the Dorian *ethnos*, Herodotus explains, are "numerous and well-known," while the Dryopes inhabit the *poleis* of Hermione and Asine, and Elis is the only *polis* that belongs to the Aetolians (8.73). It would seem, then, that the inhabitants of those areas in which *poleis* are attested from early on also subscribed – at some point – to a broader affiliation within an *ethnos*. Similarly, those regions that have traditionally been designated as *ethnê* were eventually to witness the rise of *polis* communities, even if this occurred rather later than it did in areas such as Attica, Corinthia, the Argolid, and the Aegean islands. It is for this reason that it has been suggested that the *ethnos* and *polis* are not "alternative modes" but represent "different levels" of social organization. Yet, the fact that Herodotus can describe the Chalcidians (5.77.4) and the Athenians (7.161.3) – both citizen communities commonly designated as *poleis* – as *ethnê* makes it difficult to accept that it is simply organizational level that distinguishes between the two terms.

In fact, it is not so much that *polis* and *ethnos* occupy different levels of social organization but that they belong to entirely different categories altogether. In Archaic literature, the term *ethnos* can designate flocks of birds, swarms of bees and flies, and even the ranks of the dead. Its most common application, however, is to a group of people – or, more generally, a population. Its common identity resided in the bonds of kinship, however fictive, that were recognized by its members, bolstered no doubt by shared rituals and customs. Central to the concept of the *polis*, on the other hand, was the notion of place, which was, as we have seen, inherent in the term from the outset. The members of the *polis* derived their identity from the urban center, whether or not they physically resided there, and it was in the urban center that political functions – however rudimentary at first – were housed. Regions such as Achaea or Thessaly were also home to large settlements – in the eighth century, there may have been little visible distinction between a site such as Aegium and Corinth – but these settlements do not seem to have exerted as powerful a hold on the loyalty of their residents as did *poleis* such as Sparta, Argos, or Corinth. Nor do large settlements in areas such as Achaea or Aetolia appear to have hosted political assemblies, which were instead more commonly held in regional sanctuaries such as that of Poseidon at Helike and that of Apollo at Thermon.

Particularly illuminating in this respect is the nomenclature that the Greeks employed to denote population groups. Generally speaking, the insertion of an -*i*- suffix serves an adjectival function in the Greek language, thus marking out a term as a secondary formation from a primary root. The suffix can be observed in the names of *polis* populations such as the *Athênaioi* (Athenians), *Korinthioi* (Korinthians), *Milêsioi* (Milesians), or *Surakosioi* (Syracusans), indicating that these names are ultimately derived from place-names (*Athênai*; *Korinthos*; *Milêtos*; *Surakousai*). The adjectival -*i*- grade is not, however, normally found employed for *ethnê* – e.g. *Boiotoi* (Boeotians), *Aitoloi* (Aetolians), *Thessaloi* (Thessalians), or *Makedones* (Macedonians). In fact, while the populations of a *polis* take their name from an urban center, those populations that are described as *ethnê* typically give their name to the general region they inhabit, as shown by the *-i-* suffix in *Boiotia, Aitolia, Thessalia* (Thessaly), and *Makedonia*.

Furthermore, it is increasingly difficult to maintain that the *polis* represents an evolutionary development from an earlier, more "tribal" organization in which *ethnê* were dominant. It may be helpful here to distinguish between consolidated *ethnê* and dispersed *ethnê*. Consolidated *ethnê* are represented by those groups such as the Aetolians, Achaeans, or Thessalians who inhabited a contiguous tract of territory in the historical period. Dispersed *ethnê*, on the other hand, are diaspora-type collectivities, whose members were in the historical period scattered throughout different communities – normally *poleis* – but who conceived of their unity in terms of an original homeland in which their ancestors had cohabited. Of the twelve *ethnê* who constituted the Delphic Amphictiony (Figure 4.3), two – the Ionians and the Dorians – are dispersed *ethnê*. We have already seen (pp. 47–8) that the original integrity, posited on the grounds of shared rituals, calendars, and tribal-names, of dispersed *ethnê* such as the Dorians and Ionians is far from certain and that there is good reason to suppose that the construction of such "ethnic" identities proceeded in tandem with the processes that shaped the *polis*. In a period before the populations of Greek *poleis* began to think of themselves collectively as Greeks or "Hellenes" (see pp. 270–5), it may well be that affiliation with an *ethnos* offered a broader sense of belonging that transcended parochial boundaries.

As for consolidated *ethnê*, although the Boeotians, Phocians, Locrians, Arcadians, Aetolians, Perrhaebi, and Magnesians appear already in the Homeric *Catalogue of Ships* – a section of the *Iliad* (2.494–749) that some scholars even wish to date to the Late Bronze Age – it is remarkable how long it takes for such groups to develop a sense of territoriality, let alone a political identity. The regional names that are derived from *ethnê* such as the Boeotians, Aetolians, Thessalians, and Macedonians are unattested in the poems of Homer and Hesiod. There is little support in the surviving sources for the early appearance of the *tageia*, the military authority to which all the Thessalian communities were, in the Classical period, subordinated. In Phocis, the first "federal" coinage appears ca. 510, and it is shortly after this that the Phokikon – a building, near Panopeus, that housed meetings of the Phocian League – was constructed. In Arcadia, triobols bearing the legend *ARKADIKON* and a depiction of the Arcadian patron, Zeus Lykaios, were minted shortly after the Persian War of 480–479 and may signal the earliest federal coinage in this region, though there is little other evidence for the existence of the Arcadian League in the fifth century. Similarly, the predecessor of the third-century Achaean League is unlikely to predate the end of the fifth century.

It should be reiterated that *poleis* do appear – albeit a little later – in regions inhabited by consolidated *ethnê*. Communities such as Tegea and Mantinea in Arcadia were almost certainly regarded as *poleis* by the sixth century at the latest. Hecataeus of Miletus, writing at the beginning of the fifth century, refers to the *poleis* of Chaeronea in Boeotia (fr. 116), Bouthrotos in Epirus (fr. 106), Kynos in East Locris (fr. 131), and Khaleion and Oiantheia in West Locris (fr. 113). And all the indications suggest that the more significant settlements in Aetolia were regarded as *poleis* by the fourth century. In short, for all the highly visible innovations that are attested for the eighth century, both the development of individual *poleis* and the emergence of a *polis* form of organization throughout Greece were far longer-term processes than is normally implied in the secondary literature.

It remains to ask why the *polis* should have emerged earlier in some areas than others. It has often been noted that the earliest *poleis* are attested in those regions of Greece that were most strongly influenced by the administrative structures of the Mycenaean palaces. We know from the Linear B tablets found at Pylos that Mycenaean states were divided up into provinces, districts, towns, and villages in order to facilitate military defense and the collection of taxes. Nor can it be accidental that the term *basileus*, employed to denote both the chiefs of Dark Age villages and the ruling group of the nascent *polis* (see pp. 120–1), derives from the Mycenaean *pa-si-re-u* – a term that had defined a local official at the town or village level. It has already been noted that many of the earliest *poleis* continued to be inhabited – albeit at a greatly reduced level – throughout the Dark Age: even at Eretria, once considered to be a new foundation of the eighth century, continuing investigations suggest earlier habitation. The fact, then, that physical place constituted such a crucial component within early definitions of the *polis* could well be a legacy of the administrative and territorial subdivisions of Late Bronze Age Greece.

At first sight, Boeotia appears to represent an exception: home to the Mycenaean palaces of Thebes, Orchomenus, and perhaps Gla, the Boeotians are conventionally considered to be a consolidated *ethnos*. And yet, quite apart from the fact that Boeotia stands almost as a buffer zone between, on the one hand, the city-state cultures to the south and, on the other, the Thessalians to the north and the Phocians to the west, it is probably fair to say that the *polis* enjoyed an earlier and more prolific development in Boeotia than in almost any other area settled by a consolidated *ethnos*. Eighth-century Greece was indeed a very different world from its Mycenaean predecessor, but it is difficult to deny that the Bronze Age past or the intervening centuries left no mark.

FURTHER READING

Rise of the *polis*: V. Ehrenberg, "When did the Polis rise?" *Journal of Hellenic Studies* 57 (1937), 147–59. Greek "Renaissance": Hägg 1983. Dominance of Aristotle: J. K. Davies, "The 'Origins of the Greek polis': Where should we be looking?" in Mitchell and Rhodes 1997, 24–38. For the results of the Copenhagen Polis Project: Hansen and Nielsen 2004. Importance of the urban center: M. H. Hansen, "POLLAXÔS POLIS LEGETAI (Arist., *Pol.* 1276a23). The Copenhagen Inventory of *Poleis* and the *Lex Hafniensis de Civitate*," in Hansen 1997, 9–86. Priority of state functions over urbanism: I. Morris, "The early polis as city and state," in Rich and Wallace-Hadrill 1991, 25–57. The *polis* in Homer: E. Lévy, *"Astu* et *polis* dans l'*Iliade*," *Ktema* 8 (1983): 55–73.

Definitions of the ancient city: Weber 1978, 1212–34; M. I. Finley, "The ancient city: From Fustel de Coulanges to Max Weber and beyond," in Finley 1981, 3–23. Survey of Archaic settlements: Lang 1996. Fortification walls: A. M. Snodgrass, "The historical significance of fortification in Archaic Greece," in Leriche and Tréziny 1986, 125–31. Population estimates for Early Iron Age settlements: Morris, in Rich and Wallace-Hadrill 1991; M. C. Vink, "Urbanization in late and subgeometric Greece: Abstract considerations and concrete case-studies of Eretria and Zagora ca. 700 BC," in Damgaard Andersen, Horsnaes, and Houby-Nielsen 1997, 111–41. Athenian burials: Morris 1987. Argive burials: R. Hägg, "Zur Stadtwerdung des dorischen Argos," in Papenfuß and Strocka 1982, 297–307. Physical synoecism: J. N. Coldstream, "The formation of the Greek polis: Aristotle and archaeology," *Rheinische-Westfälische Akademie der Wissenschaften* (1984), 7–22. Burials as direct index of population: Snodgrass 1980, 22–5. Drought hypothesis: J. McK. Camp, "A drought in the late eighth century BC," *Hesperia* 48 (1979): 397–411. Differential access to burial: Morris 1987. For a reassessment of population growth: W. Scheidel, "The Greek demographic expansion: Models and comparisons," *Journal of Hellenic Studies* 123 (2003), 120–40.

Public architecture: M. H. Hansen and T. Fischer-Hansen, "Monumental political architecture in Archaic and Classical Greek *poleis*: Evidence and historical significance," in Whitehead 1994, 23–90; C. Morgan and J. J. Coulton, "The *polis* as a physical entity," in Hansen 1997, 87–144. Rulers' dwellings and early temples: Mazarakis-Ainian 1997. Development of the agora: Martin 1951. Archaic agora at Athens: C. Schnurr, "Die alte Agora Athens," *Zeitschrift für Papyrologie und Epigraphik* 105 (1995), 131–8. Eretria workshop: P. G. Themelis, "An 8th-century goldsmith's workshop at Eretria," in Hägg 1983, 157–65.

Polis religion: C. Sourvinou-Inwood, "What is *polis* religion?" in Murray and Price 1990, 295–322. Prohibitions on entry to sanctuaries: P. Butz, "Prohibitionary inscriptions, *xenoi*, and the influence of the early Greek polis," in Hägg 1996, 75–95. Monumental temples: Coldstream 2003, 317–27. Extra-urban sanctuaries: Polignac 1995. For reactions: Alcock and Osborne 1994; J. M. Hall, "How Argive was the 'Argive' Heraion? The political and cultic geography of the Argive plain, 900–400 BC," *American Journal of Archaeology* 99 (1995): 577–613.

For the *ethnos*: Z. H. Archibald, "Space, hierarchy and community in Archaic and Classical Macedonia, Thessaly, and Thrace," in Brock and Hodkinson 2000, 212–33; Morgan 2003. Phocis: McInerney 1999.

5

New Homes Across the Seas

Despite appearances, the word "nostalgia" was not invented by the Greeks. It is, instead, a neologism, formed from the Greek words *nostos* ("return home") and *algos* ("pain"), that was coined in 1688 by a Swiss medical student named Johannes Hofer to describe a depressive condition among mercenary soldiers who had spent too long away from home. The *concept* of nostalgia, however, was all too familiar to the Greeks and features prominently in such well-known literary works as Homer's *Odyssey* and Xenophon's *Anabasis*. Its centrality within Greek consciousness arose from the recognition that mobility, dislocation, and migration – sometimes over very long distances – were basic and unavoidable facts of life.

It is common to draw a distinction between migration and what is conventionally, if somewhat misleadingly, termed colonization. The first, assigned to the troubled centuries that followed the collapse of the Mycenaean palaces, typically denotes the mass movements of loosely organized bands of people prior to the emergence of settled political communities. We have already discussed the literary accounts for the Dorian migration and mentioned the migration of Achaeans to the southern shore of the Corinthian Gulf and of Ionians to the coast of Asia Minor (pp. 44–5; see map 3.1). Other population movements "remembered" in the Classical period include that of the Aeolians from central Greece to northwest Asia Minor, that of the Thessalians from Thesprotia to Thessaly – ousting the Kadmeians who fled south to Boeotia – and that of the Dryopes from the Parnassus region to the Eastern Argolid, Euboea, the Cyclades, and Cyprus. Historians have reached no agreement as to the historical credibility of these migration traditions. Some accept that they contain mythical elements – for instance, the descent from Heracles or from Agamemnon, supposedly claimed by the leaders of the Dorian and Aeolian migrations respectively – but maintain that the vague contours of real events can be glimpsed behind such accounts. That people were on the move at the

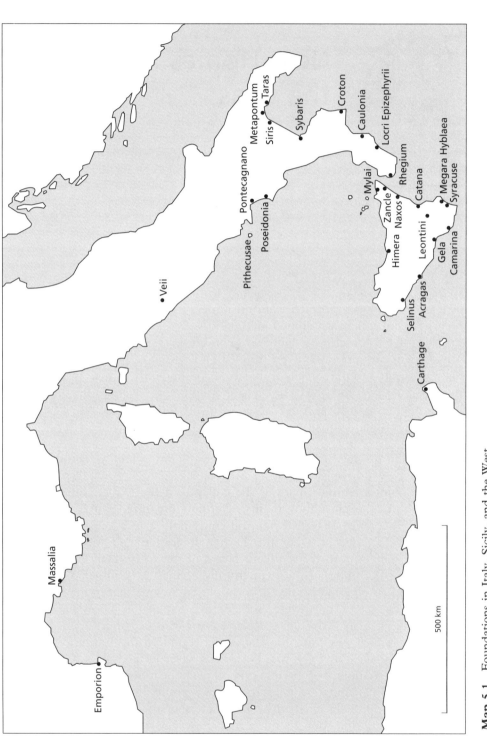

Map 5.1 Foundations in Italy, Sicily, and the West

Document 5.1

For, in the sixtieth year after the capture of Troy, those who are now called the Boeotians were expelled from Arne by the Thessalians and settled what is now Boeotia, but had previously been called the Kadmeian land (in fact, a group of them was already settled in this territory and had marched against Troy) and in the eightieth year, the Dorians together with the descendants of Heracles seized the Peloponnese. But it was with great effort and after many years that Greece became more peaceful and stable, no longer subject to demographic upheavals, and sent out overseas settlements (*apoikias*). The Athenians settled Ionia and most of the islands while the Peloponnesians settled the greater part of Italy and Sicily as well as some regions elsewhere in Greece. All these settlements were founded after the Trojan war. (Thucydides 1.12.3–4)

---

end of the Mycenaean period is beyond doubt, though we have already had reason to comment upon the evidently contrived character of the developed migration traditions – at least as regards the Dorians and the Ionians.

Colonization, instead, generally defines the more organized overseas expeditions, dispatched from city-states to locations around the Mediterranean and Black Sea from the last third of the eighth century onwards, for which the surviving literary accounts are deemed more trustworthy (Map 5.1). Yet this modern categorical distinction between migration and colonization was not one made by ancient authors. Thucydides (Document 5.1) uses the word *apoikia* (literally, "home from home") to describe not only the "Peloponnesian" foundations in South Italy and Sicily (i.e. the colonies sent out by Corinth, Sparta, and Achaea) but also the Athenian settlement of Ionia (the Ionian migration), and he regards both as a general pattern of population instability after the Trojan War, to which the Boeotian and Dorian migrations also belong. In this chapter we will ask two questions. Firstly, are the literary traditions for colonization really so much more trustworthy than they are for the migrations? Secondly, can we discern any qualitative distinction between migrations and colonial ventures?

On the Move

The first thing to note is that there is less of a chronological disjunction between the age of migration and the age of colonization than is often assumed. It is true both that the eighth century – and especially its latter part – sees a marked intensification of overseas contacts and that most Dark Age settlements on the Greek mainland are characterized by introspection and isolation (see pp. 59–64), but communication with the outside world never really ceased after the collapse of the Mycenaean palaces. That Asia Minor was settled by Greeks from further west is an archaeologically documented fact. Miletus, which seems to have been occupied by Greeks in the Mycenaean period, was destroyed ca. 1100 but resettled almost immediately afterwards. The Iron Age settlements at Ephesus and at Assarlik on the Halicarnassus peninsula probably date to the eleventh century, while the earliest houses at Old Smyrna should belong to the beginning of the tenth. Occupation at Phocaea, Clazomenae, and Iasus is probably not much later. The Protogeometric pottery from Miletus and Ephesus shows some affinities with Attic styles and this has often been taken as confirmation of the literary tradition that the settlers of Ionia set out from Athens. On the other hand, the literary tradition was by no means univocal with respect to the origins of the Ionians of Asia Minor (see p. 50) and the bulk of the earliest pottery at East Greek sites is locally made, deriving its influences as much from Euboea and Thessaly as from Attica.

Claims that the Euboeans had established a foothold in the Chalcidice as early as the eleventh century have recently been challenged by one of the excavators of Torone, a site situated on Sithonia, the central of the three promontories. On the other hand, the material from Torone and from other Chalcidian sites does include imports and imitations of Euboean, Thessalian, Cycladic, East Greek, and especially Attic vessels, so clearly there was some traffic of goods across the Aegean in these centuries. The Northern Aegean was later to become a prime destination for colonial ventures. Eretrians, Chalcidians, Achaeans, Corinthians, and Andrians are credited with establishing colonies in the Chalcidice, the poet Archilochus describes how a mixed group of settlers under Parian leadership colonized Thasos in the mid-seventh century, and Samians are said to have settled Samothrace in the second half of the sixth century.

The attestation of tenth-century pottery at the Phoenician city of Tyre is also a clear indication for contacts between the Aegean and the Levant, but the site that has excited the most scholarly controversy is Al Mina, situated on the Orontes River in the modern Turkish province of Hatay. That there is Greek pottery in the earliest levels of Al Mina is undisputed, but exactly where it comes from, when it should be dated, and how it should be interpreted are all questions that have generated heated debate. The matter is not helped by the extremely disturbed stratigraphy at the site. Many art historians and archaeologists are adamant that Euboean wares dominate the early assemblages – especially two-handled cups, or *skyphoi*, decorated with pendent compass-drawn concentric semicircles, which are often considered to be the hallmark of Euboean overseas activity. Scientific analysis confirms that at least some of these vessels do, in fact, originate from central Euboea but others have pointed to the presence, alongside the Euboean wares, of what was originally described as Attic, Samian, and Rhodian (perhaps now to be re-identified as North Ionian) pottery while it has been observed that the earliest examples of the pendent semicircle *skyphoi* come not from Euboea but from Macedonia. As for the date, it is now clear that the original chronology for the pendent semicircle *skyphoi*, which assumed a Greek presence at Al Mina a little prior to 800, was too high: the earliest class of *skyphos* found at Al Mina should probably be assigned to approximately 770–750.

More vexed is the issue of how the Greek material arrived at Al Mina. For some, the absence of Greek everyday items, Greek burials, and Greek cults argues against any permanent Greek presence. The fact that only a very restricted range of pottery shapes – primarily drinking vessels – is found at Al Mina could suggest that these were dining wares, imported through the entrepôt of Al Mina to grace the tables of Levantine elites. Such trade would have been in the hands of Phoenician merchants, who constitute a familiar character-type in the Homeric epics but whose earlier activities can be documented by the establishment of a late tenth-century Phoenician tripillar shrine at Kommos, on the southern coast of Crete, as well as by North Syrian and Phoenician artifacts deposited in tenth- and ninth-century graves in Cnossus, Athens, Lefkandi, and the Dodecanese. It is only prejudice, it is argued, conditioned by nineteenth-century racism and anti-Semitism, that conspires to deny to the Phoenicians a fundamental role in the opening up of the Mediterranean.

Others maintain, however, that a distinction should be made between items of North Syrian and of Phoenician provenance. The former enjoy an earlier, though more restricted, distribution than the latter and since the Aramaeans of North Syria were not renowned as sailors, objects of North Syrian provenance must have been carried by either Greeks or Phoenicians. Had it been Phoenicians, however, we would have to suppose that they targeted markets in Attica and Euboea only, studiously avoiding other areas until the second half of the eighth century when Phoenician goods are found throughout the Mediterranean. This is, perhaps, an unlikely hypothesis and might suggest that earlier trade was in the hands of Greeks, and particularly Euboeans. Perhaps relevant in this regard is the distribution of seals depicting a lyre-player. Of North Syrian manufacture, they are attested widely throughout the Mediterranean in the second half of the eighth century but generally at Greek rather than Phoenician sites. This may imply that it was Greeks who transported them, although we cannot exclude the possibility that they were consciously targeted at Greek consumers, much as Attic "Nikosthenic" *amphorai* were to be produced for specifically Etruscan markets in the sixth century (see p. 249). Furthermore, one may also doubt whether Levantine elites would have been particularly impressed by ceramic wares when they were more accustomed to vessels of metal. While the absence of everyday items or even burials is troubling, recent studies suggest that Greek wares account for about 93.3 percent of the early ceramics at the site, with non-Greek – especially Cypriot – ceramics only rising to prominence later in the eighth century. For some, so high a proportion can only be explained by assuming a permanent Greek – and specifically Euboean – presence at Al Mina.

As so often, the truth probably lies between the two extremes. Ethnic categories such as "Greek," "Cypriot," or "Phoenician" are almost certainly anachronistic in this period and, given that long-distance trade involved considerable absences from home, it is not entirely certain that terms such as "Athenians," "Euboeans," or "Rhodians" possess much more validity in capturing the character of ancient trade. That Greek-speakers resided on at least a temporary basis at Al Mina is a reasonable enough hypothesis, though since part of the site has been washed away by the Orontes, the apparent absence of non-Greek material from the earliest levels should not be overemphasized. That some, perhaps many, of these residents originated from Euboea is also entirely feasible, though not all Euboean wares – if that is what they are – need have been brought to Al Mina by Euboeans, making it unwise to consider Al Mina a uniquely Euboean settlement.

The contacts that the Mycenaeans had forged in the west may never have been ruptured entirely and were almost certainly not forgotten. Scoglio del Tonno, opposite the Greek city of Taras in southern Italy, seems to have been in intermittent contact with the Aegean throughout the Dark Age while three early ninth-century sherds of Corinthian provenance have been reported from Otranto, on the Adriatic coast of Puglia. Pendent semicircle *skyphoi* are known from the Quattro Fontanili necropolis in the Etruscan site of Veii, northwest of Rome, Pontecagnano in Campania, Villasmundo in eastern Sicily, and Otranto. The earliest pottery is normally considered to be Euboean in style though in the first half of the eighth century, Corinth seems to have extended its contacts to the island of Ithaca and, beyond there, to Epirus and, on the opposite side of the Adriatic, Puglia.

Evidence for settlement at Pithecusae – the modern Lacco Ameno on the island of Ischia in the Gulf of Naples – probably dates to ca. 770 and is thus contemporary with Al Mina. As at Al Mina, the character of the settlement here has been much discussed, though unlike Al Mina we do have literary sources which refer to the site. Livy (8.22.6) says it was founded by Chalcis, while Strabo (5.4.9) attributes its foundation to Eretrians and Chalcidians but adds that the latter left after an argument. Some Euboean imports have indeed been found among the earliest material from a dump on the ancient acropolis (Monte de Vico) but all the indications suggest that Pithecusae's origins were rather more diverse than the literary tradition suggests. The fact that Euboean wares were swiftly swamped by Corinthian imports and imitations is not in itself significant since this is – as we shall see – a pattern common to most Greek settlements in the west, whether or not they considered themselves to be Corinthian foundations. But there are also Cretan and East Greek imports and, more significantly, credible evidence not only for Levantine contacts but also for the actual physical presence of Phoenicians in the settlement.

Pithecusae – like Al Mina – was long considered to represent an *emporion* or trading-post, different from later, more permanent foundations (*apoikiai*) both for the mixed origins of its settlers and for the primary activity in which they were engaged (commerce in the former case, agriculture in the latter). Today, the distinction between *emporion* and *apoikia* seems less valid. That settlers were drawn to Pithecusae to exploit metal ores is still a reasonable conjecture, but the recent realization that there were other major settlements on Ischia and that the island was fairly extensively exploited probably indicates that agriculture was not of subsidiary importance. Furthermore, Pithecusae seems to be rather large for a trading-post, with an estimated population of between 5,000 and 10,000. Thirdly, the burials in the Valle di San Montano cemetery paint a picture of a hierarchically structured society in which both men and women as well as all age groups are represented – not, perhaps, what one would expect from a community of traders and craftsmen. Typically, pit inhumations and pot burials cluster around cremation burials: the latter are reserved for adults, while pits were used for adolescents and pots for infants. It is supposed that these clusters of burials represent family groups and that the different treatment afforded the different age groups serves as an index of social inclusion (i.e. the different stages by which one came to be accepted within the full sociopolitical community). But around 40 percent of adults are inhumed rather than cremated and these burials are generally unaccompanied by grave goods. If the social inclusion hypothesis is correct, then we have to reckon on the existence of a large class of adults to whom full sociopolitical recognition was not extended.

According to a tradition on which Thucydides (6.3–5) drew, the first permanent Greek colony on Sicily was Naxos, founded by Chalcidians in 734, and this initiates a spate of colonial foundations in the west and beyond. Other Chalcidian settlements were established before the end of the eighth century at Leontini, Catana, Zancle, and Rhegium, on the opposite side of the Straits of Messina (see map 5.1). Corinthians were also active on Sicily from an early period: 733 is the traditional date given for the foundation of Syracuse, a city which founded its own colonies at Acrae and Casmenae in the mid-seventh century and at Camarina at the beginning of the sixth. Megara Hyblaea, supposedly founded by Megarians in 728, founded a colony at Selinus a century later. Similarly, Gela, whose foundation is attributed to a collaborative venture between Rhodes and Crete in 688, established a daughter colony at Acragas in 580. In mainland Italy, Achaeans are credited with the foundations of Sybaris and Croton towards the end of the eighth century, Metapontum and Caulonia in the second half of the seventh century and Poseidonia (Paestum) in the early sixth, while Taras is said to have been founded by Spartan dissidents in the last decade of the eighth century and Epizephyrian Locri by Locrians at the beginning of the seventh.

Another major area of colonial activity was the region around the Hellespont, Propontis, and Black Sea. Miletus took a leading role in such ventures – especially in the seventh century with foundations such as Cyzicus, Abydos, and Sinope – but the Megarians were also active, planting colonies at Astakos, Chalcedon, Selymbria, and Byzantium in the seventh century and, with Boeotian assistance, at Heraclea Pontica in the mid-sixth century. Towards the end of the seventh century, the Athenians founded Sigeum and the Samians established Perinthus, while the Tean colony of Phanagoria probably dates to the middle of the sixth century. Meanwhile, the small island of Thera (modern

Santorini) is believed to have founded Cyrene in Libya towards the end of the seventh century; Cyrene, in turn, founded the cities of Tokra, Euhesperides, and Barka. Finally, in the far west, settlers and refugees from Phocaea are credited with the foundation ca. 600 of Massalia in southern France and Emporion in Spain. Thus, by the end of the sixth century, settlements of predominantly Greek-speaking residents dotted the shores of the Mediterranean and Black Sea areas. However, the nature of these early settlements and the circumstances under which they came to be established are questions that are worth pursuing further.

The Credibility of Colonial Foundation Stories

We are relatively well informed as to the nature of colonizing ventures in the fifth century. An inscribed bronze plaque, found at Galaxidhi on the northern shore of the Corinthian Gulf and probably dating to 500–470, sets out the regulations governing an East Locrian colony at Naupactus (ML 13 = Fornara 47). The colonists are to retain certain religious prerogatives in their original community, though without fiscal liabilities. In extreme circumstances, the right of return to East Locris is provided for (as long as no taxes are outstanding in Naupactus), and the colonists have to swear not to rebel against the Locrians. In the case of colonists who die with no heirs in Naupactus, the inheritance passes to the nearest of kin in East Locris while property in Locris may be bequeathed to a colonist in Naupactus. Violations of these conditions are to be punished with the loss of citizen-rights and the confiscation of property, with similar penalties applying to magistrates who refuse to grant trials. Somewhat later, in the third quarter of the fifth century, another inscription describes the foundation of an Athenian colony at Brea in Thrace under the direction of a man named Demokleides (ML 49 = Fornara 100). Provisions are taken for the distribution of land and for the reservation of precincts dedicated to the gods. The colony is to be founded within thirty days of the decree, though enrolled colonists who are currently away on military service are given thirty days to emigrate after their return to Athens, and the settlers are to be conscripted from the Zeugitai and the Thêtes (the two lowest property classes at Athens: see p. 165). Those who propose a reversal or modification of the conditions are subject to loss of citizen-rights and confiscation of property.

If the provisions set out in these two fifth-century decrees perpetuate habitual practices that date back to the flurry of colonial activity in the eighth century, then we would have to conclude that colonization was significantly different from earlier migratory movements in that it was more formally organized, more strictly regulated, and undertaken after considerably more advanced planning. Furthermore, it would suggest that colonization involved, from the outset, a direct and generally exclusive relationship between a single founding-city (*mêtropolis*) and its colony (*apoikia*) – something that is less apparent in the literary traditions for migrations. It is not, however, clear that earlier colonial ventures did operate along similar lines to those that are better attested in the Classical period. Certainly the expeditions that planted the Achaean colonies in South Italy cannot have been as formal or as organized as the Athenian settlement at Brea since the sorts of political and administrative structures normally associated with the *polis* are barely, if at all, attested in Peloponnesian Achaea prior to the fifth century.

Considerable attention has been given to a fourth-century decree from Cyrene (ML 5 = Fornara 18). The specific occasion for the decree was a proposal granting equal rights of citizenship to newly arrived settlers from Thera, but this proposal was justified on the grounds that the terms of the original settlement of Cyrene, in the later seventh century, had made provisions for the distribution of property to future colonists. The inscription then proceeds to record what it claims is the oath of the first Theran colonists of Cyrene. At the behest of Apollo, the Theran assembly decided to dispatch freeborn citizens under the command and rule of a man named Battos, with one son being conscripted from every family. Were the colony to prove successful, kinsmen of the original settlers would be permitted to sail to Libya where they would receive citizen-rights and a plot of unassigned land. The colonists were to persevere for five years to ensure the success of the settlement, but if ultimately unsuccessful, they would have been permitted to return to Thera and reclaim their citizen-rights there. Anybody who was conscripted and refused to sail – or who harbored somebody who refused to sail – would have been executed and have had his property confiscated. The inscription concludes by noting that both the colonists and those who remained on Thera swore an oath to uphold these provisions and invoked curses against transgressors.

The authenticity of the "original" oath cited in this decree has been the subject of much discussion. That the language adopted displays some seemingly "archaic" elements is not in itself surprising and can hardly preclude the possibility that it is a forgery. One might, perhaps, have expected even more of an emphasis on the privileges due to later arrivals had the oath been fabricated in the fourth century but, then again, it is a little surprising that a genuine foundation document did not make provisions for a whole range of issues that would have been irrelevant to the immediate concerns of fourth-century settlers. Some doubts have recently been expressed concerning Herodotus' comment (4.155.2) that the name Battos was a Libyan royal title, but had the name Battos been so indelibly associated with Cyrene's founder by the fifth century, it is strange that Pindar (*Pyth.* 5.87) should have chosen to identify him as a certain Aristoteles. Certain details mentioned in the inscription – for example, the spontaneous command from Apollo, the selection of one son/ brother per family, and the appointment of Battos as leader of the colonists – find parallels in the version of the foundation story that Herodotus (4.150–53) claims to have heard from the Therans, and this should almost certainly rule out the possibility that the oath cited in the decree was an invention of the fourth century. On the other hand, the fact that this was the tradition that was circulating on Thera in the fifth century does not in itself prove that the details had been faithfully remembered and transmitted from the time of the actual foundation.

The problem is that the earliest extant accounts of colonial foundations are invariably late. Archilochus (fr. 102) describes the settlement of Thasos and shows some familiarity with the fertile territory around the Colophonian colony of Siris in South Italy (fr. 22), but accounts that offer any details for colonial foundations in the west rarely appear before the time of Antiochus of Syracuse towards the end of the fifth century. Even then, such details as are recorded are hardly exhaustive. The provenance of the first settlers is normally given, but no *oikistês* is named for around one quarter of the thirty or so colonial foundations in South Italy and Sicily. Consultation of the Delphic oracle is mentioned for just five colonies (Croton, Gela, Rhegium, Syracuse, and Taras) while the act of dividing territory receives no treatment, save for the anecdote, recorded by Archilochus (fr. 293), that the Corinthian Aithiops exchanged his lot of land in Syracuse for a honey-cake. It might be thought that the scarcity of information to be found in the literary accounts of foundation actually argues in favor of their historicity: later inventions, it is reasoned, would have fleshed out the bare bones of the tradition with more succulent details. Yet the problem is not just that details are sketchy but that such details as there are frequently vary between sources.

Consider the case of Megara Hyblaea, near the modern industrial port of Augusta in eastern Sicily. Thucydides (6.4.1–2) says that it was founded 245 years before its destruction at the hands of Gelon of Syracuse (728 in our terms). The colonists were Megarians from mainland Greece, originally led by Lamis, who had been unsuccessful in earlier attempts to settle Trotilon, Leontini, and Thapsos (where he died). But Eusebius (*Chron.*) dates the foundation thirty years earlier; the second-century CE writer Polyaenus (*Strat.* 5.5) places the foundation of Trotilon after, not before, Leontini; and Ephorus (fr. 137) and pseudo-Scymnus (277) both say that the Megarians who founded Megara Hyblaea were led, not by Lamis, but by a man named Theokles. According to Thucydides (6.3.1–2), Theokles was the founder of Naxos, Leontini, and Catana and he seems to have been regarded as a Chalcidian, though two Byzantine lexica say he was from Eretria (*Suda*, s.v. *elegeinein*; *Etymologicum Magnum* 327.6–10) while for Ephorus (fr. 137) and pseudo-Scymnus (270–7) he was an Athenian.

Alternative founders are attested for a number of western colonies, especially on the Italian mainland. The fourth-century coins of Metapontum represent the colony's founder as a certain Leukippos, though Daulios of Crisa is named as *oikistês* by Ephorus (fr. 141), while the honor is attributed to Epeios by the third-century CE geographer Solinus (2.10) and in Justin's epitome of Pompeius Trogus' *Historiae Philippicae* (20.2). Divergent foundation dates are also offered: Syracuse is dated to 733 by Thucydides (6.4.2) but to 757 by the third-century Parian Marble; the Sicilian city of Selinus was founded in 628 according to Thucydides (6.4.2) but in 650 according to Diodorus (13.59);

and the Italian city of Cumae is said by Strabo (5.4.4) to have been the oldest foundation in the west – Eusebius (*Chron.*) actually dated it to ca. 1050 – but Livy (8.22.6) maintains that it was established after Pithecusae. Even the origin of the first settlers does not always meet with consensus: the foundation of Locri is variously attributed to East Locrians (Ephorus fr. 138), West Locrians (Strabo 9.4.9), and even Spartans (Pausanias 3.3.1), while Himera is said to be a secondary foundation of either Zancle and Syracuse (Thucydides 6.5.1), Catana and Kallipolis (pseudo-Scymnus 289–90), or Mylai (Strabo 6.2.6).

Particularly intriguing in this respect are the "double foundations" recorded for the so-called "Achaean" colonies of south Italy. Antiochus (frs. 10, 12) attributed the foundations of Metapontum, Sybaris, and Croton to Achaeans from the geographical region of Achaea in the northern Peloponnese. In the case of Croton, he also tells us that the expedition was ordained by the Delphic Oracle and entrusted to a man named Myskellos, who set out for the west in the company of Arkhias, the founder of Syracuse. According to Strabo (8.7.5), Myskellos originated from the Achaean city of Rhypes, while the *oikistês* of Sybaris was a certain Is from the nearby city of Helike (6.1.15). Pausanias (6.3.12) reports that Caulonia was established by Typhon of Aegium – though pseudo-Scymnus (318–19) and Solinus (2.10) regarded it as a secondary foundation of Croton – and Poseidonia was said to have been settled by Achaeans from Sybaris (Strabo 5.3.13).

Yet these colonists from Achaea were not believed to have been the first Greeks to settle Italian shores. According to Strabo (6.1.12), Greeks returning from the Trojan War (i.e. Achaeans in a Homeric, rather than a geographic, sense) were shipwrecked on the Italian coast and forced to settle in the territory of Croton. The hinterland of Croton was also associated with the Homeric hero Philoctetes (6.1.3), while an earlier settlement of Metapontum was attributed to Pylians sailing back from Troy with the garrulous Nestor (6.1.15). It is easy to see why historians should have dismissed these heroic foundations as fictitious fables but they are not, as is often supposed, the inventions of late mythographers. The tradition that Metapontum had been founded by veterans returning from Troy was already known to the early fifth-century lyric poet Bacchylides (11.114–23) and the specification that these were Pylians should probably be understood in terms of the hostility between Metapontum and the neighboring city of Siris, whose founding-city, Colophon, considered itself a colony of Pylos (Mimnermus fr. 9). This simultaneous appeal to Pylian origins can only really have arisen in the relatively brief period between the foundation of Metapontum ca. 630 and the sack of Siris in the mid-sixth century. The fact that traditions ascribing Italian foundations to Homeric heroes were elaborated at a relatively early date is not, of course, sufficient reason for taking them seriously. But neither does their relegation necessarily guarantee, by default, the veracity of the alternative foundation traditions concerning Is, Myskellos, and Typhon, that are first recorded by authors writing more than a century later.

In assessing the historicity of these foundation stories, it is legitimate to ask exactly how the memory of episodes that were supposed to have taken place in the eighth and seventh centuries was accurately preserved over approximately 300 years. The point is not that the ability to memorize lists is unusual in predominantly oral societies but that, if this were common practice among the western Greeks, it would markedly differentiate them from their Aegean cousins, who appear to have been totally incapable of remembering events from so early a period. It is, for example, revealing that Herodotus (3.122.2), though aware of tales concerning the naval power of mythical figures such as Minos of Crete, concedes that the late sixth-century tyrant of Samos, Polycrates, was "the first Greek *that we know* made plans to rule over the seas." The idea of dating events to the tenure of political or religious office was already well established in the sixth century: an inscription from Eretria (*IG* XII 9.1273–74) dates a law to the archonship of a certain Tollos, while a document from the sanctuary of Aphaea on Aegina (*IG* IV 1580) refers to construction-work undertaken during the priesthood of Kleoitas. It is not, however, entirely certain that sequential lists of office-holders were common in this period. An inscription from Argos (*IG* IV 614), dated to 575–550, names nine *damiourgoi* but it is probably a case of a board of concurrently-serving officials rather than a consecutive list of annual magistrates. In any event, it was not until the later fifth century that antiquarians attempted to extend these rosters back into the eighth century and beyond. A list of Athenian archons was set up in the Athenian agora ca. 425. Shortly afterwards, Hellanicus of Mytilene published his list of the priestesses of Hera at Argos and Hippias of Elis compiled the first complete list of Olympic victors stretching back to the supposed inaugural games of 776. In both cases, it is clear that imaginative guesswork, rather than consultation of written records, supplemented local memory, dedicatory inscriptions, and family genealogies. It is within this context of an awakened interest in chronography that we should situate the antiquarian works of Antiochus.

It has been argued that the nature of historical consciousness was, in fact, different in the colonial setting because of the risks involved and the trauma suffered in braving the seas and establishing settlements in hostile territory. In some colonies we hear that the founder was buried in the agora and received heroic offerings after his death, and it is suggested that the details of the original foundation were recited at these annually enacted rituals – an ancient equivalent to Independence Day celebrations in the United States. Such annual occasions, the argument continues, would also have allowed the colony's inhabitants to keep an accurate tally of the years that had elapsed since the settlement was founded. There are, however, three difficulties with this theory.

Firstly, if an "official" foundation account was recited annually in a formal setting and transmitted from generation to generation, we would expect to find considerably less variety in the literary traditions with respect to specific details than is actually the case. Secondly, there is very little evidence to support the idea that founders received heroic honors from the moment of their death. Literary testimony is invariably late – we have to wait until the time of Livy

Figure 5.1   Heröon at Megara Hyblaea (photo by author)

(40.4.9) to hear of an annually ordained sacrifice in honor of Aeneas at Aineia in the Chalcidice – and the archaeological evidence is not particularly informative. What has been identified as a hero-shrine in the northwestern sector of Megara Hyblaea (Figure 5.1) postdates the foundation of the colony by about a century, while it is by no means certain that an underground chamber at Poseidonia, dating to 520–500, has any connection with a hero cult to the city's founder. Similarly, cult is not attested to Antiphemos at Gela until the fifth century, when his name appears as part of a dedicatory offering on an Attic *kylix* (drinking cup). The most plausible occurrence of heroic honors comes from Cyrene, where an offering platform in association with a cremation burial of ca. 600 is probably to be linked to Pindar's claim that Battos "lies in death, apart, on the edges of the *agora*" (*Pyth.* 5.93–95). It would, however, be injudicious to generalize from so few examples.

Thirdly, there are good reasons for supposing that the foundation dates assigned to colonies by ancient authors were computed not on the basis of annual commemorative festivals but on an approximate count of generations. Thucydides (6.4–5) notes that Megara Hyblaea existed for 245 years, while Acrae was founded seventy years after Syracuse: both figures are almost certainly based on a thirty-five year generation (the fact that other authors appear to calculate the dates for other foundations on the basis of different generational calculations does not, in itself, invalidate the hypothesis). Generational computation is, of course, less accurate and more artificial than annual calculation but – far more importantly – it is invariably projected *backwards* from a later date. This only goes to strengthen the suspicion that it was not until the fifth century that ancient authors began to take an interest in civic foundations. This is not to say that such accounts were entirely fictitious, but we should be aware that what gets "remembered" in later periods may often have more to do with justifying the present order than with preserving an accurate account of the past for its own sake. Given our inability to distinguish between hard facts and invented traditions in foundation accounts, agnosticism is to be preferred to credulity.

Pots and Peoples

To what extent does archaeological evidence confirm or refute the information provided by literary sources? With regard to foundation dates we need to be wary about resorting to a circular argument: since our absolute ceramic chronologies are based, at least in part, on Thucydides' dates for the Sicilian colonies (see pp. 38–9), it is hardly surprising that the archaeological evidence appears to chime with the information he provides. This chronological scheme, first formulated in the 1930s, assumes that we have retrieved the earliest pottery at each site. At the Sicilian site of Selinus, for example, the earliest pottery that had come to light prior to 1931 was classified stylistically as belonging to the first phases of Early Ripe Corinthian. Since Thucydides (6.4.2) dated the foundation of Selinus to 628, it was assumed that the transition from Late Protocorinthian to Early Corinthian styles took place ca. 630. But in the 1950s, scholars came upon earlier Protocorinthian pottery in the storerooms of the Palermo museum that was alleged to have come from graves at Selinus. Two options were possible: either Thucydides' date was correct – in which case the introduction of Ripe Corinthian styles must have occurred rather later than 630 – or else he was mistaken. Since ceramic experts were reluctant to jettison a chronology that, in most respects, seemed to work well and that finds some support in "fixed points" derived from Near Eastern sites, they decided to abandon the Thucydidean date in favor of a date of 650, furnished by Diodorus (13.59). If, however, Thucydides could be mistaken in the date he gives for Selinus, why should his foundation dates for the other Greek colonies in Sicily be any more reliable? Elsewhere, in cases where earlier material has come to light – for example, Gela and Acragas – the Thucydidean dates have been maintained and the offending elements regarded as evidence for "precolonial" activity associated with exchange and commerce rather than settlement.

Let us assume that the standard chronology is basically sound (it is unlikely that future revisions will modify it radically). What the archaeological evidence actually reveals is a rather longer drawn-out process for the establishment of settlements overseas than is suggested by a simple foundation date. Thucydides dates Megara Hyblaea to 728 and this is approximately the period in which Greek ceramics begin to appear in bulk – especially a *skyphos*, assigned to the

Thapsos class, which is also known from the earliest levels at Naxos, Syracuse, Leontini, Catana, Sybaris, Croton, and Taras. But there is also some fragmentary pottery that should date to around the middle of the eighth century, nearer in time to Eusebius' foundation date of 757. Unfortunately, the earliest material found at most colonial sites is seldom associated with any secure archaeological context, meaning that its interpretation is far from straightforward. Evidence for buildings rarely predates the seventh century though, given the insubstantial nature of the materials used for construction in this period, that need not be terribly significant. Generally speaking, the earliest burials tend to be slightly later than the first Greek imports, which is perhaps what one would expect. At both Taras and the nearby site of Satyrion, for example, the earliest ceramics date to Late Geometric I (ca. 750–725) and at Scoglio del Tonno, Middle Geometric material from earlier in the eighth century has been found. Save for three or so cremations, however, the earliest burials in the cemeteries east of the city contain Early Protocorinthian pots dating to the last years of the eighth century, close enough to the date of 706 furnished by Eusebius. By and large, then, the archaeological evidence is not radically at variance with the foundation dates provided by literary sources (when they are in agreement). But it certainly does not seem to indicate the sort of highly organized, virtually instantaneous foundation anticipated by the provisions for the Athenian colony at Brea. A more likely scenario – and one which is paralleled by the process by which British settlers founded settlements in the New World – is one in which an initial party of settlers, probably relatively few in number, established a foothold in new territory and was reinforced by a steady trickle of newcomers over a period of approximately one generation and perhaps even longer.

Contrary to what has often been argued, this picture is not contradicted by the evidence from Megara Hyblaea – a site whose early urban plan can be identified thanks to the abandonment of the city after its final destruction in 214 and to its meticulous excavation by the French School in Rome. Here, a densely packed urban habitat is parceled out into approximately equal lots of land laid out on what is essentially a grid plan, although the principal avenues, which converge on a large open space that has been identified as the agora of the Archaic city, follow different orientations. Some scholars believe that these various orientations permit us to identify five different "quarters" and wish to see in this settlement pattern a replication of the five villages that are supposed to have constituted the *polis* of mainland Megara. It is widely accepted that a major programme of urbanization at Megara Hyblaea did not begin in earnest until the third quarter of the seventh century, continuing through to about 530. Nevertheless, it is generally maintained that, since the earliest houses do not encroach on the roads or on what would later be monumentalized as the agora and since they generally follow the orientation of the later grid (including the median lines of each "block"), the basic plan of the urban area was designed right from the outset, with seventh-century development merely filling in areas already earmarked for public buildings and residences.

There is, however, a danger here of committing what has been called "teleological thinking." Had the settlement been densely occupied from the start, the avoidance of areas that would later constitute public spaces could almost certainly be considered conscious and deliberate. In reality, however, perhaps only fourteen houses, for the most part partially preserved, can be assigned to the eighth century (i.e. the first generation of the colony's life if we follow Thucydides' date). These dwellings, which are generally simple, one-room structures, collectively represent such a minute portion of the excavated area (a little more than 1 percent on a rough calculation) that their absence from large parts of the later settlement is not in itself terribly meaningful (Map 5.2). Among these earliest houses there are two, not five, orientations adopted, though we cannot be certain that the difference was deliberate: all are approximately oriented north–south and since the more complete units seem to open towards the south it is not improbable that their orientation was chosen to maximize exposure to the sun for the purposes of providing both heat and light. The two different orientations are largely respected in the subsequent development of the urban area – save in the area south of Road B and east of Road C1, where the eighth-century houses follow the orientation of the houses to the northwest while the seventh-century blocks are oriented on the roads to the east of the agora. Finally, if we "think away" the seventh-century urban plan, it is not immediately clear that we could have anticipated it by examining the eighth-century houses alone. The area where the agora was later situated could have served the same function for the first inhabitants of Megara Hyblaea, but an equally plausible candidate would have been the area immediately to the south of the Archaic agora – if, that is, the early residents of the zone felt that they needed a formal open meeting-place to begin with (see pp. 80–2).

If we were to examine the material evidence without presuppositions predicated on later, fifth-century models of colonization, we would probably conclude that, for the first thirty or so years of its existence, the settlement that occupied the area of the later agora at Megara Hyblaea consisted of a few, scattered houses, roughly oriented to take advantage of natural sunlight but conforming to no overall layout (there is some evidence for another settlement approximately 500 meters to the south, though the relationship between the two zones is not yet entirely clear). Even if we were to assume that early houses are represented in equal measure in the unexcavated parts of the area around the later agora as they are in the excavated parts, the eighth-century community would still have numbered around only forty or so households – comparable to the village of Nikhoria in its heyday (see p. 60). It is far from evident that so small a community would have required a permanent, formally reserved meeting-place in this period. In the early seventh century, as the population of the settlement grew, an area that had not previously been used for habitation was reserved as an agora, receiving a more monumental form in the third quarter of that century with the construction of Building i, the North and East stoas, and the two temples along the southern side. Test trenches

Map 5.2 Plan of the zone around the Archaic agora at Megara Hyblaea in (a) the sixth and (b) the eighth centuries (after Gras, Tréziny, and Broise 2004, 452 fig. 430)

AGORA

50 m

suggest that the road network was not laid out until fairly early in the seventh century: the somewhat anomalous grid-plan that the roads create is probably determined by the formal siting of the agora and by the somewhat haphazard orientation of the earlier, eighth-century houses. Road C2, however, which is flanked by five of the earliest structures, may be a little earlier, since fragments of an eighth-century *aryballos* (perfume bottle) were discovered beneath the cobbles of the earliest surface.

Archaeological evidence is less amenable to determining the provenance of the earliest settlers. Regardless of the specific origins that the literary traditions attribute to each colony, the pattern of early imports varies little between settlements. Corinthian wares dominate the assemblages of almost every site, while pottery that has been identified as originating in the north and northwest Peloponnese is found not only in the Achaean foundations of southern Italy but also at Locri, Siris, Taras, Otranto, Pithecusae, and Cumae as well as at the Sicilian sites of Naxos, Megara Hyblaea, Syracuse, Gela, Leontini, and Himera. This almost certainly reflects the fact that most voyagers to the west chose to pass through the Corinthian Gulf rather than round the stormy capes of the southern Peloponnese. Euboean and East Greek (especially Rhodian and Chian) pottery is also commonly represented and although both Chalcis and Rhodes are said to have founded cities in Sicily, the wider distribution of these wares is certainly not restricted to colonial activities. At Megara Hyblaea itself, Corinthian imports are accompanied by imports from Attica, Euboea, the Argolid, Achaea, and Rhodes as well as by local imitations of Euboean and Corinthian pottery.

As noted above in the discussion of Al Mina and Pithecusae, traded items do not need to have been carried by residents of the area in which they were produced. An old archaeological cliché warns against equating pots with peoples. Logically speaking, if the predominance of Corinthian wares cannot be taken to indicate a Corinthian monopoly on commercial transactions, then assemblages that display a diversity of provenances should not automatically be taken as an indication of a "mixed" settlement. On the other hand, the heterogeneous character of material assemblages at colonial sites is not generally matched at sites in mainland Greece. It attests to a far wider and more extensive network of contacts and exchanges than is witnessed for "Old Greece" and it is inconceivable that human bodies did not also move along these routes. The fact that the island of Ortygia and the Arethousa spring at Syracuse share their names with natural features in the territory of Chalcis might lead one to suspect that the Euboean or Euboeanizing pottery that appears alongside Corinthian wares in the earliest levels at Syracuse does, in fact, reflect the presence of Euboeans in the settlement. If this is the case, the literary foundation stories attested from the fifth century represent a much simplified version of more complex events and processes, attributing the initiative behind foundation to those groups who were dominant within the city during the Classical period. In that respect, the literary accounts of colonial foundations are not so vastly different in kind from those for the earlier migrations.

A Spartan Foundation? Taras, Phalanthos, and the Partheniai

Some of the points made in the previous section can be developed further in relation to the foundation of Taras in South Italy. Our fullest account for this is to be found in Strabo (6.3.2–3) who claims to present, first, the version recorded by Antiochus of Syracuse (fr. 13) and, second, that provided by Ephorus (fr. 216). When we compare the two texts (Document 5.2), it becomes clear that there are very few points of overlap. Indeed the only information that is common to both authors regards the date of foundation (the time of the Spartan conquest of Messenia in the later eighth century) and the identity of the settlers (the Partheniai of Laconia). Even the figure of Phalanthos, who features prominently in Antiochus' account as the leader of the expedition, is entirely absent from Ephorus' version. One explanation that has been offered for this studied silence appeals to changed political circumstances in Ephorus' day. The figure of Phalanthos, it is argued, was intimately associated with aristocrats, some of whom probably claimed descent from the founder. When a major defeat at the hands of the neighboring Iapygians in 473 instigated a democratic revolution at Taras (Aristotle, *Pol.* 5.2.8; cf. Herodotus 7.170.3; Diodorus 11.52), Phalanthos' fortunes waned and the foundation of the city was credited instead to a more "democratic" eponymous hero named Taras. There are, however, two problems with this hypothesis.

Firstly, Phalanthos' claims to have founded Taras were never entirely eclipsed in favor of Taras: indeed, the figure of Phalanthos was particularly exploited in Ephorus' own day by the Spartan king Archidamus III, who assisted the Tarantines in their fight against the Lucanians. Secondly, if a draped, seated male figure who appears on the reverse of a series of silver staters, issued ca. 480, has been correctly identified as the eponymous Taras, then this alternative tradition would appear to predate the democratic revolution of 473. Given the complexities of numismatic dating (see p. 28), it would be unwise to insist too much on the chronological discrepancy, but there is another indication that points in a similar direction. On the obverse of the same coin series there is a representation of a youth riding a dolphin – a motif that already appears on Tarantine coins towards the end of the sixth century. The youth is normally identified as Phalanthos because Pausanias (10.13.10) describes a mid-fifth-century bronze statue group at Delphi, which included Taras and Phalanthos on the back of a dolphin. According to the legend Pausanias heard, Phalanthos was rescued by a dolphin after being shipwrecked in the Gulf of Crisa, near Delphi. But Aristotle (fr. 590), writing some five centuries earlier, says that it was Taras, not Phalanthos, who was miraculously saved by the dolphin. Furthermore, Antiochus' comment that Taras had already been named "after some hero" prior to Phalanthos' arrival demonstrates that this alternative tradition was already in existence by the fifth century. Nor can we suppose that the memory of Phalanthos' exploits was kept alive through rituals enacted at his tomb. Strabo (6.3.6) seems to imply that Phalanthos was buried at Brentesion (modern

Document 5.2

Antiochus fr. 13	Ephorus fr. 216
	The Spartans, leaving behind the young and old, swear an oath not to return home until they have destroyed
Spartans who did not take part in the **Messenian Wars** are enslaved as helots.	Messene and embark on the First **Messenian War**.
	After ten years, their wives complain that Sparta risks a manpower shortage.
	The Spartans decide to send back the youngest soldiers on the grounds that they were too young to swear the original oath.
	These sleep with Spartan maidens (*parthenoi*).
Their disenfranchised sons are named **Partheniai**.	Their children are named **Partheniai** and are denied civil rights on the grounds of illegitimacy.
They decide to revolt.	**They therefore plot** with the helots.
The Spartans send Phalanthos to infiltrate their ranks and report back.	
The revolt is set for the Hyacinthia festival at Amyclae. The signal for revolt is to be Phalanthos placing a *kyne* on his head.	The revolt is to take place in the Spartan agora. The signal for revolt is to be the raising of a *pilos*.
Phalanthos reports back.	Some of the helots reveal the plot to the Spartans.
Phalanthos is told **not to put the *kyne* on**.	Fearing the numbers of the conspirators, the Spartans refrain from a counterattack but **remove from the agora those about to raise the *pilos*.**
The Partheniai realize the plot has been betrayed and seek asylum as suppliants.	**The Partheniai realize the plot has been betrayed** and give up the attempt.
They are told to take courage and are placed under guard.	
	They are persuaded by their fathers to found a colony overseas.
Phalanthos consults Delphi: he is told to found a colony in "Satyrion and Taras" and to "become a bane to the Iapygians."	
	If the colony fails, they are told they may return and receive one fifth of Messenia.
Phalanthos leads the **Partheniai to Taras** which he names after "some hero", and is welcomed by the **indigenous peoples** and Cretans already resident there.	**The Partheniai go to Taras** and join with the Achaeans in war against the **indigenous peoples**.

Brindisi) while Justin (*Epitome* 3.4) says that he gave orders for his cremated bones to be crushed and scattered over the agora in Taras. Both accounts betray an almost embarrassed acknowledgment of the fact that Phalanthos lacked a physical presence in the city he was supposed to have founded.

As at other sites, much of the earliest archaeological material at Taras is Corinthian in style, but fragmentary Laconian Late Geometric pottery has been reported from the Città Vecchia (the Old City where the ancient acropolis was situated), Scoglio del Tonno, and Satyrion. Although the quantities are minute in proportion with other wares, the fact that Laconian Geometric is rarely found outside the area of its production is probably significant. This does not prove that all of the earliest settlers of Taras originated from the vicinity of Sparta – there is an impressive quantity of Achaean *kantharoi* at Taras and, unlike many other sites in South Italy, it seems to be imported rather than locally imitated – but it strongly suggests at the very least a Spartan component. It is, however, only in the sixth century that material associations with Sparta become most pronounced. This is when Laconian cups with conical feet and figured representations of fish and dolphins begin to appear and when Tarantine bronze figurines start to take their cue from contemporary Laconian, rather than Corinthian, styles. Towards the end of the sixth century, statuettes of reclining banqueters, though realized in a style that owes much to East Greece, appear to evoke specifically Spartan conceptions of heroizing the dead. Given the rather slight affinities in the previous two centuries, this enthusiastic adoption and adaptation of Laconian themes and styles would appear to indicate a concerted effort in the course of the sixth century to maintain – or perhaps even to forge – ties with the city that fifth-century authors were to identify as Taras' mother-city.

Associations with Sparta are also suggested by Tarantine institutions and cultural features. The script and dialect employed in Tarantine inscriptions, save for some Achaean influences regarding punctuation, find close parallels with the Laconian dialect and alphabet. The Spartan magistracy of the ephorate is attested at Taras and there is also evidence for kingship – though it is a monarchy rather than the dyarchy for which Sparta was famous. Deities that were popular at Sparta, such as Athena Polias, Persephone, and the Dioscuri, were worshipped at Taras, while according to Polybius (8.28.2), Hyacinthus – a god most famously associated with the Laconian village of Amyclae – was actually buried outside one of the city gates. Yet none of these features can assuredly be traced back to the first years of the foundation. The earliest inscriptions date to the third quarter of the sixth century even if it is a natural enough assumption that the dialect employed had been in use earlier. The ephorate is not attested at Taras itself before the early third century, though it should have existed prior to 433/2 because this is the date when Taras founded its own daughter-colony at Heraclea, a city where the magistracy is certainly documented. The first secure evidence for the worship of the Dioscuri comes with their representation on sixth-century votive tablets found in the modern Piazza del Carmine, while the figure of Hyacinthus first appears on the earliest issue of silver staters in the later sixth century. It should be emphasized that all of these features could have existed prior to their first attestation, but the fact that these earliest documented instances coincide with the first concerted efforts to establish ties with Sparta through the medium of material culture is, at the very least, worthy of note.

Taking account of all the evidence at our disposal, we would probably not be accused of excessive credulity if we were to suppose that many – though probably not all – of the first residents at Taras originated from the vicinity of Sparta. Later tradition named them the Partheniai and regarded them as a motley group of disaffected outcasts, and it may well be that social exclusion and economic difficulties prompted them to seek a better life in the west. The figure of Phalanthos is another thing entirely. In the Antiochean tradition, he is not – as is commonly supposed – one of the Partheniai but rather a representative of the Spartan authorities. His association with the foundation story of Taras contributes a more formal, official, and organized aspect to the episode that, on material and perhaps also institutional grounds, fits better a context in the sixth century. That he was not inherently tied to the tradition from the outset is strongly suggested by the fact that he could be entirely ignored by Ephorus, writing only ninety or so years after Antiochus. In short, if migrants from Laconia formed part of the original settlement, Taras did not become a fully-fledged Spartan colony until the later Archaic period.

Hunger or Greed?

It has been almost a dogma of scholarship in recent decades that the principal motivation for colonization was "land hunger." The vast majority of overseas sites were, it is argued, chosen for their agricultural potential – the coinage of Metapontum even displayed an ear of wheat. The Theran account of the foundation of Cyrene mentions a seven-year drought (Herodotus 4.151.1), and the eventual location of the colony is chosen precisely because it is situated "where the sky is pierced" (4.158.3) – that is, a place that enjoys considerable rainfall (between 400 mm and 800 mm per annum in recent history). Oracular prophecies that colonies should be founded "where water falls from a clear sky" – associated with both Taras (Pausanias 10.10.6) and Croton (Scholiast to Aristophanes, *Clouds* 371) – seem to betray a similar concern with crop productivity. When evidence came to light for demographic growth in Greece during the eighth century (see pp. 78–9), the case appeared closed. There was simply not enough land in Greece to feed an expanding population. Those cities that did not control territories as vast as those of Athens or Sparta had little option but to send young men overseas in search of sustenance.

Yet it has been objected that emigration is not the only – nor even the most obvious – response to a shortage of land. Alternative strategies could have included birth control, abortion, or infanticide, delaying the marriageable age for women – thereby decreasing the fertility cycle – or an intensification of agricultural practices by which marginal land might be brought into cultivation. Nor, despite indications for demographic growth, is there any clearly visible evidence for overpopulation in mainland Greece during the eighth century. The territory of Corinth is far more fertile than was once believed and at around 900 square kilometers in the Classical period, it ranks among the larger hinterlands, yet there are few material indications for intensive habitation in the Corinthian countryside. Achaeans are credited with founding the earliest permanent settlements in South Italy, but the results of archaeological survey around the Achaean city of Dyme suggests that the zone was only sporadically settled until the sixth century. By contrast, the island of Aegina in the Saronic Gulf almost certainly did not have the agricultural capacity to feed its population and yet it did not feel the need to dispatch a colony until shortly after 520, when it took control of the Samian colony at Kydonia (modern Khaniá) on Crete (Herodotus 3.59.3) – according to Strabo (8.6.16), a later settlement was planted in Italian Umbria. To support themselves, the Aeginetans seem to have turned to what has euphemistically been described as "negative reciprocity" – i.e. piracy – but if Thucydides (1.5) is correct that piracy and brigandage were commonplace in the Archaic period, it would be strange that the idea should have occurred to the Aeginetans alone. Furthermore, if our calculations for the early population of Megara Hyblaea are correct, there was hardly the sort of exodus that would have significantly relieved overcrowded conditions at home.

Perhaps, however, this abstract matching of agricultural resources to population levels is not the most fruitful way to approach the issue. The demographic growth hypothesized for the eighth century may have been the consequence of declining mortality rates but there can be little doubt that it was precipitated above all by higher birth rates. In real terms, sons were more likely to have brothers in the later eighth century than at any time in the previous four centuries or so. In the Classical period, it was the norm for family property to be divided equally among male heirs. That this was also the case earlier – at least in some areas of Greece – finds confirmation in Hesiod's description of his quarrel with his brother, Perses: "We divided the property between us, but you had your eyes set on seizing the larger part, bestowing excessive honours on the bribe-devouring nobles who love to adjudicate cases like this" (*WD* 37–9). It matters little whether or not Hesiod is here describing a genuine autobiographical episode: the admonitory tone of the poem as a whole would have lost its force had the supposed source of Hesiod's indignation not been fairly commonplace. Elsewhere, Hesiod notes, "There should be an only son to nourish the paternal home for in this way wealth will increase in the household; if you leave behind a second son, you should die old" (376–7). Apart from the implication that having one son was – or should ideally be – the norm, Hesiod draws attention to the fact that since partible inheritance creates smaller, fragmented landholdings, fathers of more than one son should endeavor to work as hard, and for as long, as possible to ensure a greater inheritance. We may, perhaps, infer that Hesiod's father had not heeded this advice and that it was for this reason that Perses seized a larger share of his property.

Smaller inheritances with reduced productivity could certainly offer one explanation as to why people should have moved, but resentment at what were perceived as inequitable divisions between siblings may account, at least in part, for why these new settlements were so far from home. After all, the earliest permanent settlement in the west, Pithecusae, is also the most distant from Greece. Such a pattern might explain Hesiod's otherwise surprising failure to list siblings and their families when he warns that neighbors are likely to come to one's aid sooner than kinsmen by marriage (344–5). If younger siblings chose to emigrate upon the death of their fathers and land lots were inherited in their entirety, it is far from certain that we should expect to identify major changes in the archaeology of the countryside.

For what it is worth, some hint of inheritance issues is discernible in the foundation stories. The traditions that the founders of Taras were either the sons of Spartans enslaved for "conscientious objection" (Antiochus) or born out of wedlock (Ephorus) may well be attempts to explain their name – the Partheniai – but that term in itself (from the Greek word for "virgin") carries connotations of illegitimacy and hence disputed claims to inheritance. According to the Cyrenean account of the foundation of Cyrene, Battos was the son of a Cretan princess whose moral virtue was questioned and who was sent to Thera to become the concubine (*pallakê*) of a Theran aristocrat (Herodotus 4.154–55). Battos' social marginality is signified metaphorically by a speech impediment, and a similar status may be implied in the accounts concerning Myskellos, the founder of Croton, whose name literally means "hunchbacked." Indeed, Diodorus' account (8.17) of the oracular consultation that commanded Myskellos to found Croton finds several parallels with Battos' consultation of the Delphic oracle, as recorded by the Cyreneans (Herodotus 4.155–57). Such formulaic similarities within the genre of foundation stories do little to commend their independent credibility.

However, Hesiod tells us that his father emigrated from Aeolian Cyme, on the coast of Asia Minor, to the village of Ascra in Boeotia, not only to escape poverty but also because he was "desirous of a good life" (*WD* 634). It is clear that it was not just necessity that impelled Greek-speakers to seek new homes overseas but also the realization that better opportunities awaited them there. That cultivatable land was included among these opportunities can hardly be doubted but there are also indications that commercial interests were not insignificant. This is most obviously the case with the port of trade that Greek merchants set up at Naucratis, in the western Nile delta, in the last quarter of the seventh century (see pp. 242–7), but evidence from an industrial complex on the Mezzavia ridge at Pithecusae suggests that the early occupants of the site were processing and perhaps also extracting iron ores from the island of Elba. The finished products, which certainly included fibulae, were probably designed for markets in the east where they could be exchanged for the Levantine luxury goods found in some of the tombs at Pithecusae. It is not that the Greeks lacked iron ore deposits back in the Aegean but it has been suggested that wealth generated from within the home community was, in this period, under an obligation to be redistributed to members of that community. Wealth generated overseas, on the other hand, was not subject to the same redistributive expectations, allowing for a considerable accumulation of capital. Presumably, émigrés were not held responsible either for the failings of their prodigal elder brothers.

Many of the sites in the west certainly offered vast agricultural resources – Leontini, Syracuse, Sybaris, and Metapontum in particular. But other sites, such as Naxos and Megara Hyblaea, are not blessed with vast territories and in the case of Zancle and Rhegium, strategically located either side of the Straits of Messina, it is clear that the chief preoccupation was with shipping routes rather than the hinterland. The underplaying, in the recent literature, of commercial motivations – alongside subsistence demands – as a key catalyst for colonization is probably due to two factors. In the first place, the earlier assumption that there was "trade before the flag" has been challenged on the grounds that such a conception owed more to British imperial policies than it did to the world of Greek settlements overseas. In the second, the work of Moses Finley in particular has popularized the view that the ancient economy was based primarily on agriculture and that commercial interests were of comparatively minor significance (see pp. 236–7). But recent reappraisals suggest that the ancient economy was not quite as "primitive" as Finley believed, while the notion of there being "trade before the flag" is not vitiated because there was no trade but because there was – at least initially – no flag. When we examine the evidence, unencumbered by presuppositions derived from later colonial activity, the picture that emerges is one of a less official, less formal, and more haphazard movement of various peoples for various reasons over a number of generations – in short, of a process that was not so qualitatively different from those earlier movements that followed the collapse of the Mycenaean palaces.

FURTHER READING

See generally R. Osborne, "Early Greek colonization? The nature of Greek settlement in the west," in Fisher and van Wees 1998, 251–69. Dorian migration as a type of colonial expedition: Malkin 1994, 15–45.

Foundations in Asia Minor: Lemos 2002, 148, 182, 197–200, 211–12. Euboeans in Chalcidice: A. M. Snodgrass, "The Euboeans in Macedonia: A new precedent for westward expansion," in d'Agostino and Ridgway 1994, 87–93. For a reaction: J. K. Papadopoulos, "Euboeans in Macedonia? A Closer look," *Oxford Journal of Archaeology* 15 (1996), 151–81. Al Mina: Boardman 1999, 38–46, 270–5; J. K. Papadopoulos, "Phantom Euboeans," *Journal of Mediterranean Archaeology* 10 (1997), 191–219. Pithecusae: Ridgway 1992; B. d'Agostino, "Euboean colonization in the Gulf of Naples," in Tsetskhladze 1999, 207–27. *Emporia* and *apoikiai*: J.-P. Wilson, "The nature of Greek overseas settlements in the Archaic period: *emporion* or *apoikia*," in Mitchell and Rhodes 1997, 199–207. For literary accounts of colonization: A. J.

Graham, "The colonial expansion of Greece," *Cambridge Ancient History*, vol. 3.3, 2nd edn. (Cambridge, 1982), 83–162. For the archaeological evidence: Boardman 1999.

Fifth-century colonies: Graham 1983, 40–68. Achaean colonization: C. Morgan and J. M. Hall, "Achaian *poleis* and Achaian colonisation," in Hansen 1996, 164–232. Authenticity of Cyrene decree: A. J. Graham, "The authenticity of the ORKIΩN TΩN OIKISTHRΩN of Cyrene," *Journal of Hellenic Studies* 80 (1960), 94–111; Osborne 1996, 13–15 is more skeptical. For the transmission of memory through the founder's cult: Dunbabin 1948, 11; Malkin 1987, 189; I. Malkin, "Exploring the validity of the concept of 'foundation': A visit to Megara Hyblaia," in Gorman and Robinson 2002, 195–224. Generational dating of colonial foundations: van Compernelle 1959; Miller 1970.

Ceramic chronologies: I. Morris, "The absolute chronology of the Greek colonies in Sicily," *Acta Archaeologica* 67 (1996), 51–9. Selinus: Snodgrass 1987, 54–6. Megara Hyblaea: Vallet, Villard, and Auberson 1976; de Angelis 2003, 17–39; Gras, Tréziny, and Broise 2004. "Teleological thinking": F. de Polignac, "L'installation des dieux et la genèse des cités en Grèce d'Occident, une question resolue? Retour à Mégara Hyblaea," in *La colonisation grecque en Méditerranée occidentale*. Collection de l'École Française de Rome 251 (Rome, 1999), 209–30. "Achaean" pottery: J. K. Papadopoulos, "Magna Achaea: Akhaian Late Geometric and Archaic pottery in South Italy and Sicily," *Hesperia* 70 (2001), 373–460.

Taras: M. Nafissi, "From Sparta to Taras: *Nomima, ktiseis* and relationships between colony and mother city," in Hodkinson and Powell 1999, 245–72.

Motivations for colonization: G. C. Cawkwell, "Early colonisation," *Classical Quarterly* 42 (1992), 289–303. Aegina: Figueira 1981, 22–64. Commercial motives: Tandy 1997, 59–83.

6

The Changing Nature of Authority

Charting the Genesis of the State

It was argued in chapter 4 that, from the archaeological point of view, the localization of dedicated political and administrative functions rarely predates the seventh century, while the reconstruction, proposed in chapter 5, would suggest that state organization remained comparatively underdeveloped at the time of the eighth-century settlements in the west. This, however, begs the question as to how one defines a "state." Indeed, it is sometimes argued that the Greek *polis* was actually a state*less* society. Firstly, it is reasoned, the notion of a state as an "abstract public power above both ruler and ruled" – a definition popularized by Thomas Hobbes in his *Leviathan* of 1651 – does not seem to apply to the Greek *polis*, which was simply identified with its citizens. Secondly, the *polis* lacked the coercive apparatus or "monopoly of legitimate violence" that Max Weber saw as a defining characteristic of the modern state, preferring to resort instead to self-help and self-defense. Thirdly, the fact that the *polis* lacked a standing army should suggest a certain nonchalance with regard to external sovereignty – another defining feature of the state.

The reasoning is not entirely unimpeachable. In the first place, the modern state may often be identified with the citizen body as much as with the institutions by which it is governed, while there are hints in the literary sources that the Greeks did sometimes view the *polis* as an abstract public power above the citizens. Thus, Thucydides (8.72.1) describes how, after the oligarchic coup at Athens in 411, the new government "sent ten men to Samos to reassure the camp and to show them that the oligarchy had not been established to the detriment of the *polis* and of its citizens." In the second place, although self-help certainly existed in the Greek world for crimes such as adultery, nocturnal burglary, treason, and violation of exile, similar legal provisions also continued in force in European states as late as the nineteenth century, while literary attestations of public prisons and references to the public administration of capital punishment might lead one to suppose that the *polis* did have a certain monopoly of force. In the third place, *poleis* such as Athens, Sparta, Thebes, and Argos – at least in the Classical period – do seem to have possessed standing armies comparable to those of many European states in the seventeenth and eighteenth centuries.

The concept of the "stateless society" was formulated by the anthropologists Meyer Fortes and Edward Evans-Pritchard in their research into political systems in Africa: both the Tallensi and the Nuer were categorized as such. But Fortes and Evans-Pritchard contrasted their stateless society not with Hobbes' definition of the Early Modern State, but with what they termed a "primitive state," as represented by the Zulu or the Bayankole. The features that, for them, distinguished a primitive state from a stateless society were a centralized authority with administrative and judicial institutions and cleavages of wealth, privilege, and status, corresponding to the distribution of power and authority. It should be clear that the Greek *polis* corresponded more to the primitive state than to the stateless society and, in the chapters that follow, we will consider the emergence of such characteristic features, beginning with the evidence for the nature of leadership and authority in the early Archaic period.

Kings or "Big-Men"?

In later times, the Athenians imagined that their earliest ancestors had been ruled by kings. According to Pausanias (1.2.6), hereditary succession was not always practiced: Cecrops succeeded his father-in-law, Aktaios, presumably because the latter had no male heir, while both Amphiktyon and Erichthonius seized the kingship by force. Pausanias clearly assumes, however, that the hereditary principle should have been the norm and later (1.5.3) recounts how, from Erichthonius through Pandion, Erechtheus, and Cecrops II to Pandion II, son succeeded father. The testimony is late, but it is broadly consistent with the information provided in the third-century Parian Marble (A1–16) and may ultimately derive from the genealogical works of Hellanicus of Mytilene in the later fifth century. Nor were the Athenians unique in imagining their earliest rulers to have been hereditary kings. Diodorus of Sicily (fr. 7.9.2–6) – probably following the fourth-century historian Ephorus – states that son succeeded father as king of Corinth for 447 years from the Heraclid capture of the city down to the seizure of the tyranny by Cypselus (see below). Aristotle (*Pol.* 4.10.10) certainly seems to take it for granted that monarchies preceded aristocracies.

The word that ancient authors use to describe such kings is *basileis* (singular: *basileus*). By the Classical period, *basileus* could mean one of three things. In the first place, it designated a magistrate, normally appointed on an annual basis. At Athens, for example, the *basileus* was the second-highest ranking of the nine archons, charged with administering "all the traditional sacrifices"

(Aristotle, *AC* 57.1). A decree, dated ca. 450 and regulating relations between Argos and the Cretan communities of Cnossus and Tylissos, refers to the magistracy of a *basileus* named Melantas at Argos (ML 42 = Fornara 89), while in an inscription from Chios, dated a little more than a century earlier (ML 8 = Fornara 19), an official named the *basileus* is juxtaposed with another called the *dêmarkhos* ("leader of the people"). In the second place, the term was frequently used in reference to monarchs of non-Greek peoples. The most obvious example that springs to mind is the Persian king, who was called simply *basileus* (without the definite article). Finally, the term is, as we have seen, employed to denote those mythical rulers of Greek regions such as Attica, Corinthia, and the Argolid. Is this latter usage, however, sufficient reason to suppose that hereditary kingship had once been widespread in Greece?

It is generally agreed that the Greek word *basileus* is the linguistic descendant of a term *pa-si-re-u* (or *qa-si-re-u*) that is attested in the Linear B tablets. There, however, it designates a fairly low-ranking local official rather than a supreme monarch, which is instead rendered by *wa-na-ka* – *(w)anax* in Classical Greek. The tablets from Pylos, for example, imply that somewhere between nine and twelve *basileis* were part of the kingdom's administrative bureaucracy. Were we to accept the notion of hereditary kingship in the early Archaic period, we would have to assume that the term *basileus*, having originally denoted a local administrator, then came to designate a more powerful, hereditary monarch *before* eventually coming to be used in a more restrictive sense again to indicate an appointed official with limited tenure of office. On any count, that is a rather unlikely sequence of events, which is why – for all the historical problems involved (pp. 24–6) – scholars have turned to the Homeric epics.

In the *Odyssey*, there are occasions where individuals seem to be described as rulers of populations: Odysseus' comrades ask Antiphates' daughter who the *basileus* of the Laestrygones is (10.110), while Pheidon is named as the *basileus* of the Thesprotians (14.316; 19.287) and Phaidimos the *basileus* of the Sidonians (15.118); in the *Iliad*, Rhesos is named as king of the Thracians (10.435). What is interesting is that all these cases concern populations that were considered either non-Hellenic (the Laestrygones, Sidonians, and Thracians) or something less than Hellenic (the Thesprotians) – a usage that, in some senses, anticipates the application of the term to non-Greek sovereigns in the Classical period. On the Greek side, we do hear of *basileis* of the Argives (e.g. *Il.* 10.195) and of the Achaeans (24.404), but both these names are used virtually synonymously to designate the collective forces that marched on Troy rather than specific populations rooted in particular regions. Among the Achaeans, only Agamemnon is explicitly named as king *of* anything, and in this case it is not of a population but of a place – "Mycenae, rich in gold" (*Il.* 7.180; 11.46). Other heroes, such as Achilles (1.331) or Diomedes and Odysseus (14.379–80), are simply nominated *basileis* without any further specification. Similarly, in the *Catalogue of Ships*, the Achaean heroes may sometimes be described as *arkhoi* ("leaders") of the contingents that they bring to

Troy (e.g. *Il.* 2.541, 2.685), but never as *basileis*. Agamemnon does merit the title *anax* (e.g. *Il.* 1.172), which might have suggested a more regal status were it not for the fact that the term is also applied to Aeneas (5.311) and Polydamas (15.453–4), neither of whom was a sovereign ruler.

In fact, there are three reasons why it is difficult to view Homeric *basileis* as kings in any sense we would understand today. Firstly, *basileus* appears to be a relative, rather than an absolute, term. In the *Iliad* (9.69), Nestor describes Agamemnon as *basileutatos* ("the most *basileus*") while Agamemnon himself notes that he is *basileuteros* ("more of a *basileus*") than Achilles (9.160). Some have inferred from this that Achilles belongs to a more junior cadre of princes, subordinated to a paramount ruler, Agamemnon, but a little later, Achilles refuses Agamemnon's offer of his daughter's hand in marriage and bids him to "choose another of the Achaeans who is more similar to himself and more of a *basileus*" (9.391–92). This would seem to imply that *basileus* designates a personal authority that is subject to various gradations rather than a formally constituted office. Secondly, we often hear of a plurality of *basileis*. One of Penelope's suitors, Antinous, points out that there are "many other *basileis* of the Achaeans in sea-girt Ithaca, both young and old" (*Od.* 1.394–95) and Alcinous notes that the Phaeacians have "twelve distinguished *basileis* who bear sway as leaders in the region, and I myself am the thirteenth" (8.390–91). Thirdly, the principle of hereditary succession, which would seem to be a fundamental characteristic of kingship as we understand it, is by no means guaranteed in the Homeric world. Odysseus is recognized as a *basileus* on Ithaca, but his father, Laertes, is still alive. Nor is there any certitude that his son, Telemachus, will succeed him to royal office should news of his demise be confirmed. When, in the *Odyssey*, Telemachus summons the assembly, we are told that the elders make way for him as he sits in the seat of his father (2.14) but he is utterly powerless at persuading – let alone ordering – his mother's suitors to abstain from consuming the entire wealth of his house. Nor can it be accidental that the suitors Antinous and Eurymakhos are both described as *basileis* (18.64–65; 24.179).

It is for these reasons that some historians have preferred to view Homeric *basileis* not so much as hereditary monarchs but as what the anthropologist Marshall Sahlins has termed "big-men." Sahlins was concerned with comparing political communities and structures of leadership in Melanesia and Polynesia. In the Polynesian model, a pyramidal political system is dominated by "chiefs" who occupy pre-existing and suprapersonal positions of leadership where power and status attach to the office itself rather than the personality who holds office. In the Melanesian model, by contrast, autonomous kinship-residential groups are dominated by "big-men" whose authority is more personal or charismatic rather than derived from any pre-existing office. "Big-men" emerge as a result of competition, achieving authority through public persuasion and the demonstration of skills such as magical powers, rhetoric, courage, and especially the amassment and redistribution of goods. For support, they depend initially on followers, household, and closest relatives, but then incorporate within this extended family various "strays" who, through this act of calculated generosity, are placed in a position of obligation to their patron. Because authority is vested in the person of the individual, such systems are inherently unstable and are often undermined by the death of the "big-man."

It is important to note that the distinction between "big-men" and "chiefs" is not simply typological. When Sahlins compared the political systems of Melanesia and Polynesia, he was heavily influenced by the theories of cultural evolution that had been developed by Elman Service and Morton Fried. Service believed that most human societies had passed through four evolutionary stages, characterized by different subsistence strategies, which he named "band," "tribe," "chiefdom," and "state." The band was constituted by relatively small, patrilineally-organized groups of families engaged in hunting and gathering. "Tribe" denotes a larger, united group of communities, held together by confraternal relationships, that practices simple agriculture or pastoral nomadism. In a chiefdom, a common population is united under the leadership of a chief who stands at the head of a redistributive economic system. The state, on the other hand, is a larger polity with a centralized bureaucracy that is engaged in large-scale agriculture and organized along territorial rather than kinship lines. Service's "bands" and "tribes" conform roughly with what Fried calls "egalitarian societies." In such societies, leadership is weak because all available statuses are equal and can therefore technically be occupied by anybody. In "ranked societies," by contrast, there are fewer status positions, meaning that individuals have to compete for leadership, while in "stratified societies" there is unequal access to available resources, resulting in institutionally-complex and centralized structures of domination. For purposes of comparison, Service's chiefdoms would straddle the transition between Fried's "ranked" and "stratified" societies, while Sahlins' evolution of "big-men" into "chiefs" should normally take place within a "ranked" society.

Theories of cultural evolution are not currently very fashionable. In particular, criticism has been leveled against the uniformity, unidirectionality, and teleological inevitability that they seem to presuppose. Certainly, it is patent that the political system that existed in Late Bronze Age Greece was far more complex than anything that would be seen in the centuries immediately following. There is, however, another respect in which the situation in Archaic Greece seems to have run directly counter to one of the important presuppositions of evolutionist theory. Both Service and Fried believed that the cohesion of early societies was based on kinship bonds and that, as societies became larger and institutionally more complex, such bonds weakened and were replaced by notions of territoriality. This idea has a long pedigree: in his *Ancient Law* of 1861, the English jurist and anthropologist Henry Sumner Maine argued that it was only as population groups became more sedentary that territoriality began to replace kinship as a principle of social organization. It is not at all clear, however, that this was the Greek experience.

We are poorly informed as to the situation in the Late Bronze Age, but there is precious little evidence for the importance of kinship as an organizing

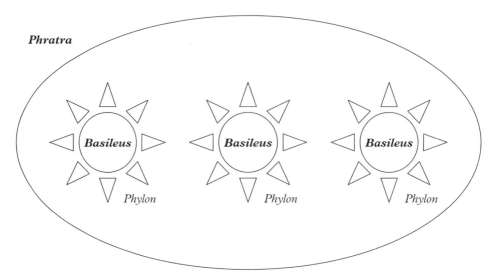

Figure 6.1   The relationship of *phyla* to the *phratra* in the Homeric epics

principle in Dark Age society. It is surely significant that, in the Homeric epics, the words *etês* ("kinsman") and *hetairos* ("companion") derive from the same Indo-European root – namely *swe-, meaning "one's own" – thus blurring the distinction between friends, companions, and kin. In the *Iliad* and *Odyssey*, the word *phylon* (plural: *phyla*) seems to denote a small group of followers united around a local leader, while the term *phratra* (plural: *phratrai*) represents an aggregative association of *phyla* (Figure 6.1). Certainly, when Nestor advises Agamemnon to "separate the men by *phyla* and by *phratrai*, so that *phratra* may help *phratra* and *phyla* may help *phyla*" (*Il.* 2.362–63), the employment of the plural, *phyla*, might suggest that they are smaller units than the *phratrai*. This seems to imply that social organization in the Homeric epics is structured around locality rather than kinship and is fully compatible with the conclusions reached in chapter 4 concerning the primacy and centrality of place within the conception of the *polis*. It also allows us to understand better why Hesiod (*WD* 344–5) should counsel Perses to rely upon neighbors rather than kinsmen by marriage – let alone genuine blood relations, who are not even mentioned.

There is, however, more to it than this. The term *phratra*, notwithstanding its adoption to designate an aggregate of *phyla*, does in fact have connotations of kinship (it is related to Latin *frater*, or "brother"). Furthermore, when we meet the term again in texts and inscriptions of the Classical period, it is as a formal subdivision of the *phylê* (plural: *phylai*) – a feminized form of the now redundant term *phylon*, indicating one of the principal subdivisions or "tribes" of the citizen body. An inscription from Argos, probably to be dated to the middle of the fifth century, lists twelve groups that have been identified as the

Temenidai
Dmasippidai
Heraieis
Sophylidai
Wariadai
Daîphonteis
Eualkidai
Diwonysioi
Melanippidai
Heraieis?
Lykotadai
Naupliadai

Figure 6.2   The twelve constituent *phratriai* of the *phylê* of the Hyrnathioi at Argos in the mid-fifth century

phratrai that constituted the *phylê* of the Hyrnathioi (Figure 6.2). What is interesting is that the suffixes adopted to indicate membership of a phratry are derived from the terminology of descent: so, for example, the Temenidai are, literally speaking, "the descendants of Temenos," the Heraclid who is supposed to have led the Dorians in their conquest of Argos. This is no less true at the level of the *phylê*: by the fourth century, members of the Athenian tribe of Antiokhis referred to themselves as Antiokhidai – descendants of Heracles' son Antiokhos, whose cult they celebrated. But there was nothing "primordial" about the Athenian *phylai* – they were the creations of Cleisthenes at the end of the sixth century (see pp. 212–13) – and, as we have already seen (pp. 47–8), earlier subdivisions of the citizen body into *phylai* can hardly predate the emergence of the *polis*. In other words, while cultural evolutionist theory would predict a shift from kinship to residence as the fundamental organizing principle of society, the Greek case appears to witness a shift from residence to kinship, even if the kinship that was recognized was more imaginary and artificial than real.

Notwithstanding these provisos, there are some interesting parallels between Sahlins' "big-men" and Homeric *basileis*. Like "big-men," Homeric heroes do not derive their authority from any office that they hold. Instead, they achieve and maintain their status and authority through martial prowess, provision of feasts, display of wealth, and acts of calculated generosity that place others under an obligation to be *therapontes* or "retainers." The example of Phoenix, welcomed as a fugitive into the household of Achilles' father, Peleus, and given both wealth and dominion by his host (*Il.* 9.478–84), is a case in point. Like "big-men," Homeric *basileis* lack true power, in the sense of controlling the sources and distribution of wealth. Rather, we are told on several occasions that the leader enjoys usufruct of agricultural land (*temenos*) that has been awarded to him by the *laos* or community. Phoenix, for example, recounts to Achilles the story of the Aetolian hero Meleager, promised an estate of arable land and a vineyard by the elders of Calydon if he would help defend the city against the Curetes (9.574–80). And like "big-men," Homeric leaders are not always capable of applying punitive measures to enforce obedience: the reason such a small contingent follows Nireus from Syme is because he is "weak" (2.671–75). In many ways, then, the relationship between the Homeric *basileus* and his followers is one based on reciprocity.

Attempts have been made to identify this sort of authority in the material record. Some settlements, such as Athens, Argos, and Cnossus, seem to have been "stable," in the sense that they were continuously occupied throughout the Dark Age, whereas others – e.g. Dhonoussa, Zagora, Nikhoria, or Emborio – were "unstable," being discontinuously occupied and often abandoned early in the Archaic period. It is in these "unstable" settlements that the "big-man" model may be most appropriate. At Lefkandi, seemingly unoccupied between ca. 1100 and ca. 950 and apparently abandoned ca. 700 after more than a century of decline, the monumental building in the Toumba cemetery could have served as a feasting-hall and as the residence of the community's "big-man." When he died, some time in the first half of the tenth century, the house with which he was so closely associated would have been demolished and buried beneath a massive earth tumulus, thus visibly symbolizing the collapse of his personal authority and prestige (see pp. 62–3). At Nikhoria, a larger structure (Unit IV–1), around which the tenth-century houses cluster, has been identified as the residence of a "big-man," while a similar function has been proposed for an apsidal building, constructed ca. 900 above the ruins of a Mycenaean palatial-like structure at Koukounaries.

As noted earlier (p. 62), the identification of the Lefkandi Toumba building as a house is not uncontroversial and it is starting to look as if renewed excavations at Xeropolis may correct the impression of settlement discontinuity there. Either way, the comparison between Lefkandi, on the one hand, and Koukounaries and Nikhoria, on the other, is not entirely valid. It is widely agreed that the Toumba building was constructed, occupied (if at all), and demolished within a relatively short period of time – at most, half a century and probably considerably less. At Koukounaries, the evidence is more ambiguous: the apsidal building was succeeded, in the eighth century, by a rectangular *megaron*, built on top of it, that continued to be occupied into the second quarter of the seventh century. Whether this represents a case of continuity across several generations is difficult to determine. Similar doubts hold at Nikhoria, where Unit IV–1, occupied for at least a century and possibly longer, was succeeded early in the eighth century by Unit IV–5, which abuts on it. In other words, it is entirely conceivable that political authority was exercised more continuously and for a longer period of time at both Koukounaries and Nikhoria, even though both would qualify as "unstable" settlements.

In fact, if we turn back to the Homeric evidence, we find that the question of political authority is far from straightforward. Although hereditary succession is not guaranteed in the epics, that does not mean that the principle might not exist. In the second book of the *Iliad*, we are told that Agamemnon's scepter – the visible symbol of his authority – had been made by the god

Hephaestus for Zeus, and that Zeus had given it to Hermes who, in turn, had presented it to Pelops. From there it had been transmitted from father to son, through Atreus and Thyestes to Agamemnon (2.100–108). The principal point behind recounting the scepter's "genealogy" is, as Nestor notes earlier (1.277–79), to demonstrate that Agamemnon's authority is greater than that of other *basileis* because it is derived ultimately from Zeus, but it is hard to ignore the hereditary implications of the scepter's transmission. Attention is also given to heredity in the *Odyssey* (4.62–64), when Menelaus tells Telemachus and Peisistratos that their demeanor betrays their descent from "god-reared, sceptre-bearing *basileis*." Along similar lines, Hesiod's description (*Th.* 80–84) of how the muses honor "*basileis* fostered by Zeus" and "look over him when he is born and pour sweet dew upon his tongue so that honeyed words stream forth from his mouth" seems to imply a fairly widespread belief that recruitment for supreme authority might be through birth.

The Homeric *basileis* are not, then, kings in the conventional sense but, while they bear some striking resemblances to "big-men," there are other features that would suggest that they are also sometimes imagined more as chieftains, occupying a formally constituted – and ideally inherited – office. One might be tempted to suppose that the society depicted by Homer is a ranked society, where the personal authority wielded by "big-men" is in the process of being transferred into a more traditional authority, occupied by hereditary chieftains. Alternatively, it might be preferable to regard the different expressions of political authority as simply typological distinctions rather than successive steps on a single evolutionary trajectory. What is far less visible in the epics, however, is evidence for the existence of a fully stratified society.

The Emergence of an Aristocracy

It is sometimes supposed that the Homeric *basileis* constitute an aristocracy. Certainly, the values that Homeric heroes hold dear – honor, status, athletic and martial prowess – were those that we find extolled later by elitist poets. From a political anthropological view, however, an aristocracy is defined not by the symbols through which it communicates its distinctiveness but by the position it holds and the influence it exerts within structures of power. As a ruling "class," rather than an ensemble of powerful individuals, the emergence of an aristocracy presupposes basic divisions of wealth and labor as well as a formalization of ascribed offices with prescribed competences – something, in other words, along the lines of Fortes' and Evans-Pritchard's "primitive state." The emergence of an aristocracy can be considered symptomatic of the rise of a state.

Collectively, whether engaging in conviviality at feasts, competing with one another at funeral games or fighting alongside each other in combat, the Homeric *basileis* may well resemble an aristocracy. But "Achaea" in the epics is not a unified state and, within their home communities, the *basileis* are simply not numerous enough to constitute a true aristocratic class. On a conservative estimate, elites would have accounted for around 10 percent of the population of the *polis* in the Late Archaic and Early Classical periods. It is hard to imagine that Scheria, ruled over by thirteen *basileis* (*Od.* 8.390–91), had an adult male population of little more than a hundred. Even taking into account married partners and kin, the size of the ruling body on the island can hardly qualify as an aristocracy.

This picture is hardly contradicted by the archaeological evidence. A sober estimate for the population of eighth-century Eretria is likely to be in the range of 1,000–2,000 (Figure 4.1), in which case the sixteen wealthy burials at the West Gate, which span more than a generation (pp. 1–2), are more reasonably those of a powerful family than of a ruling class. A late eighth-century cist grave (Tomb 45), 3 meters in length and found near the Classical Odeion in the southern sector of Argos, is probably a good candidate for the tomb of a *basileus*. The male occupant was accompanied by costly grave goods, including bronze and gold rings, two iron axes, twelve *obeloi* or iron spits (perhaps a form of proto-currency: see pp. 251–2), two fire-dogs, and – most significantly – a bronze cuirass and helmet. It should be stressed, though, that of the some one hundred eighth-century graves excavated at Argos, Tomb 45 is without parallel. A bronze helmet, apparently manufactured by the same workshop, was found in a second grave in the Stavropoulos plot, but this is located more than a kilometer to the northeast. In all likelihood, it represents the burial of a *basileus* of another small community. A third burial, in which the deceased was accompanied by a bronze helmet, two spearheads, and six iron *obeloi*, has been found near to the second in the Theodoropoulos plot but is probably, to judge from associated pottery, a generation older. Two other burials contain *obeloi* – one is roughly contemporary with, and near to, Tomb 45; the other is located in an entirely different part of the city, where five further graves, spanning a period of approximately one century, contain spearheads, swords, or daggers. These are mostly isolated occurrences – there is no evidence at Argos for aristocratic cemeteries – and reinforce the impression that eighth-century Greece was inhabited by leaders and followers rather than by aristocrats and commoners. It is surely no accident that in Hesiod's *Theogony*, *basileis* are juxtaposed directly with the *laoi* (e.g. 88, 429–30), with no mention of an intervening aristocratic class.

Nevertheless, the attestation of the plural form *basileis* in the *Odyssey*, *Theogony*, and *Works and Days* does seem to represent an evolutionary stage beyond a simple chiefdom. The most reasonable interpretation is that this is a consequence of the newly enlarged communities that the archaeological record attests for the eighth century (p. 78). The aggregation of formerly independent social groups would inevitably have raised the question as to how political authority should be exercised in the larger community. Two alternatives were possible: one *basileus* might yield – whether voluntarily or under compulsion – to the authority of another or both might agree to a "contract" whereby power was shared. The latter would seem to be the situation envisaged on Scheria, where Alcinous describes himself as one of thirteen *basileis*. The former is reflected in the legend, preserved by Conon (fr. 44), which told how the Neleid Phitres ceded the rule of Miletus to his cousin, Leodamas, after unsuccessfully challenging him to a contest in which both agreed to wage war against an enemy of the city.

It is possible that both alternatives were pursued at Sparta. One of the peculiarities of the Spartan political system was not only that it was ruled by hereditary monarchs down to as late as the third century but that there were two kings that ruled concurrently (later authors were to compare the Spartan "dyarchy" with the twin consulate at Rome). The two Spartan royal houses were known as the Agiadai and the Eurypontidai and, already by the time of Tyrtaeus (fr. 11), both traced their descent back to the hero Heracles. By the early fifth century, according to Herodotus (7.204; 8.131), both the Agiad king Leonidas and the Eurypontid king Leotychidas II reckoned themselves in the twentieth generation after Heracles. The first king of whose historical existence we can be fairly sure is the Eurypontid Theopompus, credited by Tyrtaeus (fr. 5) with the conquest of Messenia, probably towards the end of the eighth century or in the early decades of the succeeding century (pp. 172–3). Plutarch (*Lyc.* 6) seems to imply that Tyrtaeus had also named the Agiad king Polydoros as Theopompus' royal colleague. It is possible that it was Polydoros' great-grandfather, Arkhelaos, and Theopompus' grandfather, Kharilaos, who were the first kings to extend Spartan hegemony over Laconia, but since Pausanias (3.2.5), our principal source for these early events, also attributes the establishment of the Spartan kingship to Prokles and Eurysthenes in the fifth generation after Heracles, caution is warranted. Certainly some of the names of the early kings – especially in the Eurypontid branch – are suspicious. The name of Prytanis, supposedly the third Eurypontid king, derives from a common title for a magistrate while the name of his successor, Eunomos, is cognate with the Greek word *eunomia* ("good order"), which was to be a catch-phrase or slogan among sixth-century reformers.

What is interesting for our current purposes is how the Spartan dyarchy may have arisen. As we have seen (p. 75), Sparta was formed from the original union of four villages – Pitana, Mesoa, Kynosoura, and Limnai. By Pausanias' day, the Eurypontid burial ground was located at Mesoa (3.12.8), while that of the Agiads was at Pitana (3.14.2). It is a reasonable inference that there had existed long-standing and traditional links between the two royal houses and these villages and that the dyarchy arose when the *basileis* of Pitana and Mesoa agreed to share authority over the newly unified community rather than yield to one another. If Limnai and Kynosoura also had their own *basileis*, we might assume that it was this latter option that they exercised. It may not be accidental that Tyrtaeus (frs. 4, 5) should use the word *basileis* to describe the Spartan kings – especially since in official documents (see p. 184), they seem to have been called the *arkhagêtai*, or "supreme leaders."

Eventually, with the extension of authority to a number of *basileis* and, presumably, the recruitment of family-members and retainers to the more

specialized offices that larger and more complex societies demanded, an aristocracy emerged. A telling indication for this development is the appearance of
elitist terminology denoting a fairly broad-based group of "insiders" and an
even wider group of the excluded. The most common terms that appear in
Archaic poetry are *kaloi* ("beautiful" or "fair"), *agathoi* ("good"), and *esthloi*
("good" or "brave"), together with their opposites, *kakoi* ("ugly" or "bad")
and *deiloi* ("cowardly" or "wretched"). The poetry attributed to Theognis is
rife with this vocabulary. Promoting himself as a mouthpiece for the *agathoi*
(28), the poet urges his addressee, Kyrnos, not to keep company with the
kakoi but to eat, drink, and sit with the *agathoi* since it is from the *esthloi* that
one will learn noble things (31–5). The common people (*dêmos*), on the other
hand, should be trampled upon, jabbed with sharp goads, and made to bear
painful yokes around their necks (847–50). The motivation for this un_charit-
able vitriol seems to be the poet's conviction that class distinctions have been
eroded. Birth (*genos*) has been compromised by intermarriage between *esthloi*
and *kakoi* (183–92). As a result, those who formerly knew nothing about
justice or laws but wore tattered goatskins and lived outside the *polis* have now
become *agathoi* while those who were once *esthloi* are now *deiloi* (53).

It has recently been argued that the lines that are drawn in the *Theognidea*
are reflective not of true socioeconomic divisions but of violent competition
among different elite factions. Yet this is to ignore the fact that the terminology employed in the poetry attributed to Theognis is thoroughly conventional
in Archaic poetry in general and appears in specific contexts that do seem to
suggest class divisions. When Solon observes that many *kakoi* are wealthy
while many *agathoi* are poor (fr. 15), one could conceivably argue that he is
charting the volatile fortunes of elite factions. But when he writes that he was
not minded to share the rich land of Attica equally between *esthloi* and *kakoi*
(fr. 34), it is clear that he is thinking of social and economic differences and a
similar conclusion would seem to arise from his claim that he wrote laws for
kakos and *agathos* alike (fr. 36). Solon's principal role was to serve as a medi-
ator – he describes himself as a "boundary marker in no-man's land" (fr. 37)
– yet the two constituencies between which he mediated were not elite factions
but the common people (*dêmos*) and its leaders (*hêgemones*). Similar terminology is present in the poetry of Alcaeus, where notions of birth would appear to
be intrinsic to inclusion among the ranks of the nobles. Though his testimony
is undoubtedly prejudiced (see below), Alcaeus claims that Pittacus, the "base-
born" (*kakopatridas*) tyrant of Mytilene (fr. 348), rose to prominence only by
marrying into the noble family of the Penthilidai (fr. 70).

Such class-based terminology is far less evident in our earliest literary sources.
In the *Iliad*, Diomedes' affirmation that he is not a *kakos* by birth (14.216)
would seem to betray notions of belonging to a class based on birth, but the
terms *esthlos* and *kakos* in the epic generally revolve around evaluations of
bravery and cowardice. Thus, Achilles notes that those who fight get the same
respect as those who sit at home and that therefore the *kakos* and the *esthlos*
are esteemed with equal honor (9.319). Admittedly, the quality of bravery

was to be of paramount importance to elite identity but it is not immediately apparent that bravery is synonymous with noble birth. Indeed, the already cited advice that Nestor gives to Agamemnon suggests otherwise: by grouping his men according to *phyla* and *phratrai*, Agamemnon will discover which of the leaders (*hêgemones*) and which of the masses (*laoi*) is either *kakos* or *esthlos* (2.365–66). The exercise loses its point if a strict correlation is imagined between, on the one hand, the *hêgemones* and *esthloi* and, on the other, the *laoi* and *kakoi*.

The terms *esthloi* and *kakoi* do begin to display some incipient socioeconomic connotations in the *Odyssey*. When Menelaus recognizes Telemachus and Peisistratos as descendants of "god-reared, sceptre-bearing *basileis*," he adds that they are clearly not born of *kakoi* (6.63–64). Other references are more ambiguous, but Alcinous' observation that "everybody has a name, be he *kakos* or *esthlos*" (8.553) or Penelope's complaint that the suitors "honour nobody, *kakos* or *esthlos*" (23.66), could certainly support a socioeconomic interpretation. Similarly vague are the occurrences in *Works and Days*. Hesiod's injunction to avoid consorting with *kakoi* or quarreling with *esthloi* (716) or his warning that pride is an evil for both the *deilos* and the *esthlos* (214–15) could – but do not necessarily have to – be interpreted in a socioeconomic sense. Although the Homeric and Hesiodic poems cannot provide us with the sort of chronological "fix" we might want, they do not contradict the impression that significant class-based cleavages within society were weakly developed in the eighth century and only become more prominent from the seventh century onwards. That impression finds further support when we turn to the evidence for early laws.

Laws and Institutions

In the second book of the *Politics*, Aristotle distinguishes between those individuals in the past who framed laws (*nomoi*) and those who both framed laws and created constitutions (*politeiai*). To the former category belong Zaleucus of Epizephyrian Locri, Charondas of Catana, Philolaos of Corinth who legislated for the Thebans, Dracon of Athens, Pittacus of Mytilene, and Andromadas of Rhegium, who gave laws to the Chalcidian populations of Thrace. Included in the latter category are Solon of Athens and Lycurgus of Sparta (2.9). Aristotle goes on to provide some details concerning some of the laws that were proposed by these individuals. Philolaos, for example, is supposed to have passed legislation limiting the size of families in order to preserve the integrity of estates, while Pittacus decreed that offenses committed while under the influence of alcohol should carry a harsher penalty. As for the code of Charondas, "there is nothing special save for the suits against those who perjure themselves" (2.9.8). For Aristotle, Solon's most important contribution to the Athenian constitution was the establishment of the jury-courts (2.9.2–3), but for later authors Solon was the architect of a comprehensive law-code. Diogenes

Document 6.1

Our *polis* will never be destroyed by the destiny of Zeus or the will of the blessed immortal gods; for such a great-hearted overseer, Pallas Athena, born of a mighty father, holds her hands over it. But the citizens themselves, through their foolishness and being persuaded by material greed, want to destroy a great *polis*, and the mind of the leaders of the *dêmos* is unjust, and they are ready to suffer much pain for their great violence. They do not understand how to curb excess nor to organize peacefully the celebrations of the feast that is at hand, but they grow wealthy, yielding to unjust deeds; sparing neither sacred nor public property, they steal rapaciously, this one from here, that one from there, nor do they pay heed to the solemn foundations of Justice, who silently perceives what is happening and what has happened and who will, in time, certainly come to exact revenge. This irremediable wound is coming upon the whole *polis*, which has all too quickly fallen into wretched slavery and it is this that stirs up internecine strife and dormant war which bereaves many of their finest youth. For at the hands of our adversaries, our beloved town is quickly being enervated by the conflicts that are dear to the unjust. It is these evils that circulate among the *dêmos*: many of the poor go to a foreign country, sold and bound in unseemly fetters. In this way, the evil of the *dêmos* comes to the house of each man and the gates of the courtyard are no longer minded to keep it back, but it leaps over the high enclosure wall and inevitably finds him, even if he flees to the innermost recess of his bed chamber. These are the things that my heart orders me to teach to the Athenians – that Lawlessness (*Dusnomia*) provides the most ills to a *polis* but that Lawfulness (*Eunomia*) reveals everything that is decorous and fitting and frequently places chains around the unjust. She smoothens what is rough, curbs excess, attenuates violence, dries up the blooming flowers of destruction, straightens out crooked judgements, soothes insolent deeds, stops the effects of factionalism and puts an end to the anger of troublesome discord. Under her, all things among men are fitting and prudent. (Solon fr. 4)

Laertius (1.55–57), for example, credits him with enacting legislation concerning maximum rewards for athletes, compensation for the children of those who died in war, the protection of orphans, the duplication of signet rings, and the consequences that are to befall those who assault the partially sighted. The death penalty is prescribed for those who attempt to recoup a deposit they have not made or for magistrates who are caught drunk.

Certainly, the poetry attributed to Solon displays a marked interest in issues of justice (Document 6.1) and many of these concerns can be identified already in the *Works and Days* (Document 6.2). It is often argued that this notion of an abstract and universal justice, external to the world of mortals, marks a strong contrast with the understanding of judicial process in the

---

Document 6.2

You *basileis*, be heedful of this custom, for the immortals are never far away from men and they take note of those who grind down others with crooked judgements and have no concern for the vengeance of the gods. . . . One of them is the illustrious virgin Justice, born of Zeus, revered by the gods who inhabit Olympus, and whenever some perjurer harms her, she immediately sits beside her father Zeus, son of Cronus, and laments the unjust mind of men, until the *dêmos* pays the penalty for the sins of the *basileis*, who, with evil in their minds, speak crookedly and pervert their judgements. (Hesiod, *WD* 248–51, 256–62)

Homeric epics. One of the scenes on the ornate shield that the god Hephaestus forges for Achilles depicts an arbitration arising from a homicide, in which the victim's family refuses the defendant's request to pay them compensation. It is left to the elders of the community to find a solution acceptable to both parties and the elder who offers the most conducive adjudication is to be rewarded with two talents of gold (*Il.* 18.497–508). The conventional supposition is that a situation where judicial judgments aim simply to resolve feuds between families and prevent vendettas has given way to one in which the community's members are held accountable to an external, impersonal standard of comportment and that the codification of laws is designed to protect all members of the political community while simultaneously serving as an expression of a newly forged political consciousness.

The problem is that this reconstruction is at stark variance with the picture presented by the earliest epigraphically attested laws that we have. Although few in number and generally fragmentary, these tend to concern themselves with the various eventualities that might arise from very specific issues. In 409/8, for example, a decree was inscribed on stone that purported to replicate the original homicide law proposed by the Athenian legislator Dracon in 621/0 (ML 86 = Fornara 15). The law begins by prescribing exile as the penalty for involuntary homicide unless the perpetrator is pardoned by the victim's closest male relatives or – in the absence of these – by ten members of his *phratria*. Another common feature of these early inscribed laws is their concern to define the competences of various magistrates. Thus, a sacred law, found inscribed on slabs that covered the access tunnels to the Late Mycenaean cistern at Tiryns and dated to ca. 600 (*SEG* 30.380), prescribes the respective duties of the *platiwoinoi* ("the drinkers of wine"), the *platiwoinarkhoi* ("leaders of the drinkers of wine"), the *hiaromnamôn* ("sanctuary administrator"), and the *epignômôn* ("arbitrator"). Sometimes more attention is given to what should happen in cases of breaches and failure to comply than to the law itself. One of our earliest inscribed laws comes from the sanctuary of Apollo Delphinios at

Dreros on Crete and dates to the second half of the seventh century (ML 2 = Fornara 11). It prescribes that individuals may hold the office of *kosmos* only once in any ten-year period, but then goes on to stipulate that if someone flouts this law, he will be subject to double the fines that he imposes, will lose either his citizen rights or rights to hold office in perpetuity, and will have all his judgments rescinded.

There are two possible explanations for this apparent discrepancy between the systematic law-codes described by later authors and the rather specific and ad hoc responses to narrowly circumscribed situations that the earliest inscribed laws seem to present. The first is that the whole idea of the codification of statutes by early – sometimes semi-legendary, sometimes perhaps even fictional – lawgivers is a philosophical and historiographical creation of the fifth and fourth centuries. The second is that our early epigraphic evidence may not constitute a truly representative sample. It has been noted, for instance, that religious laws constitute a sizeable proportion of the surviving remains. The fact that the apparently quoted section of Dracon's law on homicide begins "And if someone kills somebody without premeditation . . ." clearly implies, as later authors claim, a broader corpus of laws attributed to Dracon. This need not mean that the legislation that was associated with figures such as Dracon, Zaleucus, or Charondas formed a coherent and singular code of simultaneously enacted ordinances, but it does suggest that the seemingly self-contained statutes that have survived on stone are only the tip of the iceberg.

It is commonly believed that the existence of laws presupposes the existence of the state since they imply both the recognition of the validity and binding-force of the regulations and the possibility and actuality of their enforcement. The problem with this conclusion is that we simply do not know to what extent, if at all, the laws actually were applied and enforced. It could well be that the enforcement of laws was, in the final resort, not as significant as their formulation and that the appearance of the earliest enactments actually speaks more about the nature of leadership in the early Archaic period than about the way civic society was regulated.

The key to the conundrum may lie in the attention given to identifying the specific officials responsible for adjudicating and punishing violations which, in many cases, seems to attract more concern than the general regulation of social behavior (the latter being rather a preoccupation of Late Classical philosophers). In Dracon's law on homicide, guilt is to be judged by the *basileis* (in this context, a specially constituted office that probably indicates the appointed leaders of the four Ionian *phylai*), while the verdict is to be given by fifty-one officials named the *ephetai*. In the Sacred Law from Tiryns, the *platiwoinarkhoi* are to fine infractions of the *platiwoinoi*, while the *hiaromnamôn* is charged with exacting fines from the *platiwoinarkhoi* if they are negligent in their duty. An inscribed limestone block from the acropolis of Argos, dated ca. 575–550, specifies that an official named the *damiourgos* shall specify the amount to be paid by an individual who damages the sacred property of Athena Polias while the *amphipolos* ("temple attendant") is to attend to the matter (*SEG* 11.314).

A contemporary law from the nearby sanctuary of Hera makes provision for when there is no *damiourgos* (*IG* IV 506), while a law from Mycenae, dated ca. 525, stipulates that if there is no *damiourgos*, the *hiaromnamones* of Perseus are to judge between parents (*IG* IV 493). Even in the Classical period, laws appear to be listed according to the magistrate responsible for enforcing them rather than the category of offense committed. The author of the Aristotelian *Athenian Constitution* notes that the eponymous archon at Athens is charged with prosecuting cases involving the maltreatment of parents, orphans, and heiresses as well as cases where an individual is charged with squandering his property through insanity, while the archon *basileus* prosecutes cases of impiety and homicide and the *polemarkhos* has particular judicial responsibilities towards *metoikoi*, or "resident alients" (56–8).

Also relevant is the fact that some of the earliest laws impose limits on the tenure of office. As we have seen, the law from Dreros prohibits an individual from holding the office of *kosmos* more than once in any ten-year period. At Gortyn, according to a sixth-century law (*IC* 4.14), one could be appointed *kosmos* again after three years, though five years had to intervene in the case of the office of *kosmos ksenios* (presumably, a magistrate responsible for non-citizens of Gortyn), and ten years in the case of the magistracy of the *gnômôn*. It has been suggested that these measures were taken to prevent political offices from being used as a stepping-stone towards tyranny though, if this is the case, they were clearly not always successful (see below). But when viewed alongside the immense detail with which individual magistrates' duties, responsibilities, and competences are spelled out in early legal inscriptions, the primary aim would appear to be to ensure that real power was shared more equally among an enlarged aristocracy both by limiting the punitive sanctions that could be levied by single officials and by guaranteeing that the most important offices would rotate.

One further significant feature of the earliest laws is the appearance of named offices and magistracies in place of the generic term *basileis*. It is not that the term itself is no longer attested: we have already seen that it is the *basileis* who are responsible for adjudging guilt in the homicide law of Dracon and that they appear also in the law from Chios. But in both cases, it is clear that it is a question of appointed officials with limited tenure rather than charismatic "big-men" or "chiefs," and the title is far outnumbered by other offices such as *arkhontes, ephetai, prytaneis, dêmarkhoi, agretai, platiwoinarkhoi, hiaromnamônes, (epi)gnômônes* and *damiourgoi*. There is, in other words, now a clear emphasis on ascribed offices rather than achieved authority. The archaeological evidence, the testimony of the Homeric and Hesiodic poems, and the data derived from early legal inscriptions all seem to point in a similar direction: the rise of the state, however loosely we define it, is more a feature of the seventh than of the eighth century.

It has been argued that Archaic elites did not constitute a true "class" because a marked emphasis on individual qualities such as physical ability, dexterity, beauty, athletic and martial prowess, and wealth, bolstered by an intensely competitive ethic, militated against any group "ethos," and because the lack of corporate descent groups precluded automatic access to high ranking positions on the basis of birth and position. It is not, however, necessarily the case that the competitive or "agonistic" spirit is incompatible with a collective consciousness. The fact that the great "Panhellenic" festivals, where athletes from different states engaged in keen competition with one another, were simultaneously important arenas for the expression of a collective Greek identity (pp. 270–2), or that Herodotus (7.9b.2) could suggest that the bloody business of hoplite combat was a defining mark of Greekness, would suggest otherwise. Furthermore, to deny the existence of an aristocratic class is to overlook the fact that terminology such as *esthloi* and *kaloi* presupposes awareness of an exclusive group, as does the principle of rotation of the most important offices.

Interesting in this respect is the information we have for the Bacchiadae of Corinth. According to Diodorus, "the Bacchiadae, descendants of Heracles and more than 200 in number, seized power and governed the *polis* in common, choosing each year one of their own to be the *prytanis*, who held the position of *basileus*, for the period of ninety years until the tyranny of Cypselus, who overthrew them" (fr. 7.9.2–6). Herodotus (5.92.b) adds the detail that the Bacchiadae married among themselves. Diodorus' testimony is, of course, late, even if it is derived from Ephorus, but the idea that the most important civic office (the *prytanis*) rotated among members of a relatively strictly defined aristocracy fits well with the evidence considered above. What fits less well is the date offered for the establishment of the regime: since Diodorus states that 447 years intervened between the return of the Heraclidae and Cypselus' seizure of the tyranny and since he dates the former event to 1104, Cypselus should have come to power in 657 while the Bacchiads should have established their rule in 747, which seems rather early for the developments that have been traced here. One solution has been to doubt the veracity of Diodorus' dating and have Cypselus come to power later, in the final decades of the seventh century. This is not, however, terribly satisfactory because the chronological information that Diodorus presents for Cypselus' reign is not widely divergent from other authors (e.g. Herodotus 5.92; Aristotle, *Pol.* 5.9.22; Nicolaus of Damascus fr. 57.8; Eusebius, *Chron.*), who are thought to be following independent traditions. Furthermore, in the list of archons that was set up ca. 425 in the Athenian agora (ML 6 = Fornara 23; see p. 31), the name Cypselus is recorded as archon for 597/6. If, as is now almost universally agreed, this is the grandson of the Corinthian tyrant then Diodorus' dating for Cypselus' accession to power may not be so wide of the mark. Perhaps a better solution would be to assume that it was in the Bacchiads' interests to promote the idea that their regime had been longer lived than it was. It could even be that the figure of ninety years is a later calculation based on three thirty-year generations: if, for example, the office of *prytanis* had been established by men in their fifties, it is entirely possible to accommodate three generations of aristocrats within the first half of the seventh century.

The other interesting feature about Diodorus' and Herodotus' information is that the office of *prytanis* was restricted to the ranks of the Bacchiadae and that the Bacchiadae preserved their exclusivity by practicing endogamy. It is within this context that we can situate Theognis' remarks about the importance of good birth and understand why Alcaeus could pretend to be so scandalized by the fact that Pittacus is alleged to have married into an aristocratic family. The early laws that we possess do not specify the precise social group among which important offices rotate, but it is a reasonable assumption that qualifications for high office were restricted – initially probably by birth and eventually by wealth also: at Athens, for example, only the top two property classes – i.e. around 20 percent of the adult male population – were eligible for the archonship until as late as 457/6 (Aristotle, *AC* 26.2). In short, the elites of seventh-century Greece contracted with one another to distribute, share, and rotate political offices as part of a voluntary self-regulation that entailed, as its necessary function, the exclusion of non-elites. There were some, however, who were not prepared to abide by this "gentleman's agreement."

The Return of the "Big-Man"

The subject of tyranny is a particularly difficult one to broach because of a strongly negative source tradition, according to which every unspeakable vice becomes attached to the figure of the tyrant. This is especially true of Cypselus' son Periander. According to Herodotus (3.48), it was only the intervention of the Samians that prevented Periander from having 300 sons of Corcyrean noblemen sent to Sardis for castration as eunuchs. He was also accused of having murdered his wife, Melissa, of having had sexual intercourse with her dead body, of gathering the women of Corinth together and stripping them naked, of banishing his younger son, Lykophron, and of embarking on a programme of extermination of his rivals (3.50; 5.92). And yet, Herodotus is also aware that Periander had a reputation as a shrewd arbitrator, adjudicating the dispute between the Athenians and the Mytileneans over Sigeion (5.95), while later tradition even included him among the seven sages of Greece (Diogenes Laertius 1.13, 30, 40–42). Conflicting traditions seem also to have existed regarding Cypselus. Herodotus comments on the evils that he was fated to inflict upon the Corinthians and how he drove many of them into exile and deprived even more of their lives. In oracular prophecies, supposedly delivered prior to his seizure of the tyranny, he is described as a "mighty lion, eater of raw flesh," who "will loosen the knees of many" and as a "rolling rock" that "will fall upon the monarchical men." And yet this last prophecy, delivered by the Pythian priestess at Delphi, also predicts that he will "set Corinth on the path of justice," while a further oracle, said to have been delivered to Cypselus himself, describes him as "fortunate, both he and his children, but not the children of his children" (5.92.b–e) – a reference to the fact that the tyranny of the Cypselids was overthrown in the third generation.

It is now generally agreed that the tyrants were normally members – albeit marginalized ones – of the aristocracy. Herodotus (5.92) says that Cypselus' mother was a Bacchiad but that none of the Bacchiadae would marry her because she was lame and so was given instead to Aetion, son of Ekhekrates. If true, Cypselus' mixed parentage might explain his hostility towards the Bacchiadae, but it is also possible that it was invented afterwards to account for this. At any rate, Nicolaus of Damascus (fr. 57.1–7) believed that Cypselus launched his coup with (non-Bacchiad) aristocratic support. The Argive ruler Pheidon was supposedly descended from Temenus (Ephorus fr. 115), while Pisistratus derived his lineage from the descendants of Nestor who ruled over early Attica (Herodotus 5.65.3). Even were we not to take literally Alcaeus' sneers (fr. 348) against Pittacus' low birth, his marriage into the family of the Penthilidai clearly qualified him for membership of the elite, just as Theagenes of Megara, whatever his origins, was evidently regarded highly enough by the Athenian aristocrat and Olympic victor Cylon, who married his daughter. Interestingly, Cylon himself attempted, without success, to establish himself as tyrant of Athens ca. 630 (Herodotus 5.71; Thucydides 1.126.3–12; Plutarch, *Sol.* 12). The capacity of intermarriage for recruiting newcomers into the elite is precisely what the poet of the *Theognidea* (183–92) attacks when he writes "It is wealth that they honour; an *esthlos* marries the daughter of a *kakos* and a *kakos* the daughter of an *agathos*. Wealth mixes up the descent group."

The only apparent exception to this rule would be the Orthagorid dynasty at Sicyon, west of Corinth. A papyrus, discovered at Oxyrhynchus in Egypt and possibly deriving from the *Universal History* of Ephorus, narrates that the first tyrant, Orthagoras, was the son of a cook named Andreas (*FGrH* no. 105, fr. 2). This information has often been placed alongside a Delphic oracle, recorded by Herodotus (5.67.2), in which Cleisthenes, perhaps the great-nephew of Orthagoras, is greeted as a "stoner" – the implication being that, in combat, those who hurl stones and other missiles are those who are too poor to afford the equipment of an infantryman. But it is entirely possible that the tradition concerning the Orthagorids' humble origins is a fabrication, invented after the fall of the tyranny. The papyrus' description of how Orthagoras' courage in battle earned him swift promotion, eventually resulting in his being elected *polemarkhos* or supreme military commander, looks suspicious. The insult leveled at Cleisthenes might refer to the type of punishment he inflicted on his rivals rather than a specific mode of combat and, in any case, Cleisthenes' standing in the Panhellenic community would seem to be vindicated by the fact that he gave his daughter to Megacles from the influential Athenian family of the Alcmaeonidae (see below).

In modern treatments, a great deal of attention is given to distinguishing the tyrant from the monarch. Both are, in principle, hereditary and both are viewed as wielding absolute power, but the former is supposed to rule unconstitutionally and often with an appetite for capricious and unbridled violence while the latter exercises authority according to custom. This definition is reasonable enough, provided we recognize that the notion of "constitutionality" was still only rudimentarily developed in the seventh century and that the capacity for violence was not limited to tyrants, even if it was often a necessity in overthrowing a former regime. In fact, tradition credits some tyrants with a special concern for justice: as we have seen, the Delphic Oracle is supposed to have predicted that Cypselus would "set Corinth on the path of justice"; the Orthagorids of Sicyon were said to have "treated their subjects moderately and in many respects enslaved themselves to the laws" (Aristotle, *Pol.* 5.9.21); and Pisistratus later had the reputation for administering everything "according to the laws," even attending court to defend himself on a homicide charge (Aristotle, *AC* 16.8). But it is also important to point out that the tendency to draw a sharp distinction between monarchy and tyranny is, in large part, a legacy of fifth- and especially fourth-century reflections on the matter.

Crucial here is a passage from the *Politics*, where Aristotle observes that the earliest tyrannies arose "from *basileis* who exceeded their ancestral prerogatives and aimed at a more despotic power"; Aristotle's prime example is Pheidon of Argos (5.8.3–4). Thucydides (1.13.1) also believed that hereditary kingship had given way to tyrannies. These supposedly historical examples generated more abstract philosophical speculation on the tendency of monarchies to degenerate into tyrannies but that does not in itself guarantee their historical credentials. In fact, as we have seen, the evidence for hereditary kingship in early Greece is, outside Sparta, extremely slight. It is also probably significant that the word *tyrannos* seems, from the outset, to have been particularly associated with the absolute monarchies of the Near East: the term first appears in a fragment of Archilochus (fr. 19), in a context which also refers to the Lydian ruler Gyges, and it is often suspected that it is a loanword of Lydian or Phoenician origin. That the Greeks should borrow a word to describe an autocratic regime only really makes sense if this was a system of government with which they were relatively unfamiliar. Similarly, when Archilochus (fr. 23) compares a woman's domination to tyranny, it is the quality of absolute rule rather than unconstitutionality that he has in mind. The poet of the *Theognidea* (51–2) uses the word *mounarkhoi* ("monarchies") for what we would describe as tyrannies and even Herodotus often appears to use the terms *basileus* and *tyrannos* interchangeably. By Aristotle's day, kingship was a very real feature in several parts of the Greek world and it was, therefore, essential to distinguish it from the negative connotations that had attached themselves to certain types of absolute autocracy in Greek thought. The important point is that, initially at any rate, the concept of tyranny does not appear to be contrasted with hereditary monarchy but with the pre-existing order – i.e. rule by a relatively circumscribed group of aristocrats in which the most important offices were shared on the principle of rotation.

Sure enough, Aristotle also notes that "some [tyrannies] arose from those chosen to fill the chief magistracies . . . and others from oligarchies that selected one of their own to the greatest offices" (*Pol.* 5.8.3). As examples, he cites the tyrants of the Ionian cities – presumably including Thrasybulus of Miletus, who was a contemporary of Periander (Herodotus 5.92.z) – and Phalaris, the early sixth-century tyrant of Acragas on Sicily. We have already seen that, according to tradition, Orthagoras seized the tyranny while he occupied the office of *polemarkhos*; Nicolaus of Damascus (fr. 57.5) reports that Cypselus too was *polemarkhos* when he launched his coup, although this is not a detail that is found in Herodotus' account. And Pittacus was, according to Aristotle (*Pol.* 3.9.5–6), initially elected to the office of *aisymnêtês* – a constitutionally ordained office designed to deal with emergencies. In many – if not all – cases, then, tyrannies arose when individual aristocrats decided to not "play by the rules," refusing to cede to their peers the offices to which they had been appointed. Although not normally classified as a tyranny in the literature, this is clearly the situation described in the Aristotelian *Athenian Constitution* (13.2), where Damasias, elected archon for 582/1, remained in office for two years and two months before being forcibly removed.

In many senses, the appearance of tyranny represents a return to the situation that had prevailed before the emergence of an aristocracy, when political leadership was exercised by Homeric- and Hesiodic-style *basileis*. Indeed, the Delphic oracle actually greets Cypselus as *basileus* (Herodotus 5.92.e2). As with the earlier *basileis*, power resided in the personal, charismatic authority of the individual rather than the political office he held. And as with the *basileis*, this sort of authority was inherently unstable and was not normally transmitted over many generations. At Corinth, Cypselus ruled for thirty years and his son, Periander, for a little over forty, but Periander's nephew Psammetichus was expelled after only three years (Aristotle, *Pol.* 5.9.22). Pisistratus is said to have died in 528/7, thirty-three years after first seizing the tyranny, and was succeeded by his sons, Hippias and Hipparchus (Aristotle, *AC* 17.1–3). But Hipparchus was assassinated in 514 and his brother lasted only another four years before being expelled by the Spartans (*AC* 19; Herodotus 5.55–65). The tyranny of the Orthagorids seems to have been longer lived, lasting around a century (Aristotle, *Pol.* 5.9.21).

The populations over whom the tyrants ruled were, of course, considerably larger than the coteries that surrounded the Homeric *basileis*. But the means by which tyrants established and maintained their authority were broadly comparable with those employed by their chiefly predecessors. In the first place, considerable *kudos* was to be derived from martial and athletic prowess. Both Orthagoras and Cypselus are said to have originally distinguished themselves in the military sphere. Herodotus (6.126.2) notes that Cleisthenes of Sicyon won the four-horse chariot race at Olympia – probably in 576 – while, according to Pausanias (10.7.6), he had won the same contest at the Pythian Games at Delphi six years earlier in 582. The French excavators of Delphi believe that the remains of a square, colonnaded pavilion, dated on stylistic grounds to ca. 580 and found within the foundations of the later Sicyonian Treasury, may have been constructed by Cleisthenes to display his victorious vehicle.

Cleisthenes' dedication at Delphi brings us to the second aspect in which tyrants legitimated their authority: self-publicity through munificence and conspicuous display. The first monumental temple at Corinth is probably too

Figure 6.3   The *diolkos* on the Corinthian isthmus (photo by author)

early to be attributed to Cypselus, as may be the first temple to Poseidon at nearby Isthmia. But Cypselus was certainly credited with costly dedications at both Delphi and Olympia (Pausanias 5.17.5; Plutarch, *Mor.* 400d) and it was probably Periander who constructed the *diolkos* or paved slipway across the Corinthian isthmus (Figure 6.3). Whether or not they were involved in commissioning the late-sixth century Temple of Athena Polias on the acropolis (p. 228), the Pisistratids were certainly responsible for beginning work on the massive temple of Olympian Zeus, even if it remained unfinished until the reign of the Emperor Hadrian. The second "dipteral" (double-colonnaded) temple of Hera at Samos was almost certainly initiated by Polycrates and major temples at Ephesus, Didyma near Miletus, Samos, and Acragas have all been plausibly associated with tyrannies. Aristotle (*Pol.* 5.9.4), at any rate, thought that major construction projects were a typical strategy practiced by tyrants, even if his explanation for it – a ploy to keep the populace busy and therefore avoid conspiracy – seems unconvincing given the lack of conclusive evidence for mass hostility to the early tyrants.

The tyrants also engaged in self-publicity through their patronage of the arts. The dithyrambic poet Arion of Methymna was entertained at the court of Periander (Herodotus 1.23–24); the lyric poet Anacreon of Teos was welcomed by both Polycrates of Samos (Herodotus 3.121) and Hipparchus of Athens (Plato, *Hipp.* 228b; Aristotle, *AC* 18.1); another lyric poet, Simonides of Ceos, was also welcomed by Hipparchus (*AC* 18.1) before his sojourn at the court of Skopas, the ruler of Crannon in Thessaly (Plato, *Prot.* 339a); and a number of non-Athenian sculptors, such as Aristion of Paros, are known to have been active in Attica during the period of the tyranny.

Thirdly, just as the Homeric *basileis* legitimated their authority by the connections they established, through intermarriage and guest-friendship, with their peers in other regions, so too did the tyrants. Although this was a common elite practice in the seventh and sixth centuries, it is one that is given considerable attention by our literary sources. The most famous example is the one-year contest that Cleisthenes is said to have organized to pick a husband for his daughter, Agariste. Herodotus, who recounts the story, says that suitors traveled from all over Greece as well as from southern Italy to prove themselves worthy husbands; in the end, the honor was awarded to the Athenian Megacles, son of Alcmaeon, after the "favorite," Hippokleides, disgraced himself over dinner (6.126–30). The narrative details of the story should not be taken too seriously (see p. 150), but it is entirely credible that Cleisthenes should have wanted to forge an influential marriage alliance for himself. Theagenes, as we have seen, married off his daughter to the Athenian Cylon; Periander's wife, Melissa, was daughter of Prokles, the tyrant of Epidaurus (Herodotus 3.50). Thrasybulus of Miletus was the guest-friend of the Lydian king Alyattes (1.22.4) and Polycrates, tyrant of Samos, maintained a guest friendship with the Egyptian Pharaoh Amasis until the latter broke it off (3.39.2). Seldom able to count on the support of their fellow aristocrats at home, such prestigious connections were indispensable to the tyrants. Pisistratus, for example, rewarded Lygdamis of Naxos for his earlier support by helping establish him as tyrant of his native island (Herodotus 1.61, 64). Lygdamis, in turn, is supposed to have assisted Polycrates in seizing power on Samos (Polyaenus, *Strat.* 1.23).

Fourthly, just as the authority of the *basileis* was based on a reciprocal relationship with the *laoi*, so the tyrants typically relied on the popular support of the *dêmos*, whose interests they were expected to champion. According to Aristotle, "the greatest number of tyrants have risen, so to speak, from leaders of the people, winning trust by slandering the nobles" (*Pol.* 5.8.3; cf. 5.4.4). Pisistratus, Theagenes, and Dionysius of Syracuse are all cited as examples. Cleisthenes, too, is said to have "promoted the interests of the *dêmos* in most respects" (5.9.21). Whereas the power of the aristocracies had rested on mutual support among peers against those deemed to be *kakoi* or *deiloi*, the tyrants returned to a system in which it was the support of retainers and clients that was essential for survival. But that support could only endure as long as the tyrant retained his personal authority.

In assessing the impact of tyranny on the political development of the Archaic Greek world, it is important to recognize that it was not a universal phenomenon: according to one estimate, only twenty-seven out of hundreds of states are known to have been subject to a tyranny over a period of 150 years. On the other hand, in an environment where "micro-states" jostled with one another for space and where intercommunication was intensive, it was only natural that reforms and developments in one state might be emulated, adopted, or adapted by its neighbors, meaning that the measures tyrants took might often have repercussions beyond their home community. It is also important to remember that there is little evidence that tyrants entertained comprehensive programmes of social and political reform. As Thucydides (1.17) notes, their primary concern was with their personal safety and with strengthening their family's hold on power. That does not mean, however, that the measures they took were without significance for the future development of the Greek states. It could be argued that the democratic revolution of the late sixth and early fifth centuries would have been difficult – if not impossible – to achieve had it not been for Pisistratus' rule (p. 233), but not every state which witnessed a tyranny was eventually destined for democracy: Corinth, save for very brief periods, was governed by oligarchies. The assassinations and exiles that tyrants undertook against their potential aristocratic rivals did not extinguish aristocracy itself. But they did weaken the authority of some of the leading families who had previously monopolized power and they also galvanized popular sentiment – a crucial step towards the crystallization of the political community.

FURTHER READING

The *polis* as a "stateless society": M. Berent, "Hobbes and the 'Greek Tongues'," *History of Political Thought* 17 (1996), 36–59; challenged by M. H. Hansen, "Was the *polis* a state or a stateless society?" in Nielsen 2002, 9–47. For "primitive states" and "stateless societies": Fortes and Evans-Pritchard 1940.

On *basileis*: Drews 1983; for an alternative view: van Wees 1992. "Big men": M. Sahlins, "Poor man, rich man, big-man, chief: Political types in Melanesia and Polynesia," *Comparative Studies in Society and History* 5 (1963), 285–303. For theories of cultural evolution: Tandy 1997, 84–111. Social groups in early Greece: W. Donlan, "The social groups of Dark Age Greece," *Classical Philology* 80 (1985), 293–308; "The relations of power in the pre-state and early state polities," in Mitchell and Rhodes 1997, 39–48; B Qviller, "The dynamics of the Homeric society," *Symbolae Osloenses* 56 (1981), 109–55; J. Whitley, "Social diversity in Dark Age Greece," *Annual of the British School at Athens* 86 (1991), 341–65; Thomas and Conant 1999, 32–59.

Post-Homeric emergence of aristocracy: Starr 1986. Factionalism in Theognis: H. van Wees, "Megara's Mafiosi: Timocracy and violence in Theognis," in Brock and Hodkinson 2000, 52–67.

Early laws: Gagarin 1986; K. J. Hölkeskamp, "Written law in Archaic Greece," *Proceedings of the Cambridge Philological Society* 38 (1992), 87–117; R. Osborne, "Law and laws. How do we join up the dots?" in Mitchell and Rhodes 1997, 74–82. Laws ensuring aristocratic dominance: W. Eder, "The political significance of the codification of law in Archaic societies: An unconventional hypothesis," in Raaflaub 1986, 262–300. For a lack of class consciousness among Greek aristocrats: Stein-Hölkeskamp 1989. For early Corinth: Salmon 1984.

Tyranny: Andrewes 1956; J. Salmon, "Lopping off the heads? Tyrants, politics and the *polis*," in Mitchell and Rhodes 1997, 60–73. For the later literary tradition: McGlew 1993. Aristocratic background of tyrants: de Libero 1996. For tyrants as "extraconstitutional" rather than "unconstitutional" leaders: G. Anderson, "Before *Turannoi* were tyrants: Rethinking a chapter of early Greek history," *Classical Antiquity* 24 (2005), 173–222. Date of the second temple at Samos: H. J. Kienast, "Topography and architecture of the Archaic Heraion at Samos," in Stamatopoulou and Yeroulanou 2002, 317–25.

Excursus I
A Cautionary Tale:
Pheidon of Argos

As we have seen (p. 139), Aristotle believed that "Pheidon of Argos and others established themselves as tyrants from a pre-existing kingship" (*Pol.* 5.8.4). Our earliest reference to Pheidon comes in Herodotus' enumeration of the suitors of Agariste, daughter of the Sicyonian tyrant Cleisthenes, where the Argive ruler is said to have introduced a system of measures and to have usurped the administration of the Olympic Games (Document I.1). Straightaway, this information is at variance with that provided by Aristotle regarding the period in which Pheidon is supposed to have lived. Cleisthenes of Sicyon was the maternal grandfather of Cleisthenes of Athens (Herodotus 5.67.1; 6.131), who held the archonship in 525/4 and instituted sweeping reforms after 508 (pp. 212–18). The elder Kleisthenes must have lived, then, in the early sixth century – the wedding of Agariste is conventionally placed in the 570s – which would make Pheidon a rough contemporary. Aristotle, on the other hand, maintains that the tyrannies that arose from monarchies predated those tyrants, such as Cypselus, who came to power by championing the *dêmos* (*Pol.* 5.8.3), which would place Pheidon before the middle of the seventh century.

Our most detailed information for Pheidon derives from Ephorus, cited by Strabo (Document I.2). Like Herodotus, Ephorus notes that Pheidon forcibly celebrated the Olympic Games, though this is part of a broader pattern of violence by which Pheidon attacked cities that had supposedly once been captured by his ancestor Heracles and celebrated other contests that were thought to have been instituted by the hero. Like Herodotus, Ephorus credits Pheidon with establishing a system of measures, though he also adds that he introduced new weight standards and minted coins from silver and other metals. But Ephorus says that Pheidon reckoned himself in the tenth generation after Temenus and since he elsewhere (fr. 223) seems to have dated the return to the Peloponnese of Temenus and his fellow Heraclids to 1069, then –

Document I.1

From the Peloponnese came Leokedes, son of Pheidon, the tyrant of the Argives.
It was this Pheidon who introduced the measures for the Peloponnesians and
who was by far the most arrogant of all the Greeks, because he dismissed
the Elean umpires and administered the contest in Olympia himself.
(Herodotus 6.127.3)

Document I.2

[Ephorus says that] the Aetolians seized the land [Elis], expelling the Epeioi, and
they also took over the administration of the sanctuary at Olympia, then in the
hands of the Achaeans. And on account of the friendship between Oxylus and the
descendants of Heracles, it was readily agreed by all on oath that Elis should be
sacred to Zeus and that anybody who invaded this territory with force of arms
should be accursed, as would he who failed to defend the land to the best of his
ability. Consequently, those who later founded the *polis* of Elis left it unwalled and
those who pass through this land with an army hand in their arms and only reclaim
them after exiting the borders. Since the Eleans were sacred, Iphitos established the
Olympic Games and for this reason these people flourished. For while other peoples
were always warring against each other, these alone, together with their guests,
enjoyed real peace and consequently became well-populated. But Pheidon of Argos,
tenth in line from Temenus, surpassed his contemporaries in power, as a result of
which he recovered the entire legacy of Temenus which had been broken up into
several parts and he invented the measures that are called "Pheidonian" as well as
weights and the coinage that is struck from silver and other metals. In addition to
this, he attacked those *poleis* that had been captured by Heracles and deemed it right
that he should celebrate the contests that Heracles had established, among which
was also the contest at Olympia. And so, attacking with force, he celebrated the
contest and the Eleans were unable to prevent him because they had no arms on
account of the peace while the others were subject to his domination. The Eleans
did not record this celebration but procured arms and began to defend themselves.
The Spartans also assisted in this, either because they envied the good fortune that
the Eleans enjoyed on account of the peace or because they thought they would
have them as allies in defeating Pheidon, who had deprived them of the hegemony
they had formerly exercised over the Peloponnesians. And, indeed, together they
defeated Pheidon, and the Spartans assisted in attaching Pisatis and Triphylia to the
Eleans. (Ephorus fr. 115 = Strabo 8.3.33)

assuming three generations per century – this would place Pheidon roughly in the third quarter of the eighth century. This date is not incompatible with that suggested by Aristotle but cannot be reconciled with that provided by Herodotus.

Ephorus adds that Pheidon "recovered the legacy of Temenus." In discussing hostilities between Argos and Sparta in the mid-sixth century, Herodotus (1.81.2) writes that "the mainland to the west as far as Malea, the island of Cythera and the other islands once belonged to the Argives," and although Pheidon is not specifically mentioned, some scholars believe that he presided over an early "empire" whose acquisition was justified in terms of an ancestral legacy from Temenus. According to tradition, Temenus' descendants had captured Sicyon (Ephorus fr. 18; Pausanias 2.6.7), Phleious (Pausanias 2.13.1), Epidaurus (Nicolaus of Damascus fr. 30), and Aegina (Herodotus 8.46.1; Pausanias 2.29.5), and some have wanted to see in this a reflection of Pheidon's own hegemony.

Other references are more cursory. Another fragment of Ephorus (fr. 176) says that Pheidon was the first to mint silver coinage on the island of Aegina, while a fragment of Aristotle (fr. 480) also refers to "Pheidonian measures." The author of the Aristotelian *Athenian Constitution* (10.1–2) says that these measures were smaller than those instituted by Solon, who raised the value of the *mina* from seventy to one hundred drachmas. Plutarch (*Mor.* 772d–773b) claims that Pheidon attempted to interfere in the internal affairs of Corinth and Nicolaus of Damascus (fr. 35), perhaps picking up the end of Ephorus' account, says that "a" Pheidon – it is unclear whether the Argive ruler is intended – was killed assisting some Corinthians in a revolt. According to Pausanias (6.22.2), in the eighth Olympiad the Pisatans invited in Pheidon, "the most arrogant of the Greek tyrants," and celebrated the Games with him. On the chronography established by Hippias of Elis in the late fifth century (p. 32), the eighth Olympiad would have fallen in 748 which corresponds well with Ephorus' date for Pheidon. Plutarch, on the other hand, offers two different dates for Pheidon, neither of which matches that of Pausanias or Ephorus. In noting that Leokedes inherited Pheidon's power (*Mor.* 893), Plutarch would seem to be following Herodotus' account which, as we have seen, dated Pheidon to the early sixth century, but elsewhere (772d–773b) he dates Pheidon to approximately two generations before the foundation of Syracuse, which would place him at the beginning of the eighth century. A similar date is offered by Eusebius (*Chron.* = Fornara 1B), who dates Pheidon to the 1,220th year of Abraham (798/7). Yet another date is offered by the fourth-century historian Theopompus (fr. 393), who considered Pheidon to be the father of Karanos, the founder of the ruling Argead dynasty of Macedonia. This would then place Pheidon in the sixth generation after Temenus – that is, the middle of the ninth century in our terms – while the Parian Marble (fr. 45 = Fornara 1A) dates him to 895/4 (though since the inscription records Pheidon in the eleventh generation after Heracles, or seventh generation after Temenus, there is clearly an error here).

895	Parian Marble
Mid-ninth century	Theopompos fr. 393
Early eighth century	Plutarch, *Moralia* 772d–773b; Eusebius
Mid-eighth century	Ephorus fr. 115; Pausanias 6.22.2
668	Pausanias 6.22.2 (emended)
Before 657	Aristotle, *Politics* 5.8.4
Early sixth century	Herodotus 6.127.3; Plutarch, *Moralia* 893

Figure I.1   The variant dates ascribed to Pheidon of Argos

To make matters worse, modern scholars have suggested an entirely different date for Pheidon's activities. Eusebius (*Chron.*) says that the Pisatans
celebrated the twenty-eighth Olympic Games of 668. Since Pausanias notes
collusion between the Pisatans and Pheidon, some have argued that his attribution of this event to the eighth Olympiad is an error of transmission and the
text should be emended to read the twenty-eighth Olympiad instead – not
least, because Strabo (8.3.30) says that the games were celebrated without
interruption down until 672. Pheidon's intervention at Olympia is then placed
in association with the Battle of Hysiae, in which the Spartans were defeated
by the Argives and which is dated by Pausanias (2.24.7) to the fourth year of
the twenty-seventh Olympiad (i.e. 669). Although Pausanias does not mention
Pheidon in reference to this battle, so great a victory, it is argued, could only
be credited to an individual noted for his power and ambition. Some go even
further and propose that the Spartan defeat encouraged the neighboring
Messenians to revolt in what is conventionally known as the Second Messenian
War (see pp. 172–6).

Faced with such a bewildering array of dates for Pheidon, spanning a period
of some three centuries (Figure I.1), it is entirely understandable that scholars
should want to assess the relative merits of each in order to arrive at *the*
definitive date for the Argive ruler. Most at risk is the seventh-century date
proposed by modern scholars because it rests on no direct ancient authority
and, as a general rule of thumb, textual emendations should only be proposed
when all other alternative options have been exhausted. That Pheidon's name
is not explicitly linked to the Battle of Hysiae in Pausanias' text is not an
insuperable obstacle. The battle should have been a great victory for Argos
and it is entirely possible that the Argives were reluctant to preserve any
association between this victory and a man deemed by posterity to have been
"the most arrogant of the Greek tyrants" – if, that is, the battle really occurred
when Pausanias says it did. There is no explicit independent testimony for the
battle and it has been suggested that Pausanias' guides confused – wilfully or
otherwise – an early and perhaps fictitious battle, which the Argives are supposed to have won, with a battle that actually took place in 417 and resulted in
a Spartan victory (Thucydides 5.83.2). Pausanias was shown the *polyandria* or
"mass graves" of the Argive victors and if these were really the final resting

---

Document I.3

Best is the land of Pelasgian Argos, the horses of Thessaly, the women of Sparta and the men who drink the water of sacred Arethousa. But better still than these are those who dwell between Tiryns and Arcadia rich in sheep, the linen-corseleted Argives, goads of war. (*Greek Anthology* 14.73)

---

places of the seventh-century warriors one wonders where the graves of those who fell in 417 were located.

Contrary to what is sometimes written, little help is offered by what purports to be a Delphic oracular response, first cited by Ion of Chios in the middle of the fifth century (Document I.3). The somewhat illogical progression ("best . . . better still") might suggest two stages of composition: an earlier phase, in which the "men who drink the water of sacred Arethousa" – i.e. the Chalcidians – were widely renowned and a later stage, when this reputation had passed to the Argives. The assumption, however, that the oracle dates to the seventh century is based on the twin suppositions that Argos' reputation should be credited to Pheidon and that Pheidon should be dated to the seventh century. Clearly, then, any argument that employs the oracle to date Pheidon would be guilty of circularity. Ultimately, however, Eusebius actually says that the Pisatans celebrated the games of 668 BCE not because they usurped this right from the Eleans but because the latter were away fighting a war against the Achaean city of Dyme. In his account, the more violent usurpations of the games by the Pisatans occurred from 660 down to 572 BCE, but neither these, nor the earlier Pisatan celebration, are associated with Pheidon. Strabo (8.3.30) dates the beginning of Pisatan dominance to the twenty-seventh Olympiad of 672 but, again, does not connect this event with the name of Pheidon, whom – following Ephorus – he dates a couple of generations earlier. These divergences make it almost certain that the Pisatan interventions did not appear in the list of Olympic victors compiled by Hippias of Elis and, even if they had, it is doubtful how much credibility would have attached to them.

The date offered by the Parian Marble can almost certainly be discounted. If the compiler believed that Pheidon belonged to the seventh generation after Temenus, then this would place him in the second half of the ninth century, shortly after the date assigned by Theopompus, who counted Pheidon in the sixth generation. The slight discrepancy is due to the fact that Theopompus regarded Pheidon as the father of Karanos while the compiler of the Parian Marble was following a tradition, attested later by the Byzantine chronicler George Synkellos (373, 498), that made Karanos the brother of Pheidon. In both cases, it is the dating of Karanos that provides the fixed point for Pheidon rather than vice versa. But according to Herodotus (8.137.1), in the fifth century it was believed that Perdiccas, not Karanos, was the founder of the

Argead dynasty. This should suggest, then, that Karanos' insertion into the Temenid lineage and, as a consequence, the early dating of Pheidon in relation to him, were developments of the fourth century.

Through a process of elimination, then, we are left with three dates: the early eighth century; shortly after the middle of the eighth century; and the early sixth century (Aristotle's information is too vague but could be compatible with both of the two earlier dates). The problem is that the choice of any one of these dates would automatically exclude some of the activities that the tradition associates with the name of Pheidon. For example, Pheidon cannot be placed in the tenth generation after Temenus and simultaneously be credited with striking the first silver coins on Aegina, as Ephorus would have us believe. It is true that Aegina was among the earliest issuers of silver currency, but the first series of "turtles" almost certainly cannot predate the sixth century (p. 250). The reference to coinage might favor Herodotus' date, but Herodotus mentions the establishment of measures, not coinage. Furthermore, some suspicion exists concerning the list of suitors in Herodotus' account of Agariste's betrothal contest: the Aetolian Titormos, whose brother Males accepted the challenge (6.127.2), was apparently a contemporary of the wrestler Milon of Croton, who is supposed to have lived towards the end of the century (Aelian, *HM* 12.22; Herodotus 3.137.5). The main point of the story concerns a contest between two important Athenian families – the Philaidai, whose representative, Hippokleides, "danced away" his marriage, and the Alcmaeonidae, the family to which Megacles, the successful suitor, belonged. The other personalities recorded could, then, simply be a *Who's Who?* of Greek worthies, whose precise chronological context was not of primary importance to the story and was not, therefore, reconciled with the supposed date of the marriage.

Furthermore, had Pheidon ruled in the early sixth century and entertained the sort of hegemonic pretensions that many of our sources attribute to him, one might have expected to find his name specifically associated with a whole series of events and campaigns. Pausanias (6.19.12–14) noted a Megarian dedication at Olympia, commemorating a victory, in alliance with the Argives, over Corinth. But he does not mention Pheidon in this context and even if Pheidon's interference in Corinthian affairs is true, it is unlikely to date to the early sixth century when the city was held by the Cypselids. Nor is this a suitable period in which to fit other interventions in the northeast Peloponnese: Epidaurus was probably ruled by the tyrant Prokles (Herodotus 3.50), while Cleisthenes held sway over Sicyon. Herodotus (5.67) does claim that Cleisthenes made war on the Argives and sought to expunge any trace of Argive cults or traditions from Sicyon but there is no mention of Pheidon. Indeed, it is hard to reconcile this account of bitter hostility between Cleisthenes and Argos with the account in which Pheidon's son was welcomed with lavish hospitality as a prospective husband for Cleisthenes' daughter, which provides further reason to suspect the historicity of the latter (if not also the former). At the very least, one might have expected Pheidon to have subjugated the neighboring communities of the Argive Plain but, in fact, there is some evidence that these enjoyed considerable autonomy in the sixth century. The early sixth-century inscription from Tiryns, mentioning the *platiwoinoi* (*SEG* 30.380), refers to both a *damos* (the Doric form for a "popular assembly") and an *aliaia* (assumed to be some sort of deliberative council), both of which would appear to attest some independence in decision-making. A law from Mycenae, dated ca. 525, implies that the *polis* is under the jurisdiction of a *damiourgos* (*IG* IV 493). The fact that only one is attested probably implies an administrative separation from Argos, where earlier inscriptions record boards of either nine (*SEG* 11.336) or six (*SEG* 11.314) *damiourgoi* – and, incidentally, these last two inscriptions, dated approximately to 575–550, leave little room for a sixth-century autocrat.

If, on the other hand, we opt for an early eighth-century date, it is difficult to see how Pheidon could have intervened in the Olympic Games, which were supposedly founded in 776 – unless there was an earlier tradition that the games were, in fact, older than this. But since it is often suspected that Hippias of Elis exaggerated the antiquity of the Olympic Games vis-à-vis the other three "stephanitic" contests at Delphi, Isthmia, and Nemea, he would surely have picked an earlier foundation date had one been available.

A date in the second half of the eighth century would fit what many view as a particularly prosperous period in Argos' history, at least as documented by the archaeological evidence, as well as information that Pausanias provides for the destruction of Asine – a coastal settlement, some 20 kilometers to the southeast of Argos (Document I.4; cf. Pausanias 3.7.4, 4.34.9). Elsewhere (4.8.3), Pausanias says that the Argives destroyed Asine in the generation before the First Messenian War, which he dates to 744–724 (4.13.7). For some scholars, this marks the opening shot in a policy of territorial expansion, continuing with the Argive destruction of nearby Nauplia (Pausanias 4.24.4, 27.8, 35.2) and broadly associated with the hegemonic aspirations that many

Document I.4

The region that follows belongs to the Argives but was once called Asinaia, and on the sea are the ruins of Asine. When the Spartans invaded the Argolid under their king, Nikandros, son of Kharillos, son of Polydektes, son of Eunomos, son of Prytanis, son of Eurypon, the people of Asine joined with them on the expedition and, together with them, ravaged the land of the Argives. But when the Spartan force returned home, the Argives together with their king, Eratos, marched against Asine. For a certain time, the Asinaians managed to defend themselves from the wall and killed, among others, Lysistratos, who was one of the most illustrious of the Argives. But when the wall was taken, they embarked their women and children on boats and abandoned their country, while the Argives razed Asine to the ground and annexed its territory, though they did spare the sanctuary of Apollo Pythaeus, which is still visible today, and they buried Lysistratos there. (Pausanias 2.36.4–5) of the literary sources ascribe to Pheidon. But since Pausanias seems to date the destruction of Nauplia to shortly after the Second Messenian War, in the first year of the twenty-eighth Olympiad, or 668 (4.23.4), it is quite clear that the same individual cannot be responsible for both events. Not only that, but in both cases the destructions are attributed to someone other than Pheidon: Eratos, in the case of Asine, and Damokratidas, in the case of Nauplia.

Modern overbuilding means that the settlement history of Nauplia (modern Náfplio) is poorly understood, but archaeological evidence certainly supports an eighth-century destruction at Asine. The walls on the Barbouna Hill, opposite the acropolis, seem to have collapsed in a violent destruction. Beyond that, the fit between the archaeological and literary evidence is not quite as close as is sometimes supposed. On the basis of the Late Geometric IIB pottery fragments found in the destruction level, the Swedish excavators of the site have suggested a date of ca. 720–710, but this is several decades later than Pausanias' dating of the event (which is, admittedly, probably too early). And the sanctuary of Apollo Pythaeus, if correctly identified with an apsidal building (Building B) on the summit of the Barbouna Hill, did not escape the conflagration as Pausanias claims, although a rectangular cult building (Building A) was established very soon afterwards and appears to have continued in use down to the fifth century. Archaeology can seldom, of course, identify aggressors, though the establishment, at the end of the eighth century, of a cult to Apollo Pythaeus on the Aspis Hill at Argos might reasonably suggest that it was the Argives who rebuilt the temple at Asine – indicating, perhaps, that it was they who were responsible for the destruction of its predecessor in the first place.

A raid on Asine, however, hardly equates with a policy of aggressive expansionism, especially since, as we have seen, the other communities of the Argive Plain appear to have maintained some independence from Argos until they were finally destroyed in the fifth century. As for intervention further afield, the evidence is extremely weak. The archaeological record of eighth-century Argos is certainly rich compared with what came before (or, for that matter, after), but it is hardly exceptional when compared with other contemporary settlements such as Athens or Corinth and there is absolutely no material evidence to suggest that Argos exercised a broad hegemony over a good part of the Peloponnese as well as the islands. It is true that the skill of Argive metalworkers was in demand: from the ninth century, tripods of Argive manufacture began to be dedicated at Olympia. But these are almost certainly prestige dedications by Homeric-style chiefs rather than trace elements of Argive hegemony and, in any case, the Argive provenance of the tripods says nothing about who actually dedicated them. There is, in fact, good evidence that itinerant metalworkers traveled to major sanctuary sites and set up shop there during festivals. In other respects – and especially ceramic production, at which Argive potters also excelled – the volume of imports and exports is singularly limited when compared with other regions. Furthermore, it is difficult to imagine any Argive hegemony within the Peloponnese on the basis of even the most generous estimate for the population of eighth-century Argos (see figure 4.1).

A total population of 2,500 would yield around 500 males of fighting age. This might be a suitable context for the famous battle which is supposed to have taken place between 300 Argive and 300 Spartan "champions" – dated to the mid-sixth century by Herodotus (1.82) and to the eighth by Plutarch (*Mor.* 231d–f) – but a consistent policy of intervention in other Peloponnesian states is hardly sustainable with a force this size.

It looks, then, as if the presumed earlier domination of the Argives was a myth and there is some evidence to suggest when it was coined. In the middle of the sixth century, the Argives built a monument that an inscribed boundary stone, later reused in a fourth-century CE hearth in the Argive agora, describes as "the hero-shrine of those in Thebes" (Figure I.2). The heroes referred to were the seven Peloponnesian chieftains, later made famous by Aeschylus' *Seven Against Thebes*, who had supported Polynices, the son of Oedipus, in his attempt to recapture the city of Thebes from his brother Eteocles. The hero-shrine was not a tomb: the phrase "in Thebes" implies that the Argives imagined the heroes to be buried in the Boeotian city, although other locations – notably Eleusis (Plutarch, *Thes.* 29.4–5; Pausanias 1.39.2) – claimed the honor for themselves. Rather, the point seems to lie in the date at which the heroön

Figure I.2   Boundary stone of the enclosure of the Seven against Thebes in the Argive agora (photo by author)

was dedicated. In precisely the middle of the sixth century, Sparta, with whom Argos seems to have engaged in a series of battles for possession of the Thyrea region along the eastern Peloponnesian seaboard (see p. 171), was rapidly expanding its influence, not least through gaining the upper hand over the Arcadian city of Tegea (Herodotus 1.67–8, 82). The promotion, then, of a cult to Peloponnesian chieftains who had marched against Thebes under the leadership of an Argive hero, Adrastus, is almost certainly an ideological attempt to assert the centrality and primacy of Argos within the Peloponnese at just the moment when Sparta had emerged as the dominant state within the region. Wistful evocations of Argos' former dominance and Pheidon's role in that could well be the products of sixth-century propaganda. One wonders whether this is not also the context in which the Argives re-elaborated an older Delphic tradition (see above) that seemed to extol their own martial superiority while making Sparta famous only for the beauty of its women.

Finally, there is the question of Pheidon's name, which literally means "miser," or somebody who is stingy. That the name really existed cannot be doubted: in around 560, a certain Aristis dedicated a monument at Nemea to commemorate four victories in the *pankration* (an extremely violent event that combined boxing and wrestling). In the dedicatory inscription (ML 9), Aristis names his father as Pheidon of Kleonai, and it is sometimes suggested that this was a relative of the Argive Pheidon, perhaps living in exile. But is it mere coincidence that the name of the Argive Pheidon should have been associated with the introduction of "Pheidonian measures," which were famously "sparing" by comparison with their Solonian counterparts? And why was it Argos – a state far less commercially oriented than either Corinth or Aegina – that should have established a standard of measures that other Peloponnesians would adopt? Ultimately, there is not much to salvage here. It is not a question of filtering out less reliable information to reach a solid core of historical fact because every single one of our literary notices for Pheidon has its flaws. Sometimes we simply have to cut our losses and accept that there are certain types of narrative histories that our sources are woefully inadequate to reconstruct.

FURTHER READING

General discussions of Pheidon: G. Huxley, "Argos et les derniers Téménides," *Bulletin de Correspondance Hellénique* 82 (1958), 588–601; Tomlinson 1972, 82–3; Kelly 1976, 94–111; Kõiv 2003, 239–97. Doubts about Hysiae: T. Kelly, "Did the Argives defeat the Spartans at Hysiai in 669 BC?" *American Journal of Philology* 91 (1970), 31–42. Argos' relations with her neighbors: J. M. Hall, "How Argive was the 'Argive' Heraion? The political and cultic geography of the Argive plain, 900–400 BC," *American Journal of Archaeology* 99 (1995), 577–613. Archaeology of the Argolid: Foley 1988. Heroon of the Seven against Thebes: A. Pariente, "Le monument argien des 'sept contre Thèbes'," in Piérart 1992, 195–229.

7
Fighting for the Fatherland

A Hoplite Revolution?

In about 485, according to Herodotus (7.8–11), the Persian king Xerxes summoned a council of nobles to gauge their opinion about his plans to invade Greece. Mardonius, a cousin of the king and the general of the Persian forces in Ionia, was particularly enthusiastic about the expedition, arguing that it would be scandalous to let a population as weak as the Greeks go unpunished for their unjust actions. "The Greeks," he says, "are accustomed to wage war in the most ill-advised way out of ignorance and ineptitude; for when they declare war on one another, they first find the fairest and most level tract of land and then go down there and fight, so that those that win meet with devastating losses while I cannot even begin to speak of the vanquished since these are utterly annihilated" (7.9b.2). Recent work suggests that casualties in Greek infantry battles may not, in fact, have been so devastating and it is possible that Herodotus' narrative intention here was to highlight the reckless-ness and even duplicity that surrounded the dispatch of Xerxes' expedition, but that does not detract from the point that, for Herodotus, there was a typically Greek way of waging war.

As with so many other areas of Archaic Greek history, treatments of warfare are all too often based on retrojections back from the better-known Classical period. It may, then, be helpful to begin by setting out what we know from later sources about the "hoplite," or heavily armed infantryman, before considering the development and chronology of this mode of combat. The full hoplite outfit, or "panoply," comprised a bronze helmet (Figure 7.1), breastplate and greaves and, most importantly, a large bronze-reinforced wooden shield, about one meter in diameter and weighing a little under seven kilograms. The shield was held by a double-grip device, whereby the hoplite passed his forearm through a small, centrally mounted strap (*porpax*) and grasped a handle (*antilabê*) on the interior of the shield's rim. According to Diodorus (15.44.3), the hoplite actually derived his name from the shield (*hoplon*) that he carried, although many believe that the term *hoplitês* simply means "armed." The main offensive weapon was a long wooden spear, about 2–2.5 meters long, with a spearhead and spear butt made of bronze (though earlier examples were made of iron). A sword, seldom longer than sixty centimeters, served as a back-up offensive weapon if, as often happened, the spear shattered in the initial charge.

In battle, the two armies would line up opposite one another in ranks and files known as the phalanx. The men in each rank would stand close to one another to present the enemy with a wall of shields. Since the center of the shield was aligned with the left elbow of its owner, it offered protection to only the left side of each combatant. By huddling together, however, each hoplite could protect his right side with the shield of his immediate neighbor to the right, which is why Plutarch (*Mor.* 220a) has the late sixth-century Spartan king Demaratus comment that soldiers put on breastplates and helmets for their own sake but hold shields for the protection of the whole line. The hoplite stationed on the extreme right of the line was not, however, so well protected and, in his description of the first Battle of Mantinea in 418, Thucydides (5.71.1) remarks on the general tendency of this man to avoid exposing his unprotected side to the enemy by edging slightly to the right, dragging the rest of the phalanx with him. The number of ranks depended

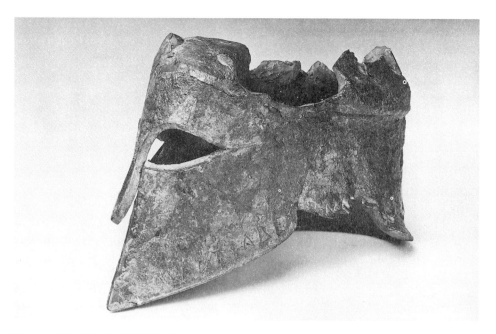

Figure 7.1 "Corinthian" hoplite helmet dedicated by Miltiades. Archaeological Museum of Olympia, © Archaeological Receipts Fund (Tap Service)

upon the desired length of the battle line: Thucydides (5.68.3) seems to suggest that the phalanx was normally at least eight ranks deep, though the Boeotian army that defeated the Athenians at Delion in 424 was drawn up in twenty-five ranks (Thucydides 4.93.4), while the Theban army that crushed the Spartans at Leuctra in 371 was fifty ranks deep (Xenophon, *Hell.* 6.4.12).

After sacrifices and exhortatory addresses, the two armies would advance – sometimes at a run – and what is called the *ôthismos* or "pushing" would ensue. There is some debate as to what the *ôthismos* involved. For some, it described a situation of intense hand-to-hand combat in fairly close formation, which eventually saw one of the two sides "pushed off" the battlefield. The more favored explanation, however, is that the front ranks of each phalanx would engage with one another, aiming to inflict wounds in the throat or groin of their adversaries, while the rear ranks would push those in front of them in what has often been likened to a rugby scrum. On this reading, this phase of pushing would have constituted the most important part of the hoplite battle and was rarely of long duration; the aim was simply to break through the enemy's ranks (Xenophon, *Hell.* 4.3.19). Once this happened, individual combats might break out between hoplites of opposing sides but most seem to have taken flight – discarding, if necessary for a fast getaway, the heavy hoplite shield. The cumbersome armor of the hoplite (estimated at around thirty-one kilograms) limited his ability to pursue fleeing opponents, but specialist units of cavalry and light-armed troops could "mop up" those who were not fast enough. After the battle, requests would be made to recover the dead and wounded and the victorious side would erect a battlefield trophy.

The hoplite battle has been described as "a wonderful, absurd conspiracy" (Hanson 1991: 6) – a highly ritualized contest fought according to "unwritten rules" that, at first sight, betray its "primordial" origins in an early phase of history. And yet many of these so-called "unwritten rules" are not actually attested until the fifth century, prompting speculation that the conventions of hoplite warfare were only formalized after the Athenian and Plataean victory over the Persians at Marathon. How, then, and when did something approximating to hoplite warfare first appear in Greece?

Once upon a time, the story was deceptively simple. Hoplite fighting in the phalanx seemed to be at variance with – and hence subsequent to – the more heroic duels between individuals that are described by Homer. The introduction of the phalanx must have gone hand-in-hand with the invention of the large hoplite shield, which has struck many as too heavy and unwieldy for individual combat. Paintings on Corinthian vases seem to indicate that the full hoplite "panoply" together with phalanx tactics were in place by ca. 675–650. The chronological coincidence between this and the earliest tyrannies (pp. 137–40) might suggest that figures such as Cypselus or Theagenes wrested power away from aristocrats through the support of the "hoplite class." And if Pheidon could be dated to this period (pp. 145–54), his victory over the Spartans at Hysiae might have been facilitated by his use of hoplite tactics against an adversary that still fought according to the old mode of combat; it was, after, all, widely believed that the hoplite shield had been invented in Argos. With the defense of the *polis* now entrusted to a larger group of "middling" farmer-warriors rather than aristocratic "champions," the hoplites began to demand political privileges on a par with their military duties – hence ushering in the egalitarian ideal considered to be so characteristic of the Greek *polis*.

This traditional interpretation is largely indebted to Aristotle, who believed that the early monarchies gave way to the rule of aristocrats who served as cavalrymen but that eventually the participation of heavily armed infantrymen led to their inclusion within a wider citizen-body (Document 7.1). Yet, Aristotle's depiction of this process is an exposition of evolutionist theory that rests on no genuine historical documentation. The idea that there might be a direct correlation between modes of combat and types of constitution is very much a product of late fifth-century writing in which the political power of the less well-off at Athens was explained in terms of their service as rowers in the fleet on which Athens' prosperity had depended. A treatise, preserved among the works of Xenophon but often ascribed to a writer that modern scholars call the "Old Oligarch," explains that "it is right that the poor and the *dêmos* have more than the noble and the wealthy, because it is the *dêmos* that crews the ships and provides strength to the *polis*. For it is the steersmen and the rowers and the stroke-callers and the commanders of the pentekontors and the prow-men and the shipwrights, rather than the noble-born and prosperous hoplites, who provide strength to the *polis*" (Xenophon, *CA* 1.2). From the notion that wider participation in combat enfranchised a greater segment of the population, it was entirely logical to suppose that the participation of infantrymen in political decision-making was a consequence of their having supplanted an earlier army of elite cavalrymen. But there is, as we have seen (pp. 120–7), little independent evidence for the existence of monarchies in early Greece and it is also clear that – outside areas such as Thessaly – specialized cavalry units were a development of the late Archaic or Classical period rather than a fossilized relic of an earlier, more elite way of war. Depictions on Archaic Attic

Document 7.1

The first citizen bodies among the Greeks after the kingships were composed of warriors. Initially, these were cavalrymen, for war had its strength and eminence in its horsemen, since without organization hoplite warfare is useless and given that experience of such matters and tactical formations did not exist among the people of old, so their strength lay in their cavalry. But as the *poleis* grew and those who were heavily armed became stronger, so more people had a share of political power. (Aristotle, *Pol.* 4.10.10) and Corinthian vases of mounted warriors represent not cavalrymen in the strict sense but heavily armed infantrymen who possessed sufficient wealth to own a horse that might transport them to the combat zone.

In fact, there are a number of problems with the traditional account concerning the emergence of the hoplite. The first is the supposed connection between the hoplite class and the emergence of tyrannies. Although some tyrants are supposed to have seized power while occupying high-ranking military offices (pp. 139–40), no source explicitly says that they seized power with the support of the hoplite class. It is, as we have seen (pp. 148–9), extremely difficult to date Pheidon to the second quarter of the seventh century. Polycrates – who, in any case, came to power roughly a century and a half later – is said to have established himself with a force of no more than fifteen hoplites (Herodotus 3.120.3). If this information – which is unfortunately presented in a taunting speech delivered by one Persian to another – possesses any reliability, it hardly testifies to popular support among the "middle class." Pisistratus' first and ultimately unsuccessful attempt at seizing the tyranny of Athens ca. 560 was apparently accomplished with a bodyguard of fifty club-bearers (Herodotus 1.59.5–6; Aristotle, *AC* 14.1; Plutarch, *Sol.* 30). His eventually successful bid was only achieved by means of, among others, Argive mercenaries (Herodotus 1.61.4). Indeed, Aristotle (*Pol.* 5.8.6) specifically states that while a king's bodyguard consists of citizen soldiers, a tyrant's is composed of "foreigners" (*xenoi*). It is difficult to understand why he should have thought this if there existed a tradition that tyrants came to power with the support of the hoplite class.

The second problem concerns the relative anteriority of the adoption of hoplite equipment and the introduction of mass fighting in the phalanx. One view, based on an examination of the archaeological and art historical evidence, suggests that items of the hoplite panoply were adopted gradually and piecemeal, largely predating the introduction of hoplite tactics. The late eighth-century warrior grave from Argos (p. 128) constitutes our earliest evidence for the re-introduction – probably from the Urnfield culture of central Europe – of the bronze breastplate. The grave also contained a bronze crested helmet of a conical shape known from contemporary vase paintings, though the more familiar "Corinthian" helmet, beaten from a single sheet of bronze and encasing most of the head save for the eyes and mouth, is not depicted on vases or bronze figurines until ca. 700. Greaves are attested on Crete in the second half of the eighth century but are not commonly represented in art until ca. 675. It is difficult to assess the significance behind the absence of a shield from the Argive grave, though the first artistic representation of the large hoplite shield is said to be on an Attic amphora, now in Berlin and dated to ca. 700. Geometric vases of the eighth century, instead, show a smaller round shield, along with rectangular shields and what is conventionally called the "Dipylon" shield – a large round shield with two "cut outs," that may derive from the Mycenaean "figure of eight" shield. On seventh-century pots, warriors are often portrayed with two spears, rather than the one that the Classical hoplite carried, and Homeric warriors also regularly carry two spears. On the assumption that one of the spears is intended to be thrown prior to the mêlée, this would seem to indicate a transitional phase from an earlier, more "open" style of fighting.

Hoplite tactics, on the other hand, do not seem to be represented in vase painting before the seventh century. One of the first unambiguous representations of the full hoplite panoply and hoplite tactics is found on an *olpê* (pitcher) manufactured in Corinth around the middle of the seventh century but found in a grave near the Etruscan site of Veii and now displayed in the Villa Giulia in Rome (Figure 7.2). The Chigi Vase – named after the princely family that formerly owned it – is decorated with three polychrome figured friezes, of which the topmost depicts two opposed ranks of hoplites, equipped with helmets, breastplates, greaves, and shields, about to either throw or thrust their spears. Behind each of the ranks is what appears to be a second rank, though a piper intervenes between the two groups on the left; it is generally supposed that his function is to "mark time" for the advancing ranks. To the far left of the scene, a hoplite arms himself for war. The vase, of course, only provides a *terminus ante quem*. Indeed, a slightly earlier *aryballos* from Thebes, almost certainly painted by the same artist (dubbed the Macmillan Painter), hints at some of the difficulties that even an accomplished painter faced trying to render perspective in depicting ranks of soldiers. The appearance of a flautist on an *aryballos* from Perachora, dated ca. 675, may suggest that knowledge of phalanx fighting preceded the skill to represent it realistically. Nevertheless, that still leaves a gap of about a quarter of a century between the introduction of the critical elements of the panoply and the first traces of massed fighting in ranks, and this has suggested to some that it was initially aristocrats who invested in heavier, more expensive armor for their own protection, and perhaps for that of some of their retainers, before the equipment became more generally available.

59

Protokorinthische Kanne Chigi (§§ 99 ff.)

Figure 7.2 Line drawing of the battle frieze from the Chigi Vase. By permission of the British Library, X.423/1337 vol. 3 Plate 13 No. 59

An alternative view looks more to literary evidence and especially the Homeric epics. Starting from the premise that changes in military equipment are the response to, rather than the catalyst for, developments in battlefield tactics, partisans of this view argue that fighting in close formation must predate the appearance of the hoplite shield ca. 700. If hoplite tactics are attested only later in art, that could be due to a lack of interest or ability on the part of vase painters. That the epics, and especially the *Iliad*, focus on individual scenes of combat between heroes is undeniable. But this, it is argued, is largely an effect of the poet "zooming in" on specific characters, who are envisaged as being embroiled in just one of many combats taking place simultaneously. By contrast, a more attentive reading of the poem suggests that mass fighting is a more decisive element in Homeric battle than had previously been realized. In the battle by the ships, for example, the Achaean army lines up, "forming a fence of spears and outstretched shields; shield rested against shield, helmet against helmet, man against man; so densely packed were they that the horse-plumed helmets with their glittering crests touched as they nodded their heads" (*Il.* 13.130–33). The same description recurs later in the case of Achilles' contingent of Myrmidones, whose densely packed helmets and shields are also compared to the "wall of a high house that a man constructs by tightly fitting together stone blocks in order to provide protection against the force of the wind" (16.212–13). Earlier, when the Achaean and Trojan forces engage each other, "there was a clash of oxhide shields and spears and men with bronze breast-plates; bossed shields were tangled and a mighty din arose" (4.447–49). According to this view, the demographic increase documented for the eighth century (pp. 78–9) would have led to increasing pressure on cultivable land, especially in marginal areas between the borders of nascent *poleis*. The task of defending the *polis*' territory fell to those who cultivated it – farmers of middling means. In other words, the emergence of hoplite warfare accompanied the rise of the *polis* and the phalanx, in which each combatant depended upon the support of his comrades, fostered the same ideology of egalitarianism that many consider to lie at the root of the *polis*.

Two counter-objections have been made to this alternative view. The first is that the assumption that the Homeric epics should be dated to the eighth century and can therefore provide a *terminus ante quem* for the introduction of mass tactics may not be legitimate. Many today believe that the poems took on their recognizable form not in the eighth but in the seventh century (pp. 24–5) and, in fact, the notion of a nascent egalitarianism hardly fits with the picture of eighth-century Greece sketched in chapter 6. The second is that the passages describing close-packed formations of infantrymen may not have much to do with the hoplite phalanx as such and that a distinction should be drawn between "mass fighting" and "massed fighting." There are, for example, scenes where missiles are fired after the two armies engage (e.g. *Il.* 8.60–65, 80–84) – something that, in a Classical hoplite battle, might have resulted in several "friendly fire" casualties – while many of the descriptions of closely-packed ranks coming to blows relate to special circumstances, such as the defense of the beached Achaean boats or the recovery of fallen heroes, rather than a pitched hoplite battle. Heroes seem to enter and exit from the field at will and break-throughs are often followed by rallies, which were rarely possible in developed hoplite warfare. Artistic representations on Archaic vases and in sculpture portray warriors in profile rather than standing frontally opposed to one another as they did in the front rank of the phalanx – a pose that would actually place them behind the center of the shield rather than to one side of it, thus dispens-ing with the need for protection within the closely packed ranks of a phalanx. Furthermore, the shield is often carried at a tilt, with the bottom part protrud-ing, which is hard to reconcile with the idea that at least seven ranks of hoplites were pushing behind the front rank. On this view, Homeric warfare was a more open style of fighting than was later the case with Classical hoplite battles, and this is why there is space for the free movement of chariots. And for those that argue that Homer's world needed to be believable for his audience, this would again suggest that the formalized conventions of hoplite battle were a later, rather than earlier, development.

At this point, however, two methodological considerations arise. The first is the well-worn question about the fundamental coherence of the society that the epics depict (see pp. 25–6). There seems to be a growing consensus among many historians that the society portrayed in the epics must have been sufficiently coherent to be comprehensible to the poet's audience and should therefore have corresponded to some current or very recent social reality. This, however, begs the question – which audience? The Homeric epics continued to be meaning-ful in oral recitation long after the dates normally ascribed to Homer: many believe that the "text" of the poems was not fixed in writing until the sixth century and some put it even later. If an audience of the fifth century could relate to a world that was detached from their immediate or recent experience, then could not the same be true for an audience of the eighth or seventh centuries, already familiar with a variety of literature transmitted orally from the Mycenaean period? And once that possibility is conceded, then the issue of coherence is no longer relevant. It is not that the epics are an undisciplined "hotchpotch" of anachronisms, but there are instances where the poet's appar-ently deliberate attempts to engage in archaism lapse. So, for example, mention of the Dorians, who are supposed to have entered the Peloponnese two gen-erations after the Trojan War, is generally studiously avoided, though they do crop up in Odysseus' description of the populations of Crete (*Od.* 19.177). Given the subject matter of the epics, it is hardly surprising that it should be in descriptions of military equipment or battle especially that we find some inconsistencies. The heroes' weapons are recognizable to the poet's audience but they are made of bronze rather than iron. Ajax's "tower-shield" (*Il.* 7.219) and Diomedes' boar-tusk helmet (10.261–65) are both artifacts that were obsolete by the end of the Mycenaean period. Agamemnon (11.15–26) dons armor that bears the closest similarity to that buried with a Mycenaean warrior at the site of Dendra in the Argolid. We cannot, then, rule out the possibility that Homer's allusions to mass fighting betray his familiarity with phalanx formations but that he transfers such combat to incongruous settings or inter-sperses it with non-hoplite fighting in order to suppress an innovation that he knows to be of recent origin.

The second methodological consideration concerns the interpretation of artistic evidence. As with epic poetry, it would be unreasonable to suppose that the primary concern of an artist was to render a faithful, realistic "snapshot" of an event or activity. It is mainly for aesthetic reasons that vase painters prefer to show the hoplite shield face-on rather than in profile, allowing them to depict either the *porpax* inside the shield or the elaborate blazon on its exterior. That they should also depict warriors in profile, however, is far from surprising: in fact, it is the exception rather than the rule for figures to be represented frontally in Archaic vase painting. Similarly, it is true that tilted shields would be less than effective in a hoplite phalanx but if aesthetic considerations do not hold also in this case, it is worth pointing out that in single combat, after the breakthrough, this would be an obvious way to hold a shield to parry spear thrusts aimed at the throat.

Some More Equal Than Others

Despite the various disagreements, there is still a lingering belief in much of the secondary literature that the obligation to defend the *polis* cannot be dis-sociated from the right to participate in its governance and that the "teamwork" that fighting in the phalanx required both reflected and corroborated a spirit of egalitarianism within the *polis*, marking the rise of a "middle class" of farmer-citizens. The underlying assumption, spoken or not, is that all members of the phalanx were equipped similarly because each might be expected to "step up" in order to take the place of those who fell in the front ranks. This assumption finds very little support, however, in the literary and material record – even in the Classical period.

Perhaps the idea derives in part from Polybius' prescription (18.29–30) that the first five ranks of the ideal phalanx will be equipped with *sarissai*, or lances. But his point is not that those in the second, third, or fourth ranks will take the place of fallen comrades in front of them but that the *sarissa* of even the fifth rank, given its length of approximately 6.5 meters, will project beyond the front rank of the phalanx. In any case, this testimony relates to tactics after the military reforms of Philip II of Macedon, who is believed to have replaced the regular spear with the *sarissa* for his elite infantry corps of *Pezhetairoi*. When we turn to the period before Philip, however, a different picture emerges. Xenophon has a young man tell Socrates that a general should put his best troops (*aristoi*) in the front and rear ranks and his worst (*kheiristoi*) in the middle, so that they may be led by the van and pushed forward by the rear (*Mem.* 3.1.8). A similar idea seems to underlie the observation of the second century CE writer Arrian (*Tactics* 12.2) that the phalanx is like a knife, where the front rank forms a cutting-edge and the rest, though weaker, add weight to the blade.

Plutarch's comment (*Pel.* 19) that the stationing of the "Sacred Band" – Thebes' elite infantry unit – in the front rank of the phalanx dissipated its strength because it was mixed with weaker troops only serves to reinforce the notion that those who fought in the front rank were generally better trained and better equipped than those behind them.

Interesting in this respect is Herodotus' description of the battle muster at Plataea in 479. Speaking of the Lacedaemonian contingent, he notes that there were 10,000 of them: "of these, five thousand were Spartiates and they were attended [or defended] by 35,000 light-armed helots, seven drawn up on each [Spartiate]" (9.28.2). It is often assumed that these helots, who were the enslaved populations of Laconia and Messenia (see below), served as attendants but seven attendants per Spartan seems a little excessive and the fact that they are equipped as light-armed infantrymen suggests that they played some role in combat. Now it is quite clear that the figure of 35,000 is a calculation, based on a ratio of seven helots for every one Spartiate and, since the Spartans typically fought in a phalanx eight ranks deep, the obvious inference would be that the lightly armed helots provided the pushing-power for a front rank of fully-equipped and fully-enfranchised Spartan hoplites. Indeed, a treatise from about a century later maintains that the Spartans rehearsed complicated drilling maneuvers precisely so that the strongest men are always facing the enemy lines (Xenophon, *CL* 11.8). In short, there is no evidence that men in the middle or rear ranks would take the place of those who fell in front of them. The function of those who fought in most ranks of the phalanx was to push the more heavily armed combatants standing in the front rank and when casualties and injuries caused the front rank to break, the chances of recuperation were minimal. At that point, lighter arms and equipment would facilitate retreat while still offering some protection.

Other considerations point in a similar direction. Outside of Sparta (Xenophon, *CL* 11.2–3), hoplites were expected to provide their own equipment. In the Classical period, a basic shield and spear is likely to have cost between twenty-five and thirty drachmas, while a bronze breastplate probably went for between seventy-five and one hundred drachmas. Given that a standard daily working wage was between one and one and a half drachmas, these are not insignificant costs. But there is also reason to believe that equipment could be far more costly: although one has to make some allowances for comic licence, Aristophanes' portrayal (*Peace* 1224–5, 1250–2) of an armorer selling breastplates for 1,000 drachmas and helmets for 100 drachmas may at least suggest that troops were differentially equipped. We lack much evidence for prices in the Archaic period, but an Athenian inscription that plausibly dates to the late sixth century sets out regulations for Athenian settlers on the offshore island of Salamis (ML 14 = Fornara 44B). Among the provisions is the requirement that the settlers provide their own military equipment to a value no less than thirty drachmas – a price that could conceivably buy a spear and shield and perhaps also a helmet but is unlikely to have included greaves or a bronze breastplate. Indeed, the description, in a Delphic oracular response (Document I.3), of the "linen-corseleted Argives, goads of war" makes it clear that bronze breastplates were not universally worn. Dedicatory practices may indicate similar trends. From the seventh century it was customary to dedicate arms and weapons at sanctuaries: Alcaeus (fr. 140) describes how he saw white-plumed helmets, bronze greaves, linen corselets, "hollow" shields, and "Chalcidian" swords adorning the walls of a "great hall" that is probably to be identified as the treasure-room of a temple. At Olympia, the fact that 350 helmets, 280 shields, and 225 greaves but only thirty-three breastplates have been found could possibly lead us to the entirely reasonable conclusion that not everybody was equipped with the full hoplite panoply, though we cannot, of course, rule out the possibility that some items of military equipment were more favored as dedications than others, nor can we necessarily assume uniform rates of archaeological retrieval.

Related to this issue is the question of the size of the hoplite "class." According to the Aristotelian *Athenian Constitution* (7.4), Solon instituted four property classes to regulate qualifications for certain offices. The highest, named the *Pentakosiomedimnoi*, included those who produced more than 500 *medimnoi* of dry or liquid measures each year (around 20,000 kilograms of wheat or 17,000 kilograms of barley meal). Below these were, respectively, the *Hippeis*, who had to produce more than 300 *medimnoi* per annum, and the *Zeugitai*, who needed to produce more than 200 *medimnoi*. Those whose property rated lower were named *Thêtes*. The term *Zeugitai* probably derives from the Greek word *zugon*, meaning "yoke": it might refer to those who could afford a pair of oxen but it is often taken as denoting those who "yoked" themselves together in the phalanx – i.e. the hoplite class. Yet the property qualification figure – if it is credible and not an extrapolation, on the part of Classical writers, from the surely genuine figure given for the *Pentakosiomedimnoi* – is unexpectedly high. Two hundred *medimnoi* would equate to about 8,000 kilograms of wheat or 6,500 kilograms of barley; a measure of this size could feed ten to fifteen people per year and would require plots of land of at least nine hectares. Given that the average landholding in the Classical period was around five hectares, it is clear that a *polis* that restricted hoplite service to those who possessed this level of wealth would not have had much of an army to field. A more reasonable expectation is that military service as a hoplite was open to all those who could afford the basic equipment. Those, however, who qualified as *Zeugitai* would certainly have been wealthy enough to afford arms and armor that were better and heavier than the bare minimum and it is fair to assume that it was these men who would be stationed in the front ranks, with the less well-equipped behind them.

Sure enough, when we turn to contemporary documentation from the Archaic period, it is the heavily-armed front rank (termed the *promakhoi*) that receives by far the most emphasis. It is often stated that the Chigi Vase (Figure 7.2) depicts the first and second ranks of two hoplite armies. The idea, however, that the hoplite frieze represents a single, "frozen" snapshot is contradicted by the hoplite to the far left, who is arming himself, as well as by the piper who intervenes between the two rows of soldiers who advance from the left. Furthermore, while the two opposed ranks in the center of the frieze stand, spears poised, about to engage with one another, the supposed second

Document 7.2

It is a fine thing for a good man (*agathos*) to die, falling in the front rank while fighting for his fatherland, but to leave his *polis* and rich fields, wandering as a beggar with his dear mother and aged father, and his small children and wedded wife is the most painful thing of all. For yielding to need and wretched poverty, he will encounter hostility from those whom he importunes and he shames his lineage and dishonours his illustrious bearing and every ignominy and evil follows him. . . . Fight, young men, remaining at each other's side and do not embark on shameful flight or fear but make the spirit in your heart great and strong; do not yearn for life when you are fighting men. Do not take flight, abandoning the revered elders, whose knees are no longer agile. For this is truly disgraceful, when an older man, with white hair and a grey beard, falls in the front rank and lies in front of the young, breathing out his valiant spirit in the dust and holding his bloodied genitals in his own hands, having been stripped down to his skin – a disgrace to the eyes and odious to see. For the young, on the other hand, everything is fair so long as he has the illustrious bloom of desirable youth. While he lives, he is a wonder for men to see and an object of desire for women, and if he falls in the front rank he is handsome. But let each man stand fast with legs placed well apart and both feet planted in the ground, biting his lip with his teeth. (Tyrtaeus fr. 10: 1–10, 15–32)

ranks are running with upright spears. The fact that some of the "second rank" hoplites on the right carry identical shield blazons to those of the first rank might suggest that the same troops are being depicted and that the frieze portrays successive moments leading up to the final confrontation represented in the center – a pictorial narrative mode that is not uncommon on figured Late Geometric vases of the eighth century. It is, of course, highly likely that the representation of the front rank is supposed to stand in for an army massed in multiple ranks, but that does not detract from the fact that it is the front rank that is given most emphasis. This focus on those who risked most for their *polis* is particularly apparent in the preserved fragments of the poetry of Tyrtaeus (Documents 7.2 and 7.3).

In many respects, Tyrtaeus' portrayal of warfare is not so dissimilar from the picture that is offered by Classical writers. It should, however, be noted that Tyrtaeus' poems were still recited at Sparta in the Classical period in order to instil martial values in the young (Lycurgus, *Against Leocrates* 106; Athenaeus 14.630f). This means that the fragments of his poetry that have been preserved are more likely to be those which remained comprehensible and meaningful for later generations, while descriptions of battle that were incompatible with later modes of combat may have been forgotten. Tyrtaeus' warriors, at any rate, are armed with spears and swords and protected by helmets and large, hollow shields; another fragment (fr. 12.26) refers to a breastplate but does

Document 7.3

Take heart, for you are the progeny of unconquered Heracles – Zeus does not yet hold his neck askance – and do not fear the mass of men nor take fright, but let each man stand straight and hold his shield towards the front rank [of the enemy], reckoning life as hateful and the black spirits of death as dear as the rays of the sun. . . . For those who dare to stand fast with one another and advance against the front rank in hand-to-hand combat die in fewer numbers and save the people (*laos*) behind them, but when men tremble, all valor is lost. . . . For it is difficult (?) in the destructive mêlée to stab a man who flees in the back, whereas a corpse, lying in the dust with a spearhead driven into the back from behind, is a shameful thing. But let each man stand fast with legs placed well apart and both feet planted in the ground, biting his lip with his teeth, concealing his thighs and shins below and his chest and shoulders within the belly of his large shield; in his right hand let him shake his strong spear and let him nod in a fearsome manner the crest above his head. Accomplishing mighty deeds, let him learn to fight and not to stand, holding his shield, outside the range of missiles. Rather, let him come close to fight hand-to-hand with his opponent, striking him with his long spear or sword. And placing foot against foot, pushing shield against shield, and interlocking crest with crest, helmet with helmet and chest with chest, let him fight his opponent, seizing the hilt of his sword or the long spear. But you light-armed men, crouching here and there beneath your shields, throw huge rocks at them and smoothed javelins, standing close to those in full armour. (Tyrtaeus fr. 11: 1–6, 11–14, 17–38)

not specify the material from which it is made. Formation in a line is indicated by the injunction to "stand fast with one another" as well as another fragment (fr. 19.7) that refers to soldiers "forming a fence from hollow shields." Furthermore, the description of shield pushing against shield is at least reminiscent of later depictions of the *ôthismos*. What is not made clear is whether other ranks also participate in the *ôthismos*, though the presence of combatants behind the front rank may be inferred both from the gruesome image of the old men falling in the front ranks and lying "in front of the young" and from the observation that those who stand fast save the *laos* behind them. Those who hold their ground also "quickly turn the bristling ranks of the enemy" (fr. 12.21–22). To fall, stabbed in the back, is doubly disgraceful: firstly, because it indicates flight and secondly because, on account of the cumbersome weight of the hoplite's equipment, it was not easy to pursue and catch up with an opponent. This is presumably why losses in hoplite battles were relatively light: at the later Battle of Delion, for example, the Athenians lost 14 percent of their troops while the Boeotians lost only 7 percent (Thucydides 4.93.3, 94.1, 101.2). The most distinctive difference from later hoplite combat is that the lighter-armed slingers and javelin throwers seem to stand near, or perhaps even among, the hoplites rather than in separate units.

What is most striking, however, is the attention given to the front rank soldiers and the imputation that they are of nobler birth. They are described as *agathoi* or *esthloi* – terms which, as we have seen (pp. 129–31), were synonymous with aristocrats. In document 7.2, the warrior who fails to hold his ground and is forced to lead the life of a beggar is told that he "shames his lineage (*genos*) and dishonours his illustrious bearing" while in document 7.3, the addressees are hailed as the "progeny of unconquered Heracles." In fact, it was only the royal houses of Sparta and their aristocratic kindred that considered themselves to be descended from Heracles; most Spartans, by contrast, thought of themselves as non-Heraclid Dorians (Tyrtaeus fr. 2). These front-rank combatants are contrasted with the *laos* – itself, an aristocratic "code-word" to describe non-elites – who are behind them, though it is not clear whether these are the same as the light-armed troops. The latter are certainly charged with an important function – elsewhere (fr. 19.19–20) there is a description of the clang of bronze helmets hit by large rocks – and yet Tyrtaeus' attitude towards these is remarkably condescending. In a passage of the *Iliad* (4.298–300), Nestor places brave men (*esthloi*) in the rear ranks and cowards (*kakoi*) in the middle, so that the latter will be compelled to fight even if they do not wish to (cf. Xenophon, *Mem.* 3.1.8; see p. 163). This is a tactic noted by Aristotle (*NE* 3.8.5), who adds that stationing such troops with their backs to trenches has a similar effect. What is interesting is that Eustratios, a commentator on Aristotle, states that this was a tactic adopted by the Spartans and alludes to a now lost poem of Tyrtaeus as evidence. An attentive reading of Tyrtaeus, in other words, reveals not so much an egalitarian ethos as an expression of class chauvinism.

This conclusion stands in stark variance to the standard picture of Sparta as the model hoplite state. At Sparta, it is normally argued, the citizen body and the hoplite class were one and the same and the egalitarianism that was expressed in the hoplite phalanx as much as in civic life was the reason why the Spartans called themselves the *homoioi* or "similars." From the middle of the seventh century, large numbers of mass-produced lead figurines of hoplites begin to be dedicated at the sanctuary of Artemis Orthia and other shrines in Sparta, testifying – so the reasoning goes – to the emergence of a unified, self-conscious hoplite class. What often goes unnoticed is that the lead figurines also include squatting archers and lighter armed warriors. The use of as many as 35,000 lightly armed helots at Plataea may have been an extraordinary measure taken in extreme circumstances but the basic concept of placing heavier armed troops in front and lighter armed troops behind can hardly have been a novelty. Indeed, it is highly unlikely that the Spartan state, which unusually seems to have assumed responsibility for equipping its warriors, could have afforded to kit out the soldiers in every rank with the full hoplite panoply.

The correspondence between nobility and martial bravery in the thick of battle continues throughout the Archaic period. An inscribed base that should probably be associated with a *kouros* (a free-standing statue of a naked male youth), dating to ca. 530 and found at Anavysos in southern Attica (Figure 7.3),

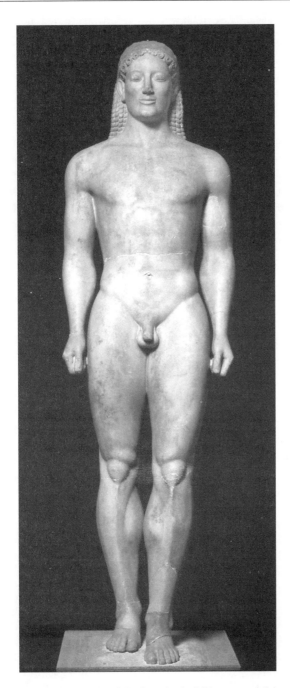

Figure 7.3   Anavysos Kouros. National Archaeological Museum, Athens, © Archaeological Receipts Fund (TAP Service)

reads: "Stand and take pity beside the memorial of the dead Croesus, whom violent Ares once destroyed in the front rank." The name Croesus is Lydian and it was once thought that this was the tomb of a Lydian mercenary who had died fighting in Attica. There are, however, good reasons to suppose that the *kouros* marked the tomb of an Athenian aristocrat. Firstly, *kouroi* were an extremely expensive type of funerary memorial, out of reach to all but the wealthiest. Secondly, Herodotus (6.125) notes that an Athenian named Alcmaeon contracted a guest-friendship with Croesus, king of Lydia, in the mid-sixth century and we know that it was fairly common practice to name a son after a guest friend. Thirdly, we have epigraphic evidence from the early fifth century that Alcmaeon's family, the Alcmaeonidae, owned land around Anaphlystos, the ancient name for Anavysos. The marked emphasis on both Croesus' social standing and his position in the battle-line only lends weight to the suspicion that, far from being an expression of egalitarianism, the hoplite phalanx visibly enshrined and perpetuated the status distinctions that characterized Archaic Greek society more generally.

Conquest, Territory, and Exploitation

In the Homeric epics, raiding represents the most common occasion for hostilities. Andromache tells her husband, Hector, how Achilles once sacked her native city, Cilician Thebes, killing her father and her seven brothers, together with their cattle and sheep (*Il.* 6.414–27), and Odysseus recounts to Alcinous how he attacked Ismaros, the city of the Kikones, killing the male population and dividing among his comrades the women, wine, and livestock (*Od.* 9.39–61). Often the motive for such raids is the opportunity to profit from plunder: while disguised as a Cretan, Odysseus describes to the swineherd Eumaeus how his former life as a freebooter brought him great wealth and, as a consequence, earned him fear and respect among his compatriots (14.211–75). Thucydides (1.5.1–3), for whom epic was an unproblematic reflection of earlier times, notes that piracy was once prevalent throughout Greece and formed a major source of livelihood with little shame being attached to the activity. Alternatively, a raid might be launched out of a desire for retribution: the obvious example here is the Trojan War itself, prompted by Paris' abduction of Helen.

What does not figure prominently in the epics is the desire for territorial conquest. And yet those same scholars who believe that the poems offer a reasonably faithful portrayal of society in the late eighth or early seventh centuries also maintain that demographic increase and a more sedentary mode of subsistence combined to create pressure on land, thus prompting wars of territorial acquisition, normally at the expense of neighbors. The supposition is not in itself unreasonable, though the evidence does not speak unambiguously in favor of it. In fact, wars in the Archaic period were not always fought over adjacent territory and the motivations ascribed to them are very often based on considerations of honor and pecuniary rewards from the spoils rather than territorial expansion. In the 480s, for example, the Athenian general Miltiades was awarded seventy ships and an army for his promise to make the Athenians rich; the target turned out to be the island of Paros (Herodotus 6.132).

Herodotus (1.82) describes how, during the reign of the Lydian king Croesus (ca. 560–547), the Spartans and the Argives fell out with one another over a place named Thyrea, some twenty kilometers south of Argos, on the east coast of the Peloponnese in a region known as Cynuria. The place, he goes on to explain, was a part of the Argolid and had been "cut off" by the Spartans. He then adds that "the whole territory to the west as far as Cape Malea used to belong to the Argives, both the mainland and the island of Cythera and the remaining islands." The notion that, prior to the mid-sixth century, the Argives had controlled the entire eastern seaboard of the Peloponnese is inherently implausible given that they do not seem to have exercised direct territorial control over even the entire Argive Plain until the middle of the fifth century (see pp. 150–3). As we have seen, Herodotus' information here is probably based on sixth-century Argive propaganda as well as on Homer's comment (*Il.* 2.108) that Agamemnon was the ruler "of many islands and the whole of Argos." Spartan activity in the Thyrea, conversely, must be taken seriously: despite Herodotus' belief (8.73.3) that the originally Ionian inhabitants of this region were "Dorianized" by the Argives, all the material cultural connections are with Laconia rather than the Argolid and Thyrea was certainly under Spartan control at the outbreak of the Peloponnesian War (Thucydides 2.27.2). But Spartan control was hardly part of a policy of territorial expansion since it was geographically separated from Laconia – a region over which, in any case, Sparta did not exercise direct, continuous control. Instead, Laconia was populated by a number of small, "perioikic" *poleis* – as many as one hundred, according to Strabo (8.4.11) – which retained their internal autonomy and the right to farm their own territory but were obliged to participate in Spartan-led military expeditions. Additionally, although his testimony cannot necessarily be taken at face value, it is nevertheless interesting that Pausanias (3.2.2) maintains that the original Spartan intervention in the eastern Peloponnese was a reaction to harassment by Cynurian bandits and adds that Cynuria was farmed by *perioikoi* rather than by the Spartans themselves.

Other reported incidents paint a similar picture. Periander is said to have marched against Epidaurus, capturing both the *polis* and his father-in-law, Prokles, because he blamed the latter for turning his son, Lykophron, against him (Herodotus 3.50–52). There is no suggestion that the territory of Epidaurus was actually annexed by Corinth. Pausanias (10.18.5) reports seeing an impressive dedication by the inhabitants of Argolic Orneai, commemorating the repulsion of a Sicyonian incursion, and it is possible that this event is related to Herodotus' information (5.67.1) that Cleisthenes of Sicyon made war on the Argives. No reason is given for the attack but it is highly unlikely to have been undertaken with the permanent conquest of territory in mind. The origins of the hostility between Athens and the island of Aegina were attributed not to Athenian irredentism but to the refusal of the Aeginetans to pay a tithe to the Athenians for the olive-wood statues of the deities Damia and Auxesia that the Athenians had given to the Epidaurians and that the Aeginetans had captured (5.82–88). And in ca. 494, the Spartan king Cleomenes launched an invasion of the Argolid, massacring the Argives at a place named Sepeia but stopping short of his original intention to capture the city of Argos (6.76–82). Again, the impression one gets of this event is rather a settling of old scores between long-term foes than an attempt to annex and exercise direct control over Argive territory.

It is not that land was not an issue. It was, as we have seen (pp. 114–16), one of several considerations behind the decision to establish new settlements overseas and this was an undertaking that must frequently have been accomplished by violent means. But the first wave of settlements in the eighth century was probably not the consequence of official, state-sponsored actions and much of the later "colonizing" activity in the Archaic period does not seem substantially different in kind. The expedition of Cleomenes' older half-brother, Dorieus, first to Libya and then to western Sicily, where he was killed in battle against the Phoenicians and the Egestans, was little more than a private initiative undertaken without the official sanction of the Delphic oracle (Herodotus 5.41–48). Similarly, according to Herodotus (6.35), it was disillusion with the rule of Pisistratus that persuaded Miltiades to accept an offer from the Dolonkoi of Thrace and set up his own fiefdom on the Gallipoli peninsula bordering the Hellespont (though this could have been part of a later apologetic tradition emphasizing the hostility of the Philaid family to the tyranny). Miltiades is said to have resettled the site of Elaious (Herodotus 6.140), though the territorial and strategic advantages of the location were only truly realized when Pisistratus captured Sigeum, on the opposite side of the Hellespont, and installed his son Hegesistratos as governor (5.94). Firm evidence for the permanent occupation of conquered territory comes towards the end of the sixth century with the Athenian *klêroukhiai* – overseas settlements in which residents retained their Athenian citizenship. Yet the establishment of a *klêroukhia* at Euboean Chalcis ca. 506 was not the cause of hostilities between Athens and Chalcis but the outcome of a defeat in a battle in which it was the Chalcidians and their Boeotian allies, rather than the Athenians, who were the aggressors (5.74–77).

It could, of course, be argued that accusations of wounded honor, religious violations, or unprovoked aggression were simply specious pretexts designed to disguise motives that were more properly territorial. That is certainly what is normally suggested in the case of the First Messenian War. According to Pausanias (4.4.2–3), the Spartans blamed the outbreak of war on the Messenians who, they said, had raped some Spartan maidens at the border sanctuary of Artemis Limnatis and had killed the Spartan king Teleklos when he tried to intervene; the war was conducted by Teleklos' son, Alkamenes, and his coruler Theopompus. Strabo (6.1.6) seems to imply that this story was already known to Antiochus of Syracuse in the fifth century. Modern scholars, conversely, are virtually unanimous in their belief that the war was provoked by territorial ambitions. The Messenians, it is commonly believed, were enslaved on their own territory – either immediately after the First Messenian War or following a later, unsuccessful rebellion (the Second Messenian War) – and forced to contribute a substantial share of their annual agricultural produce to their Spartan masters. This was a form of exploitation that had already been imposed on the inhabitants of southern Laconia and, like them, the newly enslaved Messenians were named "helots." The guarantee of a regular income from the lots of land farmed by the helots allowed the Spartans to devote their time and energy to military training which was, in any case, a necessity given the large number of helots that they had to police. Although many of the Messenian helots revolted in the 460s (the Third Messenian War) and some were expatriated by the Athenians to the *polis* of Naupactus on the Corinthian Gulf, the subjugation of Messenia continued until 369 when the Theban general Epaminondas, having defeated the Spartans at Leuctra two years earlier, liberated the region and founded a new capital at Messene on the slopes of Mount Ithome in the lower Pamisos Valley.

Pausanias (4.13.6–7) dates the First Messenian War to 743–724 and the Second to 685–668 (4.15.1, 23.4). It is probably fruitless to speculate how he may have arrived at these dates though the first set is probably derived from the fact that Tyrtaeus (fr. 5) explicitly attributes the conquest of Messene to the Spartan king Theopompus who, according to Herodotus (8.131), reigned eight generations before the Persian War. It is sometimes argued that this date is confirmed both by the destruction of Nikhoria ca. 750 (p. 60) and by the absence of Messenians from the Olympic Victor lists after 736. However, it is impossible to establish whether there really was any connection between the destruction of Nikhoria and the First Messenian War while the evidence of the Olympic lists – even if we consider them reliable, which is doubtful for the earlier entries (p. 32) – is hardly compelling since they record victors rather than participants. For what it is worth, Pausanias (4.17.9) notes that a Messenian named Phanas won an Olympic victory in the *dolikhos* (long-distance race), but this was an event that was supposedly not introduced until 720.

The date of the Second Messenian War is, as Pausanias (4.15.3) recognized, calculated on the basis of Tyrtaeus' claim (fr. 5) that Messene was first captured by "the fathers of our fathers" and the belief of ancient authors that he was a contemporary of the Second War. Pausanias' sources adopt, however, a rather short thirty-year generation. By contrast, the *Suda* says that Tyrtaeus flourished in the thirty-fifth Olympiad of 640–637 while the early Christian author Jerome dates him to 633/2. But the issue is not easily resolvable because it is entirely possible that by the phrase "fathers of our fathers," Tyrtaeus intended to indicate not his grandfather's generation specifically but rather his "forefathers" more generally. This is even more likely to be the case if the verses ascribed to Tyrtaeus are actually part of a longer, cumulative poetic tradition rather than the product of a single, historical individual (see p. 6) – in which case, all hopes of accurately dating the Second Messenian War founder.

Noting that there are no explicit references to a Second Messenian War before the fourth century, some scholars have suggested that the war was little more than a propagandistic invention, coined to equip the newly liberated state of Messenia with a "national" history that had been denied it for so long. Certainly, the detailed account that Pausanias (4.14–23) presents is a stirring story of daring resistance, centered around the larger-than-life warrior-hero, Aristomenes. But a third-century papyrus, now in Berlin, which preserves some fragmentary lines of Tyrtaeus' poetry does explicitly refer to Messenians in the context of a battle (fr. 23), while another papyrus, found at Oxyrhynchus in Egypt and dated to the early third century, seems to describe a combat scene in which Argives and probably Arcadians are participants (fr. 23a). We cannot rule out the possibility that Tyrtaeus was here describing earlier hostilities but both Strabo (8.4.10) and Pausanias (4.16.2), drawing on Tyrtaeus' poetry, say that he was a contemporary of the war and, even if they disagree as to whether he actually participated or not, it would be presumptuous to assume that they were worse informed than we are.

In the account of Pausanias, the First War was a war of conquest while the Second involved the suppression of a rebellion. A closer look, however, reveals that the theaters of operation were different. Tyrtaeus, Pausanias' principal source for the First Messenian War, does not actually say that the Spartans annexed all of Messenia. Instead, he talks about the capture of Messene (fr. 5). For a long time it was assumed – partly on the testimony of Strabo (8.5.8) and Pausanias (4.1.4) – that the toponym Messene should refer to the region of Messenia more generally since Classical Messene was a new foundation of the fourth century. Recent excavations have, however, revealed eighth-century activity on the site of Epaminondas' city. Since Messene sits at the foot of Mount Ithome, which is also explicitly mentioned by Tyrtaeus, it is reasonable to conclude that it is to the capture of this city and its immediate territory that Tyrtaeus referred. The hypothesis that the initial Spartan intervention may have been confined to the lower Pamisos Valley finds some confirmation in a tradition, recorded by Aelian (*HM* 6.1), that the Spartans took possession of half the property in Messenia after the First Messenian War.

By contrast, Pausanias' account of the Second Messenian War describes hostilities in other parts of Messenia – chiefly at Andania and in the Stenyklaros Plain in northern Messenia and around Mount Eira in the foothills of the Taÿgetos range in eastern Messenia (4.14.6, 15.8, 17.10). Since both Herodotus (3.47.1) and Antiochus of Syracuse (fr. 13) mention only "a" war between Sparta and Messenia, it is perhaps more reasonable to infer a much longer period of hostilities, perhaps commencing in the late eighth century, which saw the Spartans progressively subjugate more and more Messenian communities. That could certainly explain why Plutarch (*Mor.* 194b) has Epaminondas claim that Messenia was liberated after 230 years of subjection, which would yield a date of ca. 600. On this interpretation, the Second Messenian War would be not so much a definable historical event as a post-Epaminondan literary creation that focused – and almost certainly exaggerated – Messenian resistance to Spartan encroachments.

Furthermore, the assumption, commonly expressed in the secondary literature, that all the inhabitants of Messenia were enslaved as helots as a result of the First Messenian War is not really supported by the evidence. Thucydides (1.101.2) describes the revolt of the Messenian helots together with two perioikic communities – the Thouriatai and the Aithiaieis – in the 460s and adds that "most of the helots were descendants of the old Messenians who were then enslaved, and it is for this reason that all are called Messenians." Taken literally, the statement implies that not all of the Messenian helots were native to the region but it also seems to correct a current misapprehension, according to which all Messenians were regarded as helots. Presumably, Thucydides is here reminding his readers that, in addition to helots, there were the Messenian *perioikoi* – not only the Thouriatai and Aithiaieis but also those communities that did not participate in the revolt, such as the coastal *poleis* of Asine and Methone, said to have been populated by refugees from Argolic Asine and Nauplia respectively (Pausanias 4.34.9, 35.2). The predominantly Laconian character of dedications at many sanctuaries throughout Messenia – including a shrine beneath the later Epaminondan foundation of Messene itself – has prompted speculation that *perioikoi* may actually have inhabited significant portions of Messenia.

In fact, Pausanias (4.23.1) says that the Messenians were not enslaved as helots until the end of what, for him, constitutes the Second Messenian War (Document 7.4). It is almost certainly the case, however, that this is an inference,

---

Document 7.4

This was the treatment that the Messenians received from the Spartans. First they imposed on them an oath never to rebel nor engage in any seditious activity. Second, they did not demand a fixed tribute from them but they brought half of everything they cultivated to Sparta. It was also announced that men from Messenia, together with their wives, dressed in black, would attend the funerals of kings and others in office, and a punishment was prescribed for transgressors. Concerning the humiliating punishments that they inflicted on the Messenians, there are the verses written by Tyrtaeus:

"Just like asses oppressed by heavy burdens, bringing to their masters out of hateful necessity half of all the fruits that the earth bears."

And that it was incumbent on them to participate in mourning, he has shown in this verse:

"Bewailing their masters, both their wives and themselves, whenever the sad lot of death came upon any."

(Pausanias 4.14.4–5 = Tyrtaeus frs. 6 and 7)

based on the absence of the word "helot" from the verses of Tyrtaeus, rather than the record of a historically transmitted fact. For his part, Diodorus (11.84.8) – who, like Thucydides, distinguishes between helots and Messenians – implies that full enslavement resulted only after the revolt of the 460s. Tyrtaeus (fr. 5) explicitly says that, after twenty years of war, the Messenians "abandoned their rich plots and fled from the looming mountains of Messene" and this, together with the archaeological evidence cited above, suggests strongly that the Spartans gave the territory of Messene to somebody else – perhaps *perioikoi* – rather than enslaving Messenian farmers on their own property. Pausanias goes on to mention three conditions that were imposed on the Messenians after the First War: they had to swear never to revolt; they were required to contribute half of their annual agricultural produce to their Spartan masters, a fairly common sharecropping arrangement among other historical societies; and they were obliged to participate in mourning at the funerals of important Spartan personages. The last is of particular interest because Herodotus (6.58.3) notes that this was an obligation required of not only the helots but also the *perioikoi* of Laconia. This provides a strong hint that the social and political exploitation of dependent populations was no less significant than the economic extraction of their labor. Aelian (*HM* 6.1) also notes the obligation to provide "duty mourners" and adds that, after being defeated, some of the Messenians were left to farm the land but some were sold into slavery while others were killed. Considered together, the evidence is infuriatingly vague but it suggests a situation rather more complex than simple annexation and enslavement, with Messenia populated by a spectrum of various types of free and unfree labor.

In the end, what was truly unique about the Messenians was not their dependency upon the Spartans but rather the fact that a very vocal Messenian expatriate community or diaspora, resident in South Italy, Sicily, North Africa, and especially Locrian Naupactus, was eventually able – with Theban help – to realize its dream of establishing a new, independent state in the Peloponnese. The exploitation of dependent communities, by contrast, was fairly common throughout Greece, with evidence of its existence at Sicyon (Theopompus fr. 176), Argos (Aristotle, *Pol.* 5.12.8; Sokrates of Argos fr. 6), Syracuse (Herodotus 7.155), Byzantium (Phylarchus fr. 8), Heraclea Pontica (Plato, *Laws* 777c; Aristotle, *Pol.* 7.5.7), in Thessaly (Theopompus fr. 122) and West Locris (ML 20 = Fornara 47), and on Crete (Aristotle, *Pol.* 2.7.4). An ancient commentator on Pindar's *Nemean Odes* (7.155) says that, like the helots and *perioikoi* of Laconia and Messenia, the Megarians were once required to send mourners to the funerals of Bacchiad rulers, suggesting some relationship of dependency upon Corinth. All of this evidence suggests, then, that the acquisition of territory as such was a less important consideration in Archaic conflicts than the exploitation of populations reduced to some form of dependency vis-à-vis their victors. If so, the sort of imperialist ambitions that become particularly apparent from the fifth century onwards may well have their roots in the Archaic period.

FURTHER READING

For recent discussion of hoplite armor and tactics: Hanson 1991. For a collection of primary sources: Sage 1996. For the controversy about the *ôthismos*: van Wees 2004, 184–91; Hanson 1989, 157–9, 174–5. The role of horsemen in Archaic Greece: Greenhalgh 1973. Hoplites and tyrants: P. Cartledge, "Hoplites and heroes: Sparta's contribution to the techniques of ancient warfare," *Journal of Hellenic Studies* 97 (1977), 11–27; J. Salmon, "Political hoplites?" *Journal of Hellenic Studies* 97 (1977), 84–101; H. van Wees, "Tyrants, oligarchs and citizen militias," in Chaniotis and Ducrey 2002, 61–82. Gradual development: A. M. Snodgrass, "The hoplite reform and history," *Journal of Hellenic Studies* 85 (1965), 110–22. Massed fighting in Homer: K. Raaflaub, "Archaic and Classical Greece," in Raaflaub and Rosenstein 1999, 129–61. For an objection: A. M. Snodgrass, "The hoplite reform revisited," *Dialogues d'Histoire Ancienne* 19 (1993), 47–61; H. van Wees, "The Homeric way of war: The *Iliad* and the hoplite phalanx," *Greece and Rome* 41 (1994), 1–18; "The development of the hoplite phalanx: Iconography and reality in the seventh century," in van Wees 2000, 125–66.

Helots at Plataea: Hunt 1998, 13. Costs of equipment: W. R. Connor, "Early Greek land warfare as symbolic expression," *Past and Present* 119 (1988), 3–29; L. Foxhall, "A view from the top: Evaluating the Solonian property classes," in Mitchell and Rhodes 1997, 113–36. Dedications at Olympia: Jarva 1995, 111–2. For the non-egalitarianism of the phalanx: H. Bowden, "Hoplites and Homer: Warfare, hero cult, and the ideology of the *polis*," in Rich and Shipley 1993, 45–63; R. Storch, "The Archaic Greek phalanx, 750–650 BC," *Ancient History Bulletin* 12 (1998), 1–7.

Lack of territorial motives in war: van Wees 2004, 19–33. Laconian *perioikoi*: G. Shipley, "The Other Lakedaimonians: The dependent perioikic *Poleis* of Laconia and Messenia," in Hansen 1997, 189–291. The dating of the Messenian Wars: V. Parker, "The dates of the Messenian wars," *Chiron* 21 (1991), 25–47. For skepticism on the early traditions of Messenia: N. Luraghi, "Becoming Messenian," *Journal of Hellenic Studies* 122 (2002), 45–69; "Helotic slavery reconsidered," in Powell and Hodkinson 2002, 227–48; "The imaginary conquest of the helots," in Luraghi and Alcock 2003, 109–41. For parallels to helotage: H. van Wees, "Conquerors and serfs: Wars of conquest and forced labor in Archaic Greece," in Luraghi and Alcock 2003, 33–80.

8

Defining the Political Community

Looking to the End

Institutions, it seems, need to celebrate their origins and 1993 was marked out as the 2,500th anniversary of the invention of democracy, with celebrations in Athens, a special exhibition of Classical sculpture "from the dawn of democracy" at the National Gallery of Art in Washington DC, and the endowment of a two-year "Democracy 2500" Junior Research Fellowship in Aegean Studies at St Peter's College Oxford. The anniversary was calculated on the assumption that democracy first appeared at Athens with the reforms of Cleisthenes around 508 (see further pp. 212–18): indeed, Herodotus (6.131) explicitly says that it was Cleisthenes who established the democracy at Athens. And yet, at a meeting of historians, archaeologists, and literary critics, held at the Center for Hellenic Studies in Washington DC in 1993, Cleisthenes' contribution to the institution of democracy was called into question by many of the participants. Some put its invention later, in the fifth century; others earlier, at the beginning of the sixth century. But some credence was also given to a third viewpoint – namely, that the origins of democracy are intertwined with the origins of the *polis* itself and therefore date back to the eighth century.

We have already seen (pp. 78–9) that the number of archaeologically retrieved graves in Athens and Attica increases sharply in the course of the eighth century; the same seems to be true of the Argolid. Although these data have been variously interpreted as evidence for either higher fertility rates or else higher mortality rates, a recent influential thesis proposes that the increase in known mortuary disposals is a consequence of the fact that a broader cross-section of the political community was now granted access to formal – and hence archaeologically visible – burial and that this marks the first manifestation of what might be termed a "middling ideology." This middling ideology, which finds literary expression in the verses of Hesiod and of elegiac poets such as

Tyrtaeus, Solon, Hipponax, Phocylides, Xenophanes, and Semonides, excluded women, slaves, and outsiders to construct a community of equal male citizens. As a reaction, there emerged an "elitist ideology" – most clearly discernible in the Homeric epics and in the lyric poetry of Sappho, Alcaeus, and Anacreon – which "blurred distinctions between male and female, past and present, mortal and divine, Greek and Lydian, to reinforce a single distinction between aristocrat and commoner." With the collapse of this elitist ideology in the final quarter of the sixth century, the argument continues, "the general acceptance of middling values made democracy a real possibility" (Morris 2000: 163, 185).

Needless to say, ideology is, by definition, not the same as reality. It was argued in chapter 6 that, for much of the Archaic period, the governance of communities was in the hands of aristocracies such as the Bacchiadae at Corinth, the Eupatridai at Athens, and the Basilidai at Ephesus. We have also seen that the earliest laws were designed to regulate potential conflict among aristocratic office-holders by setting fixed procedures, competences, and terms of office and that the rise of tyranny needs to be viewed against the background of internal friction among elites rather than a desire to champion the cause of a middle class. The realities "on the ground" need not preclude a latent ideology of egalitarianism and yet, a closer examination of those poets who are supposed to have espoused a middling ideology raises some doubts. Certainly, as we saw in chapter 7, the view that Tyrtaeus celebrates the hoplite phalanx as an expression of citizen egalitarianism finds little support in the verses that actually survive.

Let us begin with Phocylides, an elegiac poet from Miletus who, according to the *Suda*, flourished during the fifty-ninth Olympiad of 544–541. In an often cited fragment, Phocylides proclaims that "Many things are best for those in the middle (*mesos*); it is in the middle that I want to be in the *polis*" (fr. 12). Many have taken *mesos* here to have a socioeconomic connotation and, indeed, this is precisely what Aristotle (*Pol.* 4.9.7), who quotes this fragment, intends us to assume when he writes that "the *polis* wishes to be composed of people who are as equal and similar as possible, and this exists especially among the middling people." But Aristotle is notorious for wrenching quotations from their original context and employing them as "sound-bites" for the development of theories that were more appropriate to his own day. Alternatively, it has been argued that what Phocylides is actually advocating is to avoid being associated with extreme factions within the *polis*. In fact, when set against the other extant fragments, it is difficult to view Phocylides as the archetypal man of middling means. His charge (fr. 1) that the inhabitants of Leros, an island south of Samos, are "base" (*kakoi*) may be an expression of local, rather than sociopolitical, chauvinism but typically elitist terms such as *aristos*, *esthlos*, and *agathos*, together with their cognates, abound in his poems. When he asks "What gain is noble birth to those who are not accompanied by grace in words or thought?" (fr. 3), it is not immediately clear that it is the concept of high birth itself that is his target. His advice to "Avoid being the debtor of a base man (*kakos*) lest he pains you by asking for repayment at an inopportune moment" (fr. 6) hardly marks him out as a man of the people. Those suspicions are strengthened by his exhortations both to obtain a rich farm to guarantee wealth (fr. 7) and to secure a livelihood in order to pursue *aretê* or "excellence" (fr. 9) as well as by his description of the circulation of wine and conversation in that most aristocratic of institutions, the symposium or drinking-party (fr. 14).

Solon's attempts to stand between warring factions at Athens in the early sixth century (see below) have often led to him being viewed as a middling man and, according to Plutarch (*Sol.* 1–2), it was partly a lack of inherited wealth that drove him to make his living from commerce. And yet Plutarch is also emphatic that he belonged to one of the noblest families of Athens, deriving his descent from the mythical king Codrus, and the elitist tone that underlies much of his surviving poetry is unmistakable. Thus, his description of how he gave to the common people (*dêmos*) "as much privilege as is sufficient" (fr. 5) or how the *dêmos* would best follow its leaders "if they are not given too much licence nor overly oppressed" (fr. 6) betrays the perspective of somebody who clearly did not see himself as a member of the *dêmos*. His observation that a wretched or cowardly man (*deilos*) "thinks that he is a good man (*agathos*) and that he is handsome (*kalos*), even though he lacks pleasing looks" (fr. 13.39–40) is typical of aristocratic prejudice. Similarly, his explanation that it did not please him "to share the rich fatherland equally between *esthloi* and *kakoi*" (fr. 34) is hardly couched in middling terminology.

Ultimately, the elegiac poets do not really challenge the aristocrats' right to rule: in fact, given that most scholars believe that their verses were composed for performance at aristocratic symposia, it could hardly be otherwise. What is more of a concern is the correct comportment that aristocrats should adopt and the necessity of avoiding abuse of the delicate relationship of reciprocity between elite leaders and the communities over which they governed. Three themes in particular stand out. Firstly, rule should be in accordance with some overarching sense of justice. Solon notes that the leaders of the *dêmos* will suffer many ills for the great violence that arises from their unjust minds and pleads that good order (*eunomia*) is the only solution to the city's ills (Document 6.1). Phocylides is more succinct: "in justice there is, in a word, the sum of excellence" (fr. 10). Secondly, the pursuit of wealth is less important than the quest for virtue and excellence. As Solon puts it, "I long to have money but I do not wish to acquire it unjustly for justice always arrives later" (fr. 13). Thirdly, the conspicuous flaunting of material trappings comes to be regarded as an unnecessary and vulgar provocation. Xenophanes (fr. 3) derides his fellow Colophonians for learning "useless luxury (*habrosynê*)" from the Lydians and going around the agora in purple robes with their hair drenched in perfumes, and Phocylides (fr. 11) observes that men who are elaborately dressed think themselves wise but are, in fact, empty-headed.

It is precisely this repugnance towards corruption and injustice rather than the principle of aristocratic rule itself that lies behind Hesiod's criticism of the "bribe-devouring *basileis*" (*WD* 36–41). All too often, Hesiod is regarded as offering a view "from below," but alongside the persona of Hesiod the farmer there is also Hesiod the divinely inspired bard, a poet who participates in the thoroughly aristocratic world of funerary games (654–5) and who has an acquaintance with Near Eastern thought and literature that can hardly have been common among Boeotian smallholders. One of the more intriguing passages of *Works and Days* is the fable of the hawk and the nightingale (202–12). A speckled nightingale, Hesiod explains, was once snatched away by a hawk and begged for pity. The hawk replied: "Good sir, why do you scream so? One far stronger than you now holds you and you will go where I lead, even if you are a minstrel. If I wish, I will make you my meal, or else I will let you go. But whoever sets himself up against those who are stronger lacks sense: he will not prevail and will suffer pains in addition to his disgrace." A great deal of ink has been spilled over the interpretation of this passage and many have been troubled by the apparent amorality of the message. Ultimately, however, it is difficult to read it as anything other than an unapologetic assertion that the vice-like rule of the community's leaders conforms to the laws of nature.

An all too common danger in studying the Archaic Greek world is that of "reading backwards." Because we have the luxury of looking to the end, of knowing how the story turns out, we are sometimes tempted to endow earlier events with a teleological inevitability. Yet, to suppose that it was a latent egalitarianism, emerging first in the course of the eighth century, that made democracy ultimately possible is to ignore the fact that democracies were not established everywhere in Greece. Although the evidence often derives from later authors, there is some reason to suppose that by ca. 500, some form of non-aristocratic governance existed in Achaea, on the islands of Chios and Naxos, and at Ambracia in western Greece, Heraclea on the shores of the Black Sea, Megara, Cyrene, Croton, and possibly Sicilian Acragas as well as, of course, Athens. What is notable is the omission from this list of powerful *poleis* such as Corinth, Argos, Thebes, Miletus and, most obviously, Sparta. But, more importantly, the thesis fails to capture the truly revolutionary achievement that is implied in the word the Greeks used to describe this type of government.

The actual term *dêmokratia* is not attested until the later fifth century though it is paraphrased by Aeschylus in the *Suppliant Maidens* (604, 699), a play that was probably first performed in the later 460s. This is also the probable date of a gravestone commemorating an individual named Demokrates. It can hardly be accidental that this was precisely the moment at which the Athenian states-man Ephialtes instituted what modern scholars term the "radical" democracy by severely limiting the powers of the aristocratic council of the Areopagus (Aristotle, *AC* 25). The word *dêmos* is used in the Homeric epics to denote the free inhabitants of a community excluding the immediate leadership – prob-ably a legacy of its employment in the Mycenaean period (p. 70) – but in the verses of Archaic poets it typically indicates the non-elite population of the *polis*. To speak, then, of the *dêmos* as exercising *kratos* or "power" is to draw attention to the fact that the masses have wrested power away from the formerly governing aristocracy. It is worth noting that, while notions of equality and freedom of speech would be intrinsic to the Classical Athenian democracy, linguistically-speaking the term itself carries no connotations of egalitarianism. In fact, it has been argued that concepts such as egalitarianism, the rule of law and civic liberties only began to become regularly associated with democracy after its reconceptualization at the end of the eighteenth century of our era. The Ancient Greek word for equality before the laws, *isonomia*, seems to have been used as a slogan by the late sixth-century Athenian reformer Cleisthenes when he wanted to enlist the support of the *dêmos* against his aristocratic rivals (see p. 212). But there is nothing inherent in the term *isonomia* that defines how widely equality should be distributed and it has been conjectured that it originally signified those very principles of power sharing and rotation of office among the elite that we have already considered (pp. 134–7).

It is perhaps understandable in this day and age, when wars are allegedly fought to impose democracies, that western ideologues should choose to regard democracy as the perfection of a natural and innate principle of egalitarianism. But even if the Athenian democracy of the fifth and fourth centuries is the direct predecessor of modern western democratic traditions – a dubious prospect at best – its inception was the consequence of a revolutionary usurpation of power on the part of the masses rather than the extension to a broader constituency of a latent egalitarianism that is, in any case, hard to document in the written sources. When considering the formation of the political community in Archaic Greece, it is important not to confuse political participation with egalitarianism. In the remainder of this chapter, we will consider how the political community began to take collective cognizance of itself.

The Role of the *Dêmos* and the Great Rhetra

In a certain sense, popular participation in decision-taking probably had a long history in the Greek world. As we have seen (pp. 120–31), the authority of the *basileus* was inherently unstable and depended on a reciprocal relationship between leader and followers. This makes it highly likely that residents of the small settlements that existed in the Dark Age would have attended gatherings presided over by the community's chief and that the latter would have endeavored to take decisions by consensus. In the Homeric epics, the massed ranks of warriors are expected to ratify by verbal assent the decisions taken by their leaders, who debate proposals in open council. Whether these onlookers are permitted actually to participate in discussion is less clear. After haranguing Agamemnon, Thersites, "the ugliest man who came to Troy," is soundly beaten by Odysseus (*Il.* 2.265–69). It could be that the tone of his complaint was judged offensive: Odysseus chastises him for having slandered the expedition's commander with insolent abuse. But the fact that Odysseus then thrashes Thersites with his scepter – an insignia traditionally held by those who wish to address Homeric councils – probably indicates that Thersites' crime was not that he had addressed his superiors impertinently but that he had addressed them at all.

With the development of a state machinery in the hands of the aristocracy, the role of the non-elite members of the community, however restricted, seems to have been formalized. The *damos* (a Doric form for *dêmos*) is explicitly mentioned in the Sacred Law from Tiryns (*SEG* 30.380), as is a body called the *aliaia*, sometimes thought to also have had a popular constituency. Of particular interest is a trachyte *stêlê* or slab, now in the Istanbul Archaeological Museum, but found near Tholopotami in the south of Chios (ML 8 = Fornara 19). All four faces of the *stêlê* were inscribed with what appears to be a single law that, on the basis of letter forms, can be dated to ca. 575–550. Three faces of the slab are extremely fragmentary, though the text refers to enactments of the *dêmos* as well as to two magistracies – that of the *basileus* and that of the *dêmarkhos* (the latter, presumably, charged with representing the interests of the *dêmos* against aristocratic office-holders). The back of the *stêlê* is better preserved and records the right of appeal to a popular council (*boulê dêmosiê*), which is to assemble on the third day after the monthly festival of the Hebdomaia in honor of Apollo and which consists of fifty elected men from each of the four tribes (*phylai*). There is mention of a fine, though it is unclear whether the popular council is itself able to levy fines or whether it is subject to a fine if it fails to meet on the ordained day. The inscription continues by stating that the council will deal with other business involving the *dêmos* and especially cases of appeal.

The fact that the term *boulê* is qualified by the adjective *dêmosiê* makes it virtually certain that this is a second, presumably more recently instituted council, in addition to an aristocratic council whose forerunner is the Homeric council of elders. The Chios inscription therefore lends some credence to the sometimes suspected testimony that Solon introduced a second council of 400 at Athens, alongside the already existing council of the Areopagus (Aristotle, *AC* 8.4). Like its counterpart on Chios, the Athenian council was recruited from each of the four "Ionian" tribes – though, in this case, each *phylê* contributed one hundred rather than fifty councilors. Plutarch (*Sol.* 19.1) adds that the Solonian council served as a "probouleutic" body, preparing business for the full assembly, though the information could be based on the function of the later "Cleisthenic" council of 500. It is, however, of considerable interest that the popular council on Chios is charged primarily with hearing judicial appeals since Solon is also credited with establishing the right of appeal to popular jury-courts even if these courts are regarded as distinct from the council of 400 (*AC* 9.1; *Sol.* 18.2).

The probouleutic and judicial functions of popular councils are likely to represent an expansion of a far more fundamental role played by the *dêmos* in decision making. An inscription from Olympia (*SEG* 41.392), dating to the end of the sixth century, proclaims the sanctity of written law by ordaining that if someone judges contrary to a written law, the sentence will be nullified. But it then continues by stating that a popular decree will have the force of law provided that it is approved by both the council of 500 and the "full" *dêmos*. The most conspicuous example, however, of the *dêmos* playing a critical role in

---

Document 8.1

Lycurgus was so zealous about this form of governance that he conveyed an oracle about it from Delphi, which they call a *rhêtra*. It runs as follows:

> Having founded a sanctuary of Zeus Syllanios and Athena Syllania, having tribed the tribes (*phylai*) and obed the obes, and having established a council of thirty elders together with the *arkhêgetai*, hold the *Apellai* each season between Babyka and Knakion and so introduce and set aside proposals, but the right to speak in opposition and power are to belong to the *dêmos*.

In these provisions, "to tribe the tribes" and "to obe the obes" are to divide and distribute the masses into divisions, some of which he named *phylai* and others *ôbai* [a Spartan word for "villages"]. The *arkhêgetai* are the kings (*basileis*) and "to hold *Apellai*" means to hold assemblies, because it was to Pythian Apollo that he attributed the origin of, and responsibility for, the constitution. They now call Babyka Kheimarros and Knakion Oinous, but Aristotle says that Knakion is a river and Babyka a bridge, and between them they hold their assemblies because there are no halls or specially designed buildings. . . . But later, when the multitude twisted and violated proposals by subtraction and addition, the kings Polydoros and Theopompus inserted the following written words into the *rhêtra*:

> But if the *dêmos* speaks crookedly, the elders and the *arkhêgetai* are to be setters-aside.

(Plutarch, *Lyc.* 6)

---

decision making appears in a Spartan document that is conventionally known as the "Great Rhetra" (Document 8.1). Plutarch is our only source for the wording of this text but, since he mentions Aristotle's name in explaining some of the more arcane provisions of the document, it is almost certain that he is drawing on the now lost *Constitution of the Lacedaemonians*, written by Aristotle or by one of his pupils (see pp. 19–20). Attempting to establish a more precise chronological context for the Great Rhetra is, however, more difficult.

It is normally assumed that the Rhetra is presupposed in some verses of Tyrtaeus. Indeed, Plutarch justifies his claim that Polydoros and Theopompus drafted an addendum or "rider" to the Rhetra by citing six lines of Tyrtaeus, which can be further supplemented by some verses quoted by Diodorus (Document 8.2). Nevertheless, quite apart from the fact that we lack secure, independent evidence for the date of Tyrtaeus' poetry and cannot even be sure if he was an individual historical personality as opposed to a name attached to a longer cumulative poetic tradition (see p. 6), some doubts have recently been expressed as to the chronological priority of the Rhetra vis-à-vis Tyrtaeus' poetry. Firstly, it is argued, the Rhetra cannot be the oracle to which Tyrtaeus

Document 8.2

Having listened to Phoebus (Apollo), they brought home from Pytho (Delphi) the prophecies and truthful words of the god: the god-honoured *basileis*, who care for the lovely *polis* of Sparta, and the aged elders are to be in charge of deliberation; then the men of the *dêmos*, responding to (or with?) straight proposals (or utterances?), *are to speak noble words and do just deeds and not give [crooked] council to the* polis. *Victory and power are to accompany the mass of the* dêmos. *For thus did Phoebus reveal about these things to the polis.* (Tyrtaeus fr. 4 and [in italics] Diodorus 7.12.5–6)

refers because it is in prose whereas oracular prophecies issued by Delphi were regularly recorded in verse and tended to be more allusive and riddling than anything we find in the text of the Rhetra. Secondly, there is a difference of emphasis between Tyrtaeus' oracle and the text of the Rhetra that Plutarch cites. The Rhetra focuses on the sovereign (albeit limited) power of the assembly while Tyrtaeus is more concerned with the rulers of the *dêmos* – the kings and the council of elders (known as the *Gerousia*) – whose proposals should always be accepted by the people since they are inherently "straight" (on the assumption that the *dêmos* is being enjoined to respond *to* straight *proposals* and not *with* straight *utterances*, as the phrase is sometimes translated).

That Tyrtaeus was a "royalist" has often been noted and, incidentally, casts further doubt on claims that he championed a "middling ideology." Elsewhere, he exhorts his listeners to obey the kings since the city of Sparta has been given to them by "Zeus himself, the son of Cronus and husband of fair-crowned Hera" (fr. 2). And yet, once allowances are made for his elitist perspective, all the central features of not only the Rhetra but also the so-called "rider" are present in Tyrtaeus' verses. Proposals are to be made by the kings and the elders while the *dêmos* is to be sovereign, provided that it does not give crooked council. It should be pointed out that the word "crooked" in the Tyrtaeus fragment is an editorial restoration for a word that seems to have dropped out of the manuscript, but it is surely significant that both the Rhetra and Tyrtaeus use variants of the same Greek word (*kartos/kratos*) to describe the power of the *dêmos*. Furthermore, the objection that the Rhetra cannot be an oracle because it is written in prose would be to suppose that, in other circumstances, the Pythian priestess was normally competent at drafting constitutional documents. Recent studies on the Delphic oracle and divination in general have suggested that petitioners would normally submit an already formulated question to which the Pythian priestess would provide a simple "yes" or "no" response which would later be embellished in poetic form. In short, it takes extraordinarily special pleading to argue that it was not the provisions of the Rhetra that Tyrtaeus had in mind.

Much of the difficulty probably arises from the association of the Rhetra with the shadowy figure of Lycurgus. Already by the time of Herodotus (1.65.4), there was a tradition that Lycurgus received the Spartan constitution from the Pythian priestess at Delphi, although Herodotus adds that the Spartans themselves believed that Lycurgus brought it from Crete. The association of Lycurgus with the Rhetra is well engrained by the time of Diodorus and Plutarch. By contrast, there is no mention of Lycurgus in the extant fragments of Tyrtaeus. Normally, an argument from silence such as this would not be compelling but, given the exceptional attention that later authors paid to the figure of Lycurgus as the founding father of virtually every Spartan institution, their inability to cite a single reference to him from the works of Tyrtaeus makes it extremely unlikely that he ever mentioned him. Indeed, there are good reasons to doubt the historical existence of the legendary lawgiver. Firstly, ancient authors were spectacularly incapable of agreeing as to when he lived: Xenophon (*CL* 10.8) makes him a contemporary of the Heraclidae – the early eleventh century in our terms – while Herodotus (1.65.4) and Simonides (fr. 628) associate him with kings who should have reigned in the ninth century, and Aristotle (*Pol.* 2.10.2) says that he was a co-founder of the Olympic Games in 776. Secondly, his human status was doubted even in antiquity. Herodotus (1.65.3) cites a Delphic oracle that debates whether to hail Lycurgus as a god or man, before deciding that he should probably be treated as a god and, by the Classical period, he was worshipped in a sanctuary on the banks of the River Eurotas at Sparta. The Sicilian historian Timaeus (fr. 127) was forced to posit the existence of two separate individuals named Lycurgus, while Plutarch prefaces his thirty-one chapter *Life of Lycurgus* by admitting that "Concerning Lycurgus the lawgiver, there is absolutely nothing that can be said that is not disputed; different stories exist concerning his lineage, his travels, his death and especially his drafting of the laws and the constitution and there is least agreement as to when the man lived."

Plutarch (*Lyc.* 6) evidently believed that Tyrtaeus had associated Polydoros and Theopompus with the Rhetra and there is little reason to suppose that he invented this, especially since Tyrtaeus elsewhere (fr. 5) credits Theopompus with the capture of Messenia. Furthermore, although Plutarch cites Tyrtaeus to support his contention that Polydoros and Theopompus sought divine legitimation only for the "rider," the verses of Tyrtaeus that can be reconstructed from Plutarch and Diodorus actually make no distinction between the main body of the Rhetra and the "rider." As we have seen, Plutarch's information is almost certainly dependent upon the work of the Aristotelian school and Aristotle dated Lycurgus to the early eighth century, almost a century before the joint rule of Polydoros and Theopompus. Faced with this apparent contradiction, Plutarch – or more probably his source – made the not unreasonable conjecture that the kings had simply added an amendment to an earlier document, once the *dêmos* had started to abuse its sovereign authority. But the tradition concerning Lycurgus is inherently untrustworthy and the verses of Tyrtaeus ought to incline us to treat the Rhetra and "rider" as part of a single document. The clause allowing the elders and *arkhêgetai* to "set aside" a "crooked" decision of the *dêmos* would then represent not a later corrective to abuses but the retention of a right of veto, should the situation so demand.

The constitution envisaged, then, in the Great Rhetra, invests most authority in the two hereditary kings and the council of elders which, according to later authors, numbered thirty with the inclusion of the two kings. By Aristotle's day (*Pol.* 2.6.15), this council was recruited from the aristocracy and this had presumably always been the case. Final decisive authority rested with the *dêmos* but, even if the popular assembly was integral to the decision-making process, the fact that the kings and council retained a veto makes it clear that the principle of consensus remained fundamental. If the right to speak against a proposal is really being granted to the *dêmos*, this seems to have been revoked by the time of Aristotle (*Pol.* 2.8.3) who notes that, unlike the Carthaginian constitution, attendees of the Spartan and Cretan assemblies were not permitted to speak against proposals. Alternatively, it is possible that the right to speak in opposition was actually limited to the five annually appointed ephors ("overseers"), who were expected to protect the rights of the *dêmos*. The ephors are not actually mentioned in the Rhetra, prompting some to suppose that the office was introduced later, though Aristotle (*Pol.* 5.9.1) certainly believed that they had been instituted by Theopompus. Finally, although absolute certainty is impossible, there is no particularly compelling reason to rule out the attribution of the document to the joint reign of Polydoros and Theopompus in the early seventh century. This would make the Rhetra one of the earliest constitutional documents from Greece and would also explain why it was that, by the Classical period, Sparta's constitution had become a byword for stable government (Thucydides 1.18.1).

Drawing Boundaries

The drafting of the Great Rhetra probably formalized a procedure of popular consensus that had a much longer history. Popular participation in governance should not, however, be confused with egalitarianism: at the same time as the Rhetra endorsed the final decision-making authority of the *dêmos*, it also made it fairly explicit that its role was primarily that of ratifying proposals formulated by the kings and the aristocratic council. Evidence for broader competences – be it drafting agendas for assembly discussion or acting as a court of appeal – does not appear until approximately a century later. This could always be due to the normal vagaries that govern the survival of evidence but it is also clear that the *dêmos* could not have emerged as a force in politics before it had acquired collective recognition of itself – before, in other words, it had defined its boundaries, establishing who belonged to the political community and who did not. The upper boundary, which divided the *kaloi* and *agathoi* from the *dêmos*, was relatively well defined from an early date; the lower boundary, by contrast, was not.

Civic organization is relevant to this question. As we have seen (pp. 47–8), the *phylai* or "tribes" that are attested in various Greek *poleis* are unlikely to be the relic of a premigratory form of social organization. The reason for this is that *phylai* served as the principal subdivisions of the citizen body for the purposes of political, social, and military organization and this necessitated a rough parity in size that would simply not have been achieved through natural evolution. It is, then, hardly surprising – as Max Weber once observed – that *phylai* are not attested in regions that were not settled in *poleis*. More importantly, the decision to divide the political community into approximately equal units presupposes some rough conception of that community and its boundaries in the first place.

The best known case of civic reorganization is that carried out at Athens by Cleisthenes in the final decade of the sixth century. According to Herodotus (5.66, 69), Cleisthenes established ten *phylai* with new names taken from predominantly local heroes. Each *phylê* was placed under the command of a *phylarkhos* or tribal leader and all of the Attic demes (or villages) were distributed among the ten *phylai*. The author of the Aristotelian *Athenian Constitution* (21) adds that the ten eponymous heroes were chosen from a pre-selected list of one hundred heroic figures, submitted to Delphi (see further pp. 212–13). Prior to Cleisthenes' reforms, the Athenians had been divided among only four *phylai* – the Hopletes, the Argadeis, the Geleontes, and the Aigikoreis.

At about the same time that Cleisthenes was reorganizing the tribal system at Athens, a similar reform seems to have taken place at Sicyon. According to one of the many bizarre tales recounted by Herodotus, Cleisthenes' homonymous grandfather, the tyrant of Sicyon, gave derogatory names to the three Dorian tribes of his city while naming his own tribe the Arkhelaoi (or "rulers of the people"); the Sicyonians continued to endure this insult for sixty years after Cleisthenes' death before reverting to the standard Dorian tribal names of Hylleis, Pamphyloi, and Dymanes, with the addition of a fourth *phylê* named the Aigialeis (Document 8.3). The tale is so obviously preposterous that few have been willing to try to understand what may lie behind it. The first interesting detail concerns the specification that sixty years passed before the Sicyonians changed the tribal names. Since this equates with two thirty-year generations and since the Athenian Cleisthenes lived two generations after his Sicyonian ancestor, we can be fairly sure that some sort of civic reorganization took place at Sicyon in the years around 500 – well within the limits of Herodotus' historical memory. At this time, three of the four Sicyonian *phylai* were given the standard Dorian tribal names, already in use at Sparta and probably also at Argos. The reform was promoted as a return to ancestral tribal names but we do not need to be so gullible. Since it is inherently unlikely that the Sicyonians would have employed derogatory names for so many years, the most likely explanation is that *Hyatai*, *Orneatai*, and *Khoireatai* were genuine local tribal names – perhaps derived from toponyms such as Hya, Orneai, and Khoreai – and that their perceived similarity to the Greek words for "pig," "ass," and "swine" led to the fabrication of a scurrilous story that they had been coined by the tyrant Cleisthenes.

Document 8.3

But he [Cleisthenes of Sicyon] gave other names to the Dorian *phylai*, so that those among the Sicyonians should not be the same as among the Argives. And in this matter he greatly mocked the Sicyonians, for he replaced the tribal names with the words for pig, ass and swine and added the usual endings to these – save, that is, for his own *phylê* to which he gave a name derived from his own rule. For these were called the Arkhelaoi, but the others were called Pigmen (*Hyatai*), Assmen (*Oneatai*) and Swinemen (*Khoireatai*). The Sicyonians employed these names for the *phylai* both during Cleisthenes' reign and for a further sixty years after his death. But then they discussed the matter and changed the names back to Hylleis, Pamphyloi and Dymanes and to these they added a fourth, named Aigialeis after Aigialeus, the son of Adrastus. (Herodotus 5.68)

If so, this would suggest that *phylai* had existed at Sicyon from at least the time of Cleisthenes' rule in the early sixth century. They are certainly documented on Chios in this period in the legal inscription discussed earlier, while *phylai* are also mentioned in an inscription, dating to the end of the seventh century, which comes from Dreros (*BCH* [1946] 590 no. 2). They are not explicitly attested in Dracon's law on homicide, dated to ca. 620 (ML 86 = Fornara no. 15), though a reference to *basileis* is often taken to refer to the *phylobasileis* who presided over each of the four original *phylai*. Once again, however, it is Sparta that may provide our earliest testimony for the existence of *phylai*. Even if we cannot date with any precision Tyrtaeus' reference (fr. 19) to the Pamphyloi, Hylleis, and Dymanes, the Great Rhetra assumes either that there has already been a tribal reorganization or else that it is the first measure to be taken before establishing regular meetings of the assembly. There was, as we have seen, a widespread belief associating the Rhetra with Polydoros and Theopompus, meaning that the population of Sparta was probably already organized according to *phylai* by ca. 700. Beyond that, it is impossible to reach, though since repartition presumes a population of a certain size, it is by no means inevitable that Dark Age communities were organized along such lines.

According to Herodotus, the fourth *phylê* at Sicyon, the Aigialeis, was named – like the Hylleis, Pamphyloi, and Dymanes – after a heroic eponymous individual. But these eponymous individuals are nearly always themselves "back constructions" and as early as Homer (*Il.* 2.575), the coastal strip of eastern Achaea in the Peloponnese, on which the territory of Sicyon abuts, had been known as Aigialos – a word meaning "seashore" or "beach" (cf. Herodotus 7.94; Strabo 8.7.1; Pausanias 7.1.1). According to a later tradition recorded by Anaxandridas (fr. 1), the Achaean city of Pellene had been destroyed by Sicyon and it is therefore tempting to suppose that the creation of a fourth *phylé* was motivated by the incorporation within the Sicyonian state of new marginal land together with its population. Something similar has been suggested for Athens in the late sixth century (see pp. 222–5), while the fourth *phylé* at Argos, the Hyrnathioi, makes an appearance only after the Argives' conquest and annexation of the territory of Mycenae and Tiryns in the 460s (Herodotus 7.137; Ephorus fr. 56; Diodorus 11.65.1–5; Strabo 8.6.11, 19; Pausanias 2.17.5, 25.8, 7.25.5–6, 8.46.3). In the case of Sparta, it is unlikely that it was hegemony over Laconia or the conquest of Messenia that prompted the civic reorganization because neither the *perioikoi* nor the helots ever had a share in Spartan citizenship. A far more likely explanation – especially given the explicit coupling of *phylai* and *ôbai* in the Great Rhetra – is that the reform was occasioned by the physical coalescence of the four villages that constituted the heart of Sparta (p. 129).

Membership in a club only becomes truly significant when others are denied admission. Bearing in mind the early centrality accorded to place in conceptions of the *polis* (see chapter 4), it is hardly surprising that the initial lines between insiders and outsiders seem to have been drawn on the basis of residence. Thus, Hesiod (*WD* 225) discusses *basileis* who give straight judgments to *endêmoi* ("local residents") and *xenoi* ("foreigners" or "strangers"). A late seventh-century inscription from the sanctuary of Apollo Pythios at Gortyn (*IC* IV 13) refers to individuals receiving the *wastia dika*, or rights of an *astos* (resident), as well as to a *xenodokos* who seems to be responsible for providing hospitality to outsiders (it may not be insignificant that it was also Pythian Apollo who was credited with drawing up the Great Rhetra). From Athens, a gravestone of about 560 bids the passer-by to mourn the deceased Tetikhos, "be you an *astos* or a *xenos*" (*IG* I³ 976).

It is often claimed that there was no clear distinction between town and country in ancient Greece but this belief may be unduly conditioned by the Athenian model, where – at least from the late sixth century – a resident of a town such as Marathon, forty kilometers to the northeast of Athens, enjoyed exactly the same civic rights and privileges as inhabitants of the city itself. In fact, there is a detectable element of prejudice in Archaic poetry against those who do not live in nucleated settlements. The Greek word *asteios* had the same connotations as the Latin-derived "urbane," while *agroikos* – literally, "someone who lives in the field" – was a synonym for a boorish individual. Alcaeus, for example, complains that he is saddled with a rustic lot, living with the wolves and longing to hear the agora being summoned (fr. 130B), and Sappho (fr. 57) refers dismissively to a country girl who wears rustic dress and is incapable of pulling her rags over her ankles. Similarly, Theognis (53–60) rails against newly ennobled individuals "who formerly knew neither justice nor convention but used to wear goatskins around their sides and used to live outside this *polis* like deer." These are admittedly reactionary comments on the part of elite authors who are likely to have remained residents of urban settlements while owning estates in the countryside. Such prejudices do, however, suggest that, prior to the archaeologically documented reoccupation of the countryside (p. 79), communities were focused on nucleated settlements. It is not by accident that *astoi* could be used synonymously with *politai* or "citizens."

Land, Labor, and the Crisis in Attica

Distinguishing insiders from outsiders is relatively easy in small, face-to-face communities. It becomes significantly more difficult once populations expand and settle outlying rural areas. At this point, other criteria necessarily come into play and scholars have often sought these in the system of land tenure. It should be stressed at the outset that this is one of the most contentious subjects in the study of Archaic Greek history. One area of disagreement concerns the precise relationship between civic, political, and juridical rights – "citizenship" in the broadest terms – and the ownership of land. In Classical Athens, the possession of landed property was not a prerequisite for citizenship; in fact, it was not so much that the landless could not be citizens but that non-citizens could not own land unless they were granted special permission (*enktêsis tês gês*). Quite how far back this prohibition extended is unclear: our earliest explicit evidence for it comes from shortly before 430, and it is widely suspected that originally – in Athens as in most other *poleis* – membership in the citizen body was dependent upon owning property. By Aristotle's day (*Pol.* 2.6.21), Spartans whose landholdings were unable to produce the required monthly contributions to the *syskania/pheiditia* or "common messes" risked losing their citizenship and the fact that in 403, a man named Phormisios proposed – ultimately without success – to restrict Athenian citizenship to those who owned property (Lysias 34) probably suggests a fairly engrained notion of a property qualification for citizenship. This might explain why an early fifth-century inscription from Gortyn (*IC* IV 64) records that an individual named Dionysios received an urban house and an outlying plot of land along with his citizen rights.

A second thorny issue concerns the nature of landholding. A great deal of debate has taken place as to whether land was privately or publicly owned and whether or not it was "alienable" – that is, whether or not it could be sold or otherwise transferred to a party outside one's immediate family or kinship group. Little credence is given today to the earlier view that land was originally inalienable, farmed by kinship groups, before the advent of private property. Informed largely by the sorts of nineteenth-century evolutionist views that have been discussed already (p. 123), the theory was also ideologically determined, playing a central role, for example, in Friedrich Engels' arguments for the historical contingency of capitalist society. Hesiod's father appears to have experienced no great difficulty in obtaining a plot of land at Ascra (*WD* 633–40) and the advice that Hesiod offers to Perses largely presupposes a system of private ownership. On the other hand, communal property does seem to have co-existed with private property. Solon (fr. 4.11–13) complains that the leaders of the *dêmos* "grow wealthy, yielding to unjust deeds; sparing neither sacred nor public (*dêmosios*) property, they steal rapaciously, this one from here, that one from there." In the *Iliad* (12.421–23), the clash between the Achaean and Lycian contingents is compared to a quarrel over boundaries between two men: "holding measuring-rods in their hands in a common field, they strive to establish equity in a narrow piece of ground." It is difficult to know how to interpret this passage. It could be that the men are squabbling over an inherited piece of property, but in that case they might more likely have been identified as brothers or at least kinsmen. It is unlikely that the simile refers to the division of land lots in a colonial settlement since the evidence suggests that such lots were far from meager. More probably, the two men are attempting to establish equal usufruct of communal land.

Ownership of property tends to be less of an issue when land is readily available. With the low population density that the archaeological record seems to attest for the Dark Age (pp. 59–62), one can easily imagine that most families farmed land that was at least sufficient for their subsistence. Since the Homeric epics seem to suggest that *temenê* or "reservations" were granted to the *basileis* by the *laos* (pp. 125–6), such property was probably envisaged as belonging formally to the community at large. This is certainly the impression one gets from the late sixth-century law regulating property in a Locrian settlement of western Greece (ML 13 = Fornara no. 33), where private land is described as "cut out of" (*apotomos*) land that is public (*damosios*). Nevertheless, given its ready availability, contestation over the use of land is likely to have been relatively rare. In such a scenario, membership within the local community would have been inextricably intertwined with more-or-less permanent usufruct of the community's land, establishing a precedent for the association between property and citizenship. Although it is important to note that the rise in population that is normally inferred for the eighth century is unlikely to have resulted in overpopulation as such, and that the Greek landscape does not appear to have reached its carrying capacity until well into the Classical period, it would have had the consequence that most of the available fertile arable land would have been brought under family cultivation. As a result, much of the common land would probably now have been located in more marginal areas. Hesiod, at any rate, talks about keeping sheep on hills (*WD* 232–4) and pasturing cattle in woodland (591) without any hint that these lands personally belong to him. But even this more marginal land might be a target for the avaricious cultivator: Solon's condemnation of the rapacious theft of public property could well be a reference to a tendency, on the part of the elite, to bring marginal land into cultivation without the consent of the community at large.

Ultimately, however, finely drawn distinctions between public and private property are probably anachronistic in this period and a more fruitful line of inquiry might be to consider the relations rather than the means of production. After all, larger landholdings were of little benefit to the elite without the labor to cultivate them. Various degrees of "unfreedom" appear to be attested in Archaic sources. At the bottom are those described in the Homeric and Hesiodic poems as *dmôes*. A distinction is sometimes made between *dmôes*, envisaged as those who have lost their freedom due to defeat in war or the failure to discharge expected obligations, and *douloi* or "chattel slaves," treated as commodities to be bought and sold in markets. But Odysseus' swineherd Eumaeus describes himself as a *dmôs* (*Od.* 17.320), even though he had been bought by Laertes from Phoenician pirates (15.403–84). The term, then, seems to signify anybody of unfree status, regardless of his or her origin, who lived in the household on a permanent basis. Laertes' isolated farm houses *dmôes* (24.210) and Hesiod (*WD* 502) seems to have at least two *dmôes* domiciled with him.

At particularly busy times within the agricultural year, cultivators of more than modest landholdings would also tend to hire casual labor. Hesiod (*WD* 441–3, 602–3) talks about hiring a forty-year-old man for the months of October through July and a (presumably cheaper) young girl for the late summer vintage, and the suitor Eurymakhos offers the disguised Odysseus waged work on an outlying farm of his (*Od.* 18.357–62). In both poems, such laborers are described as *thêtes* and they were probably individuals whose own smallholdings had failed and who therefore preferred a more steady income from working the fields of the propertied. That their status was low is implied clearly in the lament of Achilles' ghost to Odysseus that even life as a *thês*, attached to the soil and working for a poor man, would be preferable to ruling over the ranks of the lifeless dead (11.488–91). Sharecroppers constituted another type of labor. As we have seen (p. 176), the exploitation of dependent communities is attested in various regions of Greece – most notably in Laconia and Messenia with the helots. Some may have farmed ancestral property while others were probably transplanted to cultivate vacant or redistributed land but ultimately the issue of property ownership is less important than the obligation to provide a regular quota of agricultural produce to one's master.

The Greek landscape is and was heavily variegated, comprising numerous microzones whose agricultural productivity fluctuated according to varying climatic conditions and unpredictable risks. Fragmented landholdings, occasioned by the principle of partible inheritance, helped to offset some of these risks but could also result in plots of land that were too small to provide a basic level of subsistence in the absence of consolidation of property through marriage, bequest, or purchase. Smallholders who were hit by successive poor harvests would be forced to borrow – a constant theme that runs throughout the *Works and Days* – but significant loans carried serious risks since it appears to have been common practice to offer one's own person as security against a debt. Waged labor was in some ways a safer alternative, though while a loan might conceivably allow a smallholder to recuperate his losses and pay back the debt, it is unlikely that *thêtes* were compensated sufficiently to entertain the hope of securing property in the future. In both cases, it was the wealthy who were the beneficiaries, either by obtaining cheap labor for their landholdings or by deriving income from the sale of debt bondsmen who had defaulted on their repayments. In such circumstances, it was inevitable that the gap between the wealthy and the dispossessed would widen, fomenting the sort of unrest and discontent that is so discernible in the Archaic poets. At Athens, things seem to have come to a head in the early sixth century.

Our principal source is the Aristotelian *Athenian Constitution* (2, 5–6), supplemented by Plutarch's *Life of Solon* (13–16). We are told that the poor, together with their wives and children, were enslaved to the wealthy and had no share of anything. Two groups are specifically singled out – *pelatai*, perhaps to be equated with *thêtes*, and *hektêmoroi* or "sixth-parters," so called because "it was for this rent that they worked the fields of the wealthy" (*AC* 2.2). All the land was in the hands of a few and if the poor failed to pay their rents they were liable to seizure since all loans were made on the personal security of the individual. Some debt-bondsmen were enslaved in Attica while others were sold abroad. Eventually, the poor rose up against the aristocracy but both sides agreed to appoint Solon as archon and reconciler, probably in 594/3. Solon's first act was to forbid loans on the security of the individual and to cancel private and public debts, liberating those enslaved at home and repatriating those sold abroad. Ultimately, however, he pleased neither the wealthy, who were unable to recoup existing debts, nor the poor, who had hoped for a redistribution of land.

Needless to say, a certain amount of caution needs to be exercised in employing testimony as late as this – not least, because issues such as the cancellation of debts and the redistribution of land were of topical concern precisely in the Late Classical and Hellenistic periods. An obvious line of approach would be to compare these later accounts with the poems of Solon himself, though this is not as straightforward as it might seem. For one thing, Solon's poetry was constrained by the rules of the genre in which it was written: elegy is concerned primarily with moral rather than political commentary and is not therefore entirely well suited to conveying a political manifesto. But it is also important to note that we possess the fragments of Solon's poetry that appear to deal with contemporary political issues only because authors such as the compiler of the *Athenian Constitution* and Plutarch cited them in their treatments of Solon's reforms. Since these verses have been detached from their original literary context, we cannot rule out the possibility that more generic moral themes have been given a more specific historical nuance by later authors. For all that, however, it is clear that Solon's poetry can offer us important, first hand, and contemporary testimony.

We have already seen that Solon criticizes the rapacious behavior of the leaders of the *dêmos* but he is equally critical of the citizens generally, whom he accuses of foolishness and greed (fr. 4.5–6); the end result is *stasis*, or internecine civil war (fr. 4.18–20). He also notes how "many of the poor go to a foreign country, sold and bound in unseemly fetters" (fr. 4.23–25). Unfortunately, he is less explicit about the measures he took. We are told (fr. 34) that he removed boundary-markers (*horoi*), fixed everywhere in the "black earth," and liberated the land from its former slavery, that he repatriated those who had been sold abroad, legally or otherwise, and freed those "who endured shameful slavery right here," and that he wrote laws "for *kakos* and *agathos* alike, providing an equal judicial process for each man." He also admits that, in spite of expectations to the contrary, he did not redistribute land equally among the *kakoi* and *esthloi* (fr. 34). What is interesting here is not Solon's refusal to redistribute property but the mere fact that such a measure could even have been considered so early. Adopting a seemingly neutral stance, he describes himself as "a boundary-marker in no-man's land" (fr. 37), neither diminishing or increasing the status of the *dêmos* nor allowing the wealthy and powerful to suffer any indignity (fr. 5). Elsewhere (fr. 37), however, he rebukes the *dêmos* for never having imagined in their dreams the things they now possess.

There is no unambiguous reference to the cancellation of debts, unless that is what is meant by liberating those who endured shameful slavery in Attica. Nor do any of the extant fragments of Solon's poetry mention the *hektêmoroi*. The term is rare enough to make it unlikely that it is an invention of Aristotle's school, though that does not necessarily entail that the precise definition that the compiler of the *Athenian Constitution* offers is correct or anything more than an educated guess. As many commentators have pointed out, one sixth is a surprisingly low rent in a sharecropping agreement. One interpretation of the institution sees the *hektêmoroi* as smallholders who are hired to work the land of the wealthy and receive, rather than pay, one sixth of the produce they farm; over time, the procedure became a social obligation, for which defaulters could be enslaved, and it is this system that Solon abolished. A more commonly held view is that the *hektêmoroi* were impoverished smallholders who mortgaged their own land to the wealthy. The "sixth part" would have been the interest on the mortgage repayments while the *horoi* would have signaled that the plot of land in question was under mortgage. When Solon describes tearing up these *horoi*, we should understand that he canceled such mortgage agreements.

This last interpretation might explain Solon's reference to liberating the earth and those who had endured slavery on Attic soil as well as why later authors should have credited him with a cancellation of debts. There is, however, a problem. Although arguments from silence can never be conclusive, it remains the case that there is no literary or epigraphic evidence for the use of *horoi* as mortgage markers before the 360s. It could be that Solon's reference to removing *horoi* should be interpreted metaphorically as signaling an end to *stasis* between two opposing sides: Solon had, after all, described himself as a *horos*, planted between contending factions. But the argument that Solon would not have admitted to tearing up real *horoi* because authors such as Plato (*Laws* 8.842e–843b) regarded such an act as sacrilegious is only cogent if such *horoi* had been set up legitimately in the first place. Since Solon has already accused the leaders of the *dêmos* of seizing sacred and public property it could be that the *horoi* marked elite appropriation of common land, akin to the land enclosures in eighteenth- and nineteenth-century Britain, and that Solon restored such land to the community.

In the final analysis, there is much about Solon's reforms and the circumstances that motivated them that we will probably never know or understand. His contribution to the definition of the Athenian political community, on the other hand, is clear. From the perspective of the elites, the *dêmos* was regarded as a homogeneous mass, but the view from below was very different. Property holders of vastly differing means from the impoverished to the comfortably off, all of whom were presumably permitted to attend meetings of the popular assembly, shaded off into various categories of unfree status – sharecroppers, wage laborers, and debt bondsmen – who are unlikely to have been regarded as part of the political community. Aristocrats such as "Theognis" (53–68, 183–92, 555–60, 649–52, 657–82, 1109–14) may have bemoaned the fickleness of fortune but downward mobility among the lower ranks of society must have been just as, if not more, common and carried with it considerably more than a loss of pride. What Solon did was to establish a "glass floor" or lower limit, below which members of the community could no longer fall. From that time, all who were born of free Athenian fathers would be members of the political community, regardless of whether or not they owned property, and the Athenians had to begin to look to external sources for chattel slaves who would provide unfree labor. Plutarch (*Sol.* 18; cf. Aristotle, *AC* 7.3) is probably right to suggest that the right to attend the assembly and – ultimately of even greater significance – to serve on jury panels for appeal courts was now formally granted for the first time to all freeborn Athenians and it could very well be this right that Solon (fr. 37) claims the masses could never have imagined in their dreams.

From the late fifth century onwards, aristocrats of a more oligarchic persuasion reinvented Solon as the founder of the Athenian democracy so that they might disguise their reactionary proposals to restrict the franchise as a return to the "pure" form of the ancestral constitution. In truth, Solon's reforms were anything but democratic in intention. We have already had reason to consider the condescending attitude that he displayed towards the *dêmos* and that is paralleled by his decision to employ – or retain – the rather derogatory term *thêtes* to denote the lowest of the four census classes (see p. 165), which – if the qualification levels provided by the *Athenian Constitution* (7.4) are reliable – must have comprised roughly half of the Attic population, including many who were well above the breadline. But, from a longer-term perspective, it could be argued that the *dêmos* could not have seized *kratos* before it had formed a clear conception of its contours and boundaries and that it was precisely this consolidation of a political identity that Solon created. It can hardly be coincidental that a democratic regime is first attested at Argos in the 460s, a few decades after some measures appear to have been implemented formalizing the distinction between citizens and dependent laborers, described variously as *douloi* (Herodotus 6.83; Diodorus 10.26), *oiketai* (Diodorus 10.26; Pausanias 2.20.9), *perioikoi* (Aristotle, *Pol.* 5.2.8; Plutarch, *Mor.* 245f), or *gymnêtes* (Pollux 3.83). At Sparta, by contrast, the *dêmos*, though recognized from an early date as the ultimate source of authority, was a more fluid entity with frequent demotions from the citizen-body for various transgressions and failed obligations. With boundaries as porous as these, it is hardly surprising that the nominal supremacy of the Spartan *dêmos* was little more than an illusion.

The "Second Sex"

Around the exterior of the Parthenon, begun on the initiative of Pericles in the 440s, runs a frieze of metopes or panels depicting mythical battles between Gods and Giants, Greeks and Trojans, Athenians and Amazons, and Lapiths (a legendary population of Thessaly) and Centaurs. A common interpretation of these scenes is that they articulate the sort of binary oppositions that characterize Greek thought and express a citizen ideal through explicit contrast with antitypical figures such as savage beasts (Giants; Centaurs), slavish foreigners (Trojans), and warlike women (Amazons). Influenced ultimately by French structuralist thought of the 1950s and 1960s, it is precisely this type of interpretation that underpins arguments for the construction, in the course of the eighth century, of a "middling ideology" that symbolically constructed a community of equal male citizens through the systematic exclusion of women, slaves, and outsiders (see above). Yet, as satisfying as the identification of neat symmetrical patterns in Greek thought undoubtedly is, structuralism is profoundly ahistorical, concentrating usually on explaining how things are rather than how they came to be. The discussion in this chapter, for example, must necessarily cast doubt on the notion that it was the exclusion of slaves that helped construct a self-conscious political community for the simple reason that there was a wide spectrum of dependent and unfree statuses that would inevitably have blurred any clear distinction between slave and free in the earlier Archaic period. Indeed, far from being a prerequisite for the creation of a citizen ideal, the institution of chattel slavery on any significant scale – at least in Attica – seems rather to have been an economic response to a political redefinition of the political community. But what about women?

There is little doubt that, to modern sensibilities, the tone of much Archaic literature is decidedly and unattractively misogynistic. Hesiod describes Pandora, the first and prototypical woman, as possessing the beauty and charm of a goddess but the manners and morals of a bitch (*WD* 59–68). Elsewhere he cautions Perses not to be taken in by a woman, "flaunting her arse, prattling and flattering you, with an eye on your barn" (373–4) and counsels him to choose a wife carefully, "for there is no greater prize that a man can carry off than a good wife, but neither is there anything that will make him shiver more than a bad and parasitic wife who, without a fire-brand, singes her husband even if he is strong and brings him to raw old age" (702–5). Semonides of Amorgos, conventionally dated to the last quarter of the seventh century, is credited with a poem (fr. 7) classifying women according to various natural categories such as sows, vixens, bitches, the earth, the sea, asses, weasels, mares, monkeys, and bees – the last, blameless and faithful, being the only woman worth having as a wife. Phocylides (fr. 2) presents similar sentiments. Iambic poets such as Archilochus (e.g. frs. 42–3, 46, 54, 67, 82, 119, 152, 196a, 206, and 328) and Hipponax (frs. 12, 68, 70, 84, 92, and 104) betray a more loutish side to the symposium in their boasts of successful conquests, outbursts of abusive vitriol, and references to sexual violence.

In terms of explanatory power, however, the charge of misogyny is not terribly meaningful. The task of the historian is not to condone the motivations behind such negative views but to seek to understand some of them. Two of the specific complaints that Hesiod – and, to a lesser extent, Semonides – levels against women are that they are parasitic upon their husbands and that they are fundamentally untrustworthy. It has been plausibly suggested that both attitudes derive from the increasingly important role that the *oikos* or household played from the seventh century onwards. In the Dark Age, a failing farmer could probably hope for some support from the local *basileus* but the new aristocracies of Greece felt no such obligation to their social inferiors. It was left to individual *oikoi* to meet their subsistence needs and, in such a climate of imminent risk, it was essential that production match – or preferably exceed – consumption. Women were, of course, essential to the reproduction and continuation of the *oikos*, but high mortality rates meant that, on average, a woman would need to experience between four and five pregnancies to ensure the survival to adulthood of at least two children and, in agricultural regimes at any rate, the productivity of women in advanced stages of pregnancy or the early stages of nurture tends to be limited even though they and their children need to be fed. Furthermore, in the world described by Hesiod, individual households are not supported by large kin networks. When Hesiod tells Perses that the best sort of wife is one who lives nearby (*WD* 700), the implication seems to be that it was not uncommon for brides to travel some distance from the household of their father to that of their husband and it may be that this transference of women from household to household led to suspicions about their allegiance to their husband's household – eventually spawning anxiety about infidelity and the production of illegitimate heirs. Certainly, one of the fundamental themes that is treated incessantly in Attic tragedy of the fifth century concerns the ruin visited upon households when female characters in particular either value affiliation to affines (relations through marriage) over allegiance to cognates (blood relations), as is the case with Ariadne or Medea, or else rank loyalty to cognates above that to affines, as with Clytemnestra or Antigone.

The two negative attitudes towards women that Hesiod displays are fairly typical of peasant societies generally. They are sometimes contrasted with the views that are presented in the Homeric epics and lyric poetry. Homer's portrayal of the relationship between Hector and Andromache has been interpreted as validating the concept of the nuclear family over households based around more extended families, and Homeric women generally are portrayed in a positive light as paragons not only of beauty but also of domestic virtue (e.g. Arete or Penelope). It is, perhaps, not terribly surprising that the poetess Sappho should display a more tender and positive attitude towards her fellow women but the Spartan poet Alcman also reveals a sensitivity towards female camaraderie in the choral lyrics that he wrote for choirs of girls. In the opinion of some, the difference is to be explained by the fact that these authors subscribed to an "elitist ideology," that elided distinctions between – among other categories – men and women to reinforce a basic distinction between elites and commoners. There are, however, two problems with this view.

Firstly, if Homeric and lyric poetry, which was undoubtedly aimed at an aristocratic audience, testifies to an attitude of respect and affection for women, that does not mean that gender distinctions were blurred. In fact, elite women were objectified as commodities that, through marriage, served to cement alliances between powerful families. One of the most visible expressions of this attitude can be found in the production of *korai* (singular: *korê*), the statues of standing female figures that first begin to appear towards the end of the seventh century. Like their male counterpart, the *kouros* (Figure 7.3), *korai* could serve either as dedications in sanctuaries or as grave markers, but unlike the naked *kouroi* whose massive dimensions they also never attained, they were invariably clothed with elaborate drapery that became ever more luxuriant and sumptuous as East Greek fashions spread westwards. The *korai*, dedicated on the Athenian acropolis in the last third of the sixth century for example, wear variations of the "Ionic" *khitôn* – a linen garment, normally with sleeves – and the *himation* or mantle, both detailed with complex patterns of folds and pleats and decorated with brightly-colored geometric motifs. They are also bedecked with expensive jewelry and elaborate coiffures and head dresses that serve to emphasize their function as a medium of exchange – indeed some of the acropolis *korai* were actually dedicated by men (Figure 8.1). Some are accompanied by inscriptions which draw attention to the role women played in forging relations between families. So, for example, a *korê* from the sanctuary of Artemis on Delos, dated to 640–630, is inscribed "Nikandre, the excellent daughter of Deinodikes of Naxos, sister of Deinomenes and now wife of Phraxos, dedicated me to the far-shooting goddess who rejoices in the arrow" (*ID* 2). By contrast, an inscribed base of a funerary *korê*, found at Merenda (ancient Myrrhinous) to the southeast of Athens and dated approximately a century later, commemorates a girl named Phrasikleia and bewails the fact that she will "always be called 'maiden' (*korê*), having been allotted this name by the gods instead of marriage" (*IG* I^3 1261).

Secondly, as we saw earlier in this chapter, the distinction between "elitist" and "middling" or "bourgeois" poets is probably exaggerated, given that the latter's verses were undoubtedly composed for performance at the aristocratic symposium. The often offensive tone of Iambic poetry should probably be seen as reflective not of a socioeconomic class but of a masculinist environment in which expressions of bravado and machismo served as rituals of male bonding. As such, they also need to be read against homoerotic symposiastic poetry such as Solon's reference (fr. 25) to loving a boy "in the lovely flower of youth, with desiring thighs and a sweet mouth" or Theognis' admission (1341–50) that he is "in love with a soft-skinned youth who displays me to all his friends even though I am unwilling."

There may be a few hints that the exclusion of women from political life was the source of some anxiety for Greek males. According to this view, Hesiod's account in the *Theogony* of the eventual supremacy of the patriarchal Olympian

Figure 8.1 *Korê* from the Athenian acropolis, signed by Antenor and dedicated by the potter Nearkhos. Ephorate of Prehistoric and Classical Antiquities. Acropolis Museum, Athens

gods over previous generations in which female deities were more powerful or Apollo's victory over the female dragon who guarded the site of Delphi, as told in the *Homeric Hymn to Apollo*, could conceivably offer some justification for the way things were in the Archaic Greek world, seeking to cast cultural contingency in terms of natural determinism. A similar explanation has often been adduced for female religious rituals. Although there is no doubt that rituals in honor of divinities such as Artemis, Demeter and Kore, and Dionysus offered women a certain empowerment, those rituals were regulated by a society for which religious decisions were ultimately political decisions and hence in the hands of males. In the case of the Thesmophoria festival in honor of Demeter, for example, the rituals that are attested for the Classical period – including the removal of women from their homes to a sanctuary outside the civic center and the mandate that they abstain from sexual intercourse for the period of the festival – seem to reinforce, through the strategy of inversion, societal norms which expected women to attend to the household and to give birth to legitimate children. But to assume that the exclusion of women from political decision-making constituted a foundational function in imagining the political community would be to assume that their inclusion was ever entertained historically as a feasible option and for this there is no convincing evidence. Why this should have been the case is certainly an interesting question but it is not one that is unique to the Greek world.

FURTHER READING

Divergent views on the introduction of democracy at Athens: Morris and Raaflaub 1998. For "middling" and "elitist" ideologies: Morris 2000, 155–91; for a critique: E. Kistler, "Kampf der Mentalitäten: Ian Morris' 'Elitist' versus 'Middling-Ideology'?" in Rollinger and Ulf 2004, 145–75; Irwin 2005, 35–62. A non-socioeconomic interpretation of Phocylides fr. 12: Starr 1986, 96. Non-aristocratic governments outside Athens: Robinson 1997. For the meaning of *dêmos* in Archaic literature: W. Donlan, "Changes and shifts in the meaning of demos in the literature of the Archaic period," *La Parola del Passato* 25 (1970), 381–95. For the modern reconceptualization of democracy: E. Meiksins Wood, "Democracy: An idea of ambiguous ancestry," in Euben, Wallach, and Ober 1994, 59–80. For Demokrates: Hansen 1991, 70.
Homeric assemblies: K. Raaflaub, "Politics and interstate relations in the world of the early Greek *poleis*: Homer and beyond," *Antichthon* 31 (1997), 1–27. Tyrtaeus and the Great Rhetra: H. van Wees, "Tyrtaeus' *Eunomia*: Nothing to do with the Great Rhetra," in Hodkinson and Powell 1999, 1–41. The role of the Spartan assembly: de Ste Croix 1972, 126–31.
Citizenship and land tenure in Attica: Manville 1990. Various interpretations of Solon's reforms: Murray 1993, 189–94; T. W. Gallant, "Agricultural systems, land tenure, and the reforms of Solon," *Annual of the British School at Athens* 77 (1982), 111–24; T. E. Rihll, "Hektemoroi: Partners in crime?" *Journal of Hellenic Studies* 111 (1991), 101–27; E. M. Harris, "A new solution to the riddle of the *Seisachtheia*," in Mitchell and Rhodes 1997, 103–112; L. Foxhall, "A view from the top: Evaluating the

Solonian property classes," in Mitchell and Rhodes 1997, 113–36. Date of Solon's reforms: R. W. Wallace, "The date of Solon's reforms," *American Journal of Ancient History* 8 (1983), 81–9. For Solon's later role as the founder of democracy: R. Thomas, "Law and lawgiver in the Athenian democracy," in Osborne and Hornblower 1994, 119–34. Concepts of freedom and slavery in Archaic Greece: Raaflaub 2004.

For attitudes to women in Archaic literature: M. B. Arthur, "Early Greece: The origins of the western attitude toward women," in Peradotto and Sullivan 1984, 7–58. The structuralist approach to the construction of Greek gender: duBois 1982; Cartledge 2002a, 78–104.

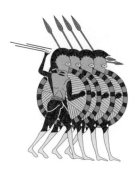

Excursus II
Evaluating the Spartan Mirage

A charge frequently leveled against Greek historians is that they too often make generalizations based on a single city – namely, Athens. Indeed, most treatments of Archaic Greece – this one included – devote at least one chapter to the history of Athens, seemingly contributing to such an "Athenocentric" focus. Nevertheless, while caution should always be exercised before assuming that Athens was either typical or atypical, there is some justification for focusing comparatively more attention on this city. Firstly, the combined literary and archaeological evidence for Archaic Athens outweighs that for any other *polis*. Much of the literary evidence is, of course, late and it cannot be employed uncritically, but neither can it be ignored. Secondly, Athens in the Classical period was one of the most powerful *poleis* in the Greek world and certainly the most important from a cultural point of view. To understand the origins of the city's ascent to such dominance, it is necessary to consider what was happening there in the preceding Archaic period.

Ideally the evidence for Athens should be compared to that available for other parts of the Greek world and such comparisons normally focus on Sparta, for which we possess almost as much evidence as for Athens. But if the testimony for Athens needs to be treated cautiously, that for Sparta should carry a formal warning. The reason for this is that much of what we think we know about Sparta – and especially Archaic Sparta – is veiled in what a French scholar once described as "the Spartan mirage," an idealized image of a pristine, static political community that has been eulogized, exaggerated, and distorted by a succession of ancient and post-antique thinkers.

The Romans, for example, liked to imagine parallels between their own constitution and that of the Spartans, and Greek authors such as Dionysius of Halicarnassus (*RA* 2.13–14, 23, 49) and Athenaeus (6.273f), influenced in good measure by Polybius (6.3, 10–11), maintained that they had deliberately set out to imitate the Spartans in this regard. The famed simplicity and austerity of the ancient Spartans was praised by Church Fathers such as Clement of Alexandria and claimed as a model for the early monastic movement. Statesmen such as Niccolò Machiavelli and Sir Walter Raleigh expressed their admiration for the stable, "mixed" constitution of the Spartans, with its popular assembly presided over by kings and an aristocratic council. The Spartans' supposed rejection of private property influenced the utopian ideas of Sir Thomas More and the Abbé de Mably and, much later, the communist philosophy of Friedrich Engels. For the eighteenth-century French philosopher Jean-Jacques Rousseau, the Spartans' subordination of their own individual interests to the good of the state offered a prototype for the "social contract," while the apparent licence accorded Spartan women constituted, for the nineteenth-century Swiss historian Johann Jakob Bachofen, the remnants of a once more universal institution of matriarchy. But Adolf Hitler also had a particular fascination with Sparta, basing the *Hitler Jugend* on the Spartan *agôgê* or public education system. In the rambling thoughts that form the *Table Talk* – itself a title borrowed from Plutarch – Hitler admired the Spartans' determination to weed out weak or inferior children and compared the fate of his own Sixth Army, cut off in Stalingrad, to that of King Leonidas and the 300 Spartans who fought to the death, defending the pass of Thermopylae against the Persians in 480.

The image of Sparta, then, has served a multitude of political, philosophical, and ideological purposes throughout the centuries but all of these ideas expand, to varying degrees, on a discourse that seems to originate in the fifth century. The Spartan authorities, no doubt, played an important role in manufacturing the image that they projected to the outside world, but our perception of that image has been refracted through the lenses of non-Spartan writers – especially Athenian authors of a more oligarchic persuasion, for whom an idealized portrayal of Sparta as a stable, just, and meritocratic society could serve as a utopian blueprint for the establishment of a new political order that did not pander to the Athenian masses. A key figure in the Athenian contribution to the Spartan mirage was Critias, who is supposed to have written two treatises on Sparta – one in prose and one in poetry, neither of which has survived save for a few fragments – and who was a relative of Plato, for whom Sparta constituted an important point of reference in more political works such as the *Republic* and especially the *Laws*.

Our most detailed accounts of Archaic Sparta are a treatise entitled the *Constitution of the Lacedaemonians* and Plutarch's *Life of Lycurgus*. The first has come down to us among the collected works of Xenophon and, although the attribution has sometimes been doubted, the author would certainly seem to fit Xenophon's profile. Like Critias, Xenophon was an associate of Socrates and, at about the time of Socrates' execution in 399, he was exiled from his native Athens and eventually given an estate in Elis by the Spartan king Agesilaus II. The debt of gratitude that Xenophon owed Agesilaus was amply repaid in the laudatory account that Xenophon wrote about his Spartan patron and a similar adulation for the Spartan way of life characterizes the *Constitution of the Lacedaemonians*. Plutarch was not so closely connected to Sparta, though the Xenophontic *Constitution of the Lacedaemonians* was an important source for the *Life of Lycurgus*, along with accounts by various Hellenistic writers who seem to have been content to allow their antiquarian research to promote more contemporary propagandistic purposes.

Both texts are already suffused with the Spartan mirage. And, although both end on a pessimistic note that comments on the state's decline from the end of the fifth century, both sketch a picture of a hitherto stable, unchanging society, living according to the laws and institutions that had been established by the famed lawgiver Lycurgus, "for it was not by imitating other cities but by actually conceiving the opposite to most that he unveiled a country that exceeded others in good fortune" (Xenophon, *CL* 1.2). Aside from his association with the Great Rhetra (*CL* 14; Plutarch, *Lyc.* 5–7), Lycurgus is credited with institutionalizing adulterous relationships to combat demographic decline (*CL* 1.7–10; *Lyc.* 15), expropriating private property and redistributing the land into 9,000 equal lots (*Lyc.* 8), establishing the *agôgê* for boys (*CL* 2–3; *Lyc.* 16–25), as well as an educational programme for girls (*Lyc.* 14), instituting the common-messes, named variously as *pheiditia*, *syssitia*, or *syskênia*, to which Spartan citizens were obliged to contribute monthly rations (*CL* 5; *Lyc.* 10, 12), banning money, save for a cumbersome iron currency (*CL* 7; *Lyc.* 9), and organizing the military (*CL* 11–12).

As we have seen (pp. 184–7), the fundamental elements of the Spartan constitution probably date back to the early seventh century though their attribution to Lycurgus appears to be a later invention – in which case, the belief that Lycurgus was responsible for virtually every Spartan institution and that such institutions had persisted unchanged over several centuries is inherently unlikely. Much more plausible is the hypothesis that various new legal and institutional developments were represented as incarnating Lycurgan ideals and prescriptions in order to stamp them with a traditional authority. The clearest example of this concerns the supposed redistribution by Lycurgus of public land into 9,000 inalienable lots. The idea that equality would be better maintained if land were not bought or sold was already current in the fourth century (Aristotle, *Pol.* 2.6.10). Yet, Aristotle also makes it clear that property was being transferred and accumulated in his own day and the widespread belief that, prior to a reform sponsored by the fourth-century ephor Epitadeus, land had been legally inalienable is found only in later sources (e.g. Plutarch, *Agis* 5). Furthermore, the figure of 9,000 is immediately suspect because the third-century King Agis IV had proposed the redistribution of Spartan land into 4,500 lots at a time when Sparta had lost half of its available territory after the liberation of Messenia (*Agis* 8). This was just one of a series of radical reforms that Agis promoted, along with the cancellation of debts and the enfranchisement of *perioikoi* and helots, and one can easily imagine that Lycurgus' name had been co-opted to disguise the revolutionary character of the proposals (for which Agis was eventually assassinated). By contrast, the marked economic differences between Spartans – notwithstanding their profession of an egalitarian ideology – together with Aristotle's observation that land had been concentrated in the hands of a few makes it virtually certain that private property and the right of alienation existed at Sparta as they did in most Greek *poleis*.

Some programme of public education certainly existed at Sparta in the last third of the fifth century: Thucydides (2.39.1) has Pericles contrast the Athenians to the Spartans, who "pursue courage from the earliest age through painful training." It is, however, unlikely to have resembled closely the detailed picture that Plutarch in particular sketches for the simple reason that the *agôgê* had been completely overhauled at least twice before Plutarch's own day. The first reincarnation of the *agôgê* was during the reign of Cleomenes III (235–222), when the Stoic philosopher Sphaerus of Borysthenes was charged with revamping a programme that may have fallen into neglect earlier in the century. Suspended by the Achaean general Philopoemen in 188, the *agôgê* was restored by the Romans after their conquest of Greece in 146 though we cannot be sure how faithfully it replicated its Hellenistic and Classical predecessors. The army too must have witnessed many changes and developments over the centuries: certainly the army that Xenophon describes in some detail is organized differently from the one depicted by Herodotos at Plataea in 479.

The supposed ban on precious metal currencies has also come under critical scrutiny. While it is true that Sparta did not mint its own currency before the mid-third century, it has been estimated that around 50 percent of *poleis* never coined at all. In fact, the Spartan state must have had some reserves of gold and silver currency minted elsewhere for purposes such as maintaining ambassadors overseas, paying mercenaries, and ransoming prisoners of war, and numerous stories about Spartans accepting or offering foreign bribes would suggest also some private ownership of precious metal currency. It may well be that the tradition concerning Lycurgus' ban on gold and silver was created as part of the moralizing reaction to the Spartan general Lysander's conquests in the east at the end of the fifth century, when Sparta was suddenly flooded by overseas revenues (Diodorus 14.10.2; Plutarch, *Lyc.* 30). At this point, some – ultimately ineffectual – provisions seem to have been taken to try to prevent the private acquisition of wealth.

As for the unbridled license supposedly afforded women, it is probably the case that Spartan women enjoyed a higher legal status than, say, women in Athens: there is, for example, good reason to suppose that they were legally entitled to inherit at least a share of their fathers' property. But the practices that Xenophon describes with some bewilderment – namely, that older Spartan husbands were required to procure younger male lovers for their wives or that men might have children by the wives of other men – appear to be a response to demographic decline. As Xenophon (*CL* 1.9) explains, "the wives want to have two households, while the men want to provide brothers to theirs sons who will share their lineage and influence but not lay claim to their property." A plausible suggestion is that these measures were taken only after the devastating earthquake of the 460s (Thucydides 1.101; Diodorus 11.63).

Ultimately, our two fullest sources for Archaic Sparta are so irredeemably affected by later invention and distortion that they possess practically no historical value for the early history of Sparta, even if they furnish important testimony for the eventual creation of the Spartan mirage itself. This is no less true of earlier, fifth-century sources. It has been claimed that Herodotus was largely immune from the effects of the mirage because his acquaintance with Sparta predated the serious distortions produced by Athenian prejudice and idealization. And yet, a different conclusion seems to emerge from the diametric oppositions that he sketches between Athens and Sparta (1.56), as well as from the fact that Sparta is the only Greek *polis* for which Herodotus offers an "ethnographic" portrait (6.56–60), akin to his descriptions of the Persians, Egyptians, and Scythians. In fact, he explicitly compares some Spartan customs to those of the Persians and the Egyptians, going as far as to claim that the Spartans were actually descendants of the Egyptians, and this all suggests that the exotically "alien" character of Sparta – a central constituent of the mirage – was already a *topos* in Herodotus' day. Thucydides is concerned primarily with contemporary, rather than early, Sparta and even there he is forced to admit that complete accuracy is impossible due to Spartan secrecy (5.68.2). When he does refer to earlier Spartan history (1.18.1), it is to say that that the Spartans were powerful because they had possessed the same, stable constitution, free from tyrannical interventions, for approximately 400 years. This belief was, as we have seen, central to the idealized image of Sparta that emerged in the fifth century. It is inherently incredible but it also meets with little support from the extant fragments of the Archaic poets Tyrtaeus and Alcman.

At first sight, the jingoistic, martial exhortations of Tyrtaeus fit well with the militaristic spirit that characterized Sparta in the Classical period. It is, however, important to remember that we only possess those fragments of Tyrtaeus' poetry that later authors saw fit to record. It is entirely possible that Tyrtaeus composed verses on a whole variety of matters but that those that were deemed incompatible with the later ideology of Sparta ceased to be recited and were therefore eventually forgotten. Alcman is another matter entirely. Although his focus on choirs, dances, and festivals is not inconsistent with later descriptions of Spartan culture and society (e.g. Plutarch, *Lyc.* 21), these are probably not the first items that come to mind when imagining Sparta. Alcman's Sparta is a Sparta not of austere egalitarianism or militaristic isolationism but rather of trans-regional elites who participate in high culture. With the British excavations of the sanctuary of Artemis Orthia between 1906 and 1910 and the discovery of a rich deposit of ceramics, terracotta figurines and masks, carved ivories, bronze statuettes and vessels, and tens of thousands of small lead figurines, it became clear that Alcman's world was not so fictitious after all. Sparta, it was argued, had not originally been so distinct from other Greek *poleis*. There must have been some sort of turning-point, and when archaeologists noted that the higher quality dedications at the sanctuary began to tail off ca. 550, scholars were quick to interpret this as a consequence of important political, economic, and ideological changes that took place in the mid-sixth century and served to isolate Sparta from the mainstream. Some even attributed the changes to the Spartan ephor Chilon, regarded as one of the seven sages of

Greece (Plato, *Prot.* 343a; Pausanias 3.16.4), and credited with strengthening the power of the ephorate (Diogenes Laertius 1.68).

Several decades on, the picture looks less straightforward. On the one hand, the terminal date of ca. 550 has little to recommend it any longer. The objects deposited in the sanctuary of Artemis prior to this date had been sealed beneath a sand layer caused by an inundation of the River Eurotas. Without the protection of this layer, dedications of the later sixth and fifth centuries could easily have been washed away by subsequent inundations or plundered. In fact, with the identification of Laconian products that the excavations offered, it became possible to recognize Laconian exports further afield and this suggested a very different story. There was, for example, a marked increase in the sixth century in the production and circulation of Laconian goods such as bronze figurines and vessels and fine black-figured pottery. Although production of the figured pottery tails off from the second half of the sixth century, it is still higher in the first quarter of the fifth century than it had been in the seventh, and plainer black-glaze wares continued to be exported long afterwards. It is the second half of the sixth century that sees a peak in the production of impressive bronze vessels – including, perhaps, the monumental bronze krater (mixing-bowl for wine), 1.64 meters high, that was found in the burial of a Celtic princess at Vix in the Seine Valley (though the Spartan provenance is contested). Bronze mirrors and figurines, instead, continued to be manufactured into the fifth century. Attempts have been made to reconcile the material evidence with later literary representations by assuming that manufacture was in the hands of the *perioikoi* rather than Spartan citizens, but it is almost certain that the more costly objects in sanctuaries were dedicated by citizens and the possible identification of a potter's burial in the center of Sparta itself hints at the distinct possibility that the supposed prohibition on "banausic" activity was nowhere near as thorough as later Spartans or their admirers liked to imagine.

There is, on the other hand, a danger of exaggerating the typicality of Archaic Sparta. Even if the conquest of Messenia was a longer, more drawn-out affair than is sometimes supposed (pp. 173–6), it remains the case that the area over which Sparta exercised some sort of control – however indirect – was, at ca. 7,500 square kilometers, exceptionally large. Furthermore, a closer look at Laconian material culture reveals some rather unusual and distinctive features. The techniques behind the production of sixth-century figured pottery may have been borrowed from Corinth and Athens, but the decorative themes are entirely original. There are now some indications that the rather atypical podium construction of the early fifth-century sanctuary of Helen and Menelaus at Therapne (Figure II.1) was a characteristic of other Spartan temples also, serving to mark them out from the canonical architectural styles adopted elsewhere. Strange objects such as the *harpax* (a bronze butcher's hook) and iron sickles are typical dedications at Spartan sanctuaries while the fact that the closest parallels for the clay masks, found in the sanctuary of Artemis Orthia and dating mainly to the seventh and sixth centuries, are with Phoenicia may provide some material support for the easternizing features that Herodotus

Figure II.1   The sanctuary of Helen and Menelaus near Sparta (photo by author)

observed for Sparta. A mirage, however distorted, has a point of reference and it is reasonable to conclude that there were some peculiarities about Sparta that were, from the fifth century onwards, capitalized upon by Spartans and non-Spartans alike. If that is the case, it would clearly be unwise to assume that Archaic Sparta can provide a benchmark against which we can assess the typicality of other Greek *poleis*.

FURTHER READING

The Spartan mirage: Tigerstedt 1965; Rawson 1969. For the history of Sparta generally: Cartledge 2002b. For the reliability of tradition: C. G. Starr, "The credibility of early Spartan history," in Whitby 2002, 26–42; M. Flower, "The invention of tradition in Classical and Hellenistic Sparta," in Powell and Hodkinson 2002, 191–217. On the *agôgê*: S. Hodkinson, "Social order and the conflict of values in Classical Sparta," *Chiron* 13 (1983), 239–81; Kennell 1995. Currency: T. J. Figueira, "Iron money and the ideology of consumption in Laconia," in Powell and Hodkinson 2002, 137–70. Women: P. Cartledge, "Spartan wives: Liberation or license?" in Whitby 2002, 131–60. For a re-evaluation of Spartan material culture: S. Hodkinson, "Lakonian artistic production and the problem of Spartan austerity," in Fisher and van Wees 1998, 93–117.

9
The City of Theseus

The End of the Tyranny

In early July 514, Pisistratus' son Hipparchus was struck down and killed while marshaling the sacrificial procession that initiated the festival of the Great Panathenaea. The assassins, Harmodius and Aristogiton, were members of a distinguished aristocratic clan named the Gephyraioi. Thucydides (6.54–57) attributes their motives to sexual jealousy and wounded pride: Hipparchus had attempted to seduce the young Harmodius, inflaming the resentment of the latter's lover, Aristogiton, and had also insulted a sister of Harmodius, thus provoking the couple to seek revenge. But elsewhere (1.20.2), he implies that the pair had originally intended to assassinate Hipparchus' older brother, Hippias, and had only changed their plans at the last minute following suspicions that their plot had been betrayed. This more mundane explanation appears more convincing and underscores the inherent instability of tyrannical regimes (see p. 140). Although, according to later traditions, Pisistratus had initially established his dominion by taking the sons of his political rivals hostage and forcing others into exile (Herodotus 1.64), he had evidently eventually reached a position of understanding with his aristocratic peers (Aristotle, *AC* 16.9). That seems to have been a delicate balance that his sons were less capable of maintaining.

Harmodius was killed on the spot, Aristogiton shortly afterwards. At some point before 480, the sculptor Antenor was commissioned to make bronze statues of the pair which were set up in the agora, the first time the likeness of an historical individual had been placed in so august a location; by the fourth century, if not much earlier, cultic honors were offered annually at the grave of the couple and their descendants were entitled to free meals in the *prytaneion* and relief from taxes (*AC* 58.1; *IG* I³ 131; Andocides 1.98; Isaeus 5.47). A series of *skolia*, or drinking songs, possibly composed soon after the assassination, lauded the fame of Harmodius and Aristogiton for having "killed the tyrant" and for "restoring equality to the Athenians" (*PMG* 474–5, 893–6). The first claim could – despite the protestations of Thucydides (1.20.2; 6.54–55) – be true if, as is likely, Hipparchus shared some authority with Hippias. The latter is not entirely accurate since Hippias continued to rule Athens for a further four years. Nevertheless, the action of Harmodius and Aristogiton was the opening salvo in a campaign of aristocratic resistance to the tyranny that was fueled further by the fact that Hippias' fears and suspicions drove him to pursue a harsher, more despotic style of leadership (Herodotus 5.62.2, 6.123.2; Thucydides 6.59.2). It is in this context that we should view the ultimately unsuccessful attempt of dissidents, led by the Alcmaeonidae, to capture the city from their base at Leipsydrion on Mount Parnes (Herodotus 5.62.2).

In the end, the tyranny was put down by the Spartan king Cleomenes. After an earlier, abortive expedition by sea under the command of Ankhimolios, Cleomenes invaded Attica by land, routed a Thessalian cavalry unit that had come to the support of Hippias, and besieged him and his family on the acropolis. Famed even in the mid-fifth century for their incapacity to conduct siege operations, the Spartans would probably have been unsuccessful had they not had the good fortune to capture members of Hippias' family whom the tyrant was trying to smuggle out of Athens to safety. In return for the restoration of these hostages, Hippias undertook to leave Attica within five days and departed for Sigeum, near the mouth of the Hellespont (Herodotus 5.63–65).

Herodotus (5.62–63) recounts an Athenian story that indirectly credits the Alcmaeonidae with the eventual expulsion of Hippias. The Alcmaeonidae had supposedly won great influence at Delphi, firstly by agreeing to contribute private funds to replace the temple of Apollo that had burned down in 548 (Pausanias 10.5.13), and then by furnishing the temple with a facade of marble rather than limestone as originally contracted. With this influence, continues Herodotus, they bribed the Pythian priestess to order any passing Spartan dignitary to liberate Athens from the Pisistratid tyrants. The story has little to recommend it – not least, because its assertion that the Alcmaeonidae were in exile throughout the Pisistratid tyranny (Herodotus 5.62.2; 6.123.1) cannot be true if the *[ ]leisthenes*, listed as eponymous archon for 525/4 on the Athenian Archon List (ML 6 = Fornara 23) is, as seems likely, the Alcmaeonid Cleisthenes. It is not even clear that the story was initially invented by the Alcmaeonids. Bribery of Apollo's oracle would surely have been viewed as an act of utmost impiety, though it is easy to understand how such a charge might have become attached to the family. In the last third of the seventh century, Cleisthenes' great-grandfather, Megacles, had supposedly violated the suppliant status of those who had supported Cylon's abortive coup d'état – a profane act that necessitated the arrival of the Cretan prophet Epimenides to purify the city (Herodotus 5.71; Thucydides 1.126; Aristotle, *AC* 1, fr. 8). But the Alcmaeonidae could have turned what was essentially a negative slur to their advantage: not only had they had no association with the Pisistratid regime, they had even been instrumental in securing its downfall. It is not at all impossible that the seemingly trivial, jealousy-based motivation ascribed to the tyrannicides was also the product of an Alcmaeonid apologist. By the fifth century, the Spartans liked to claim that it was an ideological predisposition towards stable government (*eunomia*) that impelled them to suppress tyrannical regimes throughout Greece (e.g. Thucydides 1.18.1), but their true motivations for expelling Hippias in 510 are best judged by their subsequent interventions over the next decade. Having forged asymmetrical alliances with many of the cities of the Peloponnese, the Spartans had begun to turn their attention to the states of the Saronic Gulf. Megara, for example, probably allied itself to Sparta before the end of the sixth century, and the island of Aegina seems to have come to terms with Cleomenes in the 490s (Herodotus 6.73). Under the Pisistratids, Athens had attained a strength and importance it had not known since the eighth century (see pp. 231–3) and it is highly likely that Cleomenes wanted to ensure Sparta had a docile ally north of the isthmus. There were grounds for encouragement since the Pisistratids had, up to then, enjoyed good relations with the Spartans (Herodotus 5.63.2). If, however, Hippias had baulked at actually accepting orders from Sparta, Cleomenes would certainly have had good reasons to replace him with somebody more compliant.

Cleomenes' ideal candidate was almost certainly an aristocrat named Isagoras, son of Teisandros, whom Cleomenes befriended during the siege of the acropolis in 510 and whose wife, according to scurrilous rumors, enjoyed a close relationship with the Spartan king (Herodotus 5.66.1, 70.1). Isagoras seems to have enjoyed the support of other elite families in the city, since he was appointed archon for 508/7 (Aristotle, *AC* 21.1); in response, his chief political rival, the Alcmaeonid Cleisthenes, is said to have "set about making himself the friend (*prosetairizetai*) of the *dêmos*" (Herodotus 5.66.2). The author of the *Athenian Constitution* (20.1) says that he won over the *dêmos* by "handing the constitution over to the multitude (*plêthos*)," though it is highly unlikely that the reforms were enacted until Cleisthenes' position was assured. Sensing that his grip on power was loosening, Isagoras appealed to Cleomenes, who sent a herald ordering the Athenians to rid the city of the "accursed" – a reference to the Alcmaeonidae and their role in the suppression of the Cylonian conspiracy. Following Cleisthenes' departure from Athens, Cleomenes arrived in the city with a small force and ordered the expulsion of a further 700 families. After a failed attempt to dissolve the *boulê*, Cleomenes and Isagoras seized the acropolis, where they were immediately besieged by "the rest of the Athenians who were of one mind." Three days later, the Spartan contingent was allowed to depart under truce while their Athenian supporters were executed; Cleisthenes and the other 700 exiled families were summoned back to Athens (Herodotus 5.70, 72–73; Aristotle, *AC* 20).

The Birth of Democracy?

Herodotus (6.131.1) credits Cleisthenes with "having instituted the tribes (*phylai*) and the democracy for the Athenians." The term *dêmokratia* is actually anachronistic in a late sixth-century context (p. 181) and it may not even be intended as a compliment – especially since Herodotus elsewhere (5.69) suggests that Cleisthenes' tribal reforms were motivated in part by emulation of his maternal grandfather, the tyrant of Sicyon (see pp. 188–90), and in part by his desire to distance the Athenians from their Ionian brethren by changing the names of their tribes. Nonetheless, the fact that Herodotus can associate the tribal reforms with the establishment of democracy suggests that this was a linkage that was recognized by his fifth-century contemporaries. To what extent, then, was Cleisthenes the "father of democracy"?

Prior to the end of the sixth century, the Athenian citizen body had been divided among four *phylai* (p. 188). These were not entirely disbanded – they continued to perform some religious functions, for example – but their political function was neutralized by the creation of ten new *phylai*, named after Attic heroes. Each *phylê* was divided into three *trittyeis*, one situated in the city, one in the coastal regions, and one in the inland, and to each *trittys* was assigned a variable number of demes (*dêmoi*) or villages – often, though not always, contiguous to one another. To date, some 140 demes have been identified from inscriptions and literary sources. The precise number of demes assigned to a *trittys* was directly dependent on the size of those demes, the idea being that the number of citizens assigned to each of the ten new *phylai* should be approximately equal. Let us take, by way of example, the *phylê* Pandionis (see map 9.1). The city *trittys* included the large deme of Kydathenaion, which lay to the northeast of the acropolis in the area of the modern Plaka district. The coastal *trittys* included the medium-sized deme of Myrrhinous, together with the smaller settlements of Angele, Kytherros, Steiria, and Prasia, all situated on the eastern Attic seaboard in the vicinity of the modern Pórto Ráfti. The inland *trittys* included the large deme of Lower Paiania, the smaller deme of Oai, and the tiny villages of Upper Paiania and Konthyle, situated on the eastern slopes of Mount Hymettus close to where the Eleutherios Venizelos International Airport is now situated.

A citizen's immediate loyalty was to his own deme, in which he would need to be registered upon attaining the age of eighteen if he did not want to be deprived of his citizen rights. The army, however, was brigaded by tribal regiments with ten *stratêgoi* or generals being elected annually, one for each *phylê*. In addition a council (*boulê*) of 500 was instituted, to which each *phylê* appointed by lot a slate of fifty members (known as a prytany) on an annual basis. Recruitment to the prytany was based on a fixed quota per deme, directly proportional to the number of inhabitants resident there. So, for example, the populous deme of Acharnae in the foothills of Mount Parnes seems to have sent as many as twenty-two *bouleutai* to Athens each year whereas only one councilor represented Upper Paiania. Each prytany served as the executive council for the *boulê* for each of the ten "months" of the administrative year. The *boulê*'s prime function was "probouleutic," meaning that it was charged with drafting the agenda for motions debated by the assembly, though it also oversaw administrative matters. It is unclear whether *thêtes* were admitted to

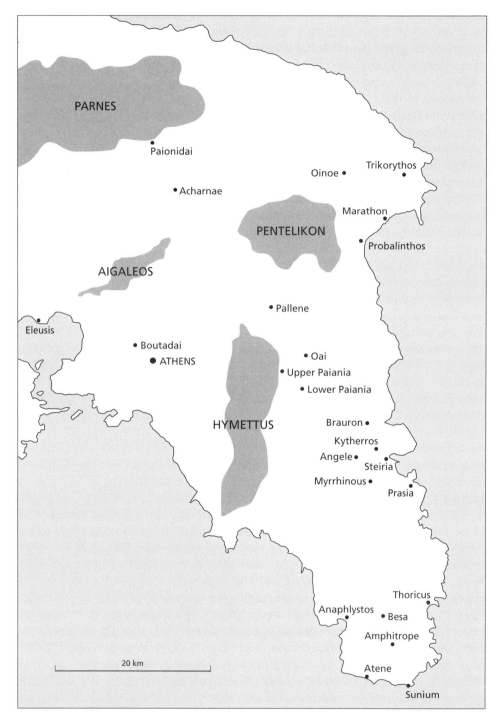

Map 9.1   Settlements in Attica

the council of 500 from the beginning although it cannot have functioned in the Classical period without their participation.

In some senses, Cleisthenes' reforms were not as radical as is sometimes claimed. The council of 500 may have assumed functions and duties from an earlier Solonian council (p. 183), while the former four *phylai* had also been divided into three *trittyeis*, with each *trittys* further subdivided into twelve *naukrariai* (Aristotle, *AC* 8.3). Intense scholarly interest in whether – and if so, why – the *naukrariai* derive their name from *naus* ("ship") has diverted attention away from the fact that many ancient sources view them as the earlier equivalents of the Cleisthenic demes (*AC* 21.5; Pollux, *Onomastikon* 8.108; Hesychius s.v. *nauklaros*; Photius, *Lexicon* s.v. *nauklêros*). In other words, the idea of distributing local territorial units among *phylai*, with the latter constituting the principal military and political units of the citizenry, had already existed prior to the reforms of Cleisthenes. Furthermore, it is highly likely that many of the new Cleisthenic demes were based on the former *naukrariai*, meaning that, at the local level, many Athenian citizens would not have noticed too many differences.

Furthermore, the old "Ionian" tribes retained, as we have seen, some ceremonial functions and the author of the *Athenian Constitution* (21.6) says that Cleisthenes did not reform "the ancestral priesthoods in each deme, the *genê* or the phratries." The phratries are poorly understood even in the fourth century – the period for which we have the most evidence – and it is not entirely clear to what extent their later functions and competences were relics of the pre-Cleisthenic period. A fragment attributed to the *Athenian Constitution* (fr. 3) says that the pre-Cleisthenic phratries were the same as the *trittyeis* and that each of them was divided into thirty *genê*, but the testimony is of dubious value for two reasons. Firstly, it is difficult to reconcile this system of subdivision with that based on the *naukrariai*, for which the evidence is more plentiful. Secondly, while all Athenian citizens belonged to a phratry in the Classical period, membership of a *genos* was limited to aristocrats and this can hardly have been an innovation of the democratic period. The author of the fragment is perhaps confusing the Athenian situation with the sociopolitical organization of other *poleis* in which the phratry does seem to be a formal subdivision of the *phylê* (see pp. 124–5). Conversely, at Athens the phratry – both before and after Cleisthenes' reforms – appears to belong to a system that is parallel to, but independent from, the *phylê–trittys*–deme/*naukraria* system. If the pre-Cleisthenic phratries were subject to the same processes of fusion and fission as their Classical successors then it is clear that, far from being subdivisions of larger units, they must have been more akin to the homonymous units that we find in Homer (pp. 123–4) – that is, aggregations of smaller, territorially-based bands (*phyla*) that orbited around the most powerful families (*genê*). By the fourth century, the phratries seem to act as microcosms of the democratic *polis* but there is no reason to believe that Cleisthenes himself did much, if anything, to overturn the informal relations of dependency that subordinated members of a phratry to the dominant *genos*.

The real innovation of the reforms was an entirely new reconfiguration of the relationships between the various components that constituted the *polis*. According to the *Athenian Constitution* (21.2), Cleisthenes' goal was "to mix up [the *phylai*] so that more should have a share in citizenship"; the author adds (21.4) that "he made the residents in each of the demes demesmen of one another so that they should not be able to mark out the new citizens by addressing them according to their parentage but should recognize them by their deme, as a result of which the Athenians call themselves by their deme name." When read alongside Aristotle's comment (*Pol.* 3.1.10) that, after the expulsion of the tyrants, Cleisthenes "enrolled in the *phylai* many resident foreigners (*xenoi*) and slaves (*douloi*)," it seems clear that the author of the *Athenian Constitution* attributed the Cleisthenic tribal reforms to an earnest desire to protect the identity of those who had been newly enrolled in the citizen body – often understood as former citizens who had been disfranchised under the tyranny (see *AC* 13.5). Yet, if that was Cleisthenes' primary aim, it was manifestly unsuccessful: there is some evidence for the use of demotics (deme names) prior to Cleisthenes and epigraphical evidence offers no substantial confirmation of a wholesale shift from patronymics to demotics in the post-Cleisthenic period. Furthermore, if Cleisthenes had wanted to protect the *neopolitai* ("new citizens") from social stigma, he surely could have achieved it in a far simpler fashion. There is, then, some reason to suppose that the precise motivation imputed here is a conjecture on the part of the author of the *Athenian Constitution*. That is not, however, to rule out that it was the "mixing up" of the population that was central to Cleisthenes' programme.

In establishing a new order it was crucial to tackle the stranglehold that powerful elite families had exerted over the old order. Areas where we know the Pisistratids to have held influence seem to have been particular targets of Cleisthenes' attention. Marathon, for example, had long formed part of a cultic – and, perhaps, originally political – union called the Tetrapolis, which also included the villages of Oinoe, Trikorythos, and Probalinthos. Indeed, the Tetrapolis continued to send its own embassies to Delphi and Delos as late as the first century. But while Marathon, Oinoe, and Trikorythos were assigned to the coastal *trittys* of the Aiantis *phylê*, Probalinthos was detached to form part of the non-contiguous coastal trittys of the Pandionis *phylê* much further south. Brauron, said to be the ancestral home of the Pisistratids (Plato, *Hipp.* 228b; Plutarch, *Sol.* 10.3), was instead renamed Philaidai, perhaps in an attempt to detach the famous cult of Artemis Brauronia from its Pisistratid patrons. At the same time, however, the bestowal of the name Philaidai on the residents of the Brauron area could be construed as an affront to another aristocratic *genos* – the Philaidai, to which Miltiades, one of the generals at Marathon, and his son Cimon belonged. The deme names Boutadai, immediately to the northwest of the city, and Paionidai, in the foothills of Mount Parnes, were also almost certainly taken from the names of *genê*: in the former case, at least, the *gennetai* responded by renaming themselves Eteoboutadai ("the true Boutadai").

Nevertheless, there is some reason to believe that certain elite families were targeted more than others. Particularly suspicious is the case of the Antiokhis *phylê*: the coastal *trittys*, which included the settlements of Anaphlystos, Besa, Amphitrope, and Atene, to the far south of Attica, contributed seventeen *bouleutai*. With the addition of the ten appointed for the city deme of Alopeke, these twenty-seven councilors would have dominated the prytany of the Antiokhis *phylê*. Is it mere coincidence that the Alcmaeonidae's base in the city was at Alopeke and that they owned rural estates and, it seems, a family cemetery at Anaphlystos (p. 170)?

The cynical view presented here is not accepted by all. For some, Cleisthenes was an altruistic idealist with "a conscious democratic aim" and if his intention had been to bestow advantage on himself and the Alcmaeonidae, then "his failure was complete" (Murray 1993: 280). But this is to infer intention from outcome. What is most surprising, perhaps, is that Cleisthenes disappears from the scene almost immediately after the reforms associated with his name. He could, of course, simply have died but, intriguingly enough, Herodotus (5.73) makes a particular point of saying that, after the recall of Cleisthenes to Athens, envoys were sent to the Persian satrap at Sardis requesting an alliance against future Spartan aggression. The alliance was granted on the condition that the envoys give the symbolic gifts of earth and water to the Persian king Darius – an act of submission for which the envoys were prosecuted on their return to Athens. This is likely to have happened before 506 when Cleomenes launched a further unsuccessful assault on Athens (Herodotus 5.74–75) and it is tempting to wonder whether Cleisthenes had been involved in the embassy and discredited on account of it.

There is one very clear effect of Cleisthenes' tribal reforms. The "reshuffling" of the Athenian citizen body promoted a new sense of unity. Although the residents of a former city *naukraria* might still find themselves demesmen of one another under the new regime, when they came to participate in political decision-making or train or fight in the tribal regiment they would now find themselves shoulder to shoulder with citizens from other parts of Attica, many of whom they are unlikely to have known previously. But, as we shall see shortly, this really only represents the continuation and extension of a policy that had been pursued by the tyranny prior to Cleisthenes' reforms and it is not entirely clear to what extent it should be labeled "democratic" in any modern sense of the term. If Cleisthenes was the "father of democracy," it was only unwittingly.

There is, however, an unsung hero of the events of 508/7 – namely, the Athenian *dêmos*. As we have seen (pp. 181–2), the term *dêmokratia*, while eventually connoting concepts such as equality and free speech, literally draws attention to the fact that the *dêmos*, the non-elite members of Athenian society, has wrested power away from the formerly governing aristocracy. One can speak of a democratic revolution so long as one does not envisage that such a revolution was instantaneous. Although the *dêmos* was not truly sovereign until the wide-ranging powers of the aristocratic Areopagus council were curtailed in the later 460s, it had already been vocal at the beginning of the sixth century when it had called for Solon's appointment as archon and arbitrator (Aristotle, *AC* 5.2; Plutarch, *Sol.* 14.2). But the events of 508/7 mark a crucial intervention by the *dêmos* in Athenian politics. Prior to this, battling elite factions had exercised power by their ability to exile their political opponents: the Pisistratidae, Alcmaeonidae, and Philaidai had all been on the receiving end of such practices. In the archonship of Isagoras, however, while Cleisthenes and 700 allied families were out of the country, the *boulê* refused Cleomenes' orders for its dissolution and the *dêmos* united in resistance against the imposition of a new regime. The exile of the Alcmaeonids and their supporters, ordered by the elite faction of Isagoras, was now annulled by the intervention and decision of the people – an action that represented an important moment of political self-definition on the part of the *dêmos*.

According to one view, the institution of ostracism needs to be viewed within this context of a popular usurpation of the aristocracy's prerogative to exile its opponents. As far as we can reconstruct the process, the Athenian assembly was asked once a year whether it wished to hold an ostracism. If so (and there are only ten known instances of the practice), citizens were invited to inscribe the name of an individual of their choice on an *ostrakon* or potsherd. Subject to a quorum of 6,000 *ostraka*, the individual who received the most votes was required to go into exile for ten years without losing his property or revenues derived from that property. In its infrequent application, the practice was largely symbolic – signifying the potential authority that the *dêmos* had over errant aristocrats – and its relative clemency, especially when compared with the harsher sentences of exile that had been imposed by Archaic aristocrats on one another, articulated a concept of democratic moderation in opposition to the extreme excesses of autocratic and aristocratic regimes. Interestingly, although the first known ostracism only occurred in 487 (see p. 269), the institution of the practice is credited by most of our sources to Cleisthenes (Aristotle, *AC* 22.1; Philochorus fr. 30; Aelian, *HM* 13, 24; Diodorus 11.55.1). If the assignment is correct, ostracism could well have been one of the most democratic of the measures proposed by Cleisthenes though once again, if the author of the *Athenian Constitution* (22.4) can be trusted, his motivations may not have been entirely altruistic.

The Unification of Attica

By the fifth century, Athens controlled a huge territory of some 2,500 square kilometers, not counting her various overseas possessions (*klêroukhiai*). Sparta exercised control over a much larger area – some 7,500 square kilometers – but this was through the intermediary of dependent and subjugated populations (the *perioikoi* and helots respectively). By contrast, all inhabitants of the rural towns and villages of Attica enjoyed the same civic rights and were expected to fulfil the same civic duties as their counterparts who resided in the city.

Document 9.1

For in the time of Cecrops and the earliest kings, Attica was – until the time of Theseus – always settled in *poleis*, each having its own *prytaneion* and magistrates. Unless there was some reason for alarm, they did not come together to deliberate with the *basileus* [of Athens] but each governed itself and took its own deliberations. Sometimes they even waged war on him, as was the case with the Eleusinians with Eumolpus against Erechtheus. But Theseus, after establishing himself as an intelligent and powerful ruler, reorganized the territory, disbanding both the *bouleutêria* and magistracies of the other *poleis* and incorporating everyone in the *polis* that exists today, designating for them a single *bouleuterion* and *prytaneion*. Although each cultivated the property that he had held before, Theseus compelled them to adopt this one *polis*. And with all working together for the benefit of the *polis*, it became great and was handed down in such a state by Theseus to his successors. In commemoration of that event, the Athenians even today celebrate the Synoikia, a public festival in honour of the goddess. (Thucydides 2.15.1–2)

Furthermore, Attica is physically divided into four distinct microzones (Map 9.1): (i) the *pedion*, or plain that surrounds the city of Athens itself, hemmed in by Mount Parnes to the north, Mount Pentelikon to the northeast, Mount Hymettus to the east, Mount Aigialeos to the west, and the sea to the south; (ii) the *paralia*, or coastal strip that runs southeast of Athens towards Cape Sunium; (iii) the *mesogaia*, or interior, beyond Mounts Pentelikon and Hymettus, which includes the eastern coast of Attica; and (iv) the Thriasian Plain to the northwest, around Eleusis. That Athens' control of such a large territory was considered a somewhat anomalous situation by Greek standards is indicated by the fact that the Athenians felt the need to explain it by means of an *aition*, or explanatory myth. According to them, the mythical hero and Athenian king Theseus decided to unite Attica by disbanding local jurisdictions and persuading residents throughout the territory to regard Athens as their political and judicial center. Theseus' "synoecism" (see pp. 77–8) was commemorated by a festival named the Synoikia, which was still celebrated in Thucydides' day (Document 9.1).

It is highly unlikely that the tradition concerning Theseus' synoecism reflects a genuine historical unification of Attica in the Late Bronze Age: the presence of elaborate *tholos* tombs outside Athens at Acharnae-Me.nídhi, Marathon, Thoricus, and Spata is not in itself sufficient reason to assume that these settlements were fully autonomous but, if such a unification had ever happened at so early a date, it cannot have survived the onset of the Dark Age when much of the Attic countryside seems to have been depopulated. It is, therefore, generally assumed that the tradition was invented to account for a political unification that happened in the distant, but post-Mycenaean, past. The most popular candidate is the Dark Age. Thoricus, Eleusis, Brauron, and Marathon were all resettled in the later tenth century with other rural areas being repopulated in the subsequent two centuries as part of what has been termed an "internal colonization" of Attica. The "colonizers," it is argued, had abandoned their rural properties for the security of Athens during the unsettled conditions that accompanied the end of the Mycenaean period. When, however, they returned to their ancestral villages, they carried out with them a new sense of loyalty to the urban center. Such a pan-Attic consciousness can be registered in the homogeneity of ceramic styles throughout the peninsula from the Late Protogeometric onwards. It is further suggested that the process should have been completed by the end of the eighth century since, in the *Catalogue of Ships* (Document 9.2), the only Attic settlement to be named is Athens whereas the contingents of other regions hail from a variety of locales.

Document 9.2

And those who held Athens, the well-built citadel,
The land of great-hearted Erechtheus, whom once Athena,
The daughter of Zeus, fostered and the grain-bearing earth bore,
Whom she made reside in Athens in her own rich temple,
550 *Where he is appeased with bulls and rams*
By the sons of the Athenians as each year rolls around,
These were led by Menestheus, son of Peteos.
No man on the earth was his equal
At marshalling horses and men with shields;
555 *Only Nestor was a match, for he was older.*
And fifty black ships accompanied him.

And Ajax led twelve ships from Salamis,
And stationed them where the ranks of the Athenians stood.

And those who held Argos and well-walled Tiryns,
560 Hermione and Asine with their deep bays,
And Troezen and Eionai and vine-clad Epidaurus,
The sons of the Achaeans who held Aegina and Mases,
These were led by Diomedes of the noble war cry
And Sthenelos, dear son of the celebrated Kapaneus,
565 And with them, as a third, godlike Euryalos,
The son of Lord Mekisteus, son of Talaos,
But ruler of them all was Diomedes of the noble war cry.
And eighty black ships accompanied them.

(Homer, *Il.* 2.546–68)

It is perhaps not overly damaging that this hypothetical model of a physical internal colonization, involving the movement of people, is a far cry from the synoecism tradition, which involved political union among pre-existing settlements. The Athenians, after all, seem to have entertained little consciousness of the "Dark Age" that we now recognize on the basis of archaeological exploration. It is, however, difficult to understand exactly how this process of political union would have resulted from internal colonization, given that the evolution of a state machinery and a sense of political community were processes that still lay, as we have seen, in the future. As for the homogeneity of ceramic styles, it is important not automatically to equate material cultural homogeneity with political unity. In the Homeric epics, craftsmen come under the category of *dêmiourgoi* – people who work "for" the *dêmos* but are often not part of it. A cautionary parallel would be the "Achaean" style pottery, found at many western colonial sites (p. 110), which belongs to a widespread cultural matrix that can hardly have been under a single jurisdiction.

Nor is the Homeric evidence especially persuasive. Although it is always tempting to argue that the Homeric text has been "tampered with" in order to corroborate whatever argument one wants to advance, there are clear signs here of interference, notably in the two verses that deal with the Salaminian contingent (lines 557–8 in document 9.2). The entry stands out, most of all, for its brevity but also for its insistence, in those two brief lines, that Ajax stationed his troops "where the ranks of the Athenians stood." The evident intentionality behind these lines serves to locate their composition within the context of the war that Athens and Megara fought for possession of Salamis. Solon's own verses (frs. 1–3) indicate that Salamis was in the Megarians' possession in his own day and there is no particular reason to doubt Herodotus' testimony (1.59.4) that Pisistratus secured an important victory in the war against Megara. Indeed, the propagandistic intention of these lines was recognized even in antiquity: Strabo (9.1.10) debated whether they had been interpolated by Solon or by Pisistratus.

The preceding verses are no less suspect, especially when compared with a more canonical entry such as that of the Argive contingent (lines 559–68). Although it is not uncommon for the compiler of the *Catalogue* to embark on narrative digressions, these normally refer to mythical episodes. This is, indeed, what we find in lines 547–8 where we are told that Erechtheus was born from the earth but raised by Athena. The reference, however, in lines 549–51 to what is evidently contemporary cult practice is far more anomalous and prompts the suspicion that all five verses have been interpolated. The typical formula, as seen in lines 559–62, lists the most important city first, followed by second-order settlements. Since a single verse typically lists two, occasionally three, settlements, it is entirely possible that the five interpolated verses have replaced an equal number of verses that originally listed the other eleven cities of the "dodecapolis" supposedly founded by Cecrops (Philochorus fr. 94). For what it is worth, the *Odyssey* (7.80–81) does seem to name Athens and Marathon as separate settlements. It is also possible that lines 553–5 have replaced a list of additional leaders of the Attic contingent – not least because the hyperbolic praise awarded Menestheus hardly matches his performance elsewhere in the epic. In later tradition, Menestheus was regarded as a usurper between Theseus and his son Demophon (Pausanias 1.17.6), which might suggest that he belongs to an originally independent – and perhaps earlier – tradition. The whole issue is complicated further by the fact that most agree that the *Catalogue of Ships*, notwithstanding individual modifications and interpolations, was composed separately from the remainder of the *Iliad*, but that only goes to weaken further the assumption that the Homeric epics can provide a *terminus ante quem* for the political unification of Attica.

It has recently been argued that full political synoecism in Attica occurred only with the reforms of Cleisthenes and that this was, in fact, one of the primary motivations behind the reforms in the first place. According to this theory, prior to the last decade of the sixth century, Athens exerted only a very weak influence over the rural Attic settlements that lay beyond the *pedion*. Had Attica been unified at an early date, it is argued, we would have expected Athens to be a more dominant force in Greek affairs of the Archaic period. Instead, Athens struggled hard and for many decades to recover Salamis from the Megarians, and the ease with which Cylon, then Pisistratus, and finally Cleomenes and Isagoras seized the acropolis has prompted the suggestion that there was no standing army at Athens until the end of the sixth century. On this view, it was the need to unify outlying rural areas of Athens with the city that prompted the "mixing" of demes within the ten new *phylai* that the author of the *Athenian Constitution* observes.

The theory also appeals to some more concrete indications that are highly suggestive. A gravestone, found at Sepolia to the northwest of the city and dating to ca. 560, bids the passer-by to mourn the deceased Tettikhos, "be you an *astos* or a *xenos*" (*IG* I³ 976). Since an *astos* can only be a resident of the city of Athens, the implication would be that all non-urban residents, be they from rural Attica, Boeotia, or the Megarid, could be addressed as *xenoi* or "strangers." At this time and, in fact, throughout the period from ca. 590 to ca. 530, inscribed gravestones are found throughout Attica but free-standing funerary sculpture is generally absent from city cemeteries save for a few possible exceptions towards the end of the period. By contrast, ten *kouroi* and *korai* are found associated with rural cemeteries, all clustered in the southern part of the peninsula. It could be that this part of Attica was considered outside the jurisdiction of Solon, who is supposed to have passed sumptuary legislation prohibiting elaborate funerary monuments, though it must be admitted that the testimony for this is late (Plutarch, *Sol.* 21; Cicero, *De Legibus* 2.26.64). It is not, however, without interest that the Alcmaeonidae, as we have seen, owned property in the area of Anaphlystos – precisely the region where three *kouroi*, including the Anavysos *kouros* which has been explicitly linked to the family, have been found (Figure 7.3). Although Cleisthenes' tenure of the archonship in 525/4 indicates that the Alcmaeonidae were, during the rule of Hippias and Hipparchus, resident in Athens, literary sources suggest that they spent much of the sixth century in exile – firstly, after the Cylonian affair (Thucydides 1.126.12; Aristotle, *AC* 1) in the late seventh century and, secondly, after Pisistratus' victory at the Battle of Pallene in ca. 546 (Herodotus 1.64). Our sources do not elaborate where the exiled Alcmaeonidae went but if, as the archaeological evidence suggests, it was southern Attica then it is difficult to imagine that this part of the peninsula was under direct Athenian control at the time.

The gravest objection to this reconstruction is that a political synoecism that occurred so late in Athenian history ought to have left some trace in the literary testimonia. On the other hand, there are some further indications that do seem to point to a relatively late unification of Attica. Firstly, there is the evidence of the *naukrariai*. As we have seen, ancient authors regarded these as the earlier equivalent of the Cleisthenic demes and it is highly likely that the deme system was based upon them. There were, however, only forty-eight *naukrariai*. If they had covered the whole of Attica, all of them would have had to be subdivided – some of them more than once – to account for the 140 Cleisthenic demes that we know by name. The fact, however, that forty-eight is approximately one third of 140 may suggest that the earlier *naukrariai* formed the basis for the demes within the city *trittyeis* only. Although it is unwise to rely on a single piece of evidence, it is not without interest that the only *naukraria* known to us by name is Kolias (Photius, s.v. *Kolias*) – probably to be identified with the modern Ayios Kosmas, south of the city and comfortably within the *pedion*.

Furthermore, the *naukrariai* were, as we have seen, sub-subdivisions of the four "Ionian" *phylai*. If they were limited to the city and the *pedion*, we would either have to suppose that rural communities in the rest of Attica formed part of some system akin to the Athenian *naukrariai* or that the population beyond the *pedion* was not divided among the same four *phylai*. In fact, the latter alternative is not nearly as odd as it may initially appear. For reasons discussed in earlier chapters (pp. 47–8, 188–90), the *phylê* system cannot be the primordial relic of some pre-migratory sociopolitical organization but rather the outcome of a rational repartition of the citizen body that is unlikely to predate the late-eighth or early seventh centuries – at least 200 years after the most important rural settlements of Attica were repopulated. Unless some anonymous Cleisthenic predecessor went to the trouble to distribute all the communities of this rather physically fragmented region among *trittyeis* and *phylai*, it is entirely possible that much of the population of Attica remained formally outside the *phylê* system until the late sixth century.

Secondly, when we turn to comparable cases, it emerges that tribal reform nearly always accompanies the incorporation within the *polis* of new territory. This may have been the case with the unification of the four *ôbai* at Sparta; it was certainly what happened with Argos' conquest of her neighbors in the 460s and possibly with Sicyon's earlier acquisition of the territory formerly controlled by Achaean Pellene (see pp. 189–90). Another interesting case is provided by Cyrene. Around the middle of the sixth century, according to

Herodotus (4.161), Cyrene faced a crisis, prompted most immediately by the loss of 7,000 soldiers in a battle against the Libyans, but rooted in longer-term causes such as discord between the various groups resident at Cyrene and tension between the *dêmos* and the monarchy. On the suggestion of the Delphic oracle, Demonax of Mantinea was invited to Cyrene and proceeded to redistribute the population of the *polis* among three *phylai*: to one were assigned those who had originally emigrated from the Greek islands; to another, those who were, by origin, Peloponnesians and Cretans; but to the third were assigned the descendants of the original settlers from Thera together with the *perioikoi*. As many commentators have noted, these *perioikoi* can only be the indigenous residents of towns and villages in the hinterland of Cyrene; their enrolment in the same ranks as the "blue-blooded" Cyreneans was almost certainly designed to curb the latter's influence but it also testifies to the enfranchisement of new citizens and, one assumes, the incorporation of their territory. In light of this, Aristotle's statement (*Pol.* 3.1275b 34–37) that Cleisthenes enfranchised many resident *xenoi* – together with the *Athenian Constitution*'s assessment (21.2) that he wanted to give more a share of citizenship – more likely refers to the full incorporation within the citizen body of the rural inhabitants of Attica than to the enfranchisement of those who had lost their civic rights under the Pisistratids.

Thirdly, an attentive reading of earlier events in Attic history suggests a far more restricted scope to the political community than is normally believed. When Solon (fr. 4) warns that the *polis* stands to be destroyed by the greed of its *astoi*, his vocabulary betrays the fact that he is not entertaining a broader vision of the *polis* and its pan-Attic citizen body but rather that he envisages the constituents of the state as being primarily those same urban residents who are contrasted with *xenoi* on the Tittakhos epitaph. Similarly, in his account of the Cylonian conspiracy, Thucydides (1.126.6) explains that Cylon's failure might have been, in part, due to his misinterpreting the instructions of the Delphic Oracle. Encouraged to seize the acropolis during "the great festival of Zeus," Cylon launched his coup during the Olympic Games. Had he instead chosen the Diasia festival, Thucydides adds, he would have found the "whole people" sacrificing "outside the city" (at Agrai, on the Ilissos River). Again, the story really suggests a rather localized focus on the city of Athens and its immediate hinterland rather than a more pan-Attic context. Indeed, had the entire rural population of Attica been present at Agrai, the risks for Cylon would have been even greater than those he actually faced.

Finally, a scenario in which Attica was not fully unified politically until the late sixth century allows us to understand better the regional factions that are described by Herodotus (1.59) and the *Athenian Constitution* (13.4) in the context of Pisistratus' first bid for the tyranny ca. 560. In Herodotus' version, the chief discord was between those of the *pedion*, led by Lykourgos, son of Aristolaides, and those of the *paralia*, led by Megacles, son of Alcmaeon; to advance his own aspirations, Pisistratus formed a third faction, to which the name of *hyperakrioi* was given. It has long been recognized that these were not political "parties" in a modern sense, though a recent attempt to cast Herodotus' tripartite factionalism as a historiographical invention on the grounds that it does not align with the bipartite Solonian division between the wealthy and the *dêmos* loses its validity if Solon is largely confining his remarks to the population of the *pedion*. If Lykourgos belonged to the same family as his more illustrious fourth-century homonym, he was of the (Eteo)Boutadai *genos*, one of the most distinguished lineages in the *pedion*. Megacles, whose family owned urban property at Alopeke, may well have found it difficult to compete against Lykourgos – especially given the scandal that had attached to the Alcmaeonidae. But, as we have seen, the family also owned property in the *paralia*, and it may be that Megacles could rely on support from the relatively prosperous communities of the Attic coast which would make him a potential threat to the Lykourgan faction. It is virtually certain that Pisistratus too had a city base, but his family held land and influence in the *mesogaia* – especially in the areas around Marathon and Brauron – and the *Athenian Constitution* (13.4–5) in particular attributes Pisistratus' popularity to his advocacy of the poor, dispossessed, and "impure of birth" that lived in this part of Attica. It is worth noting that the term *hyperakrioi* ("the men beyond the hills") betrays a perspective that is unremittingly urban and not particularly complimentary.

There are, then, reasonable grounds for doubting an early synoecism of Attica. At the same time, the Cleisthenic reforms should probably be regarded as merely the closing chapter in a process that had a longer history. In the tradition transmitted by Thucydides, the original charter for the synoecism was inextricably associated with Theseus and it is striking that Theseus suddenly becomes popular in Athenian art at the end of the sixth century. Red-figure vases depicting Theseus' exploits on the road from Troezen to Athens are generally dated to 510–500, as is part of a statue group, found on the Athenian acropolis, which may have represented Theseus' combat with the robber Procrustes. Theseus' exploits were also juxtaposed with Heracles' labors on the metopes of the Athenian Treasury at Delphi, dated – though not incontrovertibly – to ca. 500, but while Heracles' feats occupy the frieze on the northern side of the building, those of Theseus adorn the more visible, southern face. The standard interpretation for Theseus' sudden rise to prominence is that he was championed as a new, "patriotic" hero by the recently established "Cleisthenic democracy" to eclipse and neutralize the significance of the more Panhellenic Heracles, a hero whose popularity in Athenian art of the mid-sixth century is normally attributed to Pisistratid initiative. There is, however, a problem. The sacrifices at the festival of the Synoikia were made by one of the old "Ionian" *phylai*, the Geleontes. While the four pre-Cleisthenic *phylai* retained some cultic functions, we might have expected representatives of all four *phylai* to participate had this been a deliberately archaizing innovation. Instead, we have to assume that the festival was instituted before the tribal reforms of Cleisthenes and there are, in fact, some indications to suggest that the figure of Theseus was already being promoted before the expulsion of Hippias.

Theseus: Democrat or Autocrat?

While it is certainly the case that it is not until the end of the sixth century that representations of Theseus and his exploits on the road from Troezen begin to multiply, he is hardly absent from Athenian art prior to this date. On the François Vase, an Attic black-figure volute krater found at the Etruscan site of Chiusi and dated to ca. 570, Theseus is portrayed battling centaurs and instituting the *geranos* or "crane dance" on Delos. From around the middle of the sixth century, he is often depicted fighting the Minotaur while a black-figure amphora, now in Paris and dated to ca. 530, may show him battling the Bull of Marathon. A red-figure cup, on which Theseus' abduction of the Amazon Antiope is represented, has been ascribed to the potter-painter Euphronios, thought to have been active between ca. 520 and 505. Dating to the same period, a red-figure cup, found at the Etruscan site of Cerveteri, portrays Theseus in combat with the Sow of Krommyon. The common assumption that the Pisistratids cannot have been responsible for the promotion of Theseus as an Attic hero because they had championed the figure of Heracles is far from self-evident. Heracles was useful for staking Athens' new pretensions to Panhellenic status, but Theseus was better suited for internal consumption. At any rate, the iconographic evidence suggests that Theseus' rise in popularity may initially have been instigated by the Pisistratids. Indeed, his iconic importance to early fifth-century Athens was probably guaranteed by the fact that the post-Pisistratid regime co-opted and reinvented an existing figure from the mythological repertoire rather than plucking an entirely new personage from relative obscurity.

There are, in fact, several interesting parallels between the stories told of Theseus and the traditions – factual or otherwise – associated with Pisistratus. Theseus' ordeals on the road from Troezen could be considered a metaphor for Pisistratus' own repeated efforts to seize power (Herodotus 1.59–62). According to a probably Troezenian tradition, Theseus was the son of Poseidon, as was Neleus, the Pylian king from whom the Pisistratids claimed descent (Hellanicus fr. 125). Theseus is said to have instituted the *geranos* on Delos – the island that Pisistratus "purified" before reorganizing the festival of the Deleia (Herodotus 1.64.2; Thucydides 3.104.1) and, according to one scholar, the *theoria* or sacred embassy that was sent from Athens to Delos in anticipation of the festival passed through the ancient Pisistratid home of Brauron. Furthermore, Theseus' celebrated friendship with Peirithous, king of the Thessalian Lapiths, could have served as a charter for the Pisistratids' alliance with the more powerful families of Thessaly: one of Pisistratus' sons was named Thessalos and, at the time of Ankhimolios' naval invasion, Hippias was able to rely on the aid of 1,000 horsemen under the Thessalian Kineas (*AC* 17.3, 19.5).

One of Theseus' better-known exploits brought him to Marathon – another area where the Pisistratids seem to have held influence, which is presumably why the exiled Hippias led the Persians there in 490. Across the straits from Marathon, on the island of Euboea, lay Eretria, which was a particularly close ally of the Pisistratids. One of Pisistratus' wives is said to have been an aristocratic Eretrian named Koisyra (Scholiast to Aristophanes, *Clouds* 48), and the city served as a base for Pisistratid operations immediately before Pallene (Herodotus 1.61.2). It is almost certainly this Pisistratid connection that accounts for a scene depicting Theseus' abduction of Antiope that features on one of the pediments of the late sixth-century limestone temple of Apollo Daphnephoros in the center of the city.

Theseus was, however, remembered most for the synoecism of Attica and there are indications to suggest that some initial steps towards the unification of the peninsula were in fact taken by the Pisistratids. According to the *Athenian Constitution* (16.5), Pisistratus "instituted the village judges (*dikastai kata dêmous*) and he himself often went out into the *khora* to investigate and resolve differences so that they [the rural residents] should not neglect their work by coming into the *astu*." Whether a strong inclination to promote agricultural productivity was really the reason for the institution of the traveling judges, the decision to dispense the same standards of justice throughout the countryside as in the city could well have served to promote a feeling of solidarity between urban center and rural periphery. Unfortunately, it is impossible to determine whether these judges served the whole of Attica or just the *pedion*, though it is unlikely that Pisistratus would have abandoned his supporters "beyond the hills." More certainty is possible in the case of the herms – ithyphallic pillars supporting a bearded bust of the god Hermes. Hipparchus is said to have set these up on the major thoroughfares of Attica as milestones, each indicating its distance from the Altar of the Twelve Gods, dedicated in the center of the Athenian agora by Pisistratus' homonymous grandson, probably in 521 (Plato, *Hipp.* 228b–229d; Thucydides 6.54.6; ML 11). The fact that an example has been unearthed at Koropi, on the further side of Mount Hymettus, offers clear evidence that the *mesogaia* was included within this network of arterial roads radiating from the city of Athens.

It is often also believed that the Pisistratids sought to unite city and countryside through the institution of festivals and cultic processions. In an earlier chapter (pp. 86–7), we considered the theory that the establishment of "extraurban" sanctuaries served to mark out the territorial limits of the nascent *polis*. Although doubts were expressed there about the theory's applicability to the eighth-century *polis*, the hypothesis is far more credible in the case of sixth-century Attica. At Eleusis, a large square limestone *telestêrion* (initiation hall) with marble decoration may have been built in the second quarter of the sixth century to replace an earlier sixth-century predecessor – though the dating has recently been challenged – while on the northwest slopes of the Athenian acropolis, a new temple was constructed at the City Eleusinion – the starting point for the procession that set out along the Sacred Way for Eleusis on the occasion of the Great Mysteries. At Brauron, on the east coast of Attica, architectural fragments incorporated in later buildings suggest the existence of a late sixth-century temple in the sanctuary of Artemis; finds of pottery and sculpture from the sanctuary's urban counterpart on the Athenian acropolis suggest an approximately contemporaneous arrangement there. Similarly, the first temple of Dionysus Eleuthereus on the southern slopes of the acropolis, the destination of a procession from the god's native sanctuary at Eleutherai that initiated the festival of the Great Dionysia, probably predates the end of the sixth century.

Trying to establish precise dates for these various sanctuaries is more difficult. Originally, all were confidently dated to the tyranny of Pisistratus; then, many of them were cautiously downdated to the reign of Pisistratus' sons, Hippias and Hipparchus, while, in recent years, nearly all of them have been reassigned to the Cleisthenic regime of the final decade of the sixth century, even though an admittedly late source credits Pisistratus with the dedication of the temple at Brauron (Photius s.v. *Brauronia*). A case in point is the *Archaios Neos* or Old Temple of Athena Polias, constructed on the acropolis immediately south of where the Erechtheion now stands. Built of limestone, but with a marble roof and marble sculptural decoration, the pediments depicted, on one side, two lions savaging a bull and, on the other, the mythical battle between the Olympian Gods and Giants. The temple was for a long time dated to the last quarter of the sixth century and ascribed to Hippias and Hipparchus; more recently, however, arguments have been advanced that it should more properly be assigned to the decade 510–500.

Yet this tendency to downdate monuments previously attributed to the Pisistratids raises awkward historical problems. For one thing, it compresses a flurry of frenetic building activity into an extremely narrow chronological "window." For another, it leaves us wondering exactly what it was that the Pisistratids did during their thirty-six years of uninterrupted power. After all, Thucydides (6.54.5) explicitly says that the Pisistratids "beautified the city . . . and made the sacrifices in the temples" – the final detail implying, perhaps, that temples were among the monuments that they commissioned for the city. The fact is that the act of building monuments was indelibly associated in Greek thought with autocrats. When, shortly after the middle of the fifth century, the Athenian democracy, on the initiative of Pericles, embarked on its ambitious building project on the Athenian acropolis, detractors are said to have compared it not with a programme executed half a century earlier by the post-tyranny regime but with the acts of a tyrant (Plutarch, *Per.* 12). The Periclean project was largely financed by the tribute the Athenians exacted from their empire. It is difficult to comprehend how the Athenian state in the final decade of the sixth century could have funded the major works with which it has been credited. The spoils won in victory against a joint attack by Chalcidians and Boeotians in 506 BCE (ML 15) are unlikely to have been sufficient and, in any case, Herodotus (5.77) describes a bronze four-horse chariot group that stood on the acropolis as a commemoration of the triumph but does not add that the Old Temple of Athena, whose ruins were almost certainly still visible after its destruction by the Persians in 480, was also dedicated from confiscated booty. In the end, it was tyrants who were particularly well equipped to mobilize resources and manpower and it is for this reason that literary sources consistently credit them with building projects.

In fact, the dates attributed to sixth-century Athenian monuments should be approached very cautiously since they are based almost exclusively on stylistic considerations. Such a chronological scheme is predicated on the probably erroneous fallacy that stylistic evolution is unilineal, uniform and universal, but is also anchored by "fixed points" (pp. 38–40) that are very often little more than guesses. A stylistically-based chronology that assigns buildings to a particular decade can never be understood too literally, especially in cases where no more than a couple of years separate political regimes as is the case with the expulsion of Hippias and Cleisthenes' reforms. Furthermore, attempts to assign a precisely circumscribed date to a building fail to give due attention to issues of planning and execution. Both the Temple of Zeus at Olympia and the Parthenon took about fifteen years to build. Not all buildings took so long, but the fact that the sculpture of the *Archaios Neos* seems fairly advanced is not entirely surprising given that architectural sculpture was normally the last part of a building to be executed. Even if the dating is correct, the likelihood is that a building completed after 510 must originally have been conceived and commissioned before Hippias' expulsion.

The altar in front of the temple of Athena Polias was the focal point for the sacrifices that constituted the most important element of the festival known as the Great Panathenaea. A fragment, supposedly attributed to Aristotle (fr. 637), associates Pisistratus with a reorganization of the Panathenaea, but most scholars prefer Eusebius' statement (*Chron.*) that the Panathenaic athletic contests were established in 566/5 since this is approximately the date at which black-figure Panathenaic amphorae, filled with Attica's prized olive oil and awarded to victors, first appear in the archaeological record. This is probably also the date that should be assigned to architectural and sculptural fragments that have been associated with what is called the "Bluebeard Temple," named on account of a brightly painted three-bodied monster that features in the right angle of one of its pediments. It is often assumed that the Bluebeard Temple occupied that part of the acropolis where the Parthenon stands today, but it is far more likely that the southern part of the rock housed an open terrace supporting small treasury-like buildings until the construction of the unfinished "Pre-Parthenon" after the Battle of Marathon. In this case, the Bluebeard Temple would have stood on the same foundations as the *Archaios Neos* which replaced it.

If the construction of the Bluebeard Temple was conceived in conjunction with the reorganization of the Great Panathenaea, it is reasonable to infer that its replacement by the *Archaios Neos* coincided with a further reorganization. Indeed, a dialogue attributed – almost certainly erroneously – to Plato informs us that Pisistratus' son Hipparchus "was the first to convey to this land the epics of Homer and he compelled the rhapsodes at the Panathenaea to recite them, one after another in succession, as they still do today" (*Hipp.* 228b). It is tempting to suppose that it was in this context that the verses describing the

Athenian contingent in the *Catalogue of Ships* were modified to reflect a more unified Attica and, although the source is late, it is not without interest that Plutarch (*Thes.* 20.2) accused Pisistratus of tampering with verses by both Homer and Hesiod in order to cast Theseus in a better light for the Athenian people.

The (A)typicality of Athens

In light of the relative availability of evidence for sixth-century Athens as well as the city's illustrious destiny in the succeeding century, it is inevitable that treatments of Archaic Greece tend to devote more space to Athens than to any other *polis* (p. 203). In earlier studies, the better documented case of Athens was often assumed to be representative of conditions in other cities for which the evidence is less abundant. More recently, however, the tendency has been to regard Athens as the exception rather than the rule. Comparative analysis is always difficult when the evidence is unevenly distributed but, in the case of Athens, matters may have been complicated further by assumptions that must now be regarded as, at the very least, questionable.

One of the complicating factors in many studies of sixth-century Athens is what might be termed a "hyperperiodization." Much scholarly effort has been expended in determining whether certain events occurred before Pisistratus' first attempt at the tyranny, in the course of one of his two failed attempts at power, during his reign or that of his sons, or after Hippias' expulsion. The underlying assumption is that determining agency will reveal policies and counter-policies linked to tyrannical objectives or anti-tyrannical reactions. As far as the early phases of the tyranny are concerned, the whole exercise is not particularly fruitful since the chronology of Pisistratus' early career is not as securely established as we might like. More importantly, however, the assumption that the period of tyranny was qualitatively different from what preceded and succeeded it ignores the unmistakeable continuities that run throughout the entire sixth century.

Given Pisistratus' appointment to an important command during the war with Megara (Herodotus 1.59.4; Aristotle, *AC* 14.1), it is clear that he was participating in aristocratic factional politics well before his attempt to concentrate authority in his own hands. Even then, it was probably only certain aristocratic families that were unduly affected by the establishment of Pisistratus' autocracy. The author of the *Athenian Constitution* (16.2; cf. 14.3) insists that Pisistratus' administration of the state was "more constitutional (*politikôs*) than tyrannical" and Thucydides (6.54.6) says that "in other respects, the city itself continued to employ the laws that had previously been laid down, except that they [the Pisistratids] always took care that one of their own held the chief magistracies." Hippias' expulsion led not to democracy but to a return to aristocratic factionalism, and the popular riot that ushered in Cleisthenes' reforms was probably provoked more by the presence of Spartan troops in the city than by mass opposition to Isagoras. Full democracy was still several decades away at the end of the sixth century.

So, how typical was Athens' development throughout the Archaic period? In the eighth century, with what appears to be the physical coalescence of formerly distinct village communities (p. 78), the city seems to have been relatively prosperous. It had a flourishing and pioneering ceramic industry and evidently attracted skilled craftsmen from abroad – including the Levant – but eighth-century Athens was hardly exceptional when compared to contemporary settlements such as Corinth, Argos, or Eretria and even somewhat underdeveloped when compared to some of the cities on the coast of Asia Minor – especially Old Smyrna. The seventh century is a different story. Archaeologically speaking, settlement evidence is astonishingly elusive although rural cult sites are more visible in the material record. While it is unrealistic to expect material culture to reflect directly or unproblematically the conditions of its production, it is hard to avoid the suspicion that seventh-century Athens was something of a backwater compared with other *poleis* of the period.

By ca. 600, growing divisions between the wealthy and the poor and the risk of enslavement for the latter erupted into open conflict (pp. 194–6). Solon's reforms provided only limited relief to the problems of disorder, though their longer term significance was that they sharpened the category of citizenship and guaranteed to citizens the right to attend the assembly and sit on judicial appeal panels. Furthermore, a law attributed to Solon that prescribed disfranchisement for anybody who did not take sides during civil strife (Aristotle, *AC* 8.5) – a law that struck Plutarch (*Sol.* 20.1) as so paradoxical that it stands a good chance of being genuine – could be taken as prefiguring the potential interventionist role that the *dêmos* could perform in aristocratic factional politics, even if it was not until 508/7 that this potential was realized.

There are, however, reasons to suppose that the citizen body so defined was limited to the city of Athens and its immediate hinterland, the *pedion*, divided into forty-eight wards or *naukrariai*, twelve for each of the four "Ionian" *phylai*. If this is right, early sixth-century Athens was hardly exceptional in terms of the size of the territory over which it had direct control. The Classical cities of Argos and Corinth, for example, are estimated to have controlled territories of 600 and 900 square kilometers respectively. The *phylê–trittys–naukraria* system overlapped, however, with another system based on phratries, and the fact that the latter continued to remain important for evaluating claims to citizenship long after the reforms of Cleisthenes may suggest that they were a primary mode of sociopolitical organization throughout Attica, both beyond the *pedion* and – before the advent of the *naukraria* system, perhaps in the early seventh century – within it. Because phratries were formed and reformed through agglutination rather than repartition, their appearance in the Attic countryside does not presuppose the kind of act of civic definition required by an organization based on *phylai*.

How should we imagine the relationship between Athens and the rural settlements beyond the *pedion*? When invited to settle affairs at Cyrene, Demonax enrolled the Libyan *perioikoi* in the newly reconstituted citizen body and it is entirely possible that the rural Attic settlements of the *paralia* and *mesogaia* were regarded as perioikic communities – that is, communities with nominal internal autonomy but in some relationship of dependency upon the city of Athens. In this sense, the situation in early sixth-century Attica may have been fairly close to the situation in contemporary Laconia, although there is no suggestion that the relationship was based on force, as is normally supposed for the Spartan *perioikoi*. We should probably imagine a more symbiotic rapport: the city offered a valuable market for rural communities and perhaps also a more accredited system for pursuing judicial complaints; the rural communities offered valuable agricultural and mineral resources for Athens as well as manpower should the situation require. The intermediaries in this relationship are likely to have been those aristocrats such as Megacles and Pisistratus, who competed on the Athenian political stage but whose families owned property beyond the *pedion*.

There was one region over which Athens was more anxious to exert direct control. Possession of Eleusis and the offshore island of Salamis were so vital for guaranteeing free passage in the shipping lanes of the Saronic Gulf that the lengthy hostilities between Athens and Megara for control of them were retrojected in the myth that told of the epic war between King Eumolpus of Eleusis and the Athenian ruler Erechtheus. The *Homeric Hymn to Demeter*, thought to date to the late seventh century, appears to suggest an Eleusis that is not fully part of the Athenian sphere, while Solon (frs. 1–3) testifies that Salamis was in Megarian hands ca. 600. Within a generation, however, the Athenians had gained the upper hand, culminating in Pisistratus' capture of the Megarian port of Nisaia, probably in the 560s (Herodotus 1.59.4). Solon is said to have promoted manufacture at Athens, offering citizenship to those who came to Athens to ply a trade and prohibiting the export of any agricultural product save for olive oil (Plutarch, *Sol.* 24), but it was the dissipation of the Megarian threat that really paved the way for Athens' commercial revival. The second quarter of the sixth century sees a sharp rise in the production and exportation of Attic ceramics – and, of course, their contents – which effectively drive the previously popular Corinthian wares out of the overseas markets. Of particular interest are Attic-produced ceramic wares that are found almost exclusively at sites in Italy and seem to have been primarily targeted at Etruscan markets. These include the gaudy and sometimes graphically explicit "Tyrrhenian Amphorai," produced between 560 and 530, and the "Nikosthenic Amphorai" of the 530s and 520s, which are adaptations of Etruscan *bucchero* pottery (see p. 249).

In Laconia, the citizens of the perioikic cities were named "Lakedaimonioi," the same ethnonym that the Spartans used to identify themselves. The term is used in contexts that seem to indicate a political affiliation that only really makes sense if the *perioikoi* were regarded as citizens of a Spartan state even if they did not enjoy the same full civic rights as their Spartan counterparts. There is reason to believe that the appellation was endowed with a more politicized content in the sixth century when it makes its first appearance in the epigraphical record. In Attica, something similar may have occurred with the establishment, probably in the 560s, of the Great Panathenaea. Some scholars have been troubled by the apparent hyperbole in describing a festival of Attic unity as a festival of "*all* the Athenians" but, by analogy with the term "Panhellenes" (pp. 273–4), the *pan-* prefix actually emphasizes the diversity rather than the unity of the Athenians. On this reading, the establishment of the Panathenaea was designed to foster among all the communities of Attica a sense of affiliation to a state centered on Athens, though the franchise may have continued to be restricted to free-born residents of the *pedion*.

The actions attributed to the Pisistratids – the establishment of rural circuit judges, the systematization of a road-system centered on Athens, and the introduction of festal processions linking the urban center to rural sanctuaries – can then be seen as further attempts to construct a pan-Attic Athenocentric consciousness that built on, rather than repudiated, the objectives behind the institution of the Panathenaea, a festival to which Pisistratus' sons are said to have added their own innovations. This might explain why, in its plan and exterior decoration, the *Archaios Neos* actually incorporates echoes of its earlier sixth-century predecessor. Ultimately, however, full political unification had to wait until the time of Cleisthenes' reforms: the incorporation of new citizens and their territory necessitated a complete overhaul of the tribal system so that the newly-enrolled members of the citizen body would not be at a disadvantage compared with their longer-enfranchised neighbors.

The reader should be warned that the reconstruction offered here is highly conjectural. Nevertheless, one thing is clear. The gradual repopulation of the Attic countryside in the Dark Age could not have resulted in a situation where the entire population of Attica was distributed evenly across a tribal repartition of the citizen body. Nor can full political unification be diffused piecemeal across so large a territory. A situation whereby a resident of Marathon or Sunium or Brauron – let alone Halai Araphenides – could consider himself the political equal of an Athenian resident could only come about as the result of a major, deliberate reform, and the only candidate that meets the criteria is the legislation attributed to Cleisthenes. If this reconstruction is correct, then, sixth-century Athens was hardly atypical compared with Archaic *poleis* elsewhere. In fact, the parallels with sixth-century Sparta may have been closer than fifth-century Athenian patriots or Spartan apologists were willing to concede. In the final decade of the sixth century, however, the city made a choice concerning its perioikic neighbors that was not taken by Sparta. And it was that choice that marked the commencement of Athens' truly amazing ascendancy in the fifth century.

FURTHER READING

Re-evaluations of the Pisistratid tyranny: Sancisi-Weerdenburg 2000; Lavelle 1993, 2005.

Naukrariai: H. T. Wallinga, "The Athenian Naukraroi," in Sancisi-Weerdenburg 2000, 131–46. Phratries: Lambert 1998. For the epigraphical use of demotics: T. F. Winters, "Kleisthenes and Athenian nomenclature," *Journal of Hellenic Studies* 113 (1993), 162–5. Cleisthenes' possible political intentions: D. M. Lewis, "Cleisthenes and Attica," *Historia* 12 (1963), 22–40. 508/7 as a popular revolution: Ober 1996, 32–52. Ostracism and the politics of exile: Forsdyke 2005.

Synoecism as resulting from the "internal colonization" of Attica: Snodgrass 1980, 33–7. Arguments for non-existence of standing army: F. J. Frost, "The Athenian military before Cleisthenes," *Historia* 33 (1984), 283–94. Cleisthenic unification of Attica: Anderson 2003. Sixth-century factionalism as a historiographical invention: Lavelle 2005, 67–87.

For traditions and artistic representations concerning Theseus: Anderson 2003, 134–46; Shapiro 1989. Attic cults: Anderson 2003, 178–96. Downdating of *archaios neos*: W. A. P. Childs, "The date of the old temple of Athena on the Athenian Acropolis," in Coulson et al. 1994, 1–6. Buildings on the acropolis: Hurwit 1999.

On the continuities between Solon and Pisistratus: Irwin 2005, 263–80.

10

Making a Living

Conceptualizing Ancient Economic Activity

If there is a common refrain that has characterized much recent scholarship on the economy of ancient Greece, it is that it is misleading to think of an autonomous economic sphere. So, for example, Moses Finley, one of the most influential ancient economic historians of the twentieth century, argued that it was only possible to study the ancient economy because of reasons that had nothing to do with the economy. Finley's seemingly paradoxical conclusion can only truly be understood when set against two long-running theoretical debates on the subject – namely, that between modernists and primitivists and that between formalists and substantivists.

The primitivist–modernist debate is sometimes also known as the Bücher–Meyer controversy after the two German historians who first tackled the issue of the ancient economy. Karl Bücher (1847–1930), adopting an explicitly evolutionist point of view, argued that various national economies had passed through three different stages: in antiquity, there had existed only closed household economies, whereas the Middle Ages had been characterized by city economies, and the modern period by national economies. For "primitivists," there were therefore important structural differences between the economies of the present and those of the past. By contrast, the view that the ancient economy had been primitive and focused on relatively small households whose primary concern was subsistence held little appeal for historians such as Eduard Meyer (1855–1930), whose more modernist understanding of the ancient economy was not entirely unconnected from their belief that Ancient Greece had important lessons to teach the Germans concerning political unification. Meyer explicitly professed that the economy of Greece corresponded to fourteenth- and fifteenth-century Europe and, for the modernists who followed in his tracks, ancient economies differed from modern ones only in scale rather than in substance.

The Bücher–Meyer debate would probably have played itself out relatively quickly had it not become entangled in a complementary – though not identical – debate between formalists and substantivists. Formalists regard the economy as a functionally segregated, autonomous sphere of activity, characterized by the existence of a market in which actors adopt rational strategies in order to maximize their profits. By contrast, substantivists, influenced in great part by the work of the economic anthropologist Karl Polanyi (1886–1964), examine the political, social, and cultural institutions that guarantee the provision and satisfaction of material needs and regard the economy as "embedded" within society. Polanyi and many of his followers believed that a formalist approach could only be practiced in the case of industrialized modern economies, while embedded economies were typical of pre-industrial societies, thus seemingly mapping the substantivist–formalist opposition onto the primitivist–modernist divide. In reality, however, the correlation is not entirely satisfactory. One could, for example, argue that the economy of the Archaic Greek world was indeed embedded in social and political relations while still entertaining a conception of it as involving economic transactions that extended well beyond individual households.

Finley's *The Ancient Economy*, first published in 1973, has proved to be one of the most seminal contributions to the subject. An attendee of Polanyi's seminars at Columbia University, Finley was also influenced greatly by the works of the sociologist Max Weber as well as by Johannes Hasebroek, who, in 1928, had argued that ancient Greek cities lacked economic policies because trade was in the hands of a non-citizen merchant class of outsiders. In Finley's view, the principal aim of the ancient economy was self-sufficiency based primarily on agricultural production. Trade accounted for only a tiny proportion of the gross product because production exhibited few variations from place to place, transportation costs were high, there was not a sufficient market for the luxury goods that were in circulation, and the status of traders was low. Echoing Weber's distinction between the "consumer" cities of antiquity and the "producer" cities of the Middle Ages, Finley characterized the ancient *polis* as a center of consumers who paid for what they needed to subsist by extracting rents, taxes, and tributes from the rural hinterland that the urban center controlled.

Finley's position continues to exert considerable influence today – even to the extent that there have been many calls to lay the old primitivist–modernist and formalist–substantivist debates to rest. Yet scholarly opinion has hardly remained static in the thirty years or so since *The Ancient Economy* was published and, although few would now adopt an extreme modernist or formalist position, some scholars have voiced the suspicion that Finley may have underestimated the complexity of the ancient economy. So, for example, recognition of market exchange in Ancient Greece has provoked debate as to whether or not markets were interdependent and some economic historians have considered it profitable to apply analyses from modern economics even as they admit that the scale and nature of the ancient economy were very different from that of today. In the remainder of this chapter, we shall seek to explore just how embedded or underdeveloped the economy of the Archaic Greek world was.

A Peasant Economy?

Nobody disputes the dominance of agriculture within the Archaic Greek economy. The *Works and Days* presumes an audience for which agriculture was the principal means of subsistence and Phocylides (fr. 6) regards a rich farm as a prerequisite for great wealth. The probability that there was a property qualification for citizenship in many Greek *poleis* (p. 191) only serves to underscore further the centrality of cultivation to economic activity. That a commercial or industrial class was of relatively negligible importance in most Greek cities even in the Classical period is indicated by the estimate that no more than ten to fifteen vase-painters were active in Athens at any one time. Where disagreement arises is over the nature of agricultural activity and, in particular, whether most households were engaged primarily in subsistence agriculture or whether they engaged in a concerted effort to produce surpluses that could be exchanged for other goods.

The term "peasant" is regularly used in descriptions of the ancient Greek world although definitions – most of which are derived from studies of peasant societies in very different times and places – vary widely. It may, therefore, be useful to begin by defining what a peasant is not. At the lower end, a peasant is not a slave or the legal property of another, although he may be a serf – a status between free and slave where limited contracted services are expected in return for a relative degree of personal freedom, including the right to marry. At the upper end, the admittedly fuzzy boundary between peasant and farmer depends on the basis of a cultivator's attachment to the soil. Peasants typically produce at least some agricultural surplus which is used to support, through rents or taxes, other economic classes, but their economic production is geared primarily towards subsistence. Farmers, by contrast, view land as a commodity and expect regularly to derive financial gain from their labor. The distinction is important because, in a peasant economy, cultivators tend to subordinate the temptation to maximize profits to the need to minimize the risk of production failures. Within these limits, the following characteristics are common to many peasant economies: (i) the peasantry occupies just one sector within a complex, stratified society; (ii) peasants tend to possess, even if they do not own, the land they cultivate, meaning that they may be freeholders but can also be tenants or lessees; (iii) although peasants normally utilize the resources of their own household, they may occasionally employ restricted slave- or wage-labor; (iv) they tend to reside in village communities where they maintain links with other households; and (v) they typically owe obligations to the state even if they do not enjoy full political or civic rights.

It should be clear that dependent populations such as the helots of Laconia and Messenia or the Penestai of Thessaly (p. 176) qualify under this definition of peasantry. Although these populations were often described by ancient authors (e.g. Thucydides 1.101.2, 5.23.3; Antiochus fr. 13; Theopompus fr. 122) as *douloi*, a word that blurs any distinction between their position and that of a chattel slave, the second-century CE rhetorician Iulius Pollux (*Onomastikon* 3.83) described their status as between free men and slaves – i.e. as what we would now term a serf. Certainly, the helots were allowed to marry (e.g. Tyrtaeus fr. 7) and it would appear that most of the plots of land that the helots cultivated in Laconia and Messenia were worked by family units. Beyond meeting their own subsistence needs, the helots were required to contribute either a proportion (Tyrtaeus fr. 6) or a fixed amount (Plutarch, *Lyc.* 8.7) of their agricultural production to their Spartan masters and they enjoyed no political or legal rights or protection. Furthermore, although there is no unambiguous literary testimony one way or another, the results of the Pylos Regional Archaeological Project suggest that the helots of western Messenia at least resided in concentrated settlements or villages.

Populations of a similar status to the helots and Penestai are mentioned in connection with Sicyon, Argos, Syracuse, Byzantium, Heraclea Pontica, West Locris, Megara, and Crete, and it is sometimes hypothesized that this system of exploitation was once relatively widespread throughout Greece. What is more controversial is whether areas that did not rely on the labor of dependent populations can fairly be defined as peasant economies. It has, for example, been argued that the majority of rural residents in the Archaic Greek world were yeoman farmers rather than peasants because: (i) they geared their production not only towards subsistence but also with a view to the market; (ii) they did not owe excessive financial burdens, be it in rents or taxes, to the wealthy from whom they were not sharply economically differentiated; and (iii) many of them could afford to employ slaves. Unlike peasants, it is argued, most smallholders lived on isolated homesteads where they engaged in intensive agricultural practices – e.g. irrigation, crop rotation, and manuring – aimed at maximizing production. Furthermore, they played a full role in political affairs. This view of the Archaic Greek smallholder as a yeoman farmer is based in large part on a belief in an early ideology of egalitarianism that we have already had cause to question in earlier chapters. But it also relies heavily on two literary examples that may be far from representative – namely, the description of Laertes' farm in Book 24 of the *Odyssey* and Hesiod's depiction of rural life in *Works and Days*.

After slaughtering Penelope's suitors, Odysseus sets out from the *polis* of Ithaca for the fields of his father, Laertes, which the latter had "brought into cultivation through toil" (24.206–7). We are told that Laertes' house is located on the property together with buildings in which his indentured servants took their meals, sat, and slept (208–10). The farm is also home to an old Sicilian woman whose precise status is not specified though she is described as tending to Laertes (211–12, 365–7). When Odysseus finds his father, he is digging around a tree in an adjoining vineyard, dressed in a shabby, patched tunic, and wearing leggings and gloves to protect himself from the brambles (226–30).

We are also told that the estate includes fig, olive, and pear trees in addition to the vines (246–7).

Laertes' farm is characterized by a diversity of crops. There is no specific mention of cereals, though the vines and fruit trees were presumably cultivated for more than simple subsistence and the intensive care that arboriculture and viticulture require explains the necessity of slave labor on the estate. Laertes' farm also appears to be isolated though, contrary to what is sometimes written, there is no evidence that it lies in marginal territory: it is simply described as being "outside" the *polis* (212) and Odysseus is said to have "quickly" reached it from the urban center (205). It is true that the property conforms poorly to standard definitions of a peasant smallholding but why should we assume that Laertes is the representative for an entire class of smallholders? His shabby attire offers little support, since Odysseus is surprised by what he perceives as a mismatch between Laertes' appearance and the manner in which the farm is being maintained (244–55) and later, after he has taken a bath, Laertes regains a form that is likened to the "immortal gods" (371). He may have retired from political life, but the fact remains that Laertes was the former chieftain of the island, the consort of a goddess, and the father of the rightful *basileus* of Ithaca. Similarities between his property and that of other *basileis* such as Meleager (*Il.* 9.579–80) or Tydeus (14.122–24) only serve further to distinguish farms such as these from the smallholdings of most rural residents.

Much of the advice that Hesiod purports to give to his brother, Perses, is concerned with the cultivation of cereals, but he too engages in mixed farming. So, for example, we hear about viticulture (*WD* 571–3) and the herding of sheep and goats for both wool and dairy products (234, 516, 543, 585, 590), as well as beekeeping (233). For the purposes of ploughing, Hesiod has access to oxen (405, 452) and there is also mention of mules (607). His household, in addition to a wife and at least one son (376–7), includes an unspecified number of slaves (469–71, 502–3, 573, 597), one of whom is an unmarried woman who works in the fields and keeps his house in order (405–6). He also hires casual labor from time to time, including a forty-year-old man to assist with ploughing (441–6), a *thês*, or wage laborer, and a childless maidservant (602).

In terms of resources, Hesiod is far from impoverished. His household would seem to number between eight and twelve people and to support them he would probably have needed a farm of between six and eight hectares – somewhat larger than the average landholding of 3.6–5.4 hectares that has been estimated for the Classical period. Those who would see in him a comfortably-off yeoman farmer point to his advice to load a boat with the sort of cargo that would ensure a handsome profit (631–2), his comment about procuring more flocks and wealth from hard work (308), and his tendency to drink wine imported from Thrace (589). And yet, the reason he gives for engaging in overseas trade is to ward off debts and hunger (647) and his insistence on the necessity of storing up a year's supply of grain to keep hunger from the door (31–2, 299–300, 363) is more indicative of the peasant's concern to minimize risks than the farmer's desire to maximize profits. Indeed, he seems to imply that those who produce enough for subsistence do not need to take to boats (236–7). While Hesiod is self-reliant on household production for tools and implements, including his plough (407–8, 420–36), there is no hint that his farm is isolated like that of Laertes: if anything, one has the impression that he belongs to a village community (e.g. 493–5). Furthermore, his employment of fallowing (463–4) is a far cry from the intensive farming practices that would be required to maximize production. The picture is, in other words, inconsistent and perhaps this is not, in the end, all that surprising. Hesiod assumes the persona of a peasant but the poet himself was a participant in aristocratic competitions and was clearly well connected enough to have been influenced by concepts and ideas originating in Near Eastern wisdom literature. Under such circumstances, it might be unrealistic to expect systematic consistency in the values and experiences that are expressed but that only serves further to highlight how problematic the Hesiodic evidence is for the question of the peasant economy in Archaic Greece.

Questions of residence patterns and their connection to agricultural practices have recently become the topic of lively discussion. The traditional view was that partible inheritance and the acquisition of additional property through marriage led to fragmented landholdings and that practical considerations therefore prompted farmers to reside in village bases and travel out to their scattered landholdings. Biennial bare fallowing, by which certain fields are left uncultivated in alternate years to allow the soil to recover its fertility, was a natural consequence since it requires little input of labor. Although it tends to result in low yields, the very fragmentation of landholdings in different microzones acts to cushion the cultivator against the unpredictability of crop failures. It is easy to see how this system of agriculture fits well with the priority peasants are supposed to attribute to minimizing risks over maximizing returns. Nevertheless, it has recently been argued that this "traditional" picture of Greek agriculture is based on ethnographic studies of modern Mediterranean farming practices and, more importantly, on the erroneous assumption that there is an essential continuity between antiquity and the present in this regard. According to this revisionist viewpoint, Greek agriculture was more intensive than has previously been recognized. Irrigation, crop rotation – particularly the cultivation of pulses, which replenishes nitrogen in the soil – and manuring would have required a greater investment of labor but would also have resulted in higher yields, producing surpluses that could be traded. Since the demand for labor input is high, farmers in intensive agricultural regimes tend to live on their land rather than in nucleated settlements at a distance from their property.

How can we decide between these alternative viewpoints? For what it is worth and bearing in mind the provisos expressed above, Hesiod appears to sketch a picture of fallow cropping and residence in nucleated communities that accords more with an extensive than an intensive regime of agriculture. By contrast, inscriptions and speeches written for the law courts in the Classical period offer an alternative representation of rural farmsteads and concerns with irrigation and the production of cash crops that fits better a more intensive model of cultivation. It is, of course, entirely likely that agricultural regimes would have varied from region to region but the evidence of archaeological survey (see p. 29) suggests that there may also have been a chronological development, whereby extensive agricultural practices gradually yielded to more intensive ones.

Although archaeological survey techniques have witnessed enormous advances in recent years, there is still some uncertainty as to the precise relationship between subterranean features and the sherd and tile scatters that appear on the surface of the soil. There is even considerable controversy as to what constitutes a "site." Tiled structures found in the countryside, for example, need not necessarily be residential units, especially since there is later evidence (e.g. *IG* XII.5.872) that towers – once assumed to be the unmistakable index of a rural farmstead – may have been used primarily for storage purposes. What the data from various regional surveys do reveal, however, is that small isolated rural sites that might be identified with farmsteads are not common in the Archaic period until the later sixth century, with more intensive rural settlement peaking in the fifth and fourth centuries. In other words, the archaeological evidence seems to argue for a more extensive agricultural regime until the latter part of the Archaic period.

It is tempting to associate the archaeologically attested intensification of agricultural practices with the agrarian unrest in Attica that literary sources report for the early sixth century (pp. 194–5). For all the diversity of opinion concerning the crisis that faced Solon, most are agreed that the wealthy were bringing new land into cultivation for which they required more labor and that this was supplied by a mixture of impoverished wage-laborers, exploited share-croppers, and slaves. The objection that it takes at least another two generations for an increase in rural habitation to appear in the archaeological record is not entirely compelling. Firstly, the very few archaeological surveys that have been conducted in Attica are in zones such as the deme of Atene and the Skourta Plain that are largely agreed to have been somewhat atypical for the region as a whole. Secondly, the earlier stages of agricultural intensification may not have required residence on the landholding itself – especially if many of the tasks were undertaken by dependent laborers rather than freeholders themselves.

Whether or not these dependent laborers were quite as numerous as the author of the Aristotelian *Athenian Constitution* (2.2) implies, it is clear that they can be characterized as peasants. But freeholders of modest properties also meet the definition to the extent that such evidence as we possess suggests that subsistence was of primary concern even if smallholders occasionally employed unfree labor and even if they regularly generated modest surpluses. Indeed, as we have seen, a common characteristic of peasants is that such surpluses are normally extracted to support other sectors of society. It is, then, interesting to hear that Pisistratus is supposed to have levied a tax of either 10 percent (Aristotle, *AC* 16.4) or 5 percent (Thucydides 6.54) on agricultural produce and one recent interpretation of the *hektêmoroi* (p. 195) suggests that, even prior to the tyranny, the poor of Attica were expected to pay one sixth of their proceeds to the wealthy as "protection money."

In short, it seems reasonable to talk about "peasant societies" in the Archaic Greek world. Whether it is accurate to talk about a "peasant economy" is less clear cut. It has been argued that the Greek world was rather a "slave economy" because, while peasants may have constituted the majority of the population, the propertied classes derived the bulk of their surplus from the exploitation of unfree labor. Nevertheless, while that may be a fair characterization of the Classical Greek world, it is less self evident for the earlier period. The concept of a slave economy depends on a sharp definition of chattel slavery that seems not to have existed for much of the Archaic period (p. 196). The ancients believed that the institution of chattel slavery originated on Chios (Theopompus fr. 122) – probably as a consequence of the intensive viticulture for which the island was famous – but at Athens, chattel slavery only appears to assume greater importance after the legislation of Solon.

We should not, however, make the mistake of assuming that, just because a peasant economy existed in Archaic Greece, trade and the market were of no significance at all. Although subsistence was of primary concern to peasant households, they did produce modest surpluses that would need to be exchanged for goods that could not be manufactured at home. Among the propertied class, engagement with markets would have been even more pronounced. Based on information concerning the *eisphora* (property tax) that was levied in Athens in 378/7, it has been estimated that one third of the land was in the hands of the richest 10 percent of the population and it is unlikely that the figures would have been vastly different for the earlier period. If the Solonian law (Plutarch, *Sol.* 24), banning the exportation of all products except olive oil, is genuine then the implication would be that the wealthy landowners of Attica were intensifying production to generate a surplus that could be exchanged via long distance trade. There were also, however, entire regions of the Greek world that had little choice but to enter into market transactions. The population of Aegina in the early fifth century has been estimated at around 40,000 but calculations of available land and crop yields suggest that only 4,000 of these could have been supported at basic subsistence level. One option was to engage in piracy and the story of the theft of the statues of Damia and Auxesia from Epidaurus (Herodotus 5.83) might suggest that this was an activity in which several Aeginetans engaged. But simple necessity also dictated that the population of the island must have subsisted on imported foodstuffs, paid for by non-agricultural production. It is, then, little surprise that the Aeginetans seem to have engaged in long-distance trade from an early period.

Plying the Seas

The Aeginetans seem to have played a prominent role at the settlement of Naucratis in the Nile Delta. According to Herodotus (Document 10.1), the Egyptian pharaoh Amasis (569–525) allowed Greeks – perhaps former mercenaries – to settle permanently at Naucratis but he also provided land for

Document 10.1

Amasis became an admirer of the Greeks and, apart from other services that he demonstrated towards some of the Greeks, he also granted to those arriving in Egypt the *polis* of Naucratis to live in. To those, however, who regularly voyaged there but did not wish to settle permanently, he gave land so that they could erect altars and precincts to the gods. The largest and most famous of these precincts – as well as the one that is most frequented – is called the Hellenion. These are the *poleis* that founded it in common: of the Ionians, Chios, Teos, Phocaea and Clazomenae; of the Dorians, Rhodes, Cnidus, Halicarnassus and Phaselis; and of the Aeolians, Mytilene alone. These, then, are the *poleis* to whom the precinct belongs and they each provide representatives (*prostatai*) to the port of trade (*emporion*); whichever other *poleis* make claims do so without any basis. But independently, the Aeginetans established for themselves a precinct of Zeus, the Samians one to Hera and the Milesians one to Apollo. Formerly, Naucratis was the only port of trade in Egypt there was no other. If someone arrived at any of the other mouths of the Nile, he had to swear by a solemn oath that he had not come there intentionally and then sail in his own ship to the Canobic mouth. If the ship was unable to sail against contrary winds, he had to carry his cargo around the Delta in barges until he arrived at Naucratis. This was the honor in which Naucratis was held. (Herodotus 2.178–9)

Greek non-resident traders to build precincts to the gods. A coalition of East Greek cities built the so-called Hellenion but the Aeginetans, Samians, and Milesians independently built precincts for Zeus, Hera, and Apollo respectively. Other authors mention the foundation of Naucratis but differ from Herodotus on details. Strabo (17.1.18) believes that Naucratis was a Milesian foundation at the time of either Psammetichus I (664–610) or Psammetichus II (595–589); Polycharmus (fr. 1), a local historian of the Hellenistic period, thought that the *polis* was already in existence by the twenty-third Olympiad of 688–685, while Eusebius (88b) dates the foundation of Naucratis to the middle of the eighth century.

Archaeological exploration of Naucratis has been hampered by the fact that, even before Flinders Petrie's excavations of 1884, much of the site had already been destroyed by farmers who were using the soil as a high-phosphate fertilizer. Today, much of the area of the earliest excavations lies under water and attempts to determine the precise stratigraphy of the site are hampered by weathering and continued destruction. Nevertheless, enough information exists to cast more light on the literary testimonia for Naucratis. The precinct that Herodotus names the Hellenion has been identified, thanks to inscriptions to "the gods of the Hellenes" as well as to Aphrodite, Artemis, and perhaps Heracles and Poseidon. Reconstructed shortly before the middle of the fifth century, the earliest evidence stretches back to ca. 570, which would certainly allow the construction of the precinct to have been authorized by Amasis. Herodotus cannot, however, be right that the site as a whole was only granted to the Greeks in the mid-sixth century because the earliest stratified material evidence – imported Corinthian transitional pottery and a terracotta head of Cypriot manufacture – dates to the last quarter of the seventh century, thus falling towards the end of the reign of Psammetichus I.

The sanctuary of Apollo that Herodotus attributes to the Milesians has been identified by inscribed votive pottery as lying to the west of the Hellenion; the first of two temples in the precinct probably dates to shortly before 550. The Samian precinct to Hera, however, would seem to date back to the last quarter of the seventh century to judge from pottery associated with the sanctuary and a similar date may also hold for a sanctuary of Aphrodite, unmentioned by Herodotus. The sanctuary of Zeus, attributed to the Aeginetans, has not been located but it has been suggested that it might be the same precinct as that to the Dioscuri – the twin sons of Zeus – which lies to the north of the sanctuary of Apollo. A small temple with walls and pillars of mud-brick covered with stucco was probably constructed after the first temple of Apollo and may even be as late as ca. 500. On the other hand, older inscribed dedications suggest that cultic honors were being practiced for the Dioscuri at an earlier date and it is normally assumed that traders from Aegina, Samos, and Miletus may have been active at Naucratis before other Greek *poleis* collaborated in the foundation of the Hellenion.

By and large, the constituent peoples enumerated by Herodotus receive confirmation from the archaeological and epigraphic record. The distinctive white-slip pottery of Chios begins to appear from around 620 while chemical analysis on inscribed single-handed cups, dedicated in the sanctuary of Hera, has revealed that they were produced on Samos. Given the close connections that are attested between Samos and Sparta in the sixth century (e.g. Herodotus 3.47), it is likely that it was Samian traders who carried Laconian black-figure wares to Naucratis. There are also significant quantities of the so-called "Wild Goat" style of pottery (Figure 10.1), dating to the second half of the seventh century, and Fikellura pottery, which starts to be produced ca. 560: in recent years it has been recognized that Miletus was one of the most important centers of production for both styles of pottery. In addition, the more than 1,500 inscriptions found on ceramic sherds indicate the presence, however temporary, of dedicators from Teos, Phocaea, Clazomenae, Rhodes, Mytilene, and Cnidus. There is some scholarly controversy as to whether Aegina pro- duced distinctive wares, though Aeginetan traders are probably responsible for many of the Attic and Corinthian imports that are found at Naucratis. A certain Sostratus, who dedicated a Chian Wild Goat bowl in the sanctuary of Aphrodite, is almost certainly not the famous homonymous Aeginetan trader whom Herodotus (4.152.3) describes as unsurpassed in earning handsome profits on cargoes and who is probably the dedicator of a stone anchor at the Etruscan port of Gravisca. For one thing, the anchor dates to approximately a century after the inscribed bowl; for another, the script on the bowl is in the

Figure 10.1 "Wild Goat" *oinokhoe*. KB Ephorate of Prehistoric and Classical Antiquities, Rhodes

East Ionic dialect and script. By contrast, the Phanes who dedicated a black-glaze dinos at Naucratis may be the Halicarnassian mercenary who deserted Amasis' cause for the Persian king Cambyses (3.4.11) and who minted three electrum coins at Halicarnassus. There is no overall consensus as to whether another famous Halicarnassian, the historian Herodotus, is the dedicator of a fifth-century Athenian cup that bears his name.

It is often suspected that when Herodotus describes Naucratis as a *polis*, he is not using the term in any precise, political sense, but that there was indeed a residential community at the site is not in question. Many of the ceramic wares seem designed for local consumption and, to the east of the sanctuary of Aphrodite, a faience workshop was established towards the end of the seventh century. Producing Egyptianizing scarabs, heads, busts, crouching lions, and lion heads primarily for export to Greek customers, the factory almost certainly required a resident workforce. At the same time, the widespread provenance of imported materials at Naucratis confirms that it was an important port of trade for Greeks from both sides of the Aegean and the settlement developed the sorts of services and facilities that are often associated with commercial centers. For example, Naucratis was famous for its prostitutes: one of the most famous was the Thracian Rhodopis, whose freedom was bought by Sappho's brother, Kharaxos (Herodotus 2.134–35).

Naucratis conforms to what economic anthropologists term a "port of trade." Such ports are normally situated at seaside or riverside locations that permit further transportation by land. Typically they lie on the margins of a controlled territory, separated from the hinterland so as to foster a sense of neutrality, and they serve as a "checkpoint" between two societies organized according to very different principles of economic organization. Populated by either indigenous workers or by foreigners and equipped with a dedicated infrastructure, such ports of trade are usually instituted by some ceremonial act of authorization or agreement and, most importantly, serve as an exclusive locus for administered trade. All of these features are attested at Naucratis, where there is no evidence for earlier Egyptian settlement prior to the arrival of the Greeks nor for the cohabitation of other peoples such as the Phoenicians or the Cypriots alongside the Greeks.

It is, however, Herodotus' reference to official representatives (*prostatai*) and the stipulation that Naucratis was the only place in Egypt where Greeks might trade that reveals the administered nature of trade at this location. The formal agreement that, on archaeological grounds, probably goes back to Psammetichus I rather than Amasis, was of benefit to both parties. To the Greeks, the granting of exclusive trading rights may well have appeared as a gesture of favor from a pharaoh whose officials collected and controlled most of the agricultural products of the country. For the pharaoh, the collection of customs duties and taxes was greatly facilitated by concentrating foreigners in one location. Responsibility for the collection of these duties and taxes and for their dispatch to the temple of Neïth at Sais fell to the "Overseer of the Gate to the Foreign Lands of the Great Green" – an office that was held, during Amasis' reign, by a certain Nekthorheb. The *prostatai* were probably the Greek counterparts to the Overseer and, if Herodotus deliberately means to imply that the Aeginetans, Samians, and Milesians did not appoint these representatives, it is possible that the office was first instituted at the time of Amasis and the construction of the Hellenion.

The Greeks probably traded in wine, oil, and perhaps slaves, but the commodity they possessed that the Egyptians desired most was silver. Although dating much later to ca. 380, a stele of the pharaoh Nektanebis I that was found at Naucratis lists the tithe the king dedicated to the Temple of Neïth at Sais. The inventory includes gold, silver, timber, and worked wood from "the Greek sea" and gold, silver, and finished goods produced in *Pi-emrôye* (the Egyptian name for Naucratis). Gold was a resource that Egypt possessed, while timber was probably acquired from the Phoenicians, resident in what is now Lebanon. There was also, however, a pressing need for silver – not least, to pay the Greek and Carian mercenaries on whom the pharaohs relied so heavily – and it can hardly be an accident that several hoards of silver coins have been found in the area of the Nile Delta. The earliest of these dates to ca. 500 though it is highly likely that silver was flowing to Egypt at an earlier date.

One third of the coins found originate in the area of Thrace and Macedonia and it has been conjectured that the Ionians might have traded wool and other specialized products for Thracian and Macedonian silver, which they then carried to Naucratis. In return, Egypt had linen, papyrus, ivory, ebony, and resins to offer the Greeks but, as the Romans were to know all too well, the most valuable product the country possessed was grain. We have already had cause to comment on Aegina's inability to feed itself from its own agricultural resources; the situation at Miletus appears to have been little better. It is, then, hardly surprising that traders from these *poleis* should have been among the first to enter into commercial transactions with the Egyptian authorities.

The quest for an external source of grain was probably a relatively late development in the Archaic period. It certainly was not the only item that the Greeks traded. Evidence from shipwrecks testifies to a commerce in timber, oil and perfumed unguents, wine, textiles, and hides, while the traffic in food-stuffs such as olives, honey, pistachio nuts, almonds, and fish products can be tracked by finds of the amphorae used to transport them. Of particular import-ance early on was the need for non-precious metals and ores and it is generally suspected that it was the quest for iron ores from the island of Elba that motivated the foundation of Pithecusae on Ischia (p. 117). In this respect, the early Euboean settlers of the west were not behaving so differently from the Phoenicians, who traveled in search of raw materials that they could work to form metal vessels, ivory objects, cloth, and other luxury items that could then be traded for sheep, cattle, wine, and wheat (Homer, *Od.* 15.406).

It would, however, be a mistake to assume that trade was driven solely by necessity: desire for certain products was also an important component of consumption patterns. When, for example, communities in the North Levant began importing Corinthian *aryballoi*, it was not on account of a shortage of perfumed oils since factories in Cyprus and North Syria were already pro-ducing perfume containers for export to Rhodes and Cos. Similarly, imported Greek pottery in North Syria and Phoenicia indicates that Levantine populations were importing Greek wine and olive oil although the area is short of neither vines nor olives and there were already well-established customs connected with the consumption of wine (Isaiah 5.28; Jeremiah 48.11–12). Much as today, a certain cachet seems to have accrued to some brand products: Hesiod (*WD* 589), as we have seen, enjoys wine from Thrace; Archilochus (fr. 2) too is fond of the wines of Thrace as well as of Naxos; Anacreon (fr. 434) refers to the garlands of Naucratis; and the sixth-century prophet Ezekiel (27.19) mentions iron, cassia, and calamus from Javan (probably Ionia). Quite how widespread throughout Archaic Greek society this desire for imported products was is not entirely clear. A couple of bottles of Thracian wine are unlikely to have commanded the same cost as bulky worked metal items. On the other hand, the fact that references to luxury goods constitute a recognizable *topos* within poetry that was almost certainly composed for the aristocratic context of the symposium may suggest that the desire for specific brands was particularly a preoccupation of the propertied classes.

In pictorial art down to the last quarter of the sixth century, there is no discernible distinction between warships and merchant ships. So, for example, on a plaque dedicated in the sanctuary of Poseidon at Penteskouphia near Corinth, dated 550–525, a cargo of pots is being loaded onto a vessel that is indistinguishable from a warship. These dual purpose galleys are typically pentekonters – vessels, approximately 22 meters long and 2 meters wide, powered by fifty oarsmen arranged in two banks. Herodotus (1.163.2) specifies that the ships on which the Phocaeans sailed on their voyages to the Adriatic, Etruria, and Spain were pentekonters. The expenses involved in building, maintaining, and crewing a pentekonter, together with indications that the earliest cargoes consisted of luxury goods and metal ores for producing increasingly expensive weapons and armor, make it virtually certain that long-distance trade was originally undertaken on the initiative of the elite. To judge from the *Odyssey*, aristocrats undertook these voyages themselves: in Book 1 (179–84), Athena appears to Telemachus in the guise of Mentes, the lord of the Taphians, who is transporting iron to Temese in Cyprus in exchange for copper. Alternatively, it has been suggested that aristocrats might have employed impoverished elites or dependants as agents to transport goods on their behalf – a practice that we meet later in the Classical period, when a distinction is drawn between a *nauklêros*, who owns a ship, and an *emporos*, who does not.

The mechanism by which aristocrats engaged in non-specialized commerce is often classified by economic anthropologists as "balanced reciprocity," where items are exchanged within the context of a personal relationship between people who know one another and who share the same social status. As such, it is contrasted to the commerce of professional traders who buy and sell specialized commodities for the express purpose of making a profit. While the former is a positively valued "long-term transactional order," perceived to perpetuate and reproduce the larger social and cosmic order, the latter is a "short-term transactional order," geared towards individual acquisition and subject to strong censure when individual involvement becomes an end in itself. The distinction is illustrated by another passage from the *Odyssey*. When Odysseus declines Euryalos' invitation to participate in a contest, the latter likens the Ithacan to "a captain of merchant-sailors, mindful of his cargo and overseeing his merchandise and greedy gains" (8.162–64), prompting an indignant response. It can hardly be accidental that these profit-conscious characteristics are especially associated with the Phoenicians, described elsewhere in the poem as "well versed in guile and greedy" (14.288–89), though it is not so evident that this is an ethnic slur rather than the condemnation of an economic activity in which the Phoenicians played a particularly prominent role. Either way, the very recognition of a profit-oriented commerce offers an important corrective to the otherwise eminently aristocratic picture of long-distance trade that the epics promote and should caution us against assuming that an etiquette of reciprocity can be invoked for every item exchanged in the early Archaic period. After all, Hesiod (*WD* 631–2) is aware that trade may bring a profit (*kerdos*), even if maximizing gains is not his primary concern.

It is, however, the second half of the sixth century that sees a significant increase in instances of what we might characterize as professional, profit-driven trade. One indication of this is the export to Etruria of ceramic wares manufactured by the Nikosthenic workshop in Athens. It is now generally recognized that the imperishability of fired clay and the high prices that ancient vases have recently attained at auction have served to invest Greek painted pottery with a value far higher than they commanded in antiquity. Pottery is unlikely to have constituted the most important or valuable part of any cargo and its characterization as saleable ballast may not be so wide of the mark. At the same time, however, the fact that 96 percent of all Nikosthenic products whose provenance is assured have been found in Etruria and that amphorae are more likely to be found at Cerveteri while *kyathoi* are more common at Vulci and Orvieto can hardly be explained by the chance exchange of finished products to procure agricultural staples at times of unpredicted shortfalls. This is a case of the targeted marketing of a product that combined Attic pictorial designs with the familiar shapes of Etruscan *bucchero* pottery. Towards the end of the century, sail-driven round merchant vessels make their first appearance on Athenian pottery and it is surely not coincidental that this is precisely the period in which the archaeological record reveals an increase in isolated rural sites, probably to be associated with an intensification of farming techniques designed to generate higher surpluses.

Not all cargoes were intended to be traded. From around 650 onwards, marble was increasingly used for sculpture and sculptors typically hired ships to transport themselves and marble blocks from the quarry to the place of commission. We hear of Cretans in the Peloponnese, an Aeginetan on Samos, an Ionian at Sparta and a Sicyonian at Miletus, and it has been estimated that in any one year, some 270 tons of sculptural marble were being conveyed around the Aegean. From around 550, marble was increasingly being used for monumental buildings. The east facade of the temple of Apollo at Delphi, the treasuries of Cnidus and Siphnos at Delphi, and the pedimental sculpture on the temple of Aphaea on Aegina were all built from marble quarried on the island of Paros. Coinage would have been particularly useful in paying for the transportation of these raw materials and was certainly a commodity that ports of trade such as Naucratis sought from the traders who put in there.

The Introduction of Coinage

The origins of Greek coinage are normally sought in a rather unprepossessing dump of ninety-three misshapen pieces of metal found under the foundations of the sixth-century temple of Artemis at Ephesus. Made of electrum – a naturally occurring alloy of gold and silver – the pieces vary in weight from one ninety-sixth of a stater (approximately 7 grams) up to half a stater, though all but two conform to the same weight standard, known as the Milesian standard. The crudest, and presumably earliest, are simply lumps of bullion dropped onto a surface and cooled; some are punched with an incuse square on one side while others exhibit an incuse square on one side and a pattern of striations on the other. The dump also includes the earliest coins, with incuse squares on the reverse and what are known as "types" on the obverse: those with the design of a lion's head have been associated with Lydia while those that depict a seal (*phôkê* in Greek) have plausibly been identified as being issued by Phocaea, probably representing the earliest known Greek coinage.

It is widely agreed that the Artemision coins predate the first issues of silver coinage on the Greek mainland, though controversy exists as to the dating of the dump. The deposit was clearly sealed by ca. 560 at the latest, when the temple of Artemis was constructed, but scholars differ as to whether the earliest pieces in the dump date to the early sixth century or instead stretch back a further century to ca. 700. Fortunately, the chronology of the earliest mainland series is not entirely dependent on the dating of the Artemision deposit. The "owl" coins of Athens, for example, can be arranged in a relative sequence on the basis of the size and thickness of the flans (the discs on which devices were stamped), the letter forms of the written legend that appears on the coin, the arrangement of the olive sprays on the reverse of the coin, and seriation analysis of coins found in hoards. The earliest coins that display the owl of Athena are not present in hoards that predate ca. 500, suggesting that these coins were first issued in the last quarter of the sixth century. The fact that five coins, belonging to the second series of owl coinage and found in a hoard at Taranto which cannot predate 506, were in mint condition offers welcome confirmation of this dating. On this basis, it is assumed that the very first issue of Athenian coins – the so-called *Wappenmünzen*, minted with fourteen different obverse designs – was first produced shortly after the middle of the sixth century, during the rule of the Pisistratids. Corinthian coinage probably appeared a little earlier, in the second quarter of the sixth century, while the first "turtles" of Aegina have been dated to ca. 580–570, making this the earliest coinage in mainland Greece.

Aristotle (*NE* 5.5.10) argues that coinage was introduced to serve as a medium or measure for the exchange of commodities. Elsewhere, in the *Politics* (1.3.13–14), he explicitly associates the invention of coinage with long-distance trade, adding that coins were stamped so as to obviate the necessity of weighing them. Scholars of numismatics, however, have been less convinced that coinage was invented to facilitate trade. One objection that has often been made is that the earliest coins were minted in denominations that were too large for local market trade and that they are too limited in their distribution to be connected with long-distance trade. As a result, alternative hypotheses have been offered. According to one view, coinage was invented for the standardization of payments to, and expenditures by, the state. The fact that the evidence from the Artemision appears to confirm Herodotus' belief (1.94.1) that the Lydians were the first to strike coinage might suggest that the motivation was to pay the foreign mercenaries that the Lydian kings employed. Another view sees coinage as originating in bonus payments made for political, military, or judicial service;

the practice of stamping types on electrum discs combined a Near Eastern – and earlier Minoan and Mycenaean – tradition of employing seals and personal badges as symbols of authority with the disbursement of gifts of precious metal.

With the discovery of more coin finds, the objections against the trade hypothesis are less compelling than they once were. Firstly, it is becoming increasingly clear that the coinages of some – though by no means all – *poleis* did include smaller denominations. The "Lydian" coins from the Artemision at Ephesus, the *Wappenmünzen* and the early coins of Aegina and Corinth were all minted in small denominations and a hoard of 900 coins, probably originating in Colophon and dated 525–500, comprised coins that were minted to either 0.21 grams or 0.42 grams. The coins in this hoard testify to at least 400 different obverse dies and, since a single die could strike anything up to 5,000 coins before being replaced, there must have been a substantial number of coins in circulation in Colophon. The smallest known Athenian coin to date, weighing a mere 0.044 grams, is worth one sixteenth of an obol – that is, one forty-eighth of the standard daily "minimum wage" in fifth-century Athens. On pots dating to the last quarter of the sixth century, prices in obols are scratched on the feet, suggesting that customers of moderate to middling means would use cash to purchase table wares, and the fact that the prices and terms are often abbreviated may indicate a general and widespread familiarity with handling small change. Secondly, it is now known that the early coinages of Corinth and Aegina in particular circulated over a wider area than was previously realized. It is important not to exaggerate this revision but it is also worth noting that, so long as it remains valid currency, there is a natural tendency for coinage to gravitate back towards its issuing authority, meaning that we cannot always infer circulation patterns directly from find spots.

In determining why coinage came to be used in the Archaic Greek world, it is important to separate the invention of coined silver from the invention of money, defined as a medium for establishing value and for making payments. In the Homeric epics, value is measured in terms of oxen. When, in the *Iliad*, Diomedes and Glaucus recognize the age-old ties of guest friendship that bind their respective families, they decide to exchange gifts, but Zeus, we are told, must have robbed Glaucus of his wits because he exchanged gold armor, worth one hundred oxen, for bronze armor, worth nine (6.235–36). Odysseus' nurse-maid, Eurycleia, had been purchased by Laertes for twenty oxen (*Od.* 1.431); by contrast, the slave woman offered as second prize at the funeral games of Patroclus was worth only four oxen (*Il.* 23.705). In early Cretan laws, penalties are assessed in terms of semi-precious metal vessels: thus, in a law dating to the late seventh or early sixth centuries (*IC* IV.1), fines of five or one hundred cauldrons are stipulated while a sixth-century law (*IC* IV 8) mentions blood money of one tripod.

In describing the bulky iron currency of Classical Sparta, Plutarch (*Lys.* 17.5) conjectures that iron and bronze spits had once functioned as an early form of coinage for the Greeks. It is, therefore, interesting that bronze and iron spits have been found in archaeological contexts dating to the Early Iron Age. The earliest examples may be three bronze spits found in a Geometric grave at Palaipaphos on Cyprus and iron spits found on Crete which date to the tenth century. Considerable numbers of spits were deposited in graves in Argos and dedications are also attested at the Argive Heraion, Perachora, Delphi, Olympia, Nemea, Halieis, Dodona, and the Samian Heraion. The Greek word for spit, *obelos*, was eventually to designate a unit of currency in many Greek *poleis*, and six *oboloi* made up a *drachma* – literally, "a handful." It may not be coincidental, then, that spits are often – though not invariably – found in sets of six, twelve, or eighteen, though corrosion and damage make it difficult to know whether they were all produced to a single weight standard. At Athens, in laws that are plausibly ascribed to Solon, fines are levied in drachmas. Plutarch (*Sol.* 24.1), for example, claims to cite a written Solonian law to the effect that the Archon is to pay one hundred drachmas into the public treasury if he does not pronounce curses on anybody who exports agricultural goods other than olive oil. Since the earliest coinage was not to appear in Athens for another half a century, it is probable that weighed, uncoined silver bullion served as a proto-currency. A similar conclusion holds for Eretria, where a couple of inscriptions (*IG* XII 9.1273, 1274) refer to penalties of ten staters; the inscription dates to ca. 525, some twenty-five years before the city issued its first coinage.

The evidence, scant as it is, suggests that money itself emerged within the context of the political community rather than to facilitate long-distance trade. Livestock, uncoined bullion, and metal vessels could convert perishable products into storable wealth which could be used to award prizes to athletic victors, to provide daughters with dowries, or to pay fines levied by the state. Coinage, however, is a different matter. The wide range of denominations in which even the earliest issues were struck is a good indicator that coinage subsumed some of the economic functions that had formerly been exercised by uncoined money. That said, it is difficult to dissociate its development from long-distance trade entirely.

What distinguishes coinage from weighed, uncoined bullion is the presence of a stamp. The likeliest explanation for why some authority or authorities decided to stamp the earliest issues of electrum coins is that this guaranteed the value of a metal whose variable gold content was as proverbial as it was impossible to test. As an indication that the issuer would redeem his own coins for the value that he originally declared, the electrum coins found beneath the temple of Artemis at Ephesus can properly be described as a fiduciary currency. At the same time, the variable difference between the real and declared values of these electrum coins inevitably imposed limitations on their circulation and it is not therefore surprising that the numerous types attested at Ephesus tend to remain distributed close to their point of origin. With the realization, however, that the same issuing guarantee could be extended to silver coins, whose purity and therefore value was far less variable, coinage began to circulate more widely from its place of origin and to be accepted more readily as a form of payment by geographically distant economic actors. If it is also true that issuing authorities could sell silver coins for 5 percent more than their face value, then there was an additional incentive for *poleis* to establish their own mints.

It can hardly be accidental that the earliest mainland Greek coin issues appear in the sixth century when long-distance trade was becoming more specialized and when traders from numerous Greek *poleis* began to congregate more frequently at the Egyptian *emporion* of Naucratis where silver was a desirable commodity. Nor can it be accidental that Aegina, whose need to import agricultural products and whose early activity at Naucratis have already been noted, seems to have been the first city of mainland Greece to issue its own coinage. Indeed, the Aeginetan standard was used widely throughout the Aegean, including Delphi, the cities of Boeotia, Sicyon, Argos, Mantinea, Tegea, Andros, Siphnos, Naxos, Tenos, Paros, Thera, Cnidus, Camirus, Lindus, and Sinope. Corinth, whose earliest coinage follows hard on the heels of that of Aegina, was also a state that owed much to commerce (e.g. Thucydides 1.13.5), while it is difficult not to associate the introduction of the *Wappenmünzen* at Athens with the increasing presence of Athenian black-figure wares and transport amphorae attested overseas (p. 232). It would be patently anachronistic to speak of a state-directed economy in the Archaic Greek world. On the other hand, if the decision of a *polis* to establish a mint was, at least in part, designed to facilitate long-distance trade, then it is difficult to subscribe to the complete segregation of politics and commerce that is presumed by the primitivist school.

FURTHER READING

Finley 1999 remains fundamental. For discussions of the controversies: Austin and Vidal-Naquet 1977, 3–35; P. Cartledge, "The economy (economies) of Ancient Greece," in Scheidel and von Reden 2002, 11–32; J. Andreau, "Twenty years after Moses I. Finley's *The Ancient Economy*," in Scheidel and von Reden 2002, 33–49. For some critiques of the Finley position: R. Osborne, "Pots, trade and the Archaic Greek economy," *Antiquity* 70 (1996), 31–44; Horden and Purcell 2000, 105–8, 143–52.

Definitions of peasant society: de Ste Croix 1981, 208–26. Estimates for pottery production in Classical Athens: R. M. Cook, "Die Bedeutung der bemalten Keramik," *Jahrbuch des deutschen archäologischen Instituts* 74 (1959), 114–23. Pylos Survey: Davis, J. L., S. E. Alcock, J. Bennet, Y. G. Lolos, and C. W. Shelmerdine, "The Pylos Regional Archaeological Project. Part I: Overview and the archaeological survey," *Hesperia* 66 (1997), 391–494. Greek smallholders as peasants: Wood 1988. As yeoman farmers: Hanson 1999, 25–176. For the average size of landholdings: L. Foxhall, "Access to resources in Classical Greece: The egalitarianism of the polis in practice," in Cartledge, Cohen, and Foxhall 2002, 209–20. Intensive vs. extensive farming: P. Halstead, "Traditional and ancient rural economy in Mediterranean Europe: plus ça change?" in Scheidel and von Reden 2002, 53–70. Farming strategies and archaeological survey in Attica: S. Forsdyke, "Land, labor and economy in Solonian Athens: Breaking the impasse between history and archaeology," in Blok and Lardinois 2006.

For a recent treatment of Naucratis: Möller 2000. The economics of desire: L. Foxhall, "Cargoes of the heart's desire: The character of trade in the archaic Mediterranean world," in Fisher and van Wees 1998, 295–309. Development of naval architecture: Casson 1994. For a discussion of "transactional orders": von Reden 1995. For the distinction between exchange and commerce: B. Bravo, "Remarques sur les assises socials, les formes d'organisation et la terminologie du commerce maritime grec à l'époque archaïque," *Dialogues d'Histoire Ancienne* 3 (1977), 1–59; P. Cartledge, "Trade and politics revisited: Archaic Greece," in Garnsey, Hopkins, and Whittaker 1983, 1–15. Marble trade: A. Snodgrass, "Heavy freight in Archaic Greece," in Garnsey, Hopkins, and Whittaker 1983, 16–26.

For the origins and early function of coinage: J. H. Kroll and N. M. Waggoner, "Dating the earliest coins of Athens, Corinth and Aegina," *American Journal of Archaeology* 88 (1984), 325–40; R. W. Wallace, "The origin of electrum coinage," *American Journal of Archaeology* 91 (1987), 385–97; S. von Reden, "Money, law and exchange: Coinage in the Greek polis," *Journal of Hellenic Studies* 117 (1997), 154–76; "Money in the ancient economy: A survey of recent research," *Klio* 84 (2002), 141–74; Kurke 1999; H. S. Kim, "Small change and the moneyed economy," in Cartledge, Cohen, and Foxhall 2002, 44–51; Schaps 2004.

11
Imagining Greece

Greeks and Others: The External Dimension

We have already had occasion to consider the influence structuralist theories have had on the study of the ancient world in recent decades. One of the key tenets of structuralism is that meaning is created through difference rather than similarity. When applied to processes of identity formation, the principle is that self-consciousness is constructed through differentiation from outgroups or "others." Nevertheless, while it is highly likely that Greek citizens of the Classical period grounded their sense of belonging to a male political collectivity in their cognizance that they were *not* foreigners, *not* slaves, and *not* women, the structuralist approach is less helpful when it comes to explaining how such identities arose in the first place. In Athens, at any rate, widespread chattel slavery seems to have been the response to, rather than the prerequisite for, the consolidation of the free citizen community and it is inherently unlikely that the exclusion of women from political deliberation was a constitutive moment in defining the citizen body (see pp. 195–6, 197–201). But what about ancient perceptions of Greek ethnicity? Thucydides (Document 11.1) seems to imply that the terms "Hellenes" and *barbaroi* ("barbarians") presupposed, and took their meaning from, one another, and many modern scholars, drawing on anthropological studies of ethnicity, have followed suit. In the first part of this chapter, we will consider what role – if any – non-Greek populations played in allowing the Greeks to think about their own identity.

There probably never was a time when Greek-speakers were not in contact with peoples whose language and way of life were different. In the Late Bronze Age, Mycenaean products were reaching Sardinia, Egypt, the Levant, and Cyprus and there are strong hints of a more permanent Greek presence in the Italian peninsula and on the coast of Asia Minor – particularly at Ephesus and Miletus. In the tenth and ninth centuries, intercommunication declined but

---

Document 11.1

But this is, in my view, the clearest indication for the weakness of earlier times: for prior to the Trojan War, Hellas appears to have accomplished nothing in common. In my opinion, the whole territory did not even have this name yet. In fact, before the time of Hellen, son of Deucalion, this designation did not actually exist at all; rather, each people – and especially the Pelasgians – provided their own names as designations. It was only when Hellen and his sons had grown strong in Phthiotis and were being invited to lend assistance to the other cities that the inhabitants of each of these cities began to be called Hellenes through their contact with them, but even then it took a long time for the new name to prevail everywhere. The best proof of this is Homer for, although he was born considerably later than the Trojan War, he nowhere uses the name "Hellenes" to designate the assembled forces but only to denote those who accompanied Achilles from Phthiotis and who were the original Hellenes; the others are named Danaans, Argives and Achaeans in his poems. For that matter, he has not spoken of *barbaroi* – because, I assume, the Hellenes had not yet distinguished themselves under a single name in opposition to them. (Thucydides 1.3.1–3)

---

did not dry up completely: it has been argued that Levantine craftsmen were resident at Athens, Cnossus on Crete, and perhaps Lefkandi, while North Syrian grave-goods in burials on Euboea and Crete and in Attica and the Dodecanese could suggest direct contacts and possibly even intermarriage. Greek- and Aramaic-speakers certainly lived side by side at Pithecusae and perhaps also at Al Mina. It is the last third of the eighth century, however, that sees an intensification of overseas contacts with the establishment of permanent settlements in Sicily and South Italy. For many students of antiquity, it was this confrontation with indigenous populations in the colonial orbit that first promoted a sense of Hellenic unity among settlers who had hitherto defined themselves in terms of their home cities and regions.

The establishment of these overseas settlements must frequently have involved violence. According to tradition, Megara Hyblaea was founded with the acquiescence of the local Sicel king (Thucydides 6.4.1–2), but this was probably the exception rather than the rule. The Corinthian settlers of Syracuse are said to have expelled the resident Sicel population (6.3.2), while the abandonment of indigenous sites at Francavilla Marittima and Torre Castelluccia probably reflects a forcible displacement that accompanied the establishment of Sybaris and Taras respectively. In the territory of Epizephyrian Locri, the archaeological evidence suggests an initial period of cohabitation followed, after a couple of decades, by a violent expulsion of the former inhabitants – an event to which Polybius (12.1.1–6) was later to refer – and Polyaenus (*Strat.* 5.5) claims a similar scenario at Leontini.

Yet the evidence also suggests that, within a couple of generations or so, relations between settlers and indigenous populations stabilized. In some cases, it is true, this was achieved through the imposition of servile dependency on the subjected population: such seems to be the situation at Syracuse and Heraclea Pontica. In many more instances, however, we can detect a certain integration taking place between the existing population and the new arrivals. One of the key mechanisms in this integration was intermarriage: although there is some dispute on the issue, it seems likely that the first male settlers were not typically accompanied by women. Wives and sisters may have arrived subsequently from the homeland but in many cases the settlers must have taken local partners. The attestation of indigenously made jewelry in female graves at Pithecusae, Naxos, Syracuse, Megara Hyblaea, and Gela is not entirely decisive in this regard because we cannot rule out the possibility that Greek-speaking women "went native" in their attire. More suggestive is the evidence of onomastics: names such as Larth Telikles or Rutile Hipukrates, inscribed on seventh-century vessels in Etruria, plausibly identify their bearers as the children of "mixed" marriages between Greeks and Etruscans. This is also the most likely explanation for the attestation, in eastern Sicily, of the names Eurumakes, Pratomakes, Tamura, and Skutas, which are essentially Greek names (Eurymakhes, Pratomakhes, Thamyras, Skythas) written in a Sicel language that lacked aspirate occlusives. One of the catalysts for the disastrous Athenian expedition to Sicily in 415 was a war between the Greek city of Selinus and the Elymian city of Egesta. According to Thucydides (6.6.2), the dispute concerned, in part, rights of intermarriage between the two cities, though we do not know how long these might have existed.

All this is not to suggest that Greek-speaking settlers were incapable of perceiving any differences between themselves and the populations they encountered in their new homes. There is, however, little to suggest that they regarded such differences as significant or that these perceptions were instrumental in constructing a specific Greek self-consciousness. There is no convincing evidence for the existence of "federal" sanctuaries or meeting-places at which Greek cities in South Italy or Sicily might express their collective identity. Contrary to popular belief, Thucydides (6.3.1) does not say that all Greeks sacrificed on the altar of Apollo Archegetes outside Sicilian Naxos and the belief that there was a sixth-century confederation of Greek cities in South Italy, centered on the sanctuary of Hera Lakinia outside Croton, is not actually supported by the evidence normally invoked for it (Polybius 2.39.1–6). When, in the fifth century, the Syracusans coined the term "Sikeliotai" (e.g. Thucydides 4.64.3), it was a geographical designation that technically distinguished not between Hellenes and non-Hellenes on Sicily but between Sicilians and the populations of mainland Greece; indeed, the term eventually came to include the indigenous populations of the island.

Undue emphasis on the colonial orbit, however, disguises the fact that there were multiple locations where Greeks encountered other populations: the Archaic Mediterranean was a world of people perpetually on the move rather than a mosaic of discrete "ethnonations." Phoenicians regularly plied Greek waters in the Archaic period and tradition held that the sanctuary of Aphrodite in the principal settlement of the island of Cythera had been founded by Phoenicians (Herodotus 1.105.3), which might possibly explain the apparent Phoenician influence on the clay masks found at the sanctuary of Artemis Orthia in Sparta. At the sanctuary of Hera Akraia at Perachora, near Corinth, a little over three-quarters of the early metal dedications are of Phoenician manufacture. Gift exchange can hardly account for all of these dedications, especially since the possibility of a more permanent Phoenician presence in Corinthia is indicated, firstly, by the Levantine rite of temple prostitution, attested for the sanctuary of Aphrodite at Corinth (Strabo 8.6.20) and, secondly, by the existence at Isthmia of a cult to Melicertes – a Hellenized form of the Phoenician god Melqart. Conversely, Greeks sought employment overseas as craftsmen, skilled professionals, and especially mercenaries. An often cited example is provided by the Greeks in the service of the early sixth-century Egyptian Pharaoh Psammetichus II, who inscribed their names on the colossal statue of Rameses II at Abu Simbel in Egypt (Document 11.2). Another is the case of Democedes, a doctor from Croton who found employment with the Aeginetans, the Athenians, Polycrates of Samos, and finally the Persian king Darius before escaping back to South Italy (Herodotus 3.125, 3.129–36). To what extent might these multiple encounters with others have given rise to a Hellenic consciousness?

Language has always featured prominently in treatments of this subject – primarily because the term *barbaroi*, used indiscriminately in Greek literature to denote non-Greeks, is assumed to be an onomatopoeic coinage deriving from the inarticulate babbling (*bar-bar*) of allophones. Indeed, the onomatopoeic

---

Document 11.2

When King Psammetichus came to Elephantine, those who sailed with Psammetichus, son of Theokles, wrote this: they came beyond Kerkis to the extent the river allowed. Potasimto commanded the foreign-speakers and Amasis the Egyptians. Arkhon, son of Amoibikhos and Pelekos, son of Eudamos, inscribed this.
Helesibios of Teos
Telephos of Ialysus inscribed this
Python, son of Amoibikhos
[----] and Krithis inscribed this
Pabis of Colophon together with Psammetes
Anaxanor and [.....] of Ialysus when King Psammetichus marched his army for the first [time?]. (ML 7 = Fornara 24)

etymology is actually asserted by Strabo (14.2.28), but he was hardly the most astute scholar of linguistics and the hypothesis of an onomatopoeic origin is no more testable than conjectures on the relatedness of Greek and Egyptian or Near Eastern terms based on what are often little more than superficial resemblances. At least one scholar has suggested that *barbaros* is a loan-word from the Sumerian language, where it simply means "strange" or "foreign." Be that as it may, it is important to point out that the word is attested only four times in the literature of the Archaic period and in only one of these cases – Anacreon's appeal to Zeus to "silence the Solecian speech lest you utter barbarisms" (fr. 423) – does it have an unambiguously linguistic meaning. Heraclitus (fr. 107) applies it to souls in a context that privileges inner judgment over external sensory perceptions; Hecataeus (fr. 119) uses it in a generic sense to indicate non-Greek populations; and Homer's application (*Il.* 2.867) to the Carians of the compound adjective *barbarophônoi* ("barbarous with regard to their speech") is decidedly tautological if *barbaros* had a primarily linguistic sense.

In fact, there are two reasons why it is unlikely that the linguistic criterion was ever paramount in issues of Hellenic self-identification in the Archaic period. Firstly, there never existed a Greek "language" in the sense of a single linguistic idiom spoken by all those who professed Hellenic descent. What we call the Greek language was, instead, a collection of myriad regional dialects which continued to exist even after the Macedonian court adopted one of them, Attic, as a *koinê* or lingua franca in the fourth century. A modern parallel would be the Italian "language," which is actually based on the Florentine dialect and has still not entirely replaced local dialects in everyday use. It is by no means certain that these dialects were as mutually intelligible as is sometimes supposed. All that survives for us today is how these dialects were written rather than how they were spoken and the finite possibilities of a graphic system can easily conceal a far greater oral diversity. If the Aetolians spoke what they wrote, they conversed in a West Greek dialect but it was one that Thucydides (3.94.5), at any rate, found incomprehensible; the same is probably true of the Macedonian dialect. It is sometimes argued that the adoption, by various regions, of versions of the alphabet presupposes an awareness of a common language, but that assumption rests on a dubiously close identification of language and script which fails to recognize that the latter is as much a "technology" as ceramic production; it is also to forget that, already in the eighth century, the Greek alphabet was being employed to transcribe the Phrygian, Lydian, and Etruscan languages. References to "the Greek tongue" (*hê Hellas glôssa*) do appear in the fifth century (e.g. Herodotus 2.154.2) but, upon closer inspection, it emerges that this concept is based not on empirical linguistic observations but on the belief that a community of Hellenes must have its own language.

Secondly, it is highly likely that a mixed-marriage environment would have had linguistic consequences. The most obvious is bilingualism: the Pharaoh Psammetichus is said to have entrusted Egyptian children to Greek mercenaries to learn the Greek language (Herodotus 2.154.2) and the Carians and the populations of the Chalcidice were apparently fluent in Greek (Thucydides 4.109.4;

Diodorus 11.60.4, 12.68.5). Similarly, Histiaeus, the tyrant of Miletus, and the fifth-century Athenian generals Themistocles and Alcibiades are said to have been proficient in Persian (Herodotus 6.29.2; Thucydides 1.138.1; Athenaeus 12.535e). Bilingualism itself need not lead to a blurring of linguistic boundaries although the preservation of both languages is less common in cases where one of them is perceived as conferring negative prestige. On the other hand, there are also indications for linguistic interpenetration which would have served to confuse Greek and non-Greek idioms. The so-called "Elymian" language of western Sicily may owe some of its constructions to Greek while graffiti from Gela, though written in Greek, display a grammatical feature that appears to be common to many of the non-Greek languages of Sicily. Furthermore, the facility with which the Greek alphabet was transmitted to the Phrygians, Etruscans, Lydians, Carians, Lycians, Sicels, and Elymians suggests a multi-lingual environment that was hardly conducive to the construction of clearly demarcated, linguistically based identities.

Nor do the Greeks seem to have conceived of a characteristically Hellenic shared culture prior to the fifth century – the period in which the verb *hellênizein* ("to act – and eventually speak – like a Greek") makes its first appearance (e.g. Thucydides 2.68.5). In fact, one of the features that defines what we call Greek culture in the Archaic period is its tendency to borrow techniques and styles from the east – a phenomenon commonly known as "orientalizing." From the end of the eighth century into the seventh, imported North Syrian bronze cauldrons with siren attachments were imitated by Greek craftsmen, who modified them by adding attachments in the form of griffins – a mythical beast of Near Eastern origin. Other fantastic creatures from the east such as the chimera and the Triton, alongside motifs such as lotus and palmette friezes, gave Protocorinthian pottery its distinctive appeal. The "daedalic" style of sculpture of the seventh century owes many of its characteristics to North Syrian models, while the *kouroi* of the sixth century are based in part on Egyptian prototypes. Gold- and ivory-working, cosmogonies and "wisdom literature," the practice of reclining on couches to dine, and even the domestic chicken all reached Greece from the east in the course of the Archaic period. The cultural flow continued further west, however. In the Italian peninsula, the ceramic wares of Calabria, Puglia, and eastern Sicily were quick to absorb Aegean techniques, styles, and motifs from the time of the first settlements. In the seventh century, Greek-influenced items of armament and banqueting accoutrements such as spits, fire-dogs, and ceramic drinking and dining services begin to appear in indigenous cemeteries in the interior of southern Italy.

These new styles and technologies were not, of course, absorbed passively: active choices concerning selection were made and in many cases forms were borrowed and endowed with a new symbolic content that fitted the worldview of the recipients. But, more importantly for the present discussion, there is little indication that their adoption carried any ethnic signification. In the vast majority of cases, the importation of eastern artifacts preceded their local imitation and it is quite clear that these imports were prestige items acquired by the elite, especially – though not necessarily exclusively – through gift exchange. This is probably the case at Olympia, where roughly one seventh of the metal objects dedicated in the eighth and early seventh centuries are of Near Eastern manufacture. The prestige value of such items resided not in their specific place of production but in the fact that they were finely finished items that were difficult to acquire closer to home. Sappho is illuminating on this point: a self-proclaimed devotee to *habrosynê* or "luxury" (fr. 58), she is barely able to conceal her weakness for Lydian leather straps and headbands and Phrygian garments (frs. 39, 92, 98). And although Xenophanes (fr. 3) was no fan of ostentatious display, he testifies to the penchant for purple robes and hair balm among the aristocrats of Colophon. In short, the employment of luxury items from overseas was designed to create social rather than ethnic distinctiveness and once such items came to be adopted, adapted, and more widely diffused within the recipient culture they became even further divorced from any ethnically or geographically specific connotations.

When Sappho mentions the Lydian capital Sardis in the same breath as Lesbos or the cities of Ionia (fr. 98), it is difficult to imagine that she regards the ethnic distinction between Greeks and Lydians as terribly meaningful and, in fact, there are few hints in Archaic literature of the negative stereotyping of other ethnic groups. We have already seen that criticism of Phoenicians may have more to do with their profession than their eastern origins (p. 248). The Trojans are an interesting case. By the fifth century, they were assimilated with Phrygians and characterized as wily, effeminate, and cowardly but this ethnic stereotype is far less evident in earlier literature. In the *Iliad*, for example, the Trojans bear Greek names, worship the same gods as the Greeks and possess the same civic organization as them. Sappho's description (fr. 44) of Hector's marriage to Andromache is predictably focused on the luxury of the wedding paraphernalia but there is no hint of any derogatory attitude against Trojans or easterners in general – they are, rather, to be envied. In short, it simply does not seem to be the case in the Archaic period that the Greeks conceived of themselves as a single, self-conscious ethnic group by virtue of their differentiation from non-Greek populations. It was a rather different story in the fifth century and, for many, the explanation for this shift in perceptions lies in the "coming of the Mede."

The Rise of Persia and the Invasions of Greece

The fascination and admiration that Greek elites entertained towards Lydia was not unreciprocated. From the eighth century onwards, the material culture of Lydia begins to betray distinctive Greek influences and excavations at the Lydian capital Sardis testify to the popularity there of Greek products. Greeks volunteered for mercenary service in the employ of the Lydian rulers; intermarriage was practiced between the Mermnad rulers of Lydia and the Basilids of Ephesus (Nicolaus of Damascus fr. 63; Aelian, *HM* 3.26); and Gyges (reigned ca. 680–ca. 652), Alyattes (ca. 610–ca. 560), and Croesus (ca. 560–ca. 546) are all said to have dedicated costly offerings at Delphi (Herodotus 1.14.1–3, 25.2, 50–51). But the Lydian state apparatus could only support itself by means of an elaborate redistributive system that required the exploitation of vast resources and manpower. By the middle of the sixth century, the Lydian Empire embraced much of what is now Turkey. The Greek cities on the coast of Asia Minor first experienced Lydian aggression during the reign of Gyges, when Colophon was captured. During the reign of Croesus, the remaining cities, though not the offshore islands of the eastern Aegean, were conquered and made tributary to the Lydian Empire. They would never again enjoy a protracted period of liberty, free from external domination.

In perhaps 546, Croesus' empire was itself attacked and defeated by the Persian king Cyrus II. The Persians, settled in Anshan in the modern Iranian province of Fars, were an originally pastoralist, Indo-European-speaking people closely related to the Medes who, along with the Babylonians, were the inheritors of the collapsed Assyrian Empire. According to Herodotus (1.130.2), the Persians had originally been subjects of the Medes, though Near Eastern texts offer no confirmation of this. A Babylonian chronicle does, however, agree with Herodotus (1.127) that in 550/49, the Median king Ishtumegu (Astyages) marched against Cyrus, king of Anshan, and was defeated following the revolt of his army. With the incorporation of Media into the Persian kingdom, it was only a matter of time before Persia and Lydia would come to blows. Following Croesus' defeat, around half of the inhabitants of Phocaea decided to abandon their city and sail to Corsica (Herodotus 1.164–5) but the remaining Greek cities of Asia Minor were incorporated within the Persian Empire which, by the end of the sixth century, stretched from what is now Bulgaria in the northwest, to Afghanistan in the east, and Egypt in the south.

Unlike the earlier Assyrian Empire, the Persian Empire generally respected the variety of customs, languages, religious beliefs, and political organizations that existed among its various subjects provided that they remained loyal and met the tribute quotas that were levied on them and that were formalized during the reign of Darius (Herodotus 3.89–117). The Jews regarded Cyrus as chosen by Yahweh to rebuild the second temple of Jerusalem (Isaiah 44.28–45.4), while in Egypt, Cyrus' son Cambyses adopted the Egyptian throne-name Mesutire (child of the god Re). A letter from Darius to Gadatas, satrap (governor) of Ionia, threatens to punish him for levying taxes from the "Sacred Gardeners of Apollo" (ML 12). Some intellectuals fled what they perceived as servitude to an eastern despot: Xenophanes and Pythagoras, for example, emigrated to the west. But Heraclitus remained in Ephesus and, in general, the Persians' reliance on local administrators was beneficial to the aristocracies of Ionia. Miletus in particular managed to negotiate a particularly favorable status with Cyrus (Herodotus 1.141.4).

In 499, the Greek cities rose up in rebellion against their Persian masters. According to Herodotus (5.28–38), the prime instigators were Aristagoras, the tyrant of Miletus, and his father-in-law, Histiaeus. The former was anxious to save face after failing to capture the Cyclades for Persia; the latter was keen to escape the semi-imprisonment that the Persian king Darius had imposed on him in Susa and to return to Miletus, the city that he had ruled before Aristagoras. Attempts to secure the aid of the Spartans failed (5.49–54), but Athens and Eretria answered the call to arms, dispatching twenty and five ships respectively (5.97). Initially, the Ionian Revolt looked as if it might be successful: a large number of Greek cities from the Hellespont in the north to Cyprus in the south rose up and Sardis was sacked. But north–south communications were hampered by the river valleys that punctuate the Anatolian coast and, once the Persians' Phoenician fleet was mobilized, Cyprus was easily recaptured. The final major battle took place near the island of Lade, off the coast of Miletus, in 494 where a combined fleet of 353 ships confronted 600 Phoenician vessels. The one hundred ships of Chios, stationed in the center of the Greek line, put up a valiant fight but, with the departure of forty-nine Samian vessels even before combat began, the Greek effort eventually collapsed (6.5–17). The revolt was over and Miletus, under siege for six years, was sacked and its inhabitants killed or enslaved (6.18). The shock of the event was felt particularly at Athens, which viewed itself as the metropolis of Miletus: the outpouring of grief that was provoked by the production, in 493/2, of a tragedy entitled *The Capture of Miletus* resulted in its playwright, Phrynichus, being fined 1,000 drachmas (6.21).

In Herodotus' narrative, the ships that Athens and Eretria sent to aid the Ionians "were the beginning of evils for both Greeks and barbarians" (5.97) since Darius resolved to punish the Greeks for their insolence. In reality, Darius may not have needed an excuse: his doomed campaign against Scythia in the 510s (4.1–142) reveals the imperialist ambitions he harbored in general; in the same decade, a Persian force had intervened in the internal politics of Samos (3.142–49) and Artaphernes, the Persian governor of Sardis, was perfectly happy to loan Aristagoras a fleet and troops for his expedition to subjugate the Cyclades. Furthermore, in 492, Darius' nephew and son-in-law, Mardonius, began establishing vassal states in Thrace, Macedonia, and Thasos. It is however true that, alongside Naxos, it was Eretria and Athens that were the main objectives of the Persian naval expedition that set out in 490 under the command of Datis and Artaphernes. After subjugating the city of Carystus on Euboea, the city of Eretria was betrayed to the Persians after a seven-day siege, its temples plundered and sacked and its inhabitants enslaved and shipped off to the eastern reaches of the Persian Empire (6.99–101, 6.119). The Persian fleet then sailed on to Marathon, accompanied by the former tyrant, Hippias, who no doubt entertained hopes of being reinstalled in the city as a Persian vassal (6.102).

Something in the region of 9,000 Athenian troops marched to the Marathon area and set up camp near the sanctuary of Heracles to the south of the coastal plain. The long-distance runner Phidippides was dispatched to seek the help of the Spartans, though they claimed that the festival of the Carnea prevented them from marching out before the full moon; 1,000 soldiers from the Boeotian city of Plataea did, however, come to the Athenians' aid. Ancient accounts, anxious to glorify the heroism and bravery of the Athenian hoplite, invariably exaggerate the numbers of Persians that they faced, though the Persian army is likely to have outnumbered the Athenians and Plataeans by at least two to one. The Athenians were brigaded in the ten new tribal regiments that Cleisthenes had instituted, with overall command rotating among the ten *stratêgoi* or regimental generals. Opinion was divided among the *stratêgoi* as to whether or not to wait for Spartan reinforcements, and each of the generals seems to have been reluctant to commit Athenian forces against a numerically superior enemy. Indeed, Datis, concluding that the Athenians were not going to risk a battle, re-embarked his cavalry on the transport ships.

Fearing, perhaps, that the Persian forces were heading for Phaleron, at that time the harbor of Athens, the general Miltiades gave the order for the Athenians to charge the one mile of no-man's land so that the Persians would have less time to deploy their archers. To avoid being outflanked, the Athenians decided to weaken their center and strengthen their wings. The result was that the Persians easily broke through the center, where the tribal regiments commanded by Aristides and Themistocles were stationed, while the wings wheeled around and attacked the Persians in the rear. Routed, the Persians fled back to their ships but became bogged down in the marshes around the Kynosoura peninsula where their fleet was stationed. One hundred and ninety-two Athenians, including the *polemarkhos* Callimachus, fell and were buried on the battlefield with heroic honors. The toll on the Persian side was much heavier – the figure that tradition handed down was 6,400 dead. Although the Persians re-embarked and attempted to sail round Cape Sunium in order to reach Athens before the Athenian troops had the chance to regroup, they were forestalled. After a few days at anchor off Phaleron, the fleet sailed back to Asia Minor.

The Athenians were to gloat over their victory for centuries to come: the *Marathônomakhai* ("Marathon fighters") were held up as heroic exemplars of courage and discipline. From the Persian perspective, the defeat at Marathon was hardly a major catastrophe but it does seem to have irked the Persian court since, shortly after coming to the throne in 486, Darius' son and successor, Xerxes, decided to launch a new campaign against his western neighbors. A much larger army was assembled, though undoubtedly far short of the figure of 1.7 million troops that Herodotus (7.60) records, and a massive fleet was mobilized to accompany the army on its long march round the coastline of the North Aegean (Map 11.1). The Hellespont and the River Strymon were bridged and a canal dug through the Athos promontory of the Chalcidice – partly to avoid the sort of losses that were incurred eight years earlier when some 300 Persian ships had been wrecked by storms off the peninsula (Herodotus 6.44) and partly to demonstrate to the Greeks the sort of resources that Xerxes could employ. Demands for submission, in the form of earth and water, were sent to the Greek cities and many of them complied. The Spartans hurriedly assembled their Peloponnesian allies and a few other cities – Athens included – that had decided not to submit to Xerxes. Those present decided to terminate

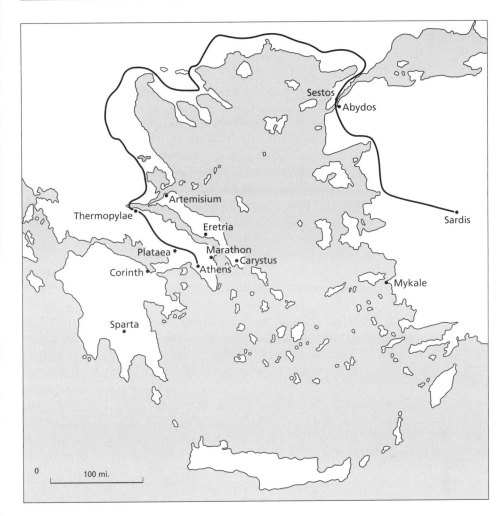

Map 11.1 Xerxes' route and the Persian War of 480–79

existing conflicts among themselves, especially the long-running conflict between Athens and Aegina; to seek the assistance of Argos, Syracuse, Corcyra, and Crete, all of whom ultimately refused to send help; and to place overall command of the defense effort in the hands of the Spartans.

At their next meeting in the spring of 480 at the Corinthian isthmus, the Greeks responded to a Thessalian request to send a force of 10,000 infantry to hold the Tempe pass between Macedonia and Thessaly but pulled back on the advice of the Macedonian king, Alexander I, who had come to terms with Persia and married his sister to a Persian nobleman. The Thessalians immediately offered submission to Xerxes and the Greeks concentrated their efforts further south, dispatching 7,000 infantry to the narrow Thermopylae pass and

271 triremes to a position just off Cape Artemisium in Euboea. The Persian superiority in numbers was to little avail in the narrow strip of land between the mountains and the sea, and numerous Persian casualties were incurred in the four days during which the Greeks held the pass. In the end, however, a Malian informed Xerxes of a back pass through the mountains. Realizing that his forces had been encircled, the Spartan king and general Leonidas, who was commanding the Greek coalition, dismissed all the troops save for the 300 Spartan hoplites he had brought with him, the Theban contingent, whose loyalty he suspected – rightly as it turned out – and the troops from Boeotian Thespiae, who refused to abandon the defense effort. So fundamental for Spartan propaganda was the image of the heroic Spartans fighting to the death that one can sometimes forget that Thermopylae was a total defeat. On the other hand, the Persian war machine had been temporarily delayed, incurring many casualties in the process, while an indecisive battle at sea off Artemisium, followed by a powerful storm, resulted in severe losses to the Persian fleet (Herodotus 8.6–16). It was, then, a somewhat reduced army that advanced south, capturing Boeotia and Attica and occupying and sacking the city of Athens itself.

The Persians found Athens virtually empty. Three years earlier, Themistocles had persuaded the assembly to use the proceeds from the discovery of a rich new silver vein in the Laurium mines to outfit a fleet of 200 triremes for the war against Aegina (Herodotus 7.144). Now, Themistocles persuaded his fellow citizens to transport their wives, families, and possessions to Salamis, Aegina, and Troezen, and to embark on the new ships. The Peloponnesian states wanted to pull back and defend the Corinthian isthmus, but Themistocles threatened to abandon the alliance and lead an Athenian colonization of Siris in South Italy unless the allies agreed to station their ships in the narrow straits between the Attic mainland and the island of Salamis. After luring the Persians into the straits, battle was joined on September 22, 480, and was vividly described by the playwright Aeschylus in his *Persians*, produced eight years later. The Greek ships were generally heavier than their Persian counterparts and they used their ramming techniques to devastating effect. The Persians are said to have lost some 200 ships, while their crews – many of whom could not swim – were drowned in the waters off Eleusis. The defeat was a major blow to the Persians' ambitions and Xerxes returned home with half of his army, leaving the rest to winter in central Greece under the command of Mardonius.

Athens was sacked again in the spring of 479 before the Persians pulled back to occupy a position near Plataea, where the broad plain offered them the possibility of finally employing their cavalry. The Greek army, led by Leonidas' nephew, Pausanias, advanced north and faced the Persian forces in the foothills of Mount Kithairon. The standoff between the two lasted for three weeks until the Greeks, in an attempt to outflank the Persians, found themselves cut off. The battle was hard fought and messy, though in the end the Greeks were victorious with only 159 casualties reported; the Spartans in particular managed to rout the Persian forces and kill Mardonius. The Persians fled in disarray

Document 11.3

These fought the war: the Lacedaemonians; the Athenians; the Corinthians;
the Tegeans; the Sicyonians; the Aeginetans; the Megarians; the Epidaurians; the
Orchomenians; the Phleiasians; the Troezenians; the Hermionians; the Tirynthians;
the Plataeans; the Thespians; the Mycenaeans; the Ceans; the Malians; the
Tenians; the Naxians; the Eretrians; the Chalcidians; the Styrians; the Eleans;
the Potidaeans; the Leucadians; the Anactorians; the Cythnians; the Siphnians;
the Ambraciots; the Lepreans. (ML 27 = Fornara 59)

back to the east. In commemoration of their victory, the Greeks set up impressive
dedications at Olympia, Isthmia, and Delphi, paid for by booty captured after
the battle. The Delphi dedication consisted of a gold tripod supported by the
heads of three entwined bronze snakes and carrying an inscription listing
the thirty-one allies who had united to repulse the Persians (Document 11.3).
The tripod was melted down by the Phocians during their occupation of Delphi
during the Third Sacred War of 356–346, while the serpentine column was
carried off by the Emperor Constantine to Constantinople (Istanbul), where
its base still stands in the hippodrome. Although Plataea marked the last battle
against Persia on Greek soil, an amphibious raid on the Persian fleet at Mykale,
opposite Samos – supposedly on the same day as the battle of Plataea –
marked a new phase of hostilities in Asia Minor that would escalate in the next
three decades and provide the justification for the hegemonic alliance that
would eventually become the Athenian Empire.

Despite a general abstention from involvement in the defense of the Greek
mainland, the western Greeks were themselves subject to hostilities launched by
the Phoenicians of Carthage: Diodorus (11.1) even suggests that it was Xerxes
who persuaded the Carthaginians to attempt to subdue the Greeks of South
Italy and Sicily. In 480, the Carthaginian general Hamilcar won a victory over
Greek forces near Himera in northern Sicily and proceeded to lay siege to the
city. Hamilcar's success was, nevertheless, short-lived and his troops were
decisively defeated by a Greek force led by Gelon, the tyrant of Syracuse who,
through a combination of brute force and alliances, had established something
of a hegemony over eastern Sicily (Diodorus 11.21–24). Surprisingly, however,
the Greek victory over the western "barbarians" was never exploited to the same
degree as its eastern counterpart.

The Invention of the Barbarian

It has been said, with some justification, that the Persian invasion offered the
Greeks the means for recognizing their identity. Within possibly only a year of

the victory at Plataea, the poet Simonides had written an elegy that specifically associated the Persian and the Trojan wars (*POxy.* 3965). The term *barbaros* is now attested with increasing frequency in Greek literature and, beginning with Aeschylus' *Persians* of 472, the figure of the barbarian in Athenian tragedy comes to be invested with all the characteristics – excess, effeminacy, cowardice, injustice, and cruelty – that were considered to be the polar opposites of cardinal Greek virtues. The comedies of Aristophanes lampoon the stupidity and savageness of barbarians such as Persians and Scythians, and the fifth century also saw a heightened, if not entirely new, fascination for depictions of Persians, Phrygians, and Thracians on Athenian red-figure vases. It is, however, important to ask whether the creation of a barbarian antitype was primarily a feature of Athenian thought and culture or a more widespread phenomenon among the Greeks. The matter is complicated considerably by the fact that nearly all of our literary and iconographic evidence comes from Athens. Simonides hailed from the island of Ceos but he worked for Athenian patrons. Herodotus – whose *History* is as much concerned with what it is that defines Greekness as with recounting the narrative of the Persian wars – was a native of Halicarnassus but spent considerable time in Athens, where he undoubtedly gave oral recitals of his research. The question cannot, then, be answered with absolute certainty but there are hints that the rampant hostility we find expressed towards the east was not as fervent in other cities of the Greek world.

Firstly, we need to remember that only thirty-one out of several hundred *poleis* were credited with the salvation of Greece on the victory monuments at Delphi, Olympia, and Isthmia. A city such as Thebes, which readily came to terms with Xerxes and fought with the Persians at Plataea, or Argos, whose professed neutrality might just as well have amounted to collusion, would have been hard placed to promote themselves as perennial enemies of barbarians. But even the Spartans, whose leadership had eventually repulsed the Persians, seem to have entertained ambiguous relations with the east. The Athenians, like many other Greeks, drew a distinction between *xenoi* (Greek-speakers from other cities and regions) and *barbaroi* (non-Greek-speakers) but, according to Herodotus (9.11.2), the Spartans called all outsiders *xenoi*, Hellenophone or not. Pausanias, the victor of Plataea, was criticized for "going native" in Byzantium – clothing himself in Median attire, surrounding himself with a bodyguard of Medians and Egyptians, dining on Persian cuisine, and making himself as inaccessible as oriental despots (Thucydides 1.130.1–2). The Spartans did take seriously evidence that Pausanias had been intriguing with the Persians and yet one gets the sense that their real fear was the charge that he had been fomenting unrest among the helot population (1.132). Certainly, the Spartans did not baulk at accepting Persian gold in order to gain the advantage over the Athenians in the final stage of the Peloponnesian War of 431–404. Secondly, it was very much in Athens' interest to promote an unbridgeable gap between Greeks and barbarians since the Delian League – which would eventually offer Athens both prosperity and hegemony over the Aegean – was founded in 478 with the explicit purpose of "avenging what they had suffered by ravaging the land of the Great King" (1.96.1). In other words, the continued "demonization" of the barbarian served as the rationale for the perpetuation of the League while legitimating Athens' continued demand for tribute from her erstwhile allies.

The history of how a barbarian stereotype functioned within Greek – and especially Athenian – self-identification leads us into the fifth and fourth centuries and so is beyond the chronological scope of this book. Considerations of ethnic self-ascription are not, however the whole story. There is also a sociopolitical dimension to the phenomenon that does relate directly to some of the developments we have been tracing in Late Archaic Athens. Although Cleisthenes is credited with having instituted ostracism (p. 218), the procedure was only used for the first time in 487, three years after the battle of Marathon. The first to be expelled was Hipparkhos, son of Kharmos – a relative, perhaps by marriage, of the Pisistratid family. In 486, it was the turn of Megakles, son of Hippokrates – an Alcmaeonid and nephew of Cleisthenes himself. The name of the Athenian ostracized in 485 is unknown, but Aristotle (*Ath. Pol.* 22.6) says that the first three victims of ostracism were "friends of the tyrants" and much modern scholarship has accepted this explanation. Interestingly enough, there does not seem to have been an immediate backlash against the Pisistratids after Hippias' expulsion in 510, which is another reason why recent attempts to interpret late sixth-century monuments as "democratic reactions" to the tyranny are unpersuasive (pp. 228–30). Hipparkhos, for example, was archon in 496/5 and an attempt in 493 to prosecute Miltiades – the victor of Marathon and a political ally of the Pisistratids – was unsuccessful (6.104). What changed public opinion was the reappearance of the exiled Hippias at Marathon. Miltiades was tried again and convicted in 489 (6.136), a decree was apparently passed in the 480s ordering the removal and melting-down of a statue of Hipparkhos, son of Kharmos, to be made into a *stêlê* on which the names of traitors would be inscribed (Lycurgus, *Against Leocrates* 117), and kinsmen and associates of the Pisistratids were ostracized. There was evidently a popular belief that the Alcmaeonidae had been implicated in the tyranny: they were accused of having communicated a signal to the Persians to sail to Athens before the troops at Marathon could make it back to the city (6.123–24) and Xanthippus, brother-in-law of Megakles and father of Pericles, was ostracized in 484. It is against this background of accusations that we must consider their professions that it had been they who contributed to the liberation of Athens in 510 (pp. 211–12).

Something more, however, than punishment for acts of treason with the enemy was in play. Among the more than 10,000 *ostraka* discovered on the acropolis and in the agora and Kerameikos cemetery, some 700 are inscribed with the name of Kallias, son of Kratios. Of these, sixteen explicitly accuse him of "Medizing" and one even depicts him in Persian costume. This could certainly be interpreted as a charge of collusion with the enemy but, if it is right that ostracism in some senses commemorated the *dêmos'* usurpation of the formerly aristocratic power of imposing exile (p. 218), the accusations of Medism resonate with a rather different tone. As we have seen, the consumption and display of eastern products was one way through which Archaic aristocrats communicated their social distinctiveness; another was by intermarrying and conducting guest friendships with wealthy, non-Greek families. In other words, the charge of "Medism" was part of a critique of aristocratic comportment leveled by a *dêmos* that had already intervened in aristocratic politics in 508 and was soon to gain even greater confidence from the role that it played in crewing the triremes that routed the Persian fleet at Salamis – a battle in which the contribution of the poorer citizens outweighed that of the wealthier hoplites. The proscription of "barbarian" customs and products was as much an attempt to "tame" the behavior of the elite as it was the outcome of ethnic chauvinism.

The Emergence of Panhellenism: The Internal Dimension

In any examination of the evolution of Greek self-consciousness, it is insufficient merely to consider how Greeks differentiated themselves from outsiders. Equally important are the similarities and commonalities that were thought to link different Greek groups to one another. The term normally employed to describe this phenomenon is "Panhellenism" and there has been near consensus in recent decades that it first becomes apparent in the eighth century with the emergence of interregional sanctuaries and the dissemination of the Homeric epics. There is, however, some reason to doubt so early a date for the self-conscious profession of Hellenic identity.

By the end of the Archaic period, a number of sanctuaries hosted athletic and musical festivals that attracted competitors from far afield, but the most prestigious games were those for which the prizes were of symbolic, rather than monetary, value. "Stephanitic" games, named after the wreath (*stephanos*) with which victors were crowned, were held every four years at the sanctuary of Zeus at Olympia and the sanctuary of Apollo at Delphi and every two years at the sanctuary of Poseidon at Isthmia and the sanctuary of Zeus at Nemea. At Delphi and Nemea, cultic activity does seem to commence in the eighth century but at Isthmia the earliest indications of ritual go back to the mid-eleventh century, while at Olympia there is an uninterrupted pottery sequence that stretches back even earlier. And while it is true that, at both sites, the eighth century witnesses a sharp increase in the number of dedications as well as a greater variety of provenance, this is a phenomenon attested at sanctuaries throughout Greece, including those that catered for a more local constituency.

In fact, three phases can be distinguished in the archaeological evidence from the great interregional sanctuaries. In the first phase, attested only at Olympia and Isthmia and commencing in the eleventh or tenth centuries, quantities of ceramic drinking vessels suggest the practice of ritual dining. Analysis of early offerings such as terracotta and bronze figurines and, from the ninth century, bronze tripods indicates that the participants in these activities did not travel from very far. The earliest activity at Olympia, for example, is indicative of a rural festival attended by chieftains from Messenia and Arcadia. In the second

Figure 11.1   Temple of Hera, Olympia (photo by author)

phase, beginning in the eighth century, the larger variety and volume of dedications at all four sanctuaries probably reflects the participation of a more diverse
personnel from further afield, though it is important to remember that the
provenance of an item may often say more about its manufacturer than about its
dedicant. Although there is no firm archaeological evidence for the construction
of temples in this phase, it is quite likely that simple cult structures first appeared
in the sanctuaries at this time. It is, however, with the third phase, commencing
in the later seventh and sixth centuries, that monumental investment in the
architectural embellishment of these interregional sanctuaries first becomes
apparent. To the seventh century belong the first stone temples of Apollo at
Delphi and Poseidon at Isthmia along with the earliest Delphic treasuries; to
the sixth belong the temples of Hera at Olympia (Figure 11.1) and of Zeus at
Nemea and the treasuries of Sybaris, Metapontum, Gela, Sicyon, Epidamnus,
Selinus, Cyrene, and Megara at Olympia. The fact that monumental religious
architecture appears in these sanctuaries a century or two later than in *polis*
sanctuaries calls for an explanation, and a reasonable conjecture would be that
investment in local, civic sanctuaries was considered a more important priority.

Nor can it be coincidental that it is in the early sixth century that many of
the great Panhellenic festivals were formalized – the Greeks talked in terms of
"refoundation" since the origins of all the most important competitions were
attributed to heroic figures of myth. The Pythian and Isthmian Games were
(re)instituted in 582 and the Nemean Games nine years later. Traditionally,
the Olympic Games were said to have begun in 776 but this figure derives

from the calculations of Hippias of Elis towards the end of the fifth century (p. 32) and, since there is nothing in the archaeological record at Olympia that suggests any reorganization of the sanctuary in the third quarter of the eighth century, it is often suspected that Hippias exaggerated the antiquity of the Olympic Games. Some believe that they too may be a creation of the early sixth century. For what it is worth, the earliest statue of an Olympic victor that was shown to Pausanias (6.18.7) dates to the fifty-ninth Olympiad of 544 – a date that falls well after the beginnings of monumental sculpture.

When set against the background of social and political developments sketched out in earlier chapters, the fit is very satisfying. The earliest frequenters of sanctuaries such as Olympia or Isthmia would have been "big men" or chieftains – more local in the case of Isthmia and perhaps from a little further afield in the case of Olympia, whose remote location may have marked it out as an ideal neutral meeting-place. The chieftains would establish relations among themselves through commensality but, increasingly, also through competitive display in the offerings they would dedicate. Competition in what the anthropologist Arjun Appadurai has termed "tournaments of value" not only guaranteed the donor's right to participate in rivalry with his peers but also enhanced his authority and status in his home community. By the seventh century, the great interregional sanctuaries became the regular arenas for communication and competition between aristocrats from various parts of Greece; although there has been some controversy on the subject of "amateurism" in the Olympic Games, it is patently clear that the earliest athletic victors in the Stephanitic games were those who possessed the resources and the leisure to train and travel.

It would, however, be mistaken to confuse the emergence of a transregional aristocracy with the crystallization of Hellenic self-consciousness. Firstly, the elites grounded their identity in the fact that they were *not* the same as the *dêmos* in their home communities: social and cultural considerations outranked ethnic or civic ones. Secondly, with the practice of guest friendship, gift exchange, and intermarriage, the borders between Greek and non-Greek aristocrats were, as we have seen, very porous. By the early fifth century, the Olympic Games were restricted to those who could prove Hellenic descent (Herodotus 5.22.1–2), but we do not know how old this restriction was and it is not clear that similar prohibitions existed at other sanctuaries; certainly, the Delphic Oracle was not restricted to solely Greeks. The important watershed in Hellenic self-definition came not when elites began competing at Olympia but when they began competing as representatives of their respective *poleis*. This was not without its dangers: a victor in a prestigious contest might arouse envy in his home community, as Xenophanes (Document 11.4) attests. A delicate balancing act was required between self-glorification within a competitive elite environment and the logic of reciprocity that governed relations between the *esthloi* and the *dêmos* in each city and this too fits best a context within the sixth century when the *dêmos* had begun to take cognizance of itself as a participant in governance – albeit not on an equal footing with the ruling aristocrats. The name of Cypselus was long associated with one of the earliest treasuries at Delphi

---

Document 11.4

But if someone should carry off victory by swiftness of foot or in the pentathlon, where the sanctuary of Zeus lies beside the streams of Pisa in Olympia, or of wrestling or engaging in painful boxing or that terrible contest that they call the *pankration*, he would have more renown in the eyes of his townsmen and he would obtain a conspicuous front seat at games and would have food from the public possessions of the *polis* and a gift that would be a treasure for him. Or if, again, he were to be victorious with horses, he would obtain all these things even though he is not as worthy as I. For my wisdom is better than the strength of men or horses. (Xenophanes fr. 2)

(Herodotus 1.14.2); in the sixth century, by contrast, such buildings – while undoubtedly still financed by the wealthiest – were dedicated in the name of the *polis*.

As for epic poetry, it is certainly true that the narrative – especially in the *Odyssey* – ranges widely over a vast geographical area and treats themes and issues of more than local significance. Furthermore, epic poetry is composed in a highly artificial literary dialect that is a blend of linguistic archaisms and the Aeolic and Ionic dialects and thus endemic to no one single locality. Nobody would dispute that epic poetry was designed to be disseminated well beyond its composer's region, whether that was in Asia Minor or Euboea. Yet, quite apart from the fact that fewer scholars are now prepared to date the dissemination of the *Iliad* and *Odyssey* before the seventh century, it is quite clear that the epics were designed for a primarily aristocratic evidence, meaning that the relevance of this type of evidence for the formation of a Hellenic ethnicity is open to the same criticisms as that of interregional sanctuaries – especially since, as we have seen, there is little evidence for ethnic differentiation between Greeks and others in the epics. In one particularly well-known episode, the Greek Diomedes and the Trojan Glaucus contemplate the ties of guest friendship that bind them (Homer, *Il.* 6.123–236). Homer's audience would more likely have identified with a Glaucus, a Sarpedon, or a Hector than with a Thersites (see p. 182).

There have seldom, if ever, existed self-conscious ethnic groups whose identity was not expressed by means of a specific name. It is a well known fact that the terms "Hellas" and "Hellenes" appear relatively late in our literary sources and initially seem to have a restricted geographical scope: Thucydides' observation of this phenomenon (Document 11.1) provides some reassurance that this is not simply an accident of the survival of evidence. In the *Iliad*, Hellas is the name given to the area around the mouth of the River Sperkheios, to the south of Thessaly. By the time of the *Odyssey*, the term seems to be used to indicate central Greece more broadly, while it is not until the end of the seventh

---

Document 11.5

The sons of the war-loving king Hellen were Doros, Xuthus and Aeolus who fights
from the chariot. . . . And by the will of the gods, Xuthus took as his wife Kreousa
of beautiful form, the fair-cheeked daughter of godlike Erechtheus, and she lay
with him in love and bore him Achaeus, Ion of the noble steeds and the beautiful
Diomede. (Hesiod frs. 9, 10(a) 20–4)

---

century, when Alcman (fr. 77) describes Paris as "an evil for man-rearing
Hellas," that its usage seems to have expanded further. Interestingly, however,
the term "Hellenes" is not attested in its inclusive sense until the first quarter
of the sixth century on an inscription that Pausanias (10.7.5–6) purportedly
saw on a tripod dedicated in 586 to commemorate the victory of an Arcadian
named Ekhembrotos at Delphi. Prior to this, the term that we find in
Archaic literature is "Panhellenes" (e.g. Homer, *Il.* 2.530; Hesiod, *WD* 526–8;
Archilochus fr. 102) – a denomination whose prefix actually emphasizes diversity rather than unity. That the chronological concurrence between the first
attestation of the term "Hellenes" and significant investment in the interregional
sanctuaries is not accidental is suggested by two other pieces of evidence.
Firstly, this is, as we have seen (pp. 242–4), precisely the period in which the
Greeks who were active at Naucratis dedicated a sanctuary to the "gods of
the Hellenes." Secondly, it has recently been argued that this was also the
period in which a genealogical poem known as the *Catalogue of Women*, erroneously attributed in antiquity to Hesiod, was composed. One of the fragments
(Document 11.5) traces the descent of the eponymous Doros, Aeolus, Achaeus,
and Ion from King Hellen, thus chartering in genealogical form the affiliation
of the principal ethnic collectivities of Greece to a single Hellenic family.

There is some reason to believe that an important role in the forging of
Hellenic self-consciousness was played by the Thessalians, dominant within
the amphictyony that governed Delphi before the end of the seventh century
and increasingly attested as victors at Olympia from the early sixth century.
The populations that inhabited Thessaly considered themselves Aeolian and,
in the Hesiodic fragment, the eponymous Aeolus is the only one of Hellen's
sons to whom an epithet is attached. Indeed, unlike the comparatively faceless
figures of Doros, Achaeus, and even Ion, myth credited Aeolus with siring
some of the most important lineages in Greece, including the heroes Nestor,
Melampus, and Sisyphus. Furthermore, Hellen's family is described in some
traditions as having once ruled over Thessaly (e.g. Strabo 8.7.1; 9.5.6). Quite
what motivated the behavior of the Thessalians is impossible to know with any
certitude, but one possibility is that the construction of a Hellenic ancestry, in
which the most important *poleis* of the Greek world shared, was intended to

exclude those populations on the fringes of Thessaly such as the Perrhaebi, the Dolopes, and the Magnesians. These populations were perioikic dependants of the Thessalians and some of them seem also to have been reduced to the status of Penestai – the serf-like population of Thessaly (Theopompus fr. 122). Certainly, in the *Catalogue of Women* (fr. 7), the eponymous Magnes is represented as the son of Zeus and Thuia, the sister of Hellen's father, Deucalion. While related to Hellen, who is his maternal uncle, Magnes cannot adduce strict lineal descent from him and this effectively denies Hellenic credentials to the Magnesians in general.

There can be no doubt that the progressive development in the fifth century of a barbarian stereotype allowed the Greeks – and especially the Athenians – to conceptualize more easily their own identity by means of differential comparison. In an age where more abstract ideas about language and culture were evolving, linguistic and behavioral factors also assisted in the process of differentiation. But Hellenic identity was no more a product of the fifth century than it was of the first encounters between Greek settlers and indigenous westerners in the eighth. Its origins lie rather in the sixth century as Greek elites sought to balance their affiliation to an international aristocracy with their obligations to their own communities.

FURTHER READING

Early Greek contacts abroad: Boardman 1999; Hall 2002, 90–124. The "ethnogenesis" of the Sikeliotai: C. M. Antonaccio, "Ethnicity and colonization," in Malkin 2001, 113–57. Non-Greek dedications in Greek sanctuaries: I. Kilian-Dirlmeier, "Fremde Weihungen in griechischen Heiligtümern vom 8. bis zum Beginn des 7. Jahrhunderts v. Chr.," *Jahrbuch des Römisch-Germanischen Zentralmuseums* 32 (1985), 215–54. *Barbaros* as Sumerian loan-word: E. Weidner, "Barbaros," *Glotta* 4 (1913), 303–4. Shifting representations of the Trojans: Erskine 2001.

For the Near East: Kuhrt 1995, 567–72, 647–701; Van de Mieroop 2004, 267–80. Persian Wars: Lazenby 1993. For a recent detailed treatment of Salamis: Strauss 2004.

The invention of the barbarian in tragedy: Hall 1989. Barbarians in comedy: Long 1986. In art: Cohen 2000. The role of Athens in stereotyping: Hall 2002, 172–205.

Panhellenic sanctuaries: Morgan 1990. For the delicate relationship between elites and their *poleis*: Kurke 1991. For the evolution of the terms "Hellas" and "Hellenes": Hall 2002, 125–71.

12

Writing the History of Archaic Greece

The First Sacred War: Fact or Fiction?

This book opened with a discussion of the Lelantine War. In this concluding chapter, I wish to turn to another famous conflict whose historicity is no less controversial. As with the Lelantine War, the problems associated with the source tradition for the First Sacred War are typical of the methodological pitfalls that characterize the study of early Greek history generally and may therefore serve as an entry-point into a final discussion of what it is that allows us to treat the Archaic Greek world as a coherent geographical unit and the period ca. 1200–479 as a single chronological entity.

According to tradition, the First Sacred War was the forerunner of successive Sacred Wars whose historicity is not in doubt. In all cases, what made the conflicts "sacred" was the fact that they were fought for control over Apollo's oracular sanctuary at Delphi (Figure 12.1). The second war broke out in 448/7, when an Athenian force wrested the sanctuary away from the Spartan-backed Delphians and gave it to the Phocians, under whose control it remained until the Peace of Nicias in 421 (Thucydides 1.112.5, 5.18.2). The third war was prompted by the accusation that the Phocians had been illegally cultivating the sacred land of Cirrha/Crisa – the names are employed interchangeably in our sources although, more properly, Cirrha was the port for Crisa. In response, the Phocians captured the sanctuary in 356, provoking the Boeotians, Thessalians, and Locrians to make war on them on behalf of the Delphic Amphictyony – the league of states that administered the sanctuary – although some amphictyonic members such as Athens and Sparta supported the Phocians. The war lasted ten years and was ended by the intervention of Philip II of Macedon and the defeat of the Phocians (Diodorus 16.23–40, 16.53–60). The fourth war occurred in 339/8; this time, those accused of cultivating the sacred land of Cirrha were the Locrians of Amphissa. Once again, an amphictyonic

Figure 12.1   Delphi (photo by author)

army under the command of Philip was victorious (Aeschines, *Against Ctesiphon* 113–58; Demosthenes, *On the Crown* 143–58).

The First Sacred War, instead, is said to have been provoked by the lawlessness of the Cirrhaeans and the Kragalidai – local populations who were harassing pilgrims to Apollo's oracular shrine. The Pylaean Amphictyony, which met at the sanctuary of Demeter at Anthela, near Thermopylae, decided to intervene to wrest Delphi from local control by sending an army in which the largest contingents were represented by the Thessalians under Eurylokhos, the Athenians under either Solon or Alcmaeon, and the Sicyonians under Cleisthenes. According to Aristotle and his nephew, Callisthenes (fr. 1), the conflict lasted ten years between 594 and 585. Various stratagems employed during the war were later to become notorious: Solon, for example, is said initially to have diverted the course of the River Pleistos to cut off a supply of drinking water to the Cirrhaeans but then, when the latter proved more than able to withstand this minor inconvenience, restored the stream's course and contaminated the water with the poisonous roots of the hellebore plant (Pausanias 10.37.7). The amphictyonic force eventually prevailed, destroying Cirrha, enslaving its inhabitants, and dedicating its land to Pythian Apollo, Artemis, Leto, and Athena Pronaia (Aeschines, *Against Ctesiphon* 112). The amphictyony, now in firm possession of the sanctuary, is said to have reorganized and, in 582, re-inaugurated the Pythian Games.

The problem is that virtually none of the literary evidence for the First Sacred War predates the fourth century, with much of it clustering in the 340s and 330s – precisely the period in which the Third and Fourth Sacred Wars were being fought. Some of our fullest information for the causes of the war and the constituent members of the amphictyony is provided by the Athenian orator Aeschines in his *On the Embassy* of 343 and his *Against Ctesiphon* of 330. Callisthenes' and Aristotle's *Table of Victors at the Pythian Games* was also compiled around 330 and, although no fragment of this work survives, it was probably an important source for the scholiasts who commented on Pindar's *Pythian Odes*. The First Sacred War was evidently treated by Antipatros of Magnesia (fr. 2), thought to be writing a history of Greece in Athens shortly after the middle of the fourth century. A little earlier, Isocrates (*Plataicus* 31) describes the Crisaean plain as a "sheep run" (*mêloboton*), though makes no explicit reference to any war or as to how the plain had fallen into this condition.

Prior to the fourth century, there are only two possible references to the First Sacred War. The first appears in the closing verses of the *Homeric Hymn to Apollo* – a poem that was probably composed in the first decades of the sixth century. Having installed Cretan pirates as priests in his oracular shrine, Apollo warns them that if they commit evil deeds or are disobedient, then "other men will be your masters, by whom you will be forcibly dominated for all your days" (542–3). The implication seems to be that control of the sanctuary will shift to the hands of others should the priests engage in lawlessness, but it is also fairly evident that these lines must have been added at a later date since the rest of the hymn provides no charter for amphictyonic control. Unfortunately, there is simply no way of telling just how soon after the initial composition of the hymn these lines were interpolated. The *Shield of Heracles*, erroneously attributed in antiquity to Hesiod and possibly dating to ca. 570, closes with a reference to the lawlessness of Cycnus, son of the god Ares, who used to plunder violently the rich hecatombs that were brought to Delphi (478–80). It is just possible that Heracles' slaughter of Cycnus stands as an allegory for the defeat of local brigands by the amphictyony on the grounds that Heracles met his death and apotheosis on Mount Oeta in the territory of Malis, one of the original members of the amphictyony, but that is far from certain. Far more troubling is Herodotus' silence about a First Sacred War. Given that he is one of our earliest sources of information for Solon, Alcmaeon, and Cleisthenes of Sicyon, it is rather surprising that he should have neglected to mention their participation in the war if it was known to him.

Our sources for the First Sacred War score poorly, then, on the test of temporal proximity. That in itself need not be decisive but, as with the traditions concerning overseas foundations (chapter 5), there are decided divergences between the testimonia concerning details and this is probably sufficient to rule out the possibility that they are following an earlier, authoritative – but now lost – source. For example, Plutarch (*Sol.* 11) maintains that an author named Euanthes of Samos was wrong to claim that Solon had been appointed general of the Athenian forces since Aeschines made no such statement and, according to the records kept at Delphi (where Plutarch at one point served as a priest), it was Alcmaeon, not Solon, who led the contingent of Athenians. Similarly, although Pausanias (10.37.7) credits Solon with poisoning the River Pleistos with hellebore root, this is a tactic that Frontinus (*Stratagems* 3.7.6) attributes to Cleisthenes.

The test of intentionality – especially regarding one of our fullest sources, Aeschines' *Against Ctesiphon* – is also revealing. The speech is an indictment of a man named Ctesiphon, for having proposed to award an honorific crown to Aeschines' chief political rival, Demosthenes. Part of Aeschines' task is to demonstrate that Demosthenes is singularly unworthy of such an honor and one of the charges he decides to lay against Demosthenes, in addition to having recklessly endangered the security of Athens, is that of impiety. Demosthenes, alleges Aeschines, had opposed the amphictyony's plans to punish the Locrians of Amphissa during the Fourth Sacred War because he had been bribed by the latter. And yet, the Locrians had been at fault in cultivating the sacred land of Cirrha and Demosthenes had violated the sacred oaths that had been taken by his Athenian ancestors, along with the other amphictyons, after the first attempt to liberate Delphi from local depredation. On that occasion, Aeschines tells us, the members of the amphictyony swore not to till the sacred land of Apollo nor allow another to till it but to go to the aid of the god and the sacred land with hand and foot and voice, and with all their might. Anybody who violated this oath, whether *polis* or individual or *ethnos*, was to be under the curse of Apollo, Artemis, Leto, and Athena Pronaia. Aeschines does not, then, mention the First Sacred War out of pure antiquarian interest. It is important for establishing a sacred law that Demosthenes is alleged to have violated and the closer the circumstances of the First War appear to match the transgressions of which Demosthenes is accused, the more patent his guilt – or so Aeschines hopes.

As for contextual fit, there is little to assist us in evaluating whether an early sixth-century context suits the circumstances of the First Sacred War. The (re)inauguration of the Pythian Games is likely to be approximately correct since it is close in time to the supposed reorganization of the Isthmian and Nemean Games. It is, then, possible that it was a change of administration that prompted or facilitated the new programme of contests. On the other hand, it is doubtful whether all the characters recorded by tradition could have participated in the war. There is, as we have seen, a discrepancy between our sources as to whether Solon or Alcmaeon commanded the Athenian forces, but this is also a chronological issue in addition to one of simple identification. Although Herodotus makes both contemporaries of the Lydian king Croesus, most scholars are agreed that the meeting the historian describes (1.29–33) between Croesus and Solon cannot be historical since Solon belongs to the beginning, not the middle, of the sixth century. Alcmaeon is more likely to have been coetaneous with Croesus, which would certainly help to explain why a youth named Croesus was buried in what appears to have been an Alcmaeonid cemetery in southern Attica (p. 170). Cleisthenes of Sicyon was probably similar in age to Alcmaeon, given that it was Alcmaeon's son, Megacles, who married Cleisthenes' daughter, Agariste (Herodotus 6.130.2), but neither can be very comfortably accommodated in the first decade of the sixth century where Aristotle and Callisthenes would place the war.

In fact, the precise dates that Aristotle and Callisthenes assign to the First Sacred War probably derive from the tradition that Solon enacted his legislation while archon in 594 and immediately afterwards left Athens for a period of ten years (Aristotle, *AC* 11.1; Plutarch, *Sol.* 11.1). Yet our sources are also virtually unanimous that Solon spent the first part of his self-imposed exile in Egypt, which would rule out his participation in the conflict. Ten years is, of course, a formulaic figure for wars – one thinks primarily of the Trojan War – but it is probably not mere coincidence that this was precisely the duration of the Third Sacred War, especially since there are two other striking parallels between that conflict and the presumed first struggle for control of Delphi. Firstly, as with the Third Sacred War, some of the accounts of the first war describe two stages of hostilities – the second taking place on Mount Kirphis. Secondly, the name of the Thessalian general, Eurylokhos, is the same as that of one of the generals in Philip II's army.

For all that, however, agnosticism is probably more warranted than outright denial. Aeschines may well have embellished details so that the "facts" of a primeval conflict fitted more closely the circumstances of the Fourth Sacred War but to have invented an original Sacred War from nothing merely for the purposes of discrediting Demosthenes offered no guarantees of success and might even have carried considerable personal risks. And while there is reason to believe that the tradition concerning the war gradually attracted a cast of famous sixth-century notables – much as with the story concerning the courting of Agariste (p. 150) – there must have been some earlier tradition that could have served as a magnet in the process. The function of an earlier, less spectacular tradition cannot have been to cause eventual trouble for Demosthenes and was probably an attempt to explain two undeniable historical facts: firstly, the prohibition against cultivating the sacred land around Delphi, which was clearly already in effect at the time of Isocrates' *Plataicus*; and secondly, the administration of Delphi by an amphictyony of various Greek states rather than local overseers – a state of affairs that seems to have existed for some time before the outbreak of the Persian War in 480, when all members of the amphictyony, save for the Phocians, the Ionians, and the Dorians, offered symbols of submission to Xerxes (Herodotus 7.132.1).

There is no particular reason to doubt the well attested tradition that the amphictyony was originally based at Anthela (Theopompus fr. 63; Parian

Marble A5; Dionysius of Halicarnassus, *RA* 4.25.3; Strabo 9.3.7; Scholiast to Euripides, *Orestes* 1094). Among the earliest members are likely to have been the Dorians, the East Locrians, the Ainianes, and the Malians, all of whom resided in the vicinity of the sanctuary. Quite how long the amphictyony had existed is impossible to determine, but even as late as the fourth century certain amphictyonic members such as the Magnesians, the Perrhaebi, and the Phthiotid Achaeans possessed the same voting power as the Thessalians who had long since reduced them to subordinates (e.g. Thucydides 4.78.6, 8.3.1; Xenophon, *Hell.* 6.1.12) and this ought to suggest that these members at least had been enrolled in the amphictyony prior to the Thessalians' hegemony over their neighbors – something that had certainly occurred by the early sixth century and may even predate the end of the seventh. Although there can be no certitude, it is extremely plausible that amphictyonic control of Delphi was connected with the Thessalians' desire to control the "Great Isthmus Corridor." This was a chain of passes and upland plains connecting the Malian and Corinthian gulfs which was dominated, to the north, by the Sperkheios Valley and Demeter's sanctuary at Anthela and, to the south, by the Crisaean plain and Apollo's sanctuary at Delphi. Just when the amphictyony assumed control over Delphi is hard to know. Some appeal to the archaeological record and argue that the appearance, ca. 725, of Cretan tripods and shields provides welcome support for the charter myth that is recounted in the *Homeric Hymn to Apollo* while the tailing off of such Cretan imports in the sixth century should reflect the transition of control to the amphictyony. On the other hand, were we only to have the material evidence without any presuppositions imported from the literary tradition concerning the First Sacred War, it would be the last quarter of the eighth century, not the sixth century, that marks the real caesura dividing a purely local sanctuary from one with a greater "international" catchment.

In short, amphictyonic control of Delphi almost certainly involved hostilities against a resistant local population which could well have lasted a number of years. But if that reasonable supposition is taken to demonstrate a kernel of truth behind the tradition on the First Sacred War, it is a kernel so minute as to be practically insignificant. The cast of characters associated with the war is inherently unlikely: although inscriptions record that Sicyon served as a representative for the Dorians on the amphictyony in the fourth century, our literary sources do not count the city among the original signatories. The oaths that the amphictyons are supposed to have sworn not to attack one another, as well as the curses they invoked against anybody cultivating the Crisaean plain, are likewise probably later elaborations. Indeed, the latter could possibly have originated from the fact that the burgeoning sanctuary needed its own arable land for the crops that would support its infrastructure and pastures for the animals that it required to be sacrificed to Apollo. We must always remember that the transmission of tradition in the Archaic Greek world served an active purpose of explaining or justifying the present, not of preserving faithfully the irrelevant circumstances of the past.

The Limits of Narrative History

The reconstruction of the Archaic Greek world that has been offered in previous chapters might well strike the reader as fairly eventless. I have had occasion to cast doubt on the value of the traditions for both the Lelantine War and the First Sacred War. I have omitted mention of the Thessalian defeat at Keressos, near Boeotian Thespiae – an "event" that Plutarch dates at one point to before 571 (*Cam.* 19.4) and at another to "shortly before" the Persian War of 480– 479 (*Mor.* 866f). There has been no account of the Phocians' acts of resistance against Thessalian encroachments – be it the successful attempt to throw the Thessalian infantry into panic by painting themselves white with gypsum and launching a night attack, the laming of the Thessalian cavalry by luring it towards trenches filled with broken amphorae, or the solemn oath to immolate their women, children, and property on a giant pyre should they be defeated in battle (Herodotus 8.27–28; Plutarch, *Mor.* 244b–d). The joint Cnidian–Rhodian expedition, under the command of Pentathlos, to colonize Lilybaeum in western Sicily has been passed over in silence (Diodorus 5.9). Nor have I attempted to reconstruct the tempestuous internal politics of Mytilene that are supposed to have ousted the Penthilid aristocracy and thrown up various autocrats such as Melankhros, Myrsilos, and Pittacus (Aristotle, *Pol.* 5.8.13; Strabo 13.2.3; Diogenes Laertius 1.4, 74), or the bitter civil war at Miletus between the *Aeinautai* (eternal sailors) and *Kheiromakhia* (manual workers?), in which Paros is said to have adjudicated in favor of the former (Herodotus 5.28; Plutarch, *Mor.* 298c–d).

I do not mean to suggest that none of these events can possibly have occurred. Rather, the evidence for them is anything but secure. In some cases we are reliant on the testimony of authors who are writing much later (Keressos; Lilybaeum; Miletus). In others, we are patently at the mercy of propagandistic exaggeration and romanticized embellishment (Phocis). The case of Mytilene, instead, involves the rather haphazard assemblage of fragments that probably are approximately contemporary to the events they seem to describe but that are clearly partisan in intention and run the risk of being severely compromised if we choose not to read Alcaeus' poetry autobiographically (p. 6). All are the products of evolving traditions whose primary purpose was not to preserve a faithful or disinterested record of the past, and attempts to strip away the accreted elements to expose some historical account of "what actually happened" are unrewarding, if not futile.

All is not lost, however. If the evidence at our disposable is not generally amenable to reconstructing an events-based narrative, it is at least possible to construct a more processual account focusing on spheres such as society, economics, and culture. Two developments within the study of this period of history have facilitated such an endeavor. The first is the increased willingness to incorporate the evidence of material culture. Settlement patterns, burial practices, votive behavior, and artifact style do not often have much to communicate about specific events – especially when detailed literary reflections on significant events are absent. They do, however, have plenty of information to offer us concerning more gradual and long-term processes such as shifting residence patterns, land use, social differentiation, and ethnic and social self-definition. The second is the marked readiness to look to disciplines in the social sciences – particularly anthropology – for possible models that might be compatible with the scant data we possess. This is not to say that we should force our data to comply with a model derived from an entirely different chronological or geographical context. The point is, rather, that the scarcity and uneven distribution of the evidence, together with the variability that exists between different types of evidence, can be configured in a number of ways, and comparative models are often useful in suggesting possible broader pictures that would not have been entirely self-evident were we to focus all of our attention on the few pieces of the jigsaw that survive. Admittedly, both of these developments were in large part responses to the particular exigencies that exist for this early period of Greek history but their application has been so successful that similar approaches are now beginning to be adopted in the study of the Classical and Hellenistic periods.

The story, then, that we can write for the Archaic period of Greek history will look rather different from that which can be told for, say, fifth-century Athens or first-century Rome but, for all its broad-brushed strokes and abstract realization, it is nevertheless a story. It is a story that, without seeking to deny the unsettled and introspective conditions of the Dark Age, nevertheless traces some important continuities from the preceding Late Bronze Age. Although it has become a virtual truism that the ancient Greek state differed from the modern nation state in the absence of any strong conception of place as opposed to community, we have instead found that spatial notions were intrinsic to political self-identification from the outset and were probably a legacy of Mycenaean administrative structures. If ancient authors chose to refer more often to the Corinthians (*hoi Korinthioi*) rather than Corinth (*hê Korinthos*), it remains the fact that the former term is derived from the latter and not vice versa.

In physical terms, then, the origins of the *polis* lie further back in the Dark Age than has often been assumed. The evolution of a fully conscious political society, on the other hand, was a far more lengthy process. Archaeological evidence suggests that the communities that emerged from the Dark Age were not entirely egalitarian or acephalous but neither were they fully stratified. Collections of households were rather grouped together under the authority of more powerful chieftains, whose status and rank depended on maintaining a delicate balance of reciprocity with their followers. It makes no sense to talk about a "state" in any recognizable modern sense until we can track the emergence of a new class of elites – something that the evidence seems to suggest did not occur prior to the seventh century. There were not commensurably more leadership positions for the new elite than there had been under their chiefly predecessors and so the ruling class decided to share power through the principle of the rotation of office; such early laws as we are able to identify

appear to have been designed to regulate such power-sharing among an aristocratic class. Those who were reluctant to relinquish their authority to their peers
would go down in later historical tradition as tyrants, though there is little to
suggest that their rule had an adverse effect on the long-term development of
the *polis* and some indications that their appeal to the populace for support
against aristocratic peers may have served as a catalyst for the emergence of a
more politicized *dêmos*.

The rights and responsibilities of the non-elite members of society were also
spelled out in this period – earlier perhaps at Sparta, rather later at Athens. It
would, however, be a mistake to confuse the participation of the *dêmos* in elite-
controlled government by consensus with a political egalitarianism. Previous
scholars were right to draw attention to the close connection between political
participation and the obligation to go to war on behalf of the *polis*. But, through
the political offices for which he was eligible or from which he was barred and
from his position in the hoplite phalanx, be it in the heavily armed front row
or the more lightly armed rear, every citizen rehearsed on a regular basis and
in full knowledge his position within a very hierarchically stratified society.

All this was to change from around the middle of the sixth century. The
contours of the political community seem to have been defined largely by
residence and the ownership of property; those who derived the maximum return
from their landed property constituted the governing class and might, from
time to time, invest some of their surplus in the procurement of merchandise
from overseas – much, though not all of it, in the form of prestige goods
designed to bolster the procurer's status at home. Non-elite smallholders
expected to derive more than simple subsistence from their plots of land but
their involvement in market exchange was almost certainly modest. In the sixth
century, however, a more professionalized, profit-driven commerce began
to assume greater importance, facilitated by the introduction of coinage and
the establishment of important trading posts in the Nile Delta, the western
Mediterranean, and the Black Sea. While earlier, landed wealth had – at least
in part – derived from status, there was now an increasing demand that the
acquisition of wealth from other sources should be recognized with a concomitant status – the poetry attributed to Theognis is pervaded by the theme of the
nouveaux riches and the threat that these presented to the traditional landed
aristocracy. It is also towards the end of the sixth century that the *dêmos* –
especially at Athens – grew cognizant of the potential role it had to play in the
governance of the *polis* and began to question the aristocrats' right to rule. The
full realization of that potential did not take place until a few decades into
the Classical period and was to some degree associated with a new ethnic self-
conception of Greekness. To demarcate oneself from the "barbarian" was,
in part, to seek to elide socioeconomic differences within Greek society. At
Athens, however, the demonization of the barbarian also served to proscribe
elite practices and thus represents an attempt, on the part of the *dêmos*, to
usurp a Hellenic identity that had originally been created a century earlier by
elite competitors at the great Panhellenic sanctuaries.

The reconstruction suggested here furnishes the Archaic period with a rather different "shape" than that under which it is normally conceived. In recent decades, there has been a virtual consensus that it was the eighth century – dubbed a "Renaissance" by some – that witnessed the epiphany of virtually everything that was significant about Archaic Greece and that the seventh and sixth centuries were primarily epochs of consolidation. Certainly, there are indications of greater settlement nucleation in the eighth century and the sharp rise in the quantity and variability of votive dedications in sanctuaries is nothing but distinctive. This is also the century in which the first overseas foundations are established in the west – though that is a process that continues well into the seventh century. In many other respects, however, the eighth century is not so significant a watershed – especially when viewed against the various gradual developments that were playing out across the whole period from ca. 1200 to 479. By contrast, the sixth century, far from being a century of consolidation, witnessed a number of significant innovations, including the introduction of coinage and escalation in long-distance commerce, a new monumentality in art and architecture, the provision of dedicated public buildings for administrative functions, the development of a circuit of "Stephanitic" games, the emergence of Hellenic consciousness, and a more concrete definition of citizenship. But what justification is there, in the first place, for considering the Archaic period as a single chronological entity?

Dividing up Space and Time

It is a longstanding convention that the lower chronological terminus for the Archaic period is marked by the Persian War of 480–479. Determining the upper limit, on the other hand, is trickier. Traditionally, the Archaic period was considered to have begun ca. 700 with the works of the lyric poets – indeed, in earlier treatments the Archaic period is sometimes referred to as the "Lyric Age." Yet this particular periodization was originally adopted at a time – the mid-nineteenth century – when the period prior to 700 was believed to represent a barely knowable "Heroic Age," for which the Homeric epics were the only contemporary witness. All that changed with Schliemann's excavations at Mycenae and Tiryns and the realization, through synchronizations with Egyptian material, that the Mycenaean civilization had gone into steep decline ca. 1200, thus opening up a "gap" of five centuries immediately before the "historical" age. Initially, this "Dark Age" attracted little scholarly interest but, with the decipherment of Linear B in 1952 and the recognition that Mycenaean Greece bore little resemblance to the world that Homer describes, an awareness emerged that archaeological evidence could go a long way in illuminating these centuries of darkness. By the 1980s, when a virtual consensus had arisen among both historians and archaeologists concerning an eighth-century "renaissance," it became clear that no account of early Greece could begin as late as 700. Even more recently, it has become increasingly clearer that the eighth-century developments cannot be satisfactorily explained without some consideration of what was going on in the tenth and ninth centuries. As a result, there has been a tendency to push back the upper terminus for the period and this is certainly not the first book to begin an account of Archaic Greece ca. 1200.

In reality, however, there is actually more rationale for the upper terminus than for the lower one. Whatever the cause of the destructions that rocked the Mycenaean palaces ca. 1200, the consequences were extremely far-reaching with few regions remaining unaffected. Lefkandi displays an almost unparalleled degree of prosperity as early as the tenth century but it had not been occupied for much of the Late Bronze Age. By contrast, at those settlements where some continuity of occupation across the transition from the Bronze to the Iron Age is suspected, there is no doubt that it was at a much lower level and density than before. The disappearance of palatial administrations had profound effects on the culture, society, and economy of the Greek world. There was little need any longer for scribal literacy or specialized manufacture, and subsistence strategies had to adapt to the new circumstances. The fraught and unsettled conditions almost certainly prompted and even compelled people to seek a living elsewhere and the traditions concerning the Ionian and Dorian migrations are best seen as later attempts to understand and explain the considerable mobility that must have existed at the beginning of our period.

By contrast, no such cataclysmic watershed divided the 470s from the 480s. There was, of course, a human cost to the conflict with Persia but in terms of politics, society, and culture, life in Athens was not so different after the repulsion of Xerxes than it was before. The Cleisthenic constitution had already been in place for a couple of decades and the final anti-aristocratic reforms of Ephialtes lay almost two decades in the future, as did the more material benefits that the Athenians were to derive from the formation of the Delian League in 478. The Greek cities in Asia Minor merely exchanged a Persian master for an Athenian one. No major upheavals or disruption took place at Sparta; there, too, it was the 460s that would witness more momentous happenings with a particularly devastating earthquake and the revolt of the Messenian helots. Indeed, we need to remind ourselves that, of the hundreds of *poleis* that existed in 480, only thirty-one took a stand against the Persian invaders. One city that sat out the conflict was Argos where there seem to be no significant changed circumstances in the early 470s. Far more traumatic was the annihilation of the Argive army at the hands of the Spartan king Cleomenes some fifteen years earlier (Herodotus 6.76–83; Plutarch, *Mor.* 245c–f; Pausanias 2.27.7–8), but, once again, the most important transformation of Argive society came in the 460s with the destruction of neighboring cities, the incorporation of their inhabitants within the Argive citizenry, and probably the introduction of democracy. In other words, had we been unaware of the circumstances of the Persian invasion, it is not at all obvious that we would have regarded the 470s as particularly distinctive. It has even been suggested that the origins of the innovations that characterize the "Severe" or "International" style of Greek sculpture, once assumed to be the cultural celebration of the freedom won at Salamis and Plataea, should actually be situated in the first two decades of the fifth century.

No doubt the picture would have looked rather different had the Persians been victorious. Some reflections on what *might have* happened had the battles of Salamis and Plataea gone differently surface in the writings of Classical authors: Herodotus (7.139) maintains that Greece would not have continued to enjoy its liberty had the Athenians not decided to resist the Persians; similarly, Plato (*Laws* 699a–d) notes that the Athenian state would have become scattered and broken up into a diaspora community had the Athenians not made the decision to unite in self-defense and defend their temples, tombs, country, relatives, and friends. But imagining the counterfactual is, by definition, the precise opposite of lived experience and there is little to indicate that such thoughts arose in the immediate aftermath of the Persian War or that they were of much widespread concern outside Athens.

Carving up space and time for the purposes of historical study is, of course, a practical necessity and it should therefore come as no surprise that the terminal dates that frame any period turn out to be artificial, if not arbitrary. But neither is it easy to identify any particular themes, issues, structures, or institutions that serve either to endow the Archaic period with a specific internal coherence or to mark it out from the periods that preceded and succeeded it. It is sometimes suggested that the concept of freedom, both personal and communal, was an especially notable feature of the period but there is no clearly identifiable transformation in the status of freedom immediately after the Persian War. The issue of communal freedom, for example, only really began to gather momentum in the late fifth and fourth centuries as *poleis* sought to preserve their autonomy within hegemonic leagues. The Archaic period certainly witnessed many innovations that had not existed in the Late Bronze Age but all of these continued to develop in subsequent periods.

There is, however, one respect in which the Archaic period is different from both the Mycenaean and the Classical periods and it is here that we return to issues of historical method and the fact that it should be the specific character of the available evidence rather than the theoretical or ideological preferences of the historian that dictate the most appropriate method to apply to a body of material. Archaeological evidence is available for all periods, but the nature of the literary evidence is different for each of the three different epochs. In the Mycenaean period, the literary evidence is restricted to the Linear B inscriptions on clay tablets and vases but this provides important contemporary testimony about the functioning of the Bronze Age palaces. In the Classical period, a burgeoning number of inscriptions on stone similarly furnish a wealth of contemporary evidence for the administration of the *polis* but this is also the period in which historiography – the self-conscious practice of recording recent or contemporary events with a view to explaining their causes and connections – is born. Fifth-century tragedy and comedy also provide an invaluable insight into the political, cultural, and moral issues that interested contemporary audiences. In short, one of the distinctive features of the Classical period –

and, to a certain extent, the Mycenaean period – is the contemporaneity of the written evidence on which our reconstructions are based.

That is a luxury that is rarely available for the Archaic period. For a start, there are very few complete works of literature that have survived. The Homeric and Hesiodic poems are obvious exceptions, but neither was composed with the needs of the future historian in mind and, in the case of the former especially, the consciously archaizing world of the heroes presents its own problems. The lyric and elegiac poets offer precious hints of the sorts of preoccupations that concerned the topmost stratum of society, but the picture that can be built up from the scattered and isolated scraps of their poetry that later authors saw fit to cite can only ever be fragmentary. Inscriptions exist, particularly in the later phases of the period, but they are notoriously scant compared with later periods and the information that they purvey is often haphazard and difficult to accommodate within any overarching, coherent set of legal or political practices. As for "events" and the circumstances that caused them, we are, as we have seen earlier in this chapter, almost entirely dependent upon the testimony of authors writing much later. The specific nature of the materials available for the Archaic period, then, requires considerable caution but also a good degree of imagination to compensate for the deficiencies of our evidence. It necessitates, in other words, a specific set of methodological skills that is rather different from those required to study other periods of Greek history.

There is, however, one final respect in which the nature of the evidence at our disposal prefigures the object of study. Greek historians are sometimes charged with too narrow a vision of their subject matter. Early Greece, it is argued, was merely part of a broader network of intellectual, cultural, and informational currents that spanned the entire Mediterranean – especially its eastern half – the Near East, and Egypt and to focus solely on one little part of this wider world is little more than parochial Hellenocentrism. That Greece was not isolated from its neighbors in the Archaic period goes without saying and much useful research has been conducted over the past few decades into the nature and frequency of such interactions. But the intellectual justification for geographically separating the Greek world from its Mediterranean context extends well beyond a simply practical decision to limit one's field of study to areas where Greek-speakers settled in significant concentrations. If one were content to limit oneself to material cultural studies, the playing field would, in a certain sense, be more level. But historians are obliged to resort to every piece of evidence at their disposal and once literary testimony is introduced into the mix, the prospect for a genuinely Mediterranean history becomes decidedly more unlikely.

The reason for this is that many of the populations with whom the Greeks came into contact have now become "people without history" – or, rather, people without their own history. From an early period, the Greeks sought to accommodate non-Greek populations within their world view by usurping the right to create myths of origins for them: the tendency becomes especially common in the ethnographies that appear in the early fifth century, beginning with the works of Hecataeus, but is already anticipated both in the *Odyssey* and in Hesiod's account (*Th.* 1011–18) of how the sorceress Circe gave birth to Latinos, the eponymous ancestor of the Latin people. It is sometimes assumed that indigenous peoples were happy to accept passively such myths from Greek authors because they lacked their own cognitive schema for the world and their place in it, although there are some hints that Greek versions of such myths were not entirely unaffected by what local populations said about themselves. It nevertheless remains the case that Greek writers reveal a particular obsession not only with coining such origin myths but also with committing them to writing and hence preserving them for posterity. The end result is – as scholars of Achaemenid Persia or Etruscan Italy admit with considerable frustration – that the literary component of the evidence for the Greeks' neighbors is often largely a product of Greek authors and carries the inevitable myopic partiality and interested agenda that one might expect under such circumstances. From a methodological point of view, then, there is not a great deal of commensurability between a reconstruction of Greek history based on archaeology and Greek written sources and a reconstruction of, say, Lydian or Etruscan history similarly based on archaeology and Greek written sources. The former may require some imagination on the part of the historian, but the latter comes dangerously close to a flight of fancy if it is set alongside and granted the same "factual" status as the former. The past may be translated in many and various meaningful ways but it cannot be written from scratch.

In the end, a sensitivity to issues of historical method serves to highlight the fundamental point that history is a practice rather than merely a synonym for the past. It is not about passively absorbing facts and figures but about engaging with a variety of materials for which appropriate methodological tools are required and that active engagement must, of necessity, result in self-interrogation as to the values and assumptions under which each one of us operates. This is why, for all the indubitable benefits that disciplines in the social sciences have contributed to our inquiries, the discipline of history will always remain firmly part of the humanities.

FURTHER READING

First Sacred War: W. G. Forrest, "The First Sacred War," *Bulletin de Correspondance Hellénique* 80 (1956), 33–52. Extremely skeptical: N. Robertson, "The myth of the First Sacred War," *Classical Quarterly* 28 (1978), 38–73. More equivocal: J. Davies, "The tradition about the First Sacred War," in Hornblower 1994, 193–212. Pylaean-Delphic amphictyony: Hall 2002, 134–54. "Great Isthmus Corridor": Kase et al. 1991. Archaeology of Delphi: Morgan 1990, 107–43.

For the "Lyric Age": Burn 1960. Periodization and the creation of a Dark Age: Morris 2000, 77–106. Osborne 1996 also starts his account of the Archaic period at 1200. Early origins of the Severe style of sculpture: Snodgrass 1980, 207–12. For the importance of individual and collective freedom: Snodgrass 1980, 204–7. By contrast, Raaflaub 2004 argues that a concept of freedom was not fully developed until the fifth century. For origin myths: E. Bickerman, "Origines gentium," *Classical Philology* 47 (1952), 65–81. For an attempt to identify an indigenous component to these myths: J. M. Hall, "*Arcades his oris*. Greek projections on the Italian ethnoscape?" in Gruen 2005, 259–84.

Abbreviations and Glossary of Literary Sources

The following abbreviations are used in the text and in the glossary below:

BCH   *Bulletin de Correspondance Hellénique.* Paris.
FGrH   F. Jacoby, *Die Fragmente der griechischen Historiker.* Berlin and Leiden, 1923–.
Fornara   C. W. Fornara, *Translated Documents of Greece & Rome,* vol. 1: *Archaic Times to the End of the Peloponnesian War,* 2ⁿᵈ edn. Cambridge, 1983.
IC   M. Guarducci, ed., *Inscriptiones Creticae Opera et Consilio Friderici Halbherr Collectae.* Rome, 1935.
ID   *Inscriptions de Délos.* Paris, 1926–.
IG   *Inscriptiones Graecae.* Berlin, 1873–.
Milet   *Milet: Ergebnisse der Ausgrabungen und Untersuchungen seit dem Jahre 1899.* Berlin, 1906–.
ML   R. Meiggs and D. M. Lewis, *A Selection of Greek Historical Inscriptions to the End of the Fifth Century BC,* rev. edn. Oxford, 1988.
PMG   D. Page, *Poetae Melici Graeci.* Oxford, 1962.
POxy.   *Oxyrhynchus Papyri.* London, 1898–.
SEG   *Supplementum Epigraphicum Graecum.* Leiden, 1923–.

In the following list of sources, an asterisk refers to the Loeb Classical Library series, published by Harvard University Press, which offers original texts in Greek or Latin with English translations on facing pages. Note, however, that since all translations in this book are the author's, they will often vary slightly from those to be found in the Loeb series.

*Aelian	Rhetorician and writer, 170–235 CE. *HM* = *Historical Miscellany*.
*Aeneas Tacticus	General and military treatise writer, mid-fourth century.
*Aeschines	Orator, ca. 397–ca. 322.
*Aeschylus	Tragedian, 525–456.
*Alcaeus	Lyric poet, (?) early sixth century. *Greek Lyric*, vol. i.
Anaxandridas	Historian, late third/early second century. *FGrH* no. 404.
*Andocides	Orator, ca. 440–ca. 390. *Minor Attic Orators*, vol. i.
Antiochus	Historian, late fifth century. *FGrH* no. 555.
Antipatros of Magnesia	Historian, mid-fourth century. *FGrH* no. 69.
*[Apollodorus]	Mythographer, first/second century CE.
*Archilochus	Iambic and elegiac poet, (?) mid-seventh century. *Greek Iambic Poetry*.
*Aristophanes	Comic poet, late fifth/early fourth century.
*Aristotle	Philosopher, 384–322. *AC* = *Athenian Constitution*; *NE* = *Nicomachean Ethics*; *Pol.* = *Politics*.
*Arrian	Historian, second century CE.
*Athenaeus	Writer, late second century CE.
*Bacchylides	Lyric poet, fifth century. *Greek Lyric*, vol. iv.
Callisthenes	Historian, fourth century. *FGrH* no. 124.
*Cicero	Roman statesman and writer, 106–43.
Conon	Mythographer, late first century/early first century CE. *FGrH* no. 26.
*Diodorus of Sicily	Historian, late first century.
*Diogenes Laertius	Biographer, (?) third century CE.
*Dionysius of Halicarnassus	Rhetorician and historian, late first century. *RA* = *Roman Antiquities*.
Ephorus	Historian, 405–330. *FGrH* no. 70.
Etymologicum Magnum	Lexicon, (?) eleventh century CE.
Eumelus	Epic poet, (?) seventh century.
Eusebius	Historian, theologian, and chronographer, ca. 260–340 CE. *Chron.* = *Chronica*.
*Frontinus	Roman politician and military theorist, ca. 30–104 CE.
Hecataeus of Miletus	Genealogist and ethnographer, early fifth century. *FGrH* no. 1.
Hellanicus of Mytilene	Chronographer and historian, late fifth century. *FGrH* no. 4.
*Herodotus	Historian, ca. 484–425.
*Hesiod	Epic poet, (?) early seventh century. *Th.* = *Theogony*; *WD* = *Works and Days*.
Hesychius	Lexicographer, (?) fifth century CE.
*Hipponax	Iambic poet, (?) mid-sixth century. *Greek Iambic Poetry*.

*Homer	Epic poet, (?) early seventh century. *Il.* = *Iliad*; *Od.* = *Odyssey*.
*Homeric Hymns	Seventh/sixth centuries.
*Isaeus	Orator, ca. 420–350.
*Isocrates	Orator, 436–338.
Justin	Epitomizer, (?) third century CE.
Kleidemos	Historian, mid-fourth century. *FGrH* no. 323.
*Livy	Roman historian, late first century/early first century CE.
*Lycurgus	Statesman, ca. 390–ca. 325. *Minor Attic Orators*, vol. ii.
*Lysias	Orator of Sicilian origin, resident in Athens, early fourth century.
*Mimnermus of Colophon	Elegiac poet, (?) late seventh century. *Greek Elegiac Poetry*.
Nicolaus of Damascus	Historian and philosopher, late first century. *FGrH* no. 90.
Parian Marble	Chronicle, mid-third century. *FGrH* no. 239.
*Pausanias	Historian and geographer, mid-second century CE.
Pherecydes	Mythographer, fifth century. *FGrH* no. 3.
Philochorus	Historian, fourth century. *FGrH* no. 328.
*Phocylides	Elegiac poet, (?) mid-sixth century. *Greek Elegiac Poetry*.
Photius	Byzantine commentator, ninth century CE.
Phylarkhos	Historian, third century. *FGrH* no. 81.
*Pindar	Lyric poet, 518–438. *Isthm.* = *Isthmian Odes*; *Nem.* = *Nemean Odes*; *Ol.* = *Olympian Odes*; *Pyth.* = *Pythian Odes*.
*Plato	Philosopher, 429–347. *Hipp.* = *Hipparchus*; *Prot.* = *Protagoras*.
*Plutarch	Philosopher and biographer, first/second century CE. *Cam.* = *Life of* Camillus; *Lyc.* = *Life of Lycurgus*; *Lys.* = *Life of Lysander*; *Mor.* = *Moralia*; *Num.* = *Life of Numa*; *Pel.* = *Life of Pelopidas*; *Per.* = *Life of Pericles*; *Sol.* = *Life of Solon*; *Thes.* = *Life of Theseus*.
Pollux	Rhetorician, second century CE.
Polyaenus	Rhetorician, mid-second century CE. *Strat.* = *Strategemata*.
*Polybius	Historian, 200–ca. 118.
*Sappho	Lyric poetess, early sixth century. *Greek Lyric*, vol. i.
[Scymnus]	Periegete, first century.
*Semonides	Iambic and elegiac poet, (?) late seventh century. *Greek Iambic Poetry*.
*Simonides	Lyric and elegiac poet, ca. 556–468. *Greek Lyric*, vol. iii.

Sokrates of Argos	Historian, (?) third century. *FGrH* no. 310.
Solinus	Geographer, (?) third century CE.
*Solon	Elegiac poet and statesman, early sixth century. *Greek Elegiac Poetry*.
Suda	Lexicon, tenth century CE.
*Strabo	Geographer and historian, 64–(?)21 CE.
Synkellos, George	Monk and chronicler, eighth/ninth centuries CE.
*Theognis	Elegiac poet, (?) sixth century. *Greek Elegiac Poetry*.
Theopompus	Historian, mid-fourth century. *FGrH* no. 115.
*Thucydides	Historian and general, late fifth century.
Timaeus	Historian, 356–260. *FGrH* no. 566.
*Tyrtaeus	Elegiac poet, (?) mid-seventh century. *Greek Elegiac Poetry*.
*Xenophanes	Elegiac poet and philosopher, (?) late sixth century. *Greek Elegiac Poetry*.
*Xenophon	Historian and general, ca. 428–ca. 354. *CA = Constitution of the Athenians*; *CL = Constitution of the Lacedaemonians*; *Hell. = Hellenica*; *Mem = Memorabilia*.

Works Cited in the Further Reading

Alcock, S. E. and R. Osborne, eds. (1994) *Placing the Gods: Sanctuaries and Sacred Space in Ancient Greece*. Oxford.

Anderson, G. (2003) *The Athenian Experiment: Building an Imagined Political Community in Ancient Attica, 508–490 BC*. Ann Arbor.

Andrewes, A. (1956) *The Greek Tyrants*. London.

Appleby, J., L. Hunt, and M. Jacob, eds. (1994) *Telling the Truth About History*. New York and London.

Austin, M. M. and P. Vidal-Naquet (1977) *Economic and Social History of Ancient Greece: An Introduction*. Berkeley, Los Angeles, and London.

Bérard, C. (1970) *Eretria 3: L'hérôon à la porte de l'ouest*. Bern.

Bickerman, E. J. (1980) *Chronology of the Ancient World*, rev. edn. London.

Biers, W. R. (1992) *Art, Artefacts, and Chronology in Classical Archaeology*. London and New York.

Blok, J. H. and A. P. M. H. Lardinois, eds. (2006) *Solon of Athens: New Historical and Philological Approaches*. Leiden.

Boardman, J. (1999) *The Greeks Overseas: Their Early Colonies and Trade*, 4th edn. London.

Bodel, J. ed. (2001) *Epigraphic Evidence: Ancient History from Inscriptions*. London and New York.

Brock, R. and S. Hodkinson, eds. (2000) *Alternatives to Athens: Varieties of Political Organization and Community in Ancient Greece*. Oxford.

Burn, A. R. (1960) *The Lyric Age of Greece*. London.

—— (1984) *Persia and the Greeks: The Defence of the West, 546–478 BC*, 2nd edn. Stanford.

Canary, R. H. and H. Kozicki, eds. (1978) *The Writing of History: Literary Form and Historical Understanding*. Madison.

Carr, E. H. (1987) *What is History?* 2nd edn. London.

Cartledge, P. A. (2002a) *The Greeks: A Portrait of Self and Others*, 2nd edn. Oxford.

—— (2002b) *Sparta and Lakonia: A Regional History 1300–362*, 2nd edn. London and New York.

Cartledge, P. A., E. E. Cohen, and L. Foxhall, eds. (2002) *Money, Labour and Land: Approaches to the Economies of Ancient Greece*. London and New York.

Casson, L. (1994) *Ships and Seafaring in Ancient Times*. London.

Chaniotis, A. and P. Ducrey, eds. (2002) *Army and Power in the Ancient World*. Stuttgart.

Cohen, B., ed. (2000) *Not the Classical Ideal: Athens and the Construction of the Other in Greek Art*. Leiden, Boston, and Cologne.

Coldstream, J. N. (1968) *Greek Geometric Pottery*. London.

—— (2003) *Geometric Greece, 900–700 BC*, 2ⁿᵈ edn. London.

Compernelle, R. van (1959) *Étude de chronologie et d'historiographie siciliotes: recherches sur le système chronologique des sources de Thucydide concernant la fondations des colonies siceliotes*. Brussels.

Connor, W. R. (1984) *Thucydides*. Princeton.

Coulson, W. D. E., O. Palagia, T. L. Shear, Jr., H. A. Shapiro, and F. J. Frost, eds. (1994) *The Archaeology of Athens and Attica under the Democracy*. Oxford.

Crawford, M. ed. (1983) *Sources for Ancient History*. Cambridge.

Crielaard, J.-P. ed. (1995) *Homeric Questions: Essays in Philology, Ancient History and Archaeology*. Amsterdam.

d'Agostino, B. and D. Ridgway, eds. (1994) *Apoikia: Scritti in onore di Giorgio Buchner*. Naples.

Damgaard Andersen, H., H. Horsnaes, and S. Houby-Nielsen, eds. (1997) *Urbanization in the Mediterranean in the 9th to 6th Centuries BC*. Acta Hyperborea 7. Copenhagen.

de Angelis, F. (2003) *Megara Hyblaia and Selinous: The Development of Two Greek City-States in Archaic Sicily*. Oxford.

de Libero, L. (1996) *Die archaische Tyrannis*. Stuttgart.

de Ste Croix, G. E. M. (1972) *The Origins of the Peloponnesian War*. London.

—— (1981) *The Class Struggle in the Ancient Greek World*. Ithaca.

Drews, R. R. (1983) *Basileus: The Evidence for Kingship in Geometric Greece*. New Haven and London.

—— (1988) *The Coming of the Greeks: Indo-European Conquests in the Aegean and in the Near East*. Princeton.

—— (1993) *The End of the Bronze Age: Changes in Warfare and the Catastrophe ca. 1200 BC*. Princeton.

duBois, P. (1982) *Centaurs and Amazons*. Chicago.

Dunbabin, T. J. (1948) *The Western Greeks. The History of Sicily and South Italy from the Foundation of the Greek Colonies to 480 BC*. Oxford.

Elton, G. (1967) *The Practice of History*. London.

Erskine, A. (2001) *Troy Between Greece and Rome: Local Tradition and Imperial Power*. Oxford.

Euben, J. P., J. R. Wallach, and J. Ober, eds. (1994) *Athenian Political Thought and the Reconstruction of American Democracy*. Ithaca and London.

Evans, R. J. (1999) *In Defense of History*. New York and London.

Figueira, T. J. (1981) *Aegina: Society and Politics*. New York.

Figueira, T. J. and G. Nagy, eds. (1985) *Theognis of Megara: Poetry and the Polis*. Baltimore.

Finley, M. I. (1981) *Economy and Society in Ancient Greece*, ed. B. D. Shaw and R. P. Saller. London.

—— (1986) *The Use and Abuse of History*, rev. edn. London.

—— (1999) *The Ancient Economy*, updated edn. Berkeley, Los Angeles, and London.

Fisher, N. and H. van Wees, eds. (1998) *Archaic Greece: New Approaches and New Evidence*. London.

Foley, A. (1988) *The Argolid, 800–600 BC: An Archaeological Survey.* Göteborg.

Forsberg, S. (1995) *Near Eastern Destruction Datings as Sources for Greek and Near Eastern Iron Age Chronology: Archaeological and Historical Studies. The Cases of Samaria (722 BC) and Tarsus (696 BC).* Uppsala.

Forsdyke, S. (2005) *Exile, Ostracism, and Democracy: The Politics of Expulsion in Ancient Greece.* Princeton and Oxford.

Fortes, M. and E. E. Evans-Pritchard, eds. (1940) *African Political Systems.* London.

Friedländer, S. ed. (1992) *Probing the Limits of Representation: Nazism and the "Final Solution."* Cambridge MA.

Gagarin, M. (1986) *Early Greek Law.* Berkeley, Los Angeles, and London.

Garnsey, P., K. Hopkins, and C. R. Whittaker, eds. (1983) *Trade in the Ancient Economy.* London.

Gorman, V. B. and E. W. Robinson, eds. (2002) *Oikistes: Studies in Constitutions, Colonies, and Military Power in the Ancient World, Offered in Honor of A. J. Graham.* Leiden, Boston, and Cologne.

Graham, A. J. (1983) *Colony and Mother-City in Ancient Greece,* 2nd edn. Chicago.

Gras, M., H. Tréziny, and H. Broise, eds. (2004) *Mégara Hyblaea 5: La ville archaïque.* Rome.

Greenhalgh, P. A. L. (1973) *Early Greek Warfare: Horsemen and Chariots in the Homeric and Archaic Ages.* Cambridge.

Gruen, E., ed. (2005) *Cultural Borrowings and Ethnic Appropriations in Antiquity.* Stuttgart.

Hägg, R., ed. (1983) *The Greek Renaissance of the 8th Century BC: Tradition and Innovation.* Stockholm.

—— ed. (1996) *The Role of Religion in the Early Greek Polis.* Stockholm.

Hall, E. (1989) *Inventing the Barbarian: Greek Self-Definition through Tragedy.* Oxford.

Hall, J. M. (1997) *Ethnic Identity in Greek Antiquity.* Cambridge.

—— (2002) *Hellenicity: Between Ethnicity and Culture.* Chicago.

Hansen, M. H. (1991) *The Athenian Democracy in the Age of Demosthenes.* Oxford.

—— ed. (1996) *Introduction to an Inventory of Poleis.* Acts of the Copenhagen Polis Center 3. Copenhagen.

—— ed. (1997) *The Polis as an Urban Centre and as a Political Community.* Acts of the Copenhagen Polis Center 4. Copenhagen.

Hansen, M. H. and T. H. Nielsen, eds. (2004) *An Inventory of Archaic and Classical Poleis.* Oxford.

Hanson, V. D. (1989) *The Western Way of War.* London.

—— (1999) *The Other Greeks: The Family Farm and the Agrarian Roots of Western Civilization,* 2nd edn. Berkeley, Los Angeles, and London.

—— ed. (1991) *Hoplites: The Classical Greek Battle Experience* (London and New York).

Hodkinson, S. and A. Powell, eds. (1999) *Sparta: New Perspectives.* London.

Horden, P. and N. Purcell (2000) *The Corrupting Sea: A Study of Mediterranean History.* Oxford and Malden MA.

Hornblower, S. (1987) *Thucydides.* London.

—— ed. (1994) *Greek Historiography.* Oxford.

Howgego, C. J. (1995) *Ancient History from Coins.* London and New York.

Hunt, P. (1998) *Slaves, Warfare and Ideology in the Greek Historians.* Cambridge.

Hurwit, J. M. (1999) *The Athenian Acropolis: History, Mythology, and Archaeology from the Neolithic Era to the Present.* Cambridge.

Irwin, E. (2005) *Solon and Early Greek Poetry: The Politics of Exhortation.* Cambridge.

James, P., with I. J. Thorpe, N. Kokkinos, R. Morkot, and J. Frankish (1991) *Centuries of Darkness: A Challenge to the Conventional Chronology of Old World Archaeology*. London.

Janko, R. (1982) *Homer, Hesiod and the Hymns: Diachronic Development in Epic Diction*. Cambridge.

Jarva, E. (1995) *Archaiologia on Archaic Greek Body Armour*. Rovaniemi.

Jeffery, L. H. (1976) *Archaic Greece: The City-States c. 700–500 BC*. London.

—— (1990) *The Local Scripts of Archaic Greece: A Study of the Origin of the Greek Alphabet and its Development from the Eighth to the Fifth Centuries BC*, rev. edn. A. Johnston. London.

Jenkins, K. (1995) *On What is History: From Carr and Elton to Rorty and White*. London and New York.

—— (2003) *Re-Thinking History*, 2nd edn. London and New York.

Jones, N. F. (1987) *Public Organization in Ancient Greece: A Documentary Study*. Philadelphia.

Kase, E. W., G. J. Szemler, N. C. Wilkie, and P. W. Wallace, eds. (1991) *The Great Isthmus Corridor Route: Explorations of the Phokis-Doris Expedition*, vol. 1. Minneapolis.

Kelly, T. (1976) *A History of Argos to 500 BC*. Minneapolis.

Kennell, N. M. (1995) *The Gymnasium of Virtue: Education and Culture in Ancient Sparta*. Chapel Hill.

Kõiv, M. (2003) *Ancient Tradition and Early Greek History: The Origins of States in Early-Archaic Sparta, Argos and Corinth*. Tallinn.

Kuhrt, A. (1995) *The Ancient Near East c. 3000–330 BC*, 2 vols. London and New York.

Kurke, L. (1991) *The Traffic in Praise: Pindar and the Poetics of the Social Economy*. Ithaca and London.

—— (1999) *Coins, Bodies, Games, and Gold: The Politics of Meaning in Archaic Greece*. Princeton.

Lambert, S. (1998) *The Phratries of Attica*, 2nd edn. Ann Arbor.

Lang, F. (1996) *Archaische Siedlungen in Griechenland: Struktur und Entwicklung*. Berlin.

Lavelle, B. M. (1993) *The Sorrow and the Pity: A Prolegomenon to a History of Athens under the Peisistratids, c. 560–510 BC*. Stuttgart.

—— (2005) *Fame, Money, and Power: The Rise of Peisistratos and "Democratic" Tyranny at Athens*. Ann Arbor.

Lazenby, J. F. (1993) *The Defence of Greece 490–479*. Warminster.

Lemos, I. S. (2002) *The Protogeometric Aegean: The Archaeology of the Late Eleventh and Tenth Centuries BC*. Oxford.

Leriche, P. and H. Tréziny, eds. (1986) *La fortification dans l'histoire de monde grec*. Paris.

Long, T. (1986) *Barbarians in Greek Comedy*. Carbondale and Edwardsville.

Luraghi, N. and S. E. Alcock, eds. (2003) *Helots and their Masters in Laconia and Messenia: Histories, Ideologies, Structures*. Washington DC.

McDonald, W. A., W. D. E. Coulson, and J. Rosser (1983) *Excavations at Nichoria in Southwest Greece*, vol. III: *Dark Age and Byzantine Occupation*. Minneapolis.

McDonald, W. A. and C. G. Thomas (1990) *Progress into the Past: The Rediscovery of Mycenaean Civilization*, 2nd edn. Bloomington and Indianapolis.

McGlew, J. F. (1993) *Tyranny and Political Culture in Ancient Greece*. Ithaca and London.

McInerney, J. (1999) *The Folds of Parnassos: Land and Ethnicity in Ancient Phokis*. Austin.

Malkin, I. (1987) *Religion and Colonization in Ancient Greece*. Leiden.

—— (1994) *Myth and Territory in the Spartan Mediterranean*. Cambridge.

—— ed. (2001) *Ancient Perceptions of Greek Ethnicity*. Washington DC.

Manville, P. B. (1990) *The Origins of Citizenship in Ancient Athens*. Princeton.

Martin, R. (1951) *Recherches sur l'agora grecque. Études d'histoire et d'architecture urbaines*. Paris.

Mazarakis-Ainian, A. (1997) *From Rulers' Dwellings to Temples: Architecture, Religion and Society in Early Iron Age Greece*. Studies in Mediterranean Archaeology 121. Jonsered.

Miller, M. (1970) *The Sicilian Colony Dates. Studies in Chronography* I. Albany.

Mitchell, L. G. and P. J. Rhodes, eds. (1997) *The Development of the Polis in Archaic Greece*. London and New York.

Möller, A. (2000) *Naukratis: Trade in Archaic Greece*. Oxford.

Morgan, C. (1990) *Athletes and Oracles: The Transformation of Olympia and Delphi in the Eighth Century*. Cambridge.

—— (2003) *Early Greek States Beyond the Polis*. London and New York.

Morley, N. (1999) *Writing Ancient History*. Ithaca.

Morris, I. (1987) *Burial and Ancient Society: The Rise of the Greek City-State*. Cambridge.

—— (2000) *Archaeology as Cultural History: Words and Things in Iron Age Greece*. Oxford and Malden MA.

Morris, I. and K. Raaflaub, eds. (1998) *Democracy 2500: Questions and Challenges*. Dubuque.

Murray, O. (1993) *Early Greece*. 2nd edn. London.

Murray, O. and S. Price, eds. (1990) *The Greek City from Homer to Alexander*. Oxford.

Nielsen, T. H. ed. (2002) *Even More Studies in the Ancient Greek Polis*. Historia Einzelschriften 162. Stuttgart.

Ober, J. (1996) *The Athenian Revolution: Essays on Ancient Greek Democracy and Political Theory*. Princeton.

Osborne, R. (1996) *Greece in the Making, 1200–479 BC*. London and New York.

Osborne, R. and S. Hornblower, eds. (1994) *Ritual, Finance, Politics. Athenian Democratic Accounts Presented to David Lewis*. Oxford.

Papenfuß, D. and V. Strocka, eds. (1982) *Palast und Hütte: Beiträge zum Bauen und Wohnen im Altertum*. Mainz-am-Rhein.

Parker, V. (1997) *Untersuchungen zum Lelantischen Krieg und verwandten Problemen der frühgriechischen Geschichte*. Stuttgart.

Peradotto, J. and J. P. Sullivan, eds. (1984) *Women in the Ancient World: The Arethusa Papers*. Albany.

Piérart, M. ed. (1992) *Polydipsion Argos: Argos de la fin des palais mycéniens à la constitution de l'état classique*. Paris.

Piérart, M. and G. Touchais (1996) *Argos: Une ville grecque de 6000 ans*. Paris.

Polignac, F. de (1995) *Cults, Territory and the Origins of the Greek City-State*. Transl. J. Lloyd. Chicago.

Popham, M. R., L. H. Sackett, and P. G. Themelis (1980) *Lefkandi* I: *The Iron Age*. London.

—— (1993) *Lefkandi* II: *The Protogeometric Building at Toumba. Part 2: The Excavation, Architecture and Finds*. London.

Powell, A. and S. Hodkinson, eds. (2002) *Sparta: Beyond the Mirage*. London.

Powell, B. B. (1991) *Homer and the Origin of the Greek Alphabet*. Cambridge.

Raaflaub, K. A. (2004) *The Discovery of Freedom in Ancient Greece*. Chicago and London.

—— ed. (1986) *Social Struggles in Archaic Rome: New Perspectives on the Conflict of the Orders*. Berkeley, Los Angeles, and London.

Raaflaub, K. A. and N. Rosenstein, eds. (1999) *War and Society in the Ancient and Medieval Worlds*. Washington DC.

Rawson, E. (1969) *The Spartan Tradition in European Thought*. Oxford.

Rich, J. and G. Shipley, eds. (1993) *War and Society in the Greek World*. London and New York.

Rich, J. and A. Wallace-Hadrill, eds. (1991) *City and Country in the Ancient World*. London.

Ridgway, D. (1992) *The First Western Greeks*. Cambridge.

Robinson, E. W. (1997) *The First Democracies. Early Popular Government Outside Athens*. Historia Einzelschriften 107. Stuttgart.

Rollinger, R. and C. Ulf, eds. (2004) *Griechische Archaik: Interne Entwicklungen, Externe Impulse*. Berlin.

Roussel, D. (1976) *Tribu et cité: études sur les groupes sociaux dans les cités grecques aux époques archaïque et classique*. Paris.

Sage, M. M. (1996) *Warfare in Ancient Greece: A Sourcebook*. London and New York.

Salmon, J. B. (1984) *Wealthy Corinth*. Oxford.

Sancisi-Weerdenburg, H. (2000) *Peisistratos and the Tyranny: A Reappraisal of the Evidence*. Amsterdam.

Schaps, D. M. (2004) *The Invention of Coinage and the Monetization of Ancient Greece*. Ann Arbor.

Scheidel, W. and S. von Reden, eds. (2002) *The Ancient Economy*. New York.

Shapiro, H. A. (1989) *Art and Cult under the Tyrants in Athens*. Mainz.

Snodgrass, A. M. (1980) *Archaic Greece: The Age of Experiment*. London.

—— (1987) *An Archaeology of Greece: The Present State and Future Scope of a Discipline*. Berkeley, Los Angeles, and London.

Stamatopoulou, M. and M. Yeroulanou, eds. (2002) *Excavating Classical Culture: Recent Archaeological Discoveries in Greece*. Oxford.

Starr, C. G. (1986) *Individual and Community: The Rise of the Polis 800–500 BC*. New York.

Stein-Hölkeskamp, E. (1989) *Adelskultur und Polisgesellschaft: Studien zum griechischen Adel in archaischer und klassischer Zeit*. Stuttgart.

Strauss, B. (2004) *The Battle of Salamis: The Naval Encounter that Saved Greece – and Western Civilization*. New York.

Syriopoulos, K. (1983) *Οι μεταβατικοί χρόνοι*. Athens.

Tandy, D. (1997) *Warriors into Traders: The Power of the Market in Early Greece*. Berkeley, Los Angeles, and London.

Thomas, C. G. and C. Conant (1999) *Citadel to City-State*. Bloomington and Indianapolis.

Tigerstedt, E. N. (1965) *The Legend of Sparta in Classical Antiquity*. Stockholm, Göteborg and Uppsala.

Tomlinson, R. A. (1972) *Argos and the Argolid from the End of the Bronze Age to the Roman Occupation*. London.

Tsetskhladze, G. R. ed. (1999) *Ancient Greeks: West and East*. Leiden, Boston, and Cologne.

Vallet, G., F. Villard, and P. Auberson (1976) *Mégara Hyblaea*, vol. 1: *Le quartier de l'agora archaïque*. Paris.

Van de Mieroop, M. (2004) *A History of the Ancient Near East ca. 3000–323 BC*. Oxford and Malden MA (2nd edn. 2006).

Vanschoonwinkel, J. (1991) *L'Égée et la Méditerranée orientale à la fin du IIe millénaire: temoignages archéologiques et sources écrites*. Louvain-la-Neuve and Providence.

van Wees, H. (1992) *Status Warriors: War, Violence and Society in Homer and History*. Amsterdam.

—— (2004) *Greek Warfare: Myths and Realities*. London.

—— ed. (2000) *War and Violence in Ancient Greece*. London.

von Reden, S. (1995) *Exchange in Ancient Greece*. London.

Weber, M. (1978) *Economy and Society*, vol. 2, ed. G. Roth and C. Wittich, transl. E. Fischoff et al. Berkeley, Los Angeles, and London.

Whitby, M., ed. (2002) *Sparta*. Edinburgh.

White, H. (1973) *Metahistory: The Historical Imagination in Nineteenth-Century Europe*. Baltimore.

Whitehead, D. ed. (1994) *From Political Architecture to Stephanus Byzantius*. Historia Einzelschriften 87. Stuttgart.

Whitley, J. (2001) *The Archaeology of Ancient Greece*. Cambridge.

Windschuttle, K. (1996) *The Killing of History: How Literary Critics and Social Theorists are Murdering our Past*. San Francisco.

Wood, E. M. (1988) *Peasant-Citizen and Slave: The Foundations of Athenian Democracy*. London.

Woodhead, A. G. (1981) *The Study of Greek Inscriptions*, 2nd edn. Cambridge.

Index

Note: page numbers in italics denote tables, maps, or illustrations

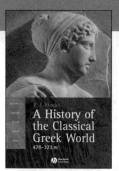
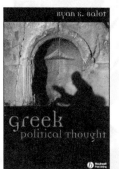
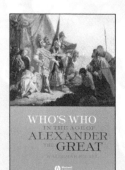